CONTEMPORARY SOCIETY: TRIBAL STUDIES

VOLUME FIVE
THE CONCEPT OF
TRIBAL SOCIETY

CONTEMPORARY SOCIETY: TRIBAL STUDIES

Edited by

GEORG PFEFFER
AND
DEEPAK KUMAR BEHERA

VOLUME ONE	—	STRUCTURE AND PROCESS
VOLUME TWO	—	DEVELOPMENT ISSUE, TRANSITION AND CHANGE
VOLUME THREE	—	SOCIAL CONCERN
VOLUME FOUR	—	SOCIAL REALITIES
VOLUME FIVE	—	CONCEPT OF TRIBAL SOCIETY
VOLUME SIX	—	TRIBAL SITUATION IN INDIA

The Editors

Georg Pfeffer is Professor and Head of the Department of Ethnology, Freie University of Berlin (Germany).

Deepak Kumar Behera is Professor in the Department of Anthropology, Sambalpur University, Sambalpur, Orissa (India).

CONTEMPORARY SOCIETY: TRIBAL STUDIES

VOLUME FIVE

CONCEPT OF TRIBAL SOCIETY

Edited by

GEORG PFEFFER
Freie Universität Berlin
Institut für Ethnologie
Drosselweg 1–3
D-14195 Berlin
Germany

DEEPAK KUMAR BEHERA
Department of Anthropology
Sambalpur University
Sambalpur–768 019
Orissa
India

CONCEPT PUBLISHING COMPANY, NEW DELHI–110 059

ISBN 81-7022-640-6 (Series)
ISBN 81-7022-983-9 (Vol. V)

First Published 2002

Published and Printed by
Ashok Kumar Mittal
Concept Publishing Company
A/15-16, Commercial Block, Mohan Garden
New Delhi-110059 (India)
Phones: 5648039, 5649024
Fax: 091-(11)-5648053
E-mail: publishing@conceptpub.com

ACKNOWLEDGEMENTS

We are grateful to all the contributors to the volume. Their academic generosity has enabled us to complete this work successfully. We offer our special thanks all others who helped us directly or indirectly for bringing the volume to its present shape. Last but not least, we are thankful to Concept Publishing Company for timely publication of the volume.

GEORG PFEFFER
DEEPAK KUMAR BEHERA

CONTENTS

SECTION II

TRIBAL SOCIETIES ABROAD

INTRODUCTION

GEORG PFEFFER AND DEEPAK KUMAR BEHERA

1. Things Indian

In India the term tribe is widely used and understood, since the constitution reserves special rights for the people classified as *Scheduled Tribes* or *Adivasi* by the President of the Union. In doing so, he is not bound by any criterion of classification. Since the passing of the Constitution in 1950, the Indian parliament is required to renew, alter, or terminate this special status of the *Scheduled Tribes* every ten years with the net result that new entities, e.g. the Badaga of the Nilgiri Hills, have been, or want to be added to the *Schedules* of the Constitution for the sake of benefits in the fields of education, land-rights, government service and parliamentary representation. In 1991 the Census of India counted 67,758,388 individuals as members of the *Scheduled Tribes*[1], i.e. a number exceeding that of the British population.

Over the last 50 years, many Indians and a few Western anthropologists have devoted their attention to problems of these people, relating to some kind of "backwardness" in the fields of health, education, and the economy. In doing so, they have assumed the *Scheduled Tribes* to suffer from certain handicaps when compared to the rest of the Indian population, just as they have seen the need to overcome such disadvantages. This attitude stands for a long tradition. One of the earliest tribal ethnographies, a general overview by a certain Colonel Dalton (1872: 123-138), summarised the chapter on the tribal people of middle India under the heading "broken tribes," indicating some unfortunate historical fate of formerly noble savages. This tradition has been kept up ever since. Unaware of the pride the people themselves express when referring to their tribal status, outsiders, particularly those of little or no local knowledge, tend to look upon the term as some kind of degradation,

1. Our source is the official report of the *Tribal Studies Committee,* 1999: 5.

comparable to "untouchability" in the plains. This attitude has, to our knowledge, never allowed a reversal of the evaluation process. Nobody so far has registered the good life in many tribal communities. "Backwardness" of Western or caste institutions, compared to the tribal conditions of life, has never been discussed. Women's Day, for example, is celebrated with great zeal all over urban India on the first of March every year, but we are unaware of anyone comparing the aspirations of the Indian women's movement to the regular status of tribal women in India.

In the *Scheduled Areas* of the country, i.e. those with a predominant population of *Scheduled Tribes*, anthropologists have very often assumed the roles of social workers, the list of their published recommendations being long. As academics they entertain a precarious relationship with the administrators, or the personnel to implement those suggestions for the better. The administrative staffs frequently offer technical help and supervision of anthropological research in the area considered to be "remote" in the eyes of the plains people. Having succeeded the colonial rulers, the foresters, policemen and revenue officers — all over the country — are responsible for practical decision-making. In the *Scheduled Areas* their power of command coincides with a cultural distance which is evident to all, but publicised by very few. It is, to mention just a single illustration, self-understood that officials, touring villages and outposts in the hills, are entertained with chicken and liquor "requisitioned" from the local population, e.g. the inhabitants of the starvation-struck tribal districts of Kalahandi, Kondhmals and Koraput. These fringe benefits of public service do not arise in those districts where the so-called "mainstream of Indian culture" and the public servants themselves are at home, or the kind of cultural, social, and economic order viewed as the ultimate goal of a policy called "tribal uplift".

In addition to the all-Indian administrative concept of *Scheduled Tribes*, provincial governments have further qualified some of the former. Thus the government of Orissa classified twelve as *Primitive Tribes*.[2] The first important consequence of such specifications seems to be the general confusion of administrative and anthropological concepts of tribe and tribal society, in use since centuries and — for decades — under severe criticism within the anthropological community. So far, we are unaware of any Indian publication differentiating the academic and the governmental terminology. A second consequence of the bureaucratic classification is an ideological reassurance, granted to the administrating lords of the land and, in fact, to most other outsiders in the *Scheduled Areas* including anthropologists. The concept of *Primitive Tribe* is associated with the idea of a definite "primitiveness," not

2. Government of Orissa, 1994; *Tribal Education in Orissa in the Context of Education for All by 2000 AD.* Tribal Welfare Department Publication.

contained in the neutral word "schedule".[3] Anyone is left to define for himself or herself the domain of such primitive conditions. Since ordinary people anywhere in the world fail to differentiate the value of institutions, structures, cultures, or individuals, the outcome is evident. Furthermore the neutral term *Scheduled Tribes* too is almost automatically associated with "backwardness" meaning little more than inferior status within the general society of *homo hierarchicus.*

Such implicit meanings are, however, not restricted to things Indian. In Russia, China, Canada and Brazil, to name just a few huge countries like India and leave out innumerable other examples, ethnic minorities have been dressed up in administrative terms such as "nationalities" or "first nations" in order to receive certain practical advantages coinciding with a general, if unwritten, discrimination of their cultural logic. Similarly, the anthropologists of these countries have been unable to disentangle themselves from the prerogatives of governmental institutions, even if they have opposed public policy.

Because of these ambiguities involving those people all over the world who used to be called tribes by anthropologists, the time has come for yet another review of the concepts of "tribe" and "tribal" society, irrespective of the pushes and pulls in the administrative domain. Perhaps the anthropological concept of tribe cannot be divorced from the growing influence of state institutions as such, but it can certainly be separated from the particular policies of particular states. Initially we should realise how the idea of the tribe was associated with and dependent upon certain schools of anthropological theory.

2. Functionalism

Anglo-Saxon literature has undoubtedly created the contours of social anthropology by supplying numerous well-known monographs concerned with tribal societies such as the classic on *The Tiv of Central Nigeria* by Laura and Paul Bohannan (1953). These societies were always located in lands ruled either by anglophone settlers, e.g. Australia and the United States, or by colonial governments in countries of Africa and Oceania. Amazingly India, one of the earliest and most important colonies of the British empire, was — during colonial times — almost completely ignored by the young academic discipline. Research in the Indian tribal areas was left to the administrators involved in "Census Ethnography". Philanthropical amateurs such as Sarat Chandra Roy, Verrier Elwin and Christoph von Fürer-Haimendorf, famous for their descriptive ethnographies, remained academic

3. This terminological neutrality must have been the reason for introducing the new designation *Scheduled Tribes* in favour of numerous 19th century remnants - including *Primitive Tribes* - in the course of the general administrative reforms of 1936.

outsiders and played absolutely no role in the theoretical or methodological development of the discipline. After independence this limitation was overcome with regard to caste society. Indian anthropologists are among the most far-sighted thinkers of the discipline. Students of tribal society, however, have continued to work in close association with the administrative apparatus. Anthropological research as such is next to impossible in the tribal areas, to this day, unless justified by some humanitarian "noble cause".

African studies — implying the concept of the tribe — undoubtedly dominated the field of social anthropology in the formative decades of the discipline. The generalisations of specific monographs were published since 1874 in a neat textbook called *Notes and Queries on Anthropology* written by the leading scholars assembled in *A Committee of the Royal Anthropological Institution* of Britain. The latest edition of 1951, frequently reprinted in the subsequent decades, offers the standard definition: "*A tribe may be defined as a politically or socially coherent and autonomous group occupying or claiming a particular territory*" (1951: 66 emphasis original). Furthermore the concept of tribal society was undoubtedly illustrated by professional accounts of a good number of tribes in anthropological classics such as *African Political Systems* of 1940[4] and *Tribes Without Rulers* of 1958[5], or Max Gluckman's *Politics, Law and Ritual in Tribal Society* of 1965, re-edited in 1982.

The latter author also indicated the important social changes since the nineteen-fifties. For him the term tribe referred to a political system in rural areas "based on...economic and social needs," while the "tribalism" of the towns was a recent development promoted by labour officers and other well-meaning but inept administrators (Gluckman, 1961: 55). Witnessing the political independence of most African states in the subsequent years, scholars of the functionalist school were keen to indicate the demise of tribal society in books named *From Tribe to Nation in Africa*[6] or *The Passing of Tribal Man in Africa.*[7] Among the many authors of this trend, Aidan Southall was perhaps the most outspoken, defining tribal society as

> "a whole society with a high degree of self-sufficiency at a near subsistence level, based on relatively simple technology without writing or literature, politically autonomous and with its own distinctive language, culture and sense of identity, tribal religion being co-terminus with tribal society" (Southall, 1970: 28).

As an unavoidable consequence, this author then pointed out that "no tribal society which has lost its political autonomy can continue to be a tribal

4. The editors were M. Fortes and E.E. Evans-Pritchard (1940).
5. The editors were J. Middleton and D. Tait.
6. The editors were R. Cohen and J. Middleton (Scranton, Chandler).
7. Edited by Peter C. Gutkind.

society in the full sense of the term, although many of its members may retain vivid and even nostalgic memories of its former full existence." Given these conditions, "they can only exist in dwindling pockets so remote..." (Southall, 1970: 29). Similar statements followed in numerous other publications until the nineteen-nineties, being also sceptical of the religious autonomy of the tribe (e.g. Ranger, 1993: 69).

All of these functionalist ethnographies of the tribe, as well as the later conclusions on the vanishing of the former subject of the discipline, were, of course, dependent upon substantialist definitions. They suffered from the defects of any "ethnic unit classification," as proposed by Naroll (1964) in an attempt to pin down the boundaries of substantial entities in anthropological research by criteria like a common territory, political organisation, and language.

As early as 1954 Edmund Leach had rebuked this kind of an approach to tribal society, as well as demarcations of the *Notes and Queries* type. "The concept of 'tribe' is of quite negative utility from the viewpoint of social analysis" (1954: XV), he wrote with reference to the complex whole of people inhabiting north-western Burma and Nagaland. He also noticed how several different languages were spoken by people involved in the same political and ideological systems. Consequently he dispatched the linguistic fallacy into the dustbin (1954: 45). The criterion of a common language as the marker of a cultural unit had, of course, much earlier been discarded by Boas[8] (1911: 139), but works of the father of American cultural anthropology had never belonged to the standard literature in British social anthropology. Perhaps the latest and most impressive testimony against the confusion of linguistic and socio-cultural criteria of tribal societies is Christine Hugh-Jones' brilliant book on the Tukano in the eastern Amazon riverian system of South America. Marriage among these longhouse-dwellers implies husband and wife to belong to different linguistisc units (1979: 17).

All functionalist attempts to devise several substantial criteria of membership, such as joint territory, language and political autonomy, in order to describe an ethnic entity[9] of tribal or non-tribal people have always been bound to fail, because evident exceptions were always at hand. It follows that the accounts of the passing of tribal society were equally fallacious, since they were dependent upon the very same untenable criteria in a prior existence of the people. In fact the functionalist logic was closely tied to political convictions. The ethnographers, women and men of great competence and integrity, had identified themselves with tribal people at a time when racist ideologies dominated much of Europe. They had also supported the independence movement and conceived nations of "new Africa," supposedly of the same content as the European nations. The concerns of these

8. *The mind of primitive man.* New York: Macmillan.
9. For the sake of brevity, we avoid the debate differentiating "groups" and "categorie".

anthropologists had always been directed towards the functional relationships between institutional establishments. If the latter meant state, church and industry, tribal society was supposed to vanish in favour of arrangements very much like the well-known nations of Europe. Any other development did not accord with the standards of political correctness. The others were to become like the own.

3. Evolutionism

Nineteenth century evolutionists had devised the scheme of a "primitive society" eventually to be transformed into a "civilisation"[10] through several stages of social evolution (Morgan, 1877: 12-13). In the famous phrase of Henry Sumner Maine, "the movement of the progressive societies has hitherto been a movement *from Status to Contract*" (1864: 165 emphasis original). Following the lead of these founding fathers of the discipline, the idea of a "general evolution" of societal types was rediscovered by Leslie White in 1959[11] and refined by several of his students in the nineteen-sixties. The ensuing debates were not without controversies regarding the nature of particular stages within such a typological sequence. Morton Fried (1967) tried to offer a coherent scheme of typological categories and, in the course of this endeavour, argued against his friends Service and Sahlins by seeing no "theoretical need for a tribal stage in the evolution of political organisation. Such a stage reveals nothing but does divert attention from the more important questions: how does ranking begin and how does it catalyse societies" (1966: 539).

Fried's evolutionary sequence was coherent, because it was concerned with a single criterion, ranking, or political and economic power. As is the case with modern north American school children, ranking sets in at an early age with the selection of the school and later continues to dominate the worlds of sororities and dating, housewives and professionals, clubs and stock exchanges, armed forces and universities. Fried, in other words, considered the dominant value of his own contemporary society[12] as the relevant guideline for grading human social evolution. The least ranked represented the earliest, those with the most elaborate and stringent form of ranking the latest stage.

Thus Fried's was an evolution of growing social inequality. In the course of his project, he found an initial stage of "simple egalitarian societies," consisting of bands involved in palaeolithic hunting and gathering, bound together by a reciprocal economy. They were followed in the next stage by "rank societies" whose members raised domestic plants and animals within

10. For the intellectual history see Kuper, 1988.
11. *The evolution of culture.* New York, McGraw-Hill.
12. Ranking is, of course, equally important in non-Western societies such as the Indian one.

a general economic order of redistribution and pooling. In the third stage of "stratified societies," equal access to the basic resources of life was no longer guarantied, and in the final one of "the state," Fried would observe "a collection of specialised institutions and agencies, some formal and others informal, that maintains an order of stratification" (1967: 235).

While Fried's evolutionary scheme neatly followed the central issue of Western ideology, his fellow evolutionists proposed stages roughly along the same lines under the headings of "hunters", "tribesmen", "peasants" and "the state".[13] When it came to "tribal" society, however, Sahlins offered a note of dissent by directing our attention to essential structural variations. As usual, he pointed to the differences between hunting and gathering bands in the preceding stage and the state in the succeeding typological formation, but "*food collectors*" (emphasis original) might also be called tribal, if they had undergone "a complicated development of clans and chiefs" (Sahlins, 1968: 3). Thus neither the modes of production, nor the degree of socio-political power alone were sufficient criteria to identify this stage. The significant aspect of the tribe was its multiplex organisation.

> "It lacks an independent economic sector or a separate religious organisation, let alone a special political mechanism. In a tribe, these are not so much different institutions as they are different functions of the same institutions" (Sahlins, 1968: 15).

For Sahlins, anthropological wisdom suggests us to abandon the conventional analysis of distinct economic, social-political, and ideological spheres, when it comes to tribes. "The tribal structure is generalised; in this lies its primitiveness" (ibid.).

4. Structuralism

Sahlins view of 1968 seems to indicate a shift, to become more obvious in his later career, away from the sole concern with cultural ecology and the development or the typology of political economies. In his book on "tribesmen" (1968), the relational patterns of a particular cultural logic gain a certain independence of the ecological and productive forces, then still very much the subject of this author. This shift must have come under the initial influence of Claude Lévi-Strauss who had earlier discussed "The Scope of Anthropology".[14]

The latter essay contains many jewels, especially the reference to the specifics of the anthropological approach in contrast to sociology, social

13. Marshall Sahlins was the editor of the most significant 'Foundations of Modern Anthropology Series' comprising books of Service (1966), Sahlins (1968), Wolf (1966) and Krader (1968) under these titles.

14. In 1960, this was his inaugural address to the College de France, the most eminent academic insitution of that country. It was initially published in *Current Anthropology*.

psychology and other particular sciences (Lévi-Strauss, 1973: 14). Today many of us, trained and preoccupied by a logic of the political economy, tend to ignore the cultural priorities, so the anthropological basics of the French school might as well be remembered for a moment: "The social facts which we study are manifested in societies, each of which is *a total, concrete, and cohesive entity*" (ibid. emphasis original). Later Dumont, in the same vain, saw "*our own modern culture and society as one particular form of humanity*" (1986: 205/6 emphasis original) and as different from "nonmodern societies" (ibid.). The message of these statements does, of course, criticise our[15] tendency to ignore other "forms of humanity," or the particular nature of other "cohesive entities," by applying the social categories — and their particular relational patterns — of our own cultural logic in the course of our anthropological analysis. This widespread tendency has been called sociocentrism by Dumont. It is also found in all political quarters of those who equate the development of administrative systems to the welfare of humanity.

Dumont's term "nonmodern society" appears to be a somewhat defensive phrasing. He opposes it to "traditional societies" like the Indian order of caste, and to the modern Western social type. Mary Douglas is more explicit in stressing "the relevance of tribal studies" (1975) and Lévi-Strauss offers a new terminology. He does talk about "so-called primitive societies" when he views their past being as old as ours, "since it goes back to the origin of the species" (1973: 28). His own phrasing makes use of the term "cold" societies. The distinction to "hot" or dynamic ones is "mainly theoretical, for there is probably no concrete society which, in its whole as well as in its components, corresponds exactly to either type" (1973: 29).

This clear rejection of substantialist definitions takes us to his central concern which is in agreement with Sahlins concept of the tribe: "Of course, so-called primitive societies belong in history" Lévi-Strauss is eager to insist: "Over thousands of years, they have undergone all sorts of transformations, gone through periods of crisis and prosperity....But they have specialised in ways different from those we have chosen" (1973: 28). The significant aspect of cold or tribal societies is that they

> "seem to have developed or retained a particular wisdom which impels them to resist desperately any modification in their structure that would enable history to burst into their midst" (ibid.).

Other authors, concerned with the cosmos of tribal religion, have similarly indicated the tribal endeavour to "take shelter from the terror of history" (Eliade, 1954: 159).

15. The term "our" may refer to the sociocentric bias of Europeans, Indians, Chinese or anyone else.

This lead, which to us is the only acceptable course, will make us abandon all substantialist efforts to conceive definitive boundaries of a human assembly called tribe, just as we will have to abandon the idea of such tribes uniting as nations with the introduction of the administrative institutions of the modern state. Western arrogance, convinced of an evolutionary concept with Western individualism at the top of the ladder of social development, should be relegated to the cabinets of nineteenth century armchair anthropologists and nowhere else.

The biased reasoning of the evolutionist concept is not dissimilar to the functionalist fallacy. Both take the priority of the political economy as self-understood, i.e. the power of the administrated economy to determine the world of ideas and values. In the footsteps of Western commonsense, the ideology of a people is conceived as a necessary consequence of events in the domain of production and as an insignificant prime mover. If such a general opinion has been relativised occasionally, e.g. by the Weberian thesis on Protestant ethics[16] or by the undeniable experience of an immortal caste system, reservations vanish when it comes to people without temples, shops and armies, organised along the lines of kinship within a subsistence economy. How could their institutions resist the onslaught of hydroelectric dams and steel mills, missionaries and schools, general elections and development aid, anthropologists and tourists?

If we understand Lévi-Strauss or Sahlins correctly, the very simplicity of these institutions, their generalised structure, is the source of the power to resist the forces of history. There being little to undo, little can be undone. The structural primitiveness is the strength of tribal concept of the world.

Such an institutional lack of differentiation regularly goes together with a superb degree of individual competence. Any fieldworker can testify this inverse relationship in primitive society, because most of us, equipped with considerable financial resources, have found it difficult to join the life in the mud huts of the forest fully over an extended period of time, whereas the people we call tribal could demonstrate their power to survive without a regular income, even if the promised salaries were not paid, the crops failed or the water had been poisoned by the nearby factory, the monument of development. The primitiveness of the tribal structure goes together with all-round individual skills and a complex world of religion,[17] normally beyond the reach of those used to writing and other "stores" of cosmological interpretations.

16. See Weber, Max 1920; die protestantische Ethik und der Geist des Kapitalismus. *In* Max Weber, *Gesammelte Aufsatze zur Religionsoziologie,* Tubingen, Mohr.
17. The best study of the religion of an Indian tribe is that of Vitebsky (1993).

6. The Past, the Present and the Future of Tribal Society

There has never been a pristine tribal society. Wolf (1982) has shown convincingly, how all peoples of the world have at times immigrated into their land and mixed with locals, adopted cultural traits from far away places and succumbed to foreign powers by the latter's direct or indirect interventions. This author has, however, ignored the amazing fact that cultural differences remained in spite of such a general subjection to the forces of history. "If the indigenous peoples were not without history, it was because they were not without culture — which is also why their modern histories have differed" (Sahlins, 1999: xii).

Culture is the key term. Anthropologists can make two elementary mistakes. One is to assume that humans of another land are different from themselves. They are not. They belong to the same species and are endowed with the same human qualities. The second basic mistake is to assume that the cultural logic or the value-ideas of others should be the same as the own, provided certain socio-economic institutions are adjusted or a certain stage of social evolution has been reached. Moral priorities and classifications of the world vary from one society to the next. Cultures differ. Cultures can, for example, go together with "hot" societies to experience a vast variety of transformations, or with "cold" societies resisting such trends.

In a seminal essay on anthropological enlightenment, Sahlins has recently shown that "the surviving victims of imperial capitalism neither became all alike nor just like us". Without belittling their hardships, he has shown that "surviving indigenous peoples aim to take cultural responsibility for what has been done to them" (1999: i). His essay argues against a widespread "sentimental pessimism," or "the encompassment of other people's lives in global visions of Western domination" (1999: vi). Observing an "indigenisation of modernity" Sahlins shows how North American hunters and gatherers continue to live by hunting and gathering. They still adhere to their subsistence economy, even if such stubbornness implies the joint purchase of "subsistence airplanes" (1999: xv). His essay is a denial of the received anthropological clichés opposing tradition and change, indigenous culture and modernity or tribesmen and townsmen. If he knew India, he might have added the opposition of "backwardness" and "uplift".

In the past, the globe was not inhabited by peoples without history, but by peoples of different cultures. A standard illustration refers to the Chinese who mostly avoid eating milk or milk products, but do consume beef, while the Indians mostly avoid beef, but certainly like to consume milk and milk products. Such differences, essential for the concerned cultures, have marked the past, are observed in the present and will rule in future.

The human condition is determined by cultural variability. Societies of hunters and gatherers, or tribal societies, are likely to retain their cultural particularities or recombine them in a new context, as they have done in the past, even if external conditions will change drastically. The culture of caste has given innumerable illustrations of such adaptability. Thus non-resident Indians, living in the USA in the fourth generation, would continue to prefer "decent marriages" and find the adequate spouses via internet rather than follow the Western style of "love marriage". Another example takes us to the island of Sriharikota in Andhra Pradesh where the government has established a space research station since 1971 launching satellites on rockets. The local population of the hunting and gathering Yanadi was evacuated and provided with farms on the mainland. Like tens of thousands of other Yanadis, however, the new farmers refused to subject themselves to the rule of the plough and trickled back to their old environment and old lives on the island in the course of two decades, developing a viable coexistence with the space research staff (Rao, 1991).

If the criticising "sentimental pessimism" is overdue, this is not to deny the past and present suffering of people ill-equipped to resist superior weapons or superior administrations. Atrocities against those citizens of the state who form a cultural minority are likely to continue, even if tribes or bands, commanding a good amount of experience, are likely to find better ways to cope with setbacks than drop-outs within the majority culture. The reasons for a more optimistic attitude refer to the phenomenon called "globalisation," usually conceived as the death-bell of tribal independence. Ulf Hannerz has pointed to the newly emerging world culture, "marked by an organisation of diversity rather than a replication of uniformity" (1990: 237). Sahlins has called it "a Culture of cultures" (1999: x) in which generalised structures like those of tribes are likely to be assets rather than liabilities.

7. Contributions to This Volume

In the present volume, the articles of Part I deal with South Asia. They indicate a general pattern, which — in Nepal — has been neatly adjusted to the organisation of the modern state. Gaenszle's contribution offers an historical overview of the Kiranti people there indicating complex changes in the course of history. In spite of these transformations, the proud tribal people have retained a distinct life world of their own, characterised by two fundamental traits: the idiom of kinship and the bond to ancestral land and territory. Gaenszle also describes the order of the house which, as everywhere in the tribal north, northeast and middle of the subcontinent, comprises the fundamental economic and social unit and, often ignored, the symbolic structure reflecting major cosmological ideas and values.

Berger's research leads to the large (old) Koraput District of Orissa, which is characterised by a tribal majority. He shows that the local society, known to differ sharply from immigrant caste people of the plains, contains a good number of segments not belonging to the administrative category of

Scheduled Tribes. Some, but not all of them, enjoy the advantages of another sort of bureaucratic status, while all interact closely in social, economic, and ritual affairs in spite of the fact that they follow different callings and frequent a number of languages of the three major Indian linguistic families.

One of these non-scheduled groups is being described at length in Hadders' article, concerned with the Jādopaṭiās in West Bengal, Bihar and Orissa. They perform priestly services for the Santal, a major Indian tribe counting some five million members. Within the twelve clans of the latter, the second one called *Murmu* used to be equated with the priestly functions in the past, particularly the *nij* or "original" *Murmu* local line in every village. Hadders describes how today outsiders have been integrated in this position with particular regard to the funeral rites and the communication with the dead, a degraded status in the Hindu context. The officiants speak both Santali and Bengali. By their empathetic skill and their extensive knowledge of the Santal world they have obtained considerable influence upon the tribal culture.

Van Schendel and Balz, working in both parts of Bengal, point to the colonial heritage of past sociological classifications and the elusive character of what might be considered tribal or indigenous. Their examples show clearly how any substantialist definition of the tribe is bound to be unworkable and how some are highly problematic. While the racism and the substantialism of Census Ethnography has been overcome with regard to caste in innumerable works on *jati* and *varna* during the last decades, modern South Asian social anthropologists tend to avoid debating the problems related to the concept of tribe. In our opinion, this gap may be explained by the lack of long-term field research in tribal societies and by the linguistic proximity of most ethnographers who command the regional *lingua franca* and thus tend to gloss over the cultural differences. East Bengal may have, after the evacuation of the great bulk of upper-caste Hindus, become culturally more homogeneous, or a society defined by cleavages of class, and yet there are these "other people" of the Chittagong Hill Tracts, outsiders for all Bengalis. Definitions of cultural boundaries have always been problematic. Communities of a cultural minority, disreputable in the eyes of the majority, have always and all over the world been in search for a label without the discriminatory meaning — mostly without much success. Such a label may refer to the naming practices of in-groups or out-groups, to the designations of the state or the political parties, and to academic considerations. If they overlap, the intentions of the users should be clarified, since any intellectual compromise is bound to lead to new problems.

Part of the distinctive cultural logic conceived by the millions of Santal, when compared to the general Hindu world-view, is the conception of time as elaborated in Carrin's article. She follows Bloch's suggestion (1998) to differentiate the semantic and the episodic past, or events of the past aiming to organise and transmit knowledge and the autobiographical memory, tinged with emotion. Thus Carrin takes up an anthropological tradition initiated by Evans-Pritchard's discussion of "ecological time" (1940: 100) when she is describing the temporality of work and seasons among the Santal, known as the "cattle-clock" among the Nuer. The world of the Santal Bongas, or transcendental beings, by contrast is involving the spacing of generations, provided the funerals have been performed correctly. Like the Australian *dreaming*, the transcendental cosmos of the Bongas is at once the past, the present and the future. Death, if experienced in proper order, implies the regeneration of life, while an unfinished person, like a woman who dies before marriage, becomes a Hinduised kind of malevolent spirit. Like the other middle Indian tribes, the Santal see themselves as *hor hopon*, or humans, a species different from the *diku*, or non-tribal outsiders who have always been known, but known as a different kind.

Trawick is among the few contributors who are native speakers of the English language. The literary style of her article is able to convey a tremendous sensitivity. It is adequately relating to her subject, the songs of the Villi of Tamil Nadu. Their themes are as heterogeneous as grief or politics, love or the ethnographer. After having spent longer periods in an Indian tribal village, most anthropologists will have experienced composition and performance of songs as a specific female medium of emotion and critique. They will be amazed over the versatile techniques employed during the singing. Trawick has the distinction to write about members of a category on the margin of caste society, called "Bowmen" in the present case, and not so different from the Vagri (see Werth, 1996) and other tribes of India who used to be branded as "Criminal Tribes" in colonial times and were then locked up in camps. All over the subcontinent they catch and charm snakes or operate as roadside dentists and medical consultants or let animals perform. The Villi may have been hunter-gatherers in the past, since they operate as foragers in the present. All urban life in India, both of the south and the north, would be unthinkable — and perhaps unbearable — without these foragers, as experienced thirty years ago, when Pfeffer (1970) studied the moiety-organisation of the vagrant Sansi in the Punjab and their relative hierarchical superiority in relation to the foraging urban Gaggera and some ten other small vagrant tribes, the so-called tent-dwellers or *pakkiwas*.

The outstanding trait the Sansi claim for themselves is their "wildness". We are particularly grateful to Tambs-Lyche for discussing "wildness" and militancy as an all-Indian value-idea, linking many tribes — such as those of the Dangs in south Gujarat — with the life-style of the Rajput rulers in western India and many other middle or upper castes of the subcontinent. Following Dumezil he is also relating them to the peoples in the epics of his home in northern Europe. Tambs-Lyche is thus able to avoid the usual stereotype of classification, linking tribes with "savage" characteristics and

Hindus with civilised order. What is described as "heroic masculinity" may belong to the tradition of both, as opposed to the Brahmin/Bania virtues of vegetarianism and restraint or to the evidently gentle bearing, which is self-understood for many tribal people. Not just in western India but also all over the subcontinent the point is applicable that "wildness" is an integral part of the whole political order, as the great wars of the Hindu epics indicate or any observer can confirm who has witnessed a modern general election in the countryside.

Apart from an excellent overview of the history of Gujarat, involving tribe-king alliances, Tambs-Lyche's article implicitly refers to a major borderline within the category of *Scheduled Tribes* which can be traced in that region for South Asia: In Gujarat it is dividing the pastoral tribes, such as the Rabari, and the cultivators, such as the Bhil. After extensive fieldwork in middle India, we think that Bhil and other tribes further east display a somewhat negligent attitude, when it comes to raising and herding cattle, while the cultivation of land — whether terraced, rain-fed, or swidden — is the core of their productive activities. Further to the south of Gujarat, however, or to the west and north, pastoralism defines the mode of production of the tribes, as it does in neighbouring Pakistan, or in Afghanistan and the Muslim countries further to the northwest.

A general comparison is the theme of Pfeffer's contribution, referring to social structure rather than the economic domain. He discusses aspects of the structural set-up in various formations within the middle Indian tribes and compares them in South Asian and African, Middle-Eastern and Polynesian tribal societies, as known from the anthropological literature. Also indicated are the elementary structural differences between tribes and such major castes as the Jat of northern India or bureaucratic organisations like that of a western European state.

The final contribution to Part I on South Asia is Demmer's article on the foraging Jēnu Kuṛumba of southern India. These hunters and gatherers are included in this volume as a deliberate structural contrast. Unlike the tribes, they lack lineages or other decent groups and categories that might define them in formal or corporate units. On a first look their social formation exhibits a considerable degree of flexibility and fluidity. Having spent about four years in a Jēnu Kuṛumba community, Demmer is, however, in a position to decipher relational patterns of this society and confirm other studies of south Indian hunter-gatherers stressing the paramount importance of social relatedness. The social praxis, the personified relational patterns observed by the ethnographer, reveal the general constitution. Demmer takes a look at the interpersonal relationships, the daily and the ritual links between kin, the structure of the camps for economic purposes and the details of the death ritual. It should also be clear that the south Indian foraging groups — like the tribes — are not and may never have been isolated from the rest of Indian society. They have their own view of the "outside world". As against popular stereotypes, the structural wealth of this "simple society" will be the lasting impression of this report.

In Part II of the volume the reader is introduced to comparable situations. Regarding the tribal societies beyond South Asia, Glatzer's introduction to the Pashtun tribal system deals with a West Asian pattern, even if about half of the Pashtun people do not live in Afghanistan but in the two western provinces of Pakistan, a part of South Asia. As in India, Pashtuns are proud of their tribal status. Belonging to a tribe is equivalent to being dependable and genuine. The former kings and the religious and political leaders of the countries highlight their tribal background, just as urban intellectuals are sure to refer to their tribal belonging. As is suitable for the West Asian pattern, Glatzer defines the tribe as a social segment based on a genealogical concept of social structure. We find the best example of such a concept in the Bible's *Book of Genesis* where Adam's tribe is introduced along with several subtribes or lineages. Tribe, for this author, is a structural concept of social order and not the description of a substantial mass of people. Glatzer shows how the idea has survived the Soviet invasion and the recent civil war in Afghanistan.

The genealogical criteria would, of course, apply to major north Indian castes (Rajput, Jat) as well, but the latter — in contrast to the Pashtuns — must observe the rule of exogamy among unilineal descent categories and castes are very much "part-societies" — one among many — depending upon the division of labour, ritual and armed services of the system as a whole. Such a division may, to a minor extent, be observed in tribal or other societies as well, but it will not be the core-value or the precondition of economic, socio-political, and religious life, as it is in the order of caste. If we keep in mind that middle Indian tribes lack genealogical concepts, and if we wish to speculate in terms of conquest theories, we might conceive — following the path of Sanskrit traditions — genealogically structured tribes coming out of West and Central Asia — perhaps as pastoralists — subjugating the indigenous tribal cultivators who are organised without such genealogical structures. The conquerors, as upper castes, might then also retain their pre-eminence by linking their elaborate pedigree to Rama or Krishna, as is the case among the major Rajput descent categories. Such speculations should, of course, by no means pave the way to a new fashion of conjectural history. They should simply indicate how partial structural overlapping of different societal types might have come about.

Braukämper's paper on the Bedouin leads to the classical West Asian and North African example of tribal society. Economically, the Bedouin are seen as Arabic (sometimes non-Arabic as well) nomadic herders of sheep, goats, and camels in opposition to sedentary peasants on the one hand and citizens of the urban centres on the other. The author offers an excellent description of the Bedouin habitat and of the evolution of Bedouin culture, which can be traced back to the 10th millennium BC. They have never lived in an isolated world of their own, but always maintained intensive relations with town-dwellers and peasants, or producers of vegetarian food. Thus some of them have supported and others have rejected the rise of the Prophet of Islam. Some political or religious leaders of the Arab world have — in the past and in the present — adhered to the modest life of the desert people. As a specialist of the Middle-Eastern ecology and traditional economy the author gives us a comprehensive and vivid description of a free and proud people, their life-cycle and their socio-political organisation and their value-ideas, such as the central concept of hospitality. He also points to recent social changes under the drastic conditions of a global oil market.

Shashahani's article discusses a central theme of such change, the use and abuse of educational programmes. She is concerned with nomads like the Bedouins, with periodically moving pastorlists of Iran where these tribes form a major section of the population. Her first-hand experience was gained among the Mamassani, a segment of the great Lor people who, like so many others, had been exposed to the "mobile schools" introduced by the government in the nineteen-fifties with the massive support of the United States of America. Shashahani rightly begins with the observation that nobody in Iran had ever undertaken research on the indigenous system of nomad education, and yet the bulk of anthropologists would do fieldwork in tribal Iran with "modernising" intentions. The mobile school system was in reality a manipulative strategy of sedentarisation. In the words of Paulo Freire (1970), the author calls it an undertaking of "oppressive pedagogy". The white tents of canvas, provided by the USA for the schools, were seen next to the black tents of goathair, the symbol of nomad independence between Pakistan and Morocco. The modernisers' effort was part of a cold war scheme to stabilise the Shah's regime and to keep communism out of the oil-rich countries. Like many efforts of "tribal education" all over the world, the modernisers were naive at best. Tribal youths who had been lured into the programme by pictures of "the educated" as doctors or teachers found themselves unemployed at the end of their school career and denounced as "lazy". As can be seen elsewhere on the globe, they were also unable to follow the traditional pursuits of the parents and were apt to ridicule elders and those who — like many women — had retained their native tribal language being less exposed to Persian. Many of the students continued to feel inferior because fluent Persian was never mastered. Significant for the tribal world in general may be Shashahani's following reference to Freire: "For cultural invasion to succeed, it is essential that those invaded become convinced of their intrinsic inferiority" (1970: 151).

Social change is also a topic of Tanner's contribution on East Africa. He is convincingly rejecting the simplistic dichotomy of townsmen and tribesmen, since — as elsewhere — individuals are on the move between the rural and the expanding urban areas. Just as Sahlins (1999: xix) has recently differentiated the social and the geographical village, Tanner points to the commuters of whom few are permanently committed to towns. His primary concern is the religion of the quasi-traditional type which, like Christianity and Islam in East Africa, includes "all activities related to or directed at metaphysical realities". Such religious practices, just as the social ones, are seen under conditions of virtually permanent dispersal. Thus a certain cult changes sharply within a period of a decade or, for example, between the region to the north of Lake Victoria and that in the south. Religious ideas and practices focus on individuals and their families, on the rites of passage and on reactions to problems experienced. The inherited religious and social paradigm does not indicate the path towards centralising and centralised religions. The basis of social segmentation is competition. Independent Christian and quasi-traditional religious leaders are in covert competition with each other within their ostensible commitment to spirituality. The author argues that — given the socio-historical background — thinking within the tribal paradigm is not only acceptable but to be expected. It fulfils important functions that can only be met by the quasi-traditional interpretations.

Van Horn's account takes us to the Micmac, settled in "reservations" or "reserves" within their original territory in the state of Maine, of the northeastern United States, and the adjoining Canadian regions. They too work as commuters in various new professions frequently crossing the international border. In spite of European influence of more than four centuries, the Micmac have retained their particular eastern Algonkian language, their bilateral kinship organisation of patrilocal extended families and their old ethical standards, the topic of the article. Van Horn describes egalitarian values which in fact imply the idea of *noblesse oblige* for the leaders: a man of influence makes it "a point of honour to be always the worst dressed of his people". Micmac humour encourages people to make puns. It is self-depreciating and full of irony. Such an attitude and its consequences are found in many tribal communities all over the world, particularly in middle India. Members of the tribe "find it virtually impossible to accept authority of any kind". This individualism goes together with sharing work and money within the kinship unit. Environmental data for hunting and fishing or material possessions are property of the group. With regard to efforts of adjustment to the general conditions of North America it is found that educational and commercial enterprises fail when competitiveness is stressed in the European manner, whereas they succeed when undertaken as a group effort.

Another specific problem faced by tribals of the native American "reservations" is discussed in Suzuki's paper, the issue of double jeopardy, or accusations of a suspected criminal in a Tribal as well as in the Federal Court of the United States. A man of the Blackfeet tribe had to face the

Winnebago Tribal Court, because he had committed crimes on the "reservation" of the latter tribe. Being charged simultaneously by a Federal Court, the problem of "over-administration" in a culture adverse to bureaucratic institutions becomes evident.

Köhler's general overview of the indigenous population of Mexico is also a history of the devastation, caused by European conquest since the second decade of the 16th century. The Spanish colonialists destroyed the pre-Columbian civilisations that had been outstanding in the fields of science and administration. The conquerors killed, enslaved or decultured the population of the former empires. When the country obtained independence three hundred years later, it continued to be ruled by the European minority making up about 10 per cent of the population. The other ethnic categories of Mexico refer to the Ladinos, or supposed descendents of the native Indios and Europeans making up about 65 per cent, and finally Indios, mostly living in the southern states of the country. The Indio majority cannot really be considered tribal, since they differ from the assimilated Spanish-speaking society of Ladinos only due to their linguistic and cultural affiliation. None of the many different linguistic groups stands for common interests or political organisation, identity being associated with the particular locality or *municipio*, even if, as is the case among the Tzotzil in Chiapas, the language group is subdivided into many "tribes" marked by a particular dress and dialect. Many Indio commuters to the cities have the opportunity to be assimilated to the Spanish-speaking Ladino category within a short period of time. Thus the majority of indigenous Mexicans have lost the cultural expressions and values of their ancestor's complex society without a comparable substitute. In the north of Mexico, however, a region without pre-Columbian civilisations — the Indios like the Tarahumara of Chihuahua, the Yaqui or the Seri — have retained their tribal social structure. Anthropologists would not class them along with the native population of Mesoamerica but rather as a part of the "Greater Southwest" which also includes well-known southwestern tribes of the USA.

Finally Gregory's article, like Demmers at the end of the South Asia section in Part I, introduces a different societal type in a different political context. The author declares himself to be a peripheral member of a self-defined "tribe," the inhabitants of the Appalachian mountain-range in the eastern United States. In choosing such an identity, he is convinced that in the year 2000 "tribal communities are typically found in the backwash of modern society, without power and control over their own destiny". Perhaps several hundred million Asian tribals would contradict such a finding, i.e. being defined only by extended ties of kinship, strong religious beliefs, weak insiders and strong outsiders. The provocation of postmodern arbitrariness must, however, be taken as an appropriate final chapter of our attempt to reconsider our categories. The inhabitants of Appalachia are said to demonstrate their "tribal" culture in several significant sketches the author has selected. Thus the hill-people of a Holler (mountain ridge) were observed to shoot systematically at outsiders' cars, or bright young people stayed home — because "family comes first" — even if this meant permanent professional stagnation and unemployment. Teachers of a university department never met for private dinners. These Appalachian "tribals" are said to have fundamentalist religious beliefs, even if their preachers are openly callous when it comes to the theft of a towel. They tell rich stories about secretly finding and selling ginseng roots in the woods outside the control of "revenooers" (government agents). For the author these are signs of "the inability to control one's own life, to stay on the side of law and order....and to maintain ever present kinship networks and alliances rather than engage in feuds". Exaggerated security arrangements for the powerful are also said to be an aspect of such "tribal" culture, just as secrecy and selfishness in financial matters or, among students, cutting out competitors by illegal means. Gregory's "tribals" celebrate weekends as fiddlers with their mountain music enthralling visitors, tourists and the musicians themselves. In short, they do not "move ahead" according to the standard American values but rather flee from "the terrors and insecurities of modern life" into the haven of an evangelical religion. They have been "vanquished and reside...in a state of plight akin to that of the Native Americans". Gregory's conclusion sees lifestyles, culture and patterns of Appalachia as "precursors for the future of all of us, around the world".

REFERENCES

Bloch, Maurice. 1998. *How We Think They Think. Anthropological Approaches to Cognition, Memory and Literacy.* Colorado: Westview Press.

Boas, Franz. 1911. *The Mind of Primitive Man.* New York: Macmillan.

Bohannan, Laura and Paul. 1953. *The Tiv of Central Nigeria.* London: International African Institute.

Cohen, Ronald and John Middleton (eds.). 1970. *From Tribe to Nation in Africa.* Swanton: Chandler.

Dalton, Edward Tuite. 1872. *Descriptive Ethnology of Bengal.* Calcutta: Govt. Printing.

Douglas, Mary. 1975. "Couvade and Menstruation. The Relevance of Tribal Studies," (pp. 60-73) in Mary Douglas (ed.), *Implicit Meanings. Essays in Anthropology.* London: Routledge.

Dumont, Louis. 1986. *Essays on Individualism.* Chicago: The University of Chicago Press.

Eliade, Mircea. 1954. *The Myth of the Eternal Return or Cosmos and History.* London: Penguin.

Evans-Pritchard, E.E. 1940. *The Nuer.* London: Oxford University Press.

Fortes, Meyer and E.E. Evans-Pritchard. 1940. *African Political Systems.* London: Oxford University Press.

Freire, Paulo. 1970. *Pedagogy of the Oppressed.* New York: Seabury Press.

Fried, Morton H. 1966. "On the Concepts of 'Tribe' and 'Tribal Society'," (pp. 527-540) *Transactions of the New York Academy of Science*, Ser. 2, vol. 28.

Fried, Morton. 1967. *The Evolution of Political Society. An Essay in Political Anthropology*. New York: Random House.

Gluckman, Max. 1960. "Tribalism in Modern British Central Africa," *Cahiers D'etudes Africaines*, 1: 55-70.

Gluckman, Max. 1965 (1982). *Politics, Law and Ritual in Tribal Society*. Oxford: Blackwell.

Government of Orissa. 1994. *Tribal Education in Orissa in the Context of Education for All by 2000 AD*. Bhubaneswar. Tribal Welfare Department Publication.

Gutkind, Peter W. (ed.). 1970. *The Passing of Tribal Man in Africa*. Leiden: Brill.

Hannerz, Ulf. 1990. "Cosmopolitans and Locals in World Culture," (pp. 237-51) in M. Featherstone (ed.), *Global Culture*. London: Sage.

Hugh-Jones, Christine. 1979. *From the Milk River. Spatial and Temporal Processes in Northwest Amazonia*. Cambridge: Cambrige University Press.

Krader, Lawrence. 1968. *Formation of the State*. Englewood Cliffs: Prentice Hall.

Kuper, Adam. 1988. *The Invention of Primitive Society. Transformations of an Illusion*. London: Routledge.

Leach, E. R. 1954. *Political Systems of Highland Burma. A Study of Kachin Social Structure*. London: Athlone.

Lévi-Strauss, Claude. 1973. *Structural Anthropology 2*. Harmondsworth: Penguin.

Maine, Henry Sumner. 1864. *Ancient Law*. New York: H. Holt.

Middleton, John and David Tait. (eds.). 1958. *Tribes Without Rulers. Studies in African Segmentary Systems*. London: Routledge.

Morgan, Lewis Henry. 1878. *Ancient Society*. New York: H. Holt.

Naroll, Raoul. 1964. "On Ethnic Unit Classification," *Current Anthropology*, 5: 283-91; 306-12.

Pfeffer, Georg. 1970. *Pariagruppen des Pandschab*. Munich: Renner.

Ranger, Terence. 1993. "The Local and the Global in Southern African Religious History," (pp.65-98) in H. Hefner Robert (ed.), *Conversion to Christianity*. Berkeley: University of California Press.

Rao, Memalladinne Sudharkar. 1991. Marriage Alliance, Family and Kinship in an Island Community: A Case of Yanadi of Sriharikota Island. Unpublished Ph.D. Dissertation, University of Hyderabad.

Royal Anthropological Institution. 1951. *Notes and Queries on Anthropology* (6th edition). London: Routledge.

Sahlins, Marshall D. 1968. *Tribesmen*. Englewood Cliffs: Prentice Hall.

Sahlins, Marshall D. 1999. "What is Anthropological Enlightenment? Some Lessons of the Twentieth Century," *Annual Review of Anthropology*, 28: i-xxiii.

Service, Elman R. 1966. *The Hunters*. Englewood Cliffs: Prentice Hall.

Southall, Aidan W. 1970. "The Illusion of the Tribe," (pp. 28-50) in Peter W. Gutkind (ed.), *The Passing of Tribal Man in Africa*. Leiden: Brill.

Tribal Studies Committee, Indian Council of Social Sciences Research. 1999. *Draft Executive Report*. New Delhi: Ministry of Human Resource Development.

Vitebsky, Piers. 1993. *Dialogues with the Dead. The Discussion of Mortality among the Sora of Eastern India*. Cambridge: Cambridge University Press.

Werth, Lukas. 1996. *Von Göttinnen und ihren Menschen. Die Vagri, Vaganten Südindiens*. Berlin: Das Arabische Buch.

White, Leslie. 1959. *The Evolution of Culture*. New York: McGraw-Hill.

Wolf, Eric R. 1966. *Peasants*. Englewood Cliffs: Prentice Hall.

Wolf, Eric R. 1982. *Europe and the People without History*. Berkeley: University of California Press.

SECTION I

SOUTH ASIA

ONE

THE KIRANTI GROUPS OF EAST NEPAL

MARTIN GAENSZLE

When the Gorkhali troops of Prithvi Narayan Shah, the founder of modern Nepal, entered the Kirat region in 1772 in their attempt to conquer the eastern territories controlled by the petty kings of the Sen dynasty, they met with strong resistance by the local people. Being skilled archers Kiranti youths inflicted heavy losses on the Gorkhali side, so that Prithvi Narayan Shah had to send reinforcements. However, in spite of their courage their bows and arrows eventually had no chance against the muskets of the invaders (Acharya, 1973). Today the Kiranti peoples are one of the largest ethnic units, well integrated within the Hindu Kingdom and nation-state of Nepal. But though to the outsider they appear not very much different from the Hindu castes in the hills (known generally as Parbatiya), on closer view one can still recognise a strong and distinct tribal heritage.

1. Profile

So who are the Kiranti? First of all it must be stressed that the ethnic unit known as Kiranti is far from being homogenous. It comprises the Rai groups (over a dozen "subtribes" with distinct languages), the Limbu, Yakha, Sunuwar and Ḥayu, but also is often understood to include the Mechi, Rajbamsi, Danuwar in the Tarai (plains) as well as the Thami and Chepang. Sometimes the term is even used in a very general sense to include all the Tibeto-Burman speaking ethnic groups in the Central Himalayas (cf. Chemjong, 1966). In fact, the term Kiranti has a complex history (see below) and so there is reason to be cautious in using this ethnonym. But nevertheless, there are various features which justify considering these groups as closely related. Linguistically they form a special family within the Bodic language group, and culturally they can be seen as distinct due to common characteristics in the structure and content of their social institutions. Though influenced both by the Great Tradition of the South, Hinduism, as well as the Great Tradition of the North, Lamaist Buddhism, they share the cultural core of a tribal culture, which is dependent on neither of these.

1.1. Ethnic Categories

To begin with, I will take a closer look at the background of the ethnonyms. Of particular interest is the history of the term Kiranti (Kirāti). This word has rather rich connotations due to the fact that it is related to the Sanskrit term Kirāta. In the old Sanskrit texts, particularly in the epics (*Mahābhārata* and *Rāmāyaṇa*), this refers to an infamous warring "race" inhabiting the mountains of the north and northeast of the subcontinent. For the most part they were looked upon as uncouth barbarians on the border to civilised India, living as gatherers of fruits and tubers, and by hunting and fishing. Among other things, their "golden" skin color, the hair knot tied on the top of their head and a knife related to the Nepalese *khukuri* are cited as being characteristic of them (Lévi, 1985 II: 74-78 provides a survey of the textual references; see the commentary of this classic work by Riccardi, 1975: 52-55; Chatterji, 1974). Famous above all other stories about them is the episode in the *Mahābhārata* in which Shiva, disguised as a *Kirāta*, turns against Arjuna but in the end presents him with the miraculous pāśupata weapon. Moreover, according to the Nepalese chronicles (vaṃśāvati Sk), there were *Kirāta* who ruled over the Kathmandu Valley for a period of more than 1,000 years, until they were driven out by the direct ancestors of the Licchavi, the earliest dynasty of Nepal documented inscriptionally (Lévi, 1985 II: 78-85).

Does this mean that the *Kirāta* were a well-defined group, a kind of ancient Himalayan tribe, which has been there for times immemorial (as popular usage often implies)? A critical look at the evidence leads to different considerations. Already the Indologist Sylvain Lévi concluded that *Kirāta* was a general term used by the Hindus of the plains to designate the Tibeto-Burman speaking groups of the Himalayas and Northeast India (Lévi, 1985 II: 77). Thus it is unlikely that the *Kirāta* who ruled the Kathmandu Valley were a particular ethnic group. Rather the evidence suggests that they were forefathers of the present day Newar (the Tibeto-Burman speaking indigenous people of the valley) and were described as *Kirāta* primarily by outsiders. Similarly it can be shown that up to the 19th century the term *Kirāt* was mainly used by the people (especially administrators) in the Kathmandu Valley to designate the eastern regions (Burghart, 1984: 107), and that only gradually the peoples there took up *Kirāti* ("those of *Kirāt*") as a self-designation.[1] Today, to call oneself a Kiranti means identification with a prestigious and ancient past, even though once it may have been a pejorative term (according to one theory it can be derived from Sanskrit *kira* "edge" + *at* "to roam").

Early reports of the 19th century leave the impression that there was a multitude of ethnic categories with often unclear referents and confusing classificatory status (e.g. Campbell, 1840; Hodgson, 1880 I). This basically reflects the segmentary character of the local groups which at this time had little reason to develop an identity beyond the local level. Nevertheless, it seems that some broader terms were used in self-designation already then: Khambu was used by certain Kiranti groups in the Western Kirat region, and Yakthumba in the east. But only in the course of the consolidation of the Gorkhali state the latter became known as Limbu, and most of the remaining groups took up the ethnonym "*Rai*". This term derives from the title *rāi* (Skt *rājan*, "king"), which was given to the local headmen by the Gorkhali rulers. Thus this category developed into an ethnonym by metonymic extension. A similar process can be observed with the term *Jimi*, which is used for certain Rai in the Arun Valley: it is related to *jimmāwāl* ("headman").

1.2. Linguistic Diversity

From a linguistic perspective there is ample evidence that Kiranti is a

1. In an article first publishd in 1858 the B.H. Hodgson notes. "Adverting to the high recorded antiquity of the terms Kirāt of Kirānt and Kirāti or Kirānti (vague nasal), as applied respectively to the country and people even to this hour, it is remarkable that the Kirāntis themselves do not readily admit the genuineness or propriety of those terms, but prefer the names Khwombo vel Khombo and Kirāwa as their general personal designations, and seem to have none at all for their country" (Hodgson 1880 I: 398).

distinct unit. Following the pioneer work of Hodgson (1847, 1880[2]), hardly any new, authentic material on the languages of East Nepal was made available up to the sixth decade of this century, but since then a number of new field studies have confirmed that there are indeed a number of features which justify to treat Kiranti languages as group (van Driem, 1987; Ebert, 1994). For me most among these is the complex verbal system, which is characterised by grammatical markings of speech act participants (a property which was earlier described as "complex pronominalisation"). Another unique feature is the grammaticalised coding of space, which gives special emphasis to the vertical, or altitudinal, dimension (uphill vs. downhill)(see Gaenszle, forthcoming a).

The variety of more than fifty (more or less) distinct Kiranti languages continues to puzzle linguists. There is wide agreement that they belong to the Bodic branch of the Tibeto-Burman language family, but their position within Bodic (which includes among others the Tibetan languages, Tamang, Gurung, and Lepcha) is still being debated. An earlier scheme classed the various languages as part of the "East Himalayish section" (Shafer, 1955), but by now the distinctness of Kiranti as a single unit is beyond doubt. According to one recent classification scheme one can even speak of a Mahakiranti sub-branch, which includes the Newar language (van Driem, 1992).

Within Kiranti the Limbu language has by far the greatest number of speakers (ca. 200.000). Numerous Rai languages are spoken only in a few villages and many are in danger to become extinct (such as Sangpang or Dumi). Kulung is probably the "biggest" among the Rai languages, as it is spoken also outside the traditional home valley (the Hongu Valley) by those Kulunge who have migrated to other areas further east. The great linguistic variety of the Rai idioms is proverbial: *jati Rāi uti kurā* ("there are as many languages as there are Rai"). Nevertheless, this does not prevent interaction. Marriages between speakers of different Rai languages are rather common, and as we will see, there are indeed grounds to see the Rai as somewhat more closely related to each other than to the Limbu.

---

2. Hodgson published several articles on grammar and, most importantly, compiled vocabulary lists for various Kiranti languages, such as Bahing, Vayu, Thulung, Sunuwar and other "broken tribes".

1.3. A History of Disempowerment

At the time of the Gorkhali expansion into east Nepal the Kiranti still practiced slash and burn agriculture (planting dry rice), and hunting was of major importance. Nevertheless there is evidence that besides this they had already adopted certain agricultural techniques (like cultivating irrigated rice) from their Hindu neighbours to the south (Sagant, 1976a: 32-41). In the course of the nineteenth century the landscape of the Kirat region underwent a drastic change. More and more land came under cultivation, dry fields were converted into irrigated terraces fields and in the midhills the jungles were diminished to a minimum. Already at the beginning of the 20th century land had become a scarce resource. There was an increasing population pressure, and for many the only way out was emigration. Many Kiranti left their villages to go further east to seek employment, e.g. in the tea plantations in Darjeeling, or Assam (English, 1985).

These developments were closely linked to the political history of the consolidating Gorkhali state. After the conquest the Shah kings granted considerable autonomy to the Kiranti, knowing that these tribal populations at the eastern fringe of the kingdom had to be treated carefully: There was always the danger that they would switch allegiance and ally themselves with the Sikkimese. The single most important privilege which the Kiranti were granted was that they could retain their traditional rights over the land through a system known as *kipaṭ*. This was a communal form of land tenure, which meant that land was held by the kinship group and not by individuals (Regmi, 1978: 534). Among other things this implied that land under *kipaṭ* tenure could not be alienated to outsiders. This conferred considerable powers to the local population *vis-à-vis* immigrant settlers.

At the same time, however, the state strongly encouraged settlement of Hindu castes in the eastern region (Regmi, 1978: 537). Due to scarcity of land in the west numerous families, in particular high caste Hindus, took the opportunity and migrated to the east. In the beginning these settlers were given land they had cleared in exchange for a symbolic gifts to the local headman. In the course of time it became more difficult for outsiders to acquire rights over *kipaṭ* lands in this way. But there were other ways in which the newcomers gained control over the land. Lionel Caplan has described in a classic field study how Brahmans in Ilam managed to get hold of large tracts of Limbu *kipaṭ* lands through an unscrupulous practice of money-lending (Caplan, 1970). Towards the end of the nineteenth century state legislation gradually undermined the traditional *kipaṭ* system, and land which was mortgaged or lacked clear documentary evidence could be easily converted into freehold land (*raikar*). More and more the Limbu felt annoyed that their ancestral territory was encroached upon by non-Limbus, and already in 1920 a resistance movement, led by a religious leader called Phagunanda, came into being (Jones, 1976: 73).

That the situation did not turn against the rulers in Kathmandu is largely due to the crucial position of the local headmen and the clever state policy by which they were dealt with. In the beginning the indigenous chiefs, who had been given the titles of *subbā*, *rāi*, or *jimmāwāl*, were treated like vassals, they were the "younger brothers" of the King of Nepal and enjoyed considerable powers. They were in charge of collecting taxes, and above all, they were responsible to uphold (customary) law and order. As these rights, which brought them not only power but also a special income (Sagant, 1996a), were guaranteed by the state, they had good reason to feel loyal to the monarchy. This position enabled them to act as mediators between the local people and the state, but increasingly they became mere agents of the administrative machinery. As more and more persons were given titles, the territory of a headman fissioned to ever-smaller units and thus the traditional power base slowly eroded. The Kiranti chiefs no longer posed any danger. Moreover, the headmen were ideal agents of Hinduisation. As local representatives of the Hindu monarchy they identified with its religious and social values and significantly contributed to the fact that these spread in the Kirat region.

Thus the indigenous culture of the Kiranti has been subject to complex historical changes. Yet in spite of these transformations they have retained a distinct life world, which will be introduced in more detail in the following sections.

2. Social Groups and Categories

The social structure of the Kiranti groups is characterised by two fundamental traits: the idiom of kinship and the bond to ancestral land and territory. Both of these traits are encompassing, as they are effective on different levels and scales. The principle of descent and the fissioning of segmentary units is not only applied on the level of the local kinship system but also affects the different kinds of Kiranti "ethnic" units, and extends even further up to the first living creatures at the beginning of the world (see below). Likewise the principle of territorial linkage can be recognised on the level of the smallest unit, the household, but also on the level of larger units, such as the local clan or the Kiranti as a whole who have appropriated the landscape of Eastern Nepal in a history of migration and settlement. Due to the segmentary structure of the social organisation the following description of the major levels can only be seen as an ideal-type kind of abstraction from the complexities in actual fact.

2.1. The House

Among the Kiranti the house is an important focus of both ordinary social as well as religious action. Not only is it the basis of the household as a fundamental economic and social unit, but it is also a symbolic structure which reflects major cosmological ideas and values. The majority of the numerous Kiranti rituals takes place in or in front of the house and are held for the benefit of the house and household as a closely interconnected and "animate" entity. In fact, one can speak here of a "living house," similar to the ones found in other parts of the world.

Kiranti settlements generally are of a dispersed kind, i.e. houses are not clustered but tend to be autonomous units (with only secondary buildings attached). In most cases the houses as seen from the outside resemble the Indo-Nepalese Parbatiya house found throughout the midhills: built of stone and mud, whitewashed walls with red clay colouring, a verandah in front, and a thatched roof. In some (lower) areas one can still find the older type, which is built on poles, has walls made of bamboo and a protruding platform. Below this construction (which is similar to certain types in the Eastern Himalayas and insular South East Asia) domestic animals are kept, while grains are stored in a separate building.

The household is the residential unit with a common budget, common property of domestic animals and, most importantly, land. Agricultural work is generally organised on a household basis, and when teams are formed which include other persons it is always for the benefit of one household. As a rule Kiranti households are of the elementary or joint lineal type. Brothers tend to separate soon after marriage, the elder ones setting up their own households (after receiving their share of the inheritance), while the youngest one stays with the parents (ultimogeniture).

The interior of the Kiranti house is conceptually divided along two axes: one divides domestic space into the "upper" and "lower" halves (facing uphill, resp. downhill), and the other divides it into the "front" half, which is entered via the verandah through the main door, and the "back" half. The intersection of these divisions is generally marked by the central pillar. The upper half is held to be more auspicious than the lower, and this is particularly so in the case of the upper quarter containing the fireplace (which in some areas is in the front, and in some areas in the back part), as this important focus is associated with the ancestors and possesses special sanctity. Among the Rai this quarter also contains the altar of the ancestral house-deity, located in a wooden shelf just above the fire-place. During certain ritual occasions (such as the offering for the three hearth stones) and at the time of menstrual "pollution" women are prohibited from entering this quarter. Affines in general are associated with the lower half; this is where the wife's relatives are seated when they visit.

The full symbolic significance of the Kiranti house, however, becomes only clear if one understands its mythological background, such as the building of the first house by the culture-hero (see below). Even today building a house continues to be a reenactment of mythical precedents. For example, a blood sacrifice is offered to the central pillar as laid down in the mythic narrative. Thus domestic space and structural elements derive their origin and meaning from the deeds of the ancestors in the mythic past. This explains why most ritual activities focus on the house: it is the visible link with the ancestral world.

2.2. The Kin Group

The kinship unit of persons who can fully trace unilineal descent from a known individual is generally known as the lineage. Among the Kiranti this unit is usually recognised as that of "close" agnatic relatives (it has a depth of around 5-6 generations) who tend to be cooperative, but it is rarely named and can hardly be regarded as a corporate group.[3] More important as an overt unit of tribal social organisation is the patrilineal clan, i.e. the descendants of a mythic ancestor who share a common name and — ideally at least — constitute the exogamous

3. Among the Limbu the lineage has become the tax-paying unit (Caplain 1970: 28), but this is not generally the case among other Kiranti groups.

group. Both, the lineage and the clan are termed thar ("clan", "tribe" and "class") in Nepali.

The clan is generally conceived of as sharing common substance of "bone," which is distinguished from the "milk" or "flesh" inherited from the maternal side (cf. Sagant, 1976b: 162; McDougal, 1979: 91f). The minimal depth of a clan is seven generations. As soon as the genealogical distance to a common ancestor of seven generations is reached marriage between members of the same clan becomes possible: this effects the formal fission of the clan, commonly called *hāḍphorā*, "breaking of the bones". Though this is mostly regarded as an irregularity which is to be avoided, this has led, particularly in times of general population growth, to a wide-spread multiplication of clans which retained the feasible size of an exogamous unit.

Clans are generally grouped into sets of several "brother" clans which are seen as descendants of a "first settler" who has taken possession of a particular territory. Among the Mewahang Rai, for example, the legendary first settler is described as a "chief" or "king" (called *hang* in most Kiranti languages), and the names of his sons (often four brothers) tend to be identical with the names of contemporary clans (Gaenszle, 1991: 148). In this way the sets of clans are ordered by the principle of seniority: the clan descending from the senior brother is regarded as the senior clan, and this commonly implies a certain status distinction. Though it would be an exaggeration to say that the order of clans implies a straightforward hierarchy, it is generally the case that the senior clan enjoys a more pronounced position. As a rule, it is the senior line of the senior clan in which the office of village headman is transmitted.

Looking at the actual distribution of clans, one finds that clans of the same name are often resident in various, sometimes even distant, villages, as there has been migration and dispersal. It turns out that the clan as a named entity tends to have only a nominal existence. What counts is the clan group of a particular locality, i.e. what is called the local clan segment or the local clan group (Caplan, 1970: 24ff; McDougal, 1979: 135ff; Gaenszle, 1991: 149ff). Often it is this unit which can be regarded as the actual exogamous unit, and which has features of a corporate group. Though, after the abolishment of the *kipaṭ* system this is no longer the land-holding unit, there is evidence that before the land reform it was membership in the local clan group which validated right to land (Caplan, 1970: 28). Moreover, the local clan group is marked in symbolic terms. Among various Rai groups it is obligatory that at the time of marriage of a clan-"sister" the households of her local clan group receive symbolic payments from the wife-takers (Gaenszle, 1991: 150; McDougal, 1979: 25, 114). And among most Kiranti groups the death of a kin belonging to this group implies ritual pollution, which requires the observance of certain food taboos during the period of mourning (Gaenszle, 1991: 150f).

Thus it shows that in terms of culturally marked social solidarity it is the localised kinship group, which is of prime significance. Not infrequently this group also shares certain food taboos, which at one time have been called totemistic, such as the abstinence from goat, chicken or soybeans (Gaenszle, 1991: 155). Common descent, then, is important, but of equal, if not greater importance is the bond to a particular territory. This becomes evident in the case of adoptions of immigrants, which have been relatively common: co-resident outsiders were transformed into kin and thus obtained legitimate access to ancestral land.

2.3. The Village Territory

The territory which has been appropriated by a first settler ancestor is a major focus of Kiranti life, both on the level of social and political organisation as well as on the level of religious ideas and practices. Mythological accounts emphasise that the first settler was the first truly legitimate settler who established a special link with the autochthonous forces of local land and water (Gaenszle, 1991: 306-312, also cf. Allen, 1996; Forbes, 1998). Only when this link is regularly renewed through ritual offerings to the territorial spirit can the fertility of the soil and its inhabitants be maintained.

As was noted above it was membership in the local kin group, which in the traditional system of land tenure validated rights to the land. These rights were controlled by the local headman, i.e. the *subbā* (Limbu), *dewān* (Yakha), *rāi* or *jimmāwāl* (Rai). When new land was to be cultivated it was the headman who had to be asked for permission. Or when immigrant settlers wanted to acquire usufructory rights to land they turned to the headman, presented him with a symbolic gift, and asked for an allotment (later annual presentations were mandatory). The headman not only controlled cultivated land, but also the high pastures, the forests (wood-cutting, hunting, collecting wild honey), the rivers (fishing). He took care that access to the products of the territory was regulated in a proper way, and acted as arbitrator in cases of conflicts over land, inheritance strife, boundary disputes etc. In short: he was in charge of managing the communal property of the ancestral territory (cf. Sagant, 1996a: ch.5).

The religious qualities of the link to this territory come out most clearly in the rituals celebrated for the ancestral soil and water. Among the Rai there is a wide-spread tradition of making offerings to the territorial spirit, who is often identified with *Bhume*, the Hindu deity of the soil (McDougal, 1979: 37f; Gaenszle, 1991: 134ff). These rituals (often a series which accompany agricultural growth) are undertaken to ensure fertility, abundant rainfall (but no hail), and protection from malevolent spirits who could spoil the harvest. Significantly these rituals are community festivals, involving all the *kipaṭ* households of the village whose members gather for a joyful celebration. At the same time there is generally a clear political aspect to it. The ritual is often focused on the headman who receives presentations from his subjects and, acting as the host, redistributes food to the community. In a way he can be regarded as the human representative of the territorial forces.[4]

2.4. The Subtribe

It has already been indicated in the beginning that the ethnic groups which make up the Kiranti, in particular the Rai and the Limbu, are more or less heterogeneous and have emerged as such only in the course of the last two centuries. The units which are linguistically and also, to a certain degree, culturally distinct, are commonly called "subtribe". In Nepali the term *thar* is used which, as we have seen, can refer to various kinds of segmentary sections. In the case of the Limbu there are only four major linguistic units, the *Phedāppe,* the *Pãcthare*, the *Chathare*, and the *Tāplejuṅge* (van Driem, 1987: xxii). These also were names associated with the ancient Limbu "kingdoms" (Jones & Jones, 1976: 6), of which, however, there are said to have been ten. In the case of the Rai, there is a much greater number of linguistic units, and a cultural identity on this level is generally much stronger. Thus groups

4. Among the Limbu, where the community festival appears to have been lost, the powerful men were seen as Masters of the Soil. In older times they were also Masters of the Forest who practiced ritual hunts in order to control the territory (Sagant 1996b).

like the Kulunge Rai, the Camling Rai, the Lohorung Rai, the Athpahariya Rai, or the Mewahang Rai have such distinct traditions that they can also be seen — and in fact increasingly do so — as ethnic groups in their own right.

But one has to be careful not to overestimate the existence of clear-cut ethnic boundaries. There are several indications that these boundaries are rather fluid. First of all there may be discrepancies in the usage of the subtribal name: not infrequently the self-ascription of a name is not in full agreement with outsider's ascriptions. For example, the Mewahang tend to call all the western Rai by the term Khambuhang, but these have more specific denominations for themselves (e.g. Kulunge, Camling, Thulung, Bahing, etc.). Even a term like Kulunge Rai, which is ultimately derived from a locality (Mahakulung, "the great Kulung region"), is rather unspecific as a social category, as it can be taken in a wider as well as a narrower sense.

Also in a linguistic perspective, things are often far from clear-cut. Many of the named subtribes do not speak a homogenous language but have various, sometimes rather distinct, dialects. For example, the Lingustic Survey of Nepal lists no less than seven variants of Sampang, even though there are hardly more than a dozen of Sampang villages. It is no surprise then that also in terms of culture there is considerable variety. Often it is not only villages which have their own ritual traditions and practices, but even clans emphasise their cultural distinctiveness. The subtribe is therefore not to be seen as a bounded group. Rather it may be regarded as a more or less loose collection of kin groups which identify with a name, are part of a field of communication and interaction, and share a number of "family resemblances" (Gaenszle, 1991: 115-128).

2.5. *Affinal Relationships*

As comes out in the symbolism of domestic space (see above) as well as other cultural domains there is a clear categorical distinction between one's own kin (in the narrow sense) and one's affines. Marriage is seen as a bond with people who are "others" and live at a certain distance from oneself. In the older times it was often from one's enemies that wives were taken in order to establish an affinal relationship. But this is a cultural ideal. Today suitable marriage partners are generally available close by and matches within the village are rather common.

The typical way to marry is "by theft" (Sagant, 1970): assisted by intermediaries and friends a boy elopes with a girl of his choice, thus ignoring the authority of her parents (but not usually her personal will). After this affront, which has qualities of a ritual drama, there follows a long sequence of negotiations and reparations, which eventually lead to the stepwise legitimisation of the union. Marriages "by request" are seen as more prestigious and gain increasing popularity, but this has to be seen as the result of Hindu influence. Nevertheless, in both cases marriage among the Kiranti is a lengthy process, which usually takes many years to be completed. It involves a series of presentations (beer and liquor, pork, cash money, etc.), and only with the final part of the bridewealth being transferred the bride becomes a full member of her husband's clan. Among the Rai groups there are generally two weddings: a "small" wedding which gives full legitimacy to the children of the couple, and a "big" wedding which finalises the marriage process and the transfer of rights. During the interim period the groom remains indebted to his wife-givers (in some cases he also has to provide labour services for them) and the marriage is considered to be on a trial basis: divorce at this stage is relatively easy. Due to this processual character of marriage it is quite common that by the time of the concluding rites the couple has already several children.

The relationship between the category of "wife-takers" and "wife-givers" is generally marked by a certain asymmetry. A common term of address for the latter is *māitirājā,* lit. "wife-giver kings". Since the wife-takers are in a position of request whereas the wife-givers are in the position of granting this request, the bride's side is considered to be "higher" (e.g. one says "the wife-givers are high as the mountains"). Though this metaphoric resembles that of other Himalayan tribes with a consistent asymmetric kinship system of matrilateral cross-cousin marriage (such as the Magar, cf. Oppitz, 1991), among the Kiranti this asymmetry is only temporary. The direction of marriage may be reversed, if not in the same generation (through sister exchange, which is not particularly preferred but condoned) then in a following generation (at least on the clan level). The marriage of a real cross-cousin is generally prohibited by the marriage rules, but where they are terminologically distinguished classificatory cross-cousins are the preferred spouses (e.g. among the Limbu, cf. Sagant, 1976b: 155; Davids & van Driem, 1985: 150). In fact, there is evidence that Kiranti kinship terminologies were once of the prescriptive, symmetrical kind implying bilateral cross-cousin marriage (Allen, 1978; Gaenszle, 1991: 173ff) but that in the course of historical and demographic developments this character has been blurred.

What, then, is the character of the Kiranti marriage system? Rather than being determined by positive rules which require marriage with a particular category of persons the choice of spouses is mainly determined by negative rules which exclude certain categories of "close" kin. One of these rules has already been mentioned: the 7-generation rule which allows the "breaking of the bones" specifies the minimal genealogical distance within the agnatic kin group. In a similar way, there is another rule which prohibits marriage with descendants of matrilateral kin within 3 generations. Thus it emerges that the actual exogamous group is not only the (local) clan but a unit which is defined by both agnatic and cognatic principles and which may be referred as the kindred.

Looking at the *de facto* marriage practice one can observe a tendency to look for spouses in the nearby neighbourhood (Gaenszle, 1991: 227ff; McDougal, 1979: 141ff). One might say that the Kiranti marriage system is characterised by the attempt to marry as "far" as required (in genealogical terms as defined by the negative rules), but as close as possible (spatially but also genealogically).

2.6. Politics of "Soul"

Whereas the norms and rules outlined above form the base of Kiranti social organisation, it should be stressed that its functioning was and is not simply a matter of mechanical reproduction; rather the formation of groups and marriage alliances must be seen in the context of processes which are determined by the action of eminent individuals and their struggle for power and influence. It has already been indicated that the headman had a powerful position in the former system, but whereas this position tended to be fixed through written documents by the Gorkhali administration, in the older, tribal system there was much more fluidity and open competition. Until today it can be recognised in the religious ideas that in principle each householder is a little "king" who has his personal "head-soul" which can rise and fall according to his fortunes. (As Sagant writes in the motto to one of his articles: "In the old days, each Limbu was a king," Sagant, 1982). Regular household rituals ensure that the "head-soul" will be raised, so that its possessor is strong, fertile and successful. If the "head-soul" is high, others will obey;

formerly outsiders could be chased away, or else be incorporated in one's group by adoption, or marriage ties were forged which further increased influence. Typically a powerful headman had a somewhat bigger house, he had command over his lineage and co-clan members, and he had several wives. But he had to be always careful not to lose the goodwill of the ancestors, i.e. he had to make sure that the link with them was properly maintained through ritual. And, of course, he had to be careful not to lose the loyalty of his following. This could be done, for example, by hosting sumptuous feasts, displaying his power and generosity.

In the Kiranti worldview, then, the perpetuation — and manipulation — of a social order and the enactment of a religious tradition are intrinsically linked. In the following I will look more closely at two major aspects of this tradition: mythology and ritual.

3. Mythological Foundations

The religious tradition is generally referred to by a single term in the various Kiranti languages, and though these terms may be different they are mostly cognate. Among the Limbu, for example, it is known as *mundhum*, among the Mewahang Rai as *muddum*, among the Yakha Rai as *mintum*, among the Kulunge as *ridum*, or among the Camling Rai simply as *dum*: thus there is apparently a common root (**dum*) which points to a shared conceptual base. All these terms designate the essentially oral tradition of the group, including both the spoken "texts" as well as their ritual performance. The Tradition (written with a capital initial letter this is perhaps the best translation of the indigenous designations) may be seen as the way through which the Kiranti maintain their link to the ancestors: remembering their deeds in mythological narratives, speaking to them in ritual invocations, and interacting with them in ritual exchanges (Gaenszle, 1992).

There is evidence that at one time the major myths of origin where fully embedded in ritual action and only were performed in this context in the distinct ritual language. In fact, this appears to be still the case among the Limbu. However, among the Rai the mythology today is part of ordinary narrative practice, i.e. the myths can be told in non-ritual contexts and may be recounted even in the Nepali language. This might be one of the reasons why very little has been published on Limbu mythology whereas Raï mythology has been documented by several scholars (Gaenszle, 1991; Allen, 1976a, Toba, 1983). Though still only a small fragment of this vast tradition has been recorded and it is therefore too early for comparative propositions, there are indications that Rai mythologies are more closely related among themselves than with the Limbu mythology. In the following I will give a short outline of the major Rai myths, with some references to Limbu parallels.

The mythology can be divided in roughly three major sections: the myths of creation, the myths about the culture hero, and the myths of ancestral migration and settlement. The myths of origin recount how the first living creatures, the variety of species, came into being. Generally emphasis is given to the duality of earth and sky, or the soil and water, which combine to produce life. Among the Thulung, for example, Heaven rained and a lake formed on Earth into which leaves were swept by the wind: from these moistened leaves sprang the first plant, and this again produced the creator goddess (Allen, 1976a: 37). Whereas there is considerable variance, and often uncertainty, concerning these primordial events, with the appearance of the creator goddess one reaches firmer ground. This figure, known by various names (Somnima, Naima, Miyapma, etc.) is depicted as a woman who — living in a world without men (but only mothers and grandmothers) — is desperately in search of a husband. Eventually she hears about a male person living up in the sky (Paruhang, Paruhõ, Ruwasila, etc.) and sends out intermediaries to bring him down. But seeing him she is struck by his ugliness (in some versions because of a huge goitre) and rejects him. The would-be groom then resorts to a trick: he dries out the world and leaves his semen as the only liquid on a leaf. When the woman is about to die of thirst she is forced to drink the semen (unknowingly) whereupon she becomes pregnant. In due course she gives birth to the variety of species: bamboo, tiger, bear, monkey — and the First Man (Gaenszle, 1991: 257-265). Evidently this myth about the creator couple combines images of a primordial marriage with those of divine creation. At this point, however, culture and nature are not yet distinguished.[5]

The next section recounts the origin of Kiranti cultural institutions, such as hunting, agriculture, house-building, and ritual (Gaenszle, 1991:

5. No variants of this myth are found among the Limbu, but there is also a creator couple. The two have an incestuous relationship out of which 17 children are born. A part of these become the ancestors of present day Limbu (Sagant 1976c: 79).

271-291). The major actor is the culture hero known by rather similar names among the different Rai groups (Khakculukpa, Khocilipa, Khakcilik, etc.). Though he is seen as a descendant of the First Man he is generally depicted as an orphan who is left by his two elder sisters. Completely on his own he has to make a living in the jungle and only through his cunning he survives the malevolent attacks of evil beings. One day, as he is fishing he repeatedly catches a stone. At first he throws it back, but it turns out that it is his would-be spouse who, while at home, makes his cooking. After their first child is born they decide to build a proper house, and when it is finished the hero plans to hold a house inauguration ritual.[6] He remembers his lost sisters and eventually manages to find them and bring them back. They all reunite in a big festive celebration, which resembles both a house inauguration and a wedding. This myth, then, can be seen as founding, or laying the precedent for, present day Kiranti cultural practice. That the culture hero is particularly associated with the house may be seen as further indication of the symbolic significance of domestic space (see above). In some cases he is also associated with shamanism (cf. Hardman, n.d.), i.e. ritual expertise for the protection of the house.

The migration myths of the third section are of special importance for an understanding of the social system. These myths are very prominent among all Kiranti groups. In the Rai narratives the migration begins at the Place of Origin situated down in the plains, "where all the waters drain" (Gaenszle, 1991: 292-305). This place is described as a hole in the ground, or a primal lake; today it is often said to be close to Barachetra, the Hindu pilgrimage site located near the confluence of the Seven Rivers (Saptakosi), which form the drainage system of East Nepal. From there four brothers, whose names differ according to the teller's group identity, migrated up towards the mountains. Among the Mewahang Rai, for example, they are Khambuhang, Mewahang, Limbuhang and Mece Koce (in order of seniority). Along with the four brothers travelled their four sisters. However, the youngest brother and the youngest sister were left behind and stayed in the plains. The elder siblings crossed the river near Barachetra with the help of blood offerings. But at this point a quarrel erupted among the brothers, because the eldest one had tricked the younger ones. They decided to split and divide up

6. In Limbu mythology there is also a hero who built the first house. According to one author he is called Lokphademba Hangphademba (Subba, 1995: 59).

the territory, and each of the remaining three brothers eventually migrated up along one of the three big rivers in Kirat country, the Dudh Kosi, the Arun and the Tamur. There, in the course of time, they settled down and further split up in different valleys. The myths eventually recount how one's forefathers' group found the present territory and established a legitimate link with its spirit (see above), how the first settlers interacted with other groups, and how the present day clans evolved. Thus the myths generally lead to an account of the teller's own genealogical affiliation, thus positioning him/her within the grand genealogy of Kiranti mythical ancestry.

Among the Limbu migration myths are equally prominent. The migration also begins at a Place of Origin, but here this place — called *co-lung* — is located in the hills: it is the place where one of the ancestral being fell from the sky and the earth opened (Sagant, 1976c: 79f). Here also the first priests came into being. Departing from this Place of Origin the Ten Limbus split, and five of them migrated to the north, to Lhasa in Tibet, and the other five migrated to Kashi (i.e. Benares) in the South. Later on, however, they migrated back to the Nepalese hills and settled on their present territories. Due to these events the Limbu distinguish between those groups which are called "Lhasa gotra" (i.e. the line from Lhasa) and those which are classed as "Kashi gotra" (i.e. the line from Kashi, cf. Sagant, 1976b: 162). In fact, the distinction is also found among various Rai groups, even though it is not used very consistently (Gaenszle, 1991: 126f). It is possible that this particular dichotomy results from historical influences: as the Limbu (more than the Rai) have been in contact with Lamaist Buddhism from Sikkim as well as the Hindu kingdom of the Sen-Makwanpur dynasty these two Great Traditions may well have left their traces in Kiranti oral traditions. Though this can no longer be traced with certainty, it is likely that the dichotomy at one time reflected different political affiliations.

To sum up, it can be observed that Kiranti mythology is a grand genealogical account of the origin of life, the variety of the species, mankind, Kiranti culture and the diversity of Kiranti social groups: it is an account of continuous differentiation in time and space. The migration of the ancestors represents the fissiparous tendencies of the segmentary kinship system as well as the all-important territorial linkages. As the ancestors migrate up the rivers they split up and appropriate their respective share of land. It emerges that the myths reflect the various levels of the social structure: the migration stories depict the division of subtribes, the first settler stories describe the division of village territories and eventually lead to an account of the division of kin groups. And the origin stories, among other things, highlight the significance of the house and the institution of marriage. Thus the mythology of the Tradition may be seen as a comprehensive template — or "charter" — for cultural institutions and social divisions.

4. Ritual Links

As noted above, the Tradition of the Kiranti groups comprises both the spoken — or oral — "texts" (such as mythological narratives) and the performance in ritual. It must be emphasised at this point that rituals among the Kiranti are focused very much on the spoken word. Many rituals consist of lengthy invocations and recitations, accompanied only by a minimum of ritual gestures and actions. What is unique about this form of speaking is that it requires the use of a special ritual language. This language is distinct from ordinary language. Though there is certain continuity with everyday language, in particular on the level of grammar, the ritual code is largely made up of a special lexical inventory. Thus most of the ritual nouns have the form of binomials: for example, in Mewahang Rai ritual speech the word for house is *khatiru dungmaru,* whereas in ordinary speech the word would be *khùm*. This kind of parallelism is typical of Kiranti ritual speech, it recurs also on the syntactic level in the form of grammatical parallelism (cf Allen, 1978b). In other words, ritual speech has poetic, i.e. aesthetic, qualities: it is a particularly elegant and "sweet" way of speaking. It is an ancient language inherited from the ancestors, and hence it is the proper way of communicating with them. The ritual language is the single most important medium to maintain a link with the ancestral world (Gaenszle, forthcoming b).

The performance of ritual and ritual speech is not restricted to specialists. There are various rituals and ceremonies, which may be carried out by ordinary men as well as women. For example, the invocation of the dead's soul during the funerary ceremonies or the calling of the ancestors in the context of the first fruits offering in autumn are generally done by all adult household members and close relatives. These invocations are not very complex and are relatively close to ordinary speech forms in style. Other speech genres are more formalised and require greater competence. Certain rites can only be performed by knowledgeable elders (called *purkhā* in Nepali). Among these are the ceremonial dialogues, i.e. ritualised negotiations in the context of funerals, marriages and other elaborate ritual occasions. Also smaller domestic rituals, such as that for the three hearth stones, may be performed by an experienced elder. Thus competence in the use of ritual speech is generally acquired in the course of time, through repeated listening and repeated practice. In principle, the ancestral world is accessible to everyone.

However, communication with the more powerful ancestral beings or deities and the performance of certain additional tasks requires special competence. Among all the Kiranti groups there are at least two classes of ritual experts who have to undergo a period of initiation in order to be able to perform the respective rituals. Generally this kind of initiation cannot be chosen at will. Rather it is the divinity itself, which selects its adept. At first the candidate has recurrent dreams in which he or she encounters the tutelary deity and is shown certain paraphernalia, which are needed for performance. Eventually he may become possessed by the divinity, in some cases suffering fits and illness or even lengthy periods of confusion and "madness". But with the help of initiated ritual experts the adept learns to control his contact with the divine forces and to communicate with them in a regular manner.

Though the system of ritual specialists differs considerably among the Kiranti groups, it is striking that there is always a pronounced duality of ritual office. On the one hand, there is what is generally termed the "tribal priest" (e.g. *phedangma* in Limbu, *ngo:pa* in Mewahang Rai, *dewa nokcho* in Thulung Rai), on the other hand there is the "shaman" (e.g. *yaba* or *yama* in Limbu, *makpa* or *mangmani* in Mewahang, *jhākri* among the Thulung Rai). The latter can be easily distinguished by his/her professional outfit and paraphernalia: feathered headdress, a harness of bells, and, most importantly, the handheld drum (*dhyanro*). In fact, this is the typical outfit of the pan-Nepalese shaman, who is found among almost all ethnic groups and castes (including untouchables and Brahmans!) and is generally known as *jhākri*. The tribal priest usually does not have a special dress, except for a turban which some of them wear. He may use a metal plate to accompany his chanting, but he rarely uses a drum. If one tries to characterise the duality of ritual office in terms of different functions things become more complicated. An early ethnographer of the Sunuwar attempted to depict the system as one of dual classification, opposing the tribal priest to the shaman as right : left :: sacrifice : trance :: ancestral spirits : evil spirits :: auspicious : inauspicious, etc. (Fournier, 1978). But in a comparative perspective the situation is far from clear-cut. In many of the groups both may become possessed, both may do sacrificial offerings, and both may deal with dangerous spirits. In fact there are good reasons to term both ritual specialists "shamans," but in order to avoid confusion the above terminology has become generally accepted. In spite of these ambiguities, however, one can say that the tribal priest is generally in charge of maintaining a good relationship with the ancestral beings (which involves regular blood sacrifice), whereas the shaman is responsible for warding off harmful influences. Moreover, the former often has the task and capability to deal with the territorial spirits, whereas the latter also deals with many non-Kiranti spirits and deities (such as Siva, Devi, etc.). While the tribal priest never uses the Nepali language, a good deal of the shaman's ritual chanting is done in an "archaic" version of the national idiom. This indicates that the duality of ritual office has also been subject to historical influences (Allen, 1976b).

It becomes clear that the core of Kiranti religion is an ancestral religion. The Tradition is basically a way to keep intact the crucial link with the ancestors. Mythological narratives keep up the memory of ancestral creations, deeds and migrations, reminding the living of the origin of the natural and cultural order. Ritual performances make use of an ancestral speech (it is both the speech of the ancestors and for the ancestors), and by communicating with the ancestors in a pleasant idiom, presenting offerings of good food (rice, meat) and other coveted items (beer, liquor) the ancestors are made and kept happy, so that they "look benevolently" on their descendants, refrain from making troubles but ensure the prosperity of the living.

Again the notion of head-soul is crucial for understanding Kiranti traditions. A good deal of ritual activity ultimately aims at "raising the head-soul," or strengthening other such life-forces.[7] By making the ancestors happy and benevolent, i.e. by raising their head-soul, the vitality of the living can be renewed. The well-being of both is intrinsically linked. If this link is disrupted (through neglect, ignorance, emigration,

7. A ritual text used to "raise soul" among the Mewahang Rai has been documented in Gaenszle 1996.

etc.) it ultimately leads to disaster: illness, infertility misfortune etc. Thus there is an immense pressure to live according to the Tradition. Clearly, the Tradition is not simply a collection of customs and rituals, but an all-encompassing way of life.

5. Conclusion

It has been noted at the beginning that to an outsider the Kiranti groups in East Nepal do not appear to be very different from the Hindu castes (Parbatiya). Longstanding interaction and political integration into the Gorkhali state have led to a considerable degree of cultural assimilation. Agricultural techniques (in particular irrigated rice cultivation), house constructions, or forms of dress are similar in many respects. Moreover, the Kiranti groups celebrate many pan-Nepalese Hindu festivals, such as Dasai, Tihar, and Nag Pancami, and worship Hindu deities such as Siva, Laksmi, Durga.

Nevertheless, on closer view it shows that there is still a distinct "Kiranti way of life," which may be described as a tribal heritage. When I use the term "tribal" I do not mean to imply that the Kiranti conform to the ideal-typical image of a tribal society. As critics have often pointed out it is problematic to speak of tribes in the contemporary context (Dahal, 1978). However, if taken as a heuristic device which also takes past conditions into account the characterisation of cultural and social institutions as "tribal" still makes good sense (cf. Gellner, 1991: 106ff).

The social organisation of the Kiranti groups in East Nepal is based on a kinship system, which combines in a unique way patrilineal descent, affinity and territoriality. Though the idea of hierarchy is not absent in Kiranti cosmology (there is a strong emphasis on seniority), this systems stands in clear contrast to that of Hindu caste society. Whereas in the latter case there is a strong tendency toward closure and stratification (endogamy, rules of commensality etc.) and territorial bonds are minimised (cf. Dumont, 1979), among the Kiranti a major concern seems to have always been with exogamy (leaving considerable room for the incorporation of outsiders) and the maintenance of a proper link with the territory. It is due to this fundamental "openness" of the kinship system that the formation of ethnic groups has only been a recent phenomenon.

We have further seen that Kiranti religion is basically an ancestral religion: almost all the divine beings worshiped in the (oral) Tradition are ancestors, both patrilineal and affinal ones. And through mythological narratives and ritual performances the memory of these ancestors, their deeds and foundations, their migrations and appropriations is kept alive. As the ancestors are closely associated with the landscape, the Tradition periodically renews the link between the past and the present, and between person and territory. The Kiranti have their own religious specialists, mainly the tribal priest and the shaman. Though they sometimes may call Brahmans or Lamas, this is rather the exception.

In recent times, the Kiranti assert with new pride that they have a tradition of their own which does not require assimilation. It is a religion without written texts and without a name (some now call it animism), but it certainly is a tradition which is very rich on its own terms and many see it as standing on an equal footing with the Great Traditions, Hinduism and Buddhism. Since the Democracy Movement of 1990 the Kiranti have formed various ethnic organisations in order to preserve their languages and cultural traditions, but also to strengthen their position within the multi-ethnic nation state (Gaenszle, 1997). There is an new awareness of the Kiranti being an indigenous people with a great and ancient tradition which has been subjugated and underprivileged for a long time. Increasingly demands for better representation within the national arena are brought forth, such as claims for more proportional access to education and employment in national institutions. There have also been more radical demands for a Kiranti autonomy (Krämer, 1996: 273f). These have largely remained peaceful and — so far at least — have not led to serious political tensions.

REFERENCES

Acharya, Baburam. 1973. "Annexation of the Sen Kingdoms," *Regmi Research Series*, 5 (5): 81-85.

Allen, Nicholas J. 1976a. *Studies in the Myths and Oral Traditions of the Thulung Rai of East Nepal.* Unpublished Dissertation, Oxford.

____. 1976b. "Approaches to Illness in the Nepalese Hills," (pp. 500-552) in J.B. Loudon (ed.), *Social Anthropology and Medicine*. London, New York: Academic Press.

____. 1978a. "Fourfold Classification of Society in the Himalayas," (pp. 7-25) in James F. Fisher (ed.), *Himalayan Anthropology: The Indo-Tibetan Interface*. The Hague: Mouton.

____. 1978b. "Sewala Puja Bintila Puja: Notes on Thulung Ritual Language," *Kailash*, 6 (4): 237-256.

____. 1996. "Animal Guides and Himalayan Foundation Myths," (pp. 375-390) in Samten Karmay & Philippe Sagant (eds.), *Les habitants du toit du monde*. Paris: Société d'Ethnologie.

Burghart, Richard. 1984. "The Formation of the Concept of Nation-state in Nepal," *Journal of Asian Studies,* 44 (1): 101-125.

Campbell, A. 1840. "Note on the Limboos, and Other Hill Tribes Hitherto Un-described," *Journal of the Asiatic Society of Bengal*, 9: 595-615.

Caplan, Lionel. 1970. *Land and Social Change in East Nepal: A Study of Hindu-Tribal Relations.* London: Routledge and Kegan Paul.

Chatterji, Suniti Kumar. 1974 (1951). *Kirāta Jana Kṛti: The Indo-Monogoloids: Their Contribution to the History and Culture of India.* Calcutta: The Asiatic Society.

Chemjong. 1966. History and Culture of the Kirat People. 2 vols., Phidim: Tumeng Hang.

Dahal, Dilli Ram. 1979. Tribalism as an Incongruous Concept in Modern Nepal," in Marc Gaborieau & A. Thorner (eds.), *Asie du sud: traditions et changements.* Paris: CNRS.

Davids, I.M.H. & G.L. van. Driem. 1985 "Limbu Kinship Terminology. A Description," *Kailash*, 12 (1-2): 115-156.

Driem, George van. 1987. A Grammar of Limbu. Berlin etc.: Mouton de Gruyter.

____. 1992. "In Quest of Mahakiranti," *Contributions to Nepalese Studies,* 19 (2): 242-247.

Dumont, Louis. 1979 (1966). *Homo Hierarchicus: Le système des castes et ses implications.* Paris: Éditions Gallimard (Collection Tel).

Ebert, Karen. 1994. *The Structure of Kiranti Languages: Comparative Grammar and Texts.* Zürich: Seminar für Allgemeine Sprachwissenschaft.

English, Richard. 1985. "Himalayan State Formation and Impact of British Rule in the Nineteenth Century," *Mountain Research and Development,* 5 (1): 61-78.

Forbes, Ann Armbrecht. 1998. "Sacred Geography on the Cultural Borders of Tibet," (pp. 111-121) in Anne-Marie Blondeau (ed.), *Tibetan Mountain Deities: Their Cults and Representations.* Wien: Verlag der Österreichischen Akademie der Wissenschaften.

Fournier Alain. 1978. "The Role of the Priest in Sunuwar Society," (pp. 167-178) in James F. Fisher (ed.), *Himalayan Anthropology: The Indo-Tibetan Interface.* The Hague: Mouton.

Gaenszle, Martin, 1991. *Verwandtschaft und Mythologie bei den Mewahang Rai in Ostnepal. Eine ethnographische Studie zum Problem der 'ethnischen Identität'.* Wiesbaden: Franz Steiner Verlag.

____. 1992. "Ancestral Types: Mythology and the Classification of 'Deities' among the Mewahang Rai," (pp. 197-218) in Véronique Bouillier & Gérard Toffin (eds.), *Classer les dieux? Des panthéons en Asie du Sud.* (Puruṣārtha 15) Paris: EHESS.

____. 1996. "Raising the Head-soul: A Ritual Text of the Mewahang Rai," *Journal of the Nepal Research Centre,* 10: 77-93.

351-373) in David Gellner, Joanna Pfaff-Czarnecka & John Whelpton (eds.), *Nationalism and Ethnicity in a Hindu Kingdom: The Politics of Culture in Contemporary Nepal.* Amsterdam: Harwood Academic Publishers.

____. forthcoming a. "Travelling up and Travelling down: The Vertical Dimension in Mewahang Rai Ritual Texts," in Balthasar Bickel & Martin Gaenszle (eds.), *Himalayan Space: Cultural Horizons and Practices.* Zurich: Ethnological Museum of the University of Zurich.

____. forthcoming b. *Ancestral Voices: Oral Ritual Texts and their Social Contexts among the Mewahang Rai in East Nepal.* Unpublished Habilitation Thesis, Heidelberg University.

Gellner, David N. 1991. "Hinduism, Tribalism and the Position of Women: The Problem of Newar Identity," *Man* (N.S.), 26: 105-125.

Hardman, Charlotte. n.d. *Conformity and Self-expression: A Study of the Lohorung Rai of East Nepal.* Unpublished dissertation, School of Oriental & African Studies, London.

Hodgson, Brian Houghton. 1847. "On the Aborigines of the Sub-Himalayas," *Journal of the Asiatic Society of Bengal,* 16: 1235-1244.

____. 1880. *Miscelleneous Essays Relating to Indian Subjects.* 2 vols. London: Trübner.

Jones, Shirley Kurz & Rex L. Jones. 1976. *The Himalayan Woman: A Study of Limbu Women in Marriage and Divorce.* Palo Alto: Mayfield Publishing Company.

Jones, Rex L. 1976. "Sanskritisation in Eastern Nepal," *Ethnology,* 15 (1): 63-75.

Krämer, Karl-Heinz. 1996. *Ethnizität und nationale Integration in Nepal: eine Untersuchung zur Politisierung der ethnischen Gruppen im modernen Nepal.* Stuttgart: Franz Steiner Verlag.

Lévi, Sylvain. 1985 (1905-1908). *Le Népal: Étude historique d'un royaume hindou.* 2 vols. Kathmandu, Paris: Raj de Condappa, Toit du Monde, Errance. (Reprint)

McDougal, Charles. 1979. *The Kulunge Rai: A Study in Kinship and Marriage Exchange.* Kathmandu: Ratna Pustak Bhandar.

Oppitz, Michael, 1991. *Onkels Tochter, Keine Sonst.* Frankfurt: Suhrkamp Verlag.

Regmi, Mahesh Chandra. 1978. *Land Tenure and Taxation in Nepal.* Kathmandu: Ratna Pustak Bhandar. Bibliotheca Himalayica Series 1, 26.

Riccardi, Theodore Jr. 1975. "Sylvain Lévi: The History of Nepal", Part I (Introduction, translation and commentary to S. Lévi: Le Népal, vol.II, part I) *Kailash,* 3 (1): 5-60.

Sagant, Philippe. 1970. "Mariage par enlèvement chez les Limbu (Népal)," *Cahiers internationaux de Sociologie,* 48: 71-98.

____. 1976a. *Le Paysan Limbu, sa Maison et ses Champs.* Paris: Mouton.

____. 1976b. "Les Limbu, population du Népal oriental," *L'Ethnographie* (Nouvelle Série), 72: 146-173.

____. 1976c. "Becoming a Limbu Priest: Ethnographic Notes," (pp. 56-99) in John Hitchcock & Rex Jones (eds.), *Spirit Possession in the Nepal Himalayas.* Warminster: Aris & Phillips Ltd.

____. 1982. "L'hindouisation des Limbus — 'Tout Limbu était roi, autrefois'," (pp. 209-239) in Alexander Macdonald (ed.), *Les royaumes de l'Hima-laya.* Paris: Imprimerie Nationale.

____. 1996a. *The Dozing Shaman: The Limbus of Eastern Nepal.* Delhi: Oxford University Press.

____. 1996b. "Dasaī et le double pouvoir chez les Yakthumba," (pp. 283-314) in Krauskopff, Gisèle & Marie Lecomte-Tilouine (eds.), *Célébrer le pouvoir: Dasaī, une fête royale au Népal.* Paris: Editions du CNRS.

Shafer, Robert. 1955. "Classification of the Sino-Tibetan Languages," *Word,* 11 (1): 94-111.

Subba, Chaitanya. 1995. *The Culture and Religion of the Limbus.* Kathmandu: K.B. Subba.

Toba, Sueyoshi. 1983. *Khaling Texts.* Yak 7. Tokyo: Institute for the Study of Languages and Cultures of Asia and Africa (ILCAA).

TWO

THE GADABA AND THE "NON-ST" DESIA OF KORAPUT, ORISSA

PETER BERGER

1. Introduction

As in every other region of India the government categorised the people of the Koraput District (Orissa) according to administrative requirements. Thus some indigenous inhabitants, or Desia, of this part of the Eastern Ghats are defined as "Scheduled Castes" ("SC"), some as "Scheduled Tribes" ("ST") and some as "Other Backward Classes" ("OBC"). For social scientists this mix of the sociological categories of "class", "caste" and "tribe" is highly problematic. Each term is controversial in itself and to find them applied in such a close proximity may lead to some confusion. Generally sociologists and anthropologists are not solely guided by bureaucratic categories. Instead they define these terms with reference to their subject. Strangely enough, anthropologists writing on society and culture of Koraput or Orissa in general do this very much along the lines set by the government. With some exceptions (Bailey, 1957, 1960) they concentrate on "tribes," leaving out the so-called "castes" and "classes" of the region or treating them as peripheral.

This chapter does not want to discuss whether or not some social categories are rightly defined as "tribe", "caste" or "class". Based on ongoing ethnographic research[1] it wants to focus on the interrelations

1. Fieldwork has been done for three months in spring 1999 supported by the FAZIT foundation and has been continued for one year from September 1999 to August 2000 financed by the German Research Foundation (DFG). Further research will soon be conducted in the same area. The main focus of research is on the ritual system of the Gadaba and Desia. The author wants to thank the Asha Kiran Society in Lamtaput which provided him with a Computer to write a raw draft of this paper in the field.

of the different Desia categories and groups. Living in a Desia village it became very soon apparent that the different groups frequently interact in all spheres of social life.

Thus the material presented here lends support to the thesis of a unified *Koraput complex* as set forth by Pfeffer (1997) in the first volume of these series. There he points out that all "inhabitants of the land" or *Desia* of Koraput are parts of one social system. All Desia, speaking an Oriya dialect of the same name,[2] share a patrilineal and patrilocal kinship system and use the same clan categories to differentiate between agnates and affines. The Boro Gadaba use only four of the total repertoire of eight exogamous clan categories, namely cobra (Hantal), leopard or tiger (Killo), monkey (Golori) and sun clan (Kora) are found among them. The others are vulture or hawk (Pangi or Gidh), cow (Goru), fish (Macho) and bear (Kimdu) (ibid.: 17). Some Desia employ only a selection of the whole, while among others all eight are found.[3] As far as marriage is concerned all Desia practice symmetric exchange and among all forms marriage with the menabai ('MBS'/'FZS') or menabouni ('MBD'/'FZD') is the stated preference. But in contrast to south and north Indian patterns the value of tribal affinity is holistic and does not relate to individuals (ibid.: 24f).

As Pfeffer is further keen to show that this unity does not presuppose equality, but rather rests within hierarchical structures not altogether similar with those of the *homo hierarchicus* in the plains (ibid.: 5). First, part of the general middle Indian pattern is the complementary relationship between "tribal" patrons and "SC" clients. Although the most obvious feature with regard to the property of land is a major difference in their sacred and profane status. Thus Pfeffer opposes the patrons as "communicators with divine" to the clients as "communicators with

2. The Oriya dialect called Desia is the *lingua franca* of the district. Desia is quite different from coastal Oriya and even if the words are the same they are pronounced differently. The Oriya word for "brother" *bhai* is pronounced *bai* in Desia, i.e. without aspiration. The Desia words are therefore not transcribed like Oriya but written as they are spoken by the people. If Oriya or Gutob words are cited they are marked with a capital "O" or "G" respectively. Throughout the text Desia or Gutob words referring to groups or social categories are written with a capital letter at the beginning, like "Gadaba" or "Hantal". Specific persons or office-holders are written in italics with a capital letter, like "*Pujari*" or "*Barik*". All other Desia or Gutob words are written only in italics and small letters, like "*puja*" or "*biru*".

3. To my knowledge the Dombo, Sundi and Rona employ all eight clan categories, among the Mali and Kumar no fish-clan is found. Kamar don't have the clans of bear and fish and also Goudo have only six clans, bear and cow-clan is missing.

human beings" (ibid.: 13). This point will be dealt with in detail later. Second status is expressed in the idiom of seniority, "subtribes" are hierarchically ordered as "elder" and "younger" brothers (ibid.: 13f). In my own work among the Desia, especially the Gadaba, of Koraput I also found both aspects to be present: unity and hierarchy. All Desia people share a common life-style, wear the same dress, build their houses in the same manner, believe in the same gods and spirits and participate in the same festivals. Existing peculiarities of each category therefore seem to be embedded in a more general framework. More ethnographic work is needed to get a clearer view of the similarities as well as the differences. As shown by Pfeffer status is conceived in the language of seniority. I also found the opposition of *boro* ("big" or "elder") and *sano* ("small" or "younger") to be ubiquitous. It is applied at all levels of society to distinguish groups, persons, things or gods[4].

The area of my study concentrates on the Lamtaput Block of Koraput, where we find Boro and Sano Gadaba, Parenga, Kui Kond and Joria who all belong to the category of "ST". In the south-western Malkangiri District, previously a part of undivided Koraput, the famous Bondo and the less known Didaye have their villages. Potters (Kumar), blacksmiths (Kamar), gardeners (Mali), liquor distillers (Sundi), herdsmen (Goudo) and the former militia of the king in Jeypore (Rona), are labelled as "OBC". The omnipresent musicians, traders and weavers (Dombo) belong to the "SC" category.

Generally a Desia village is comprised of one of the "ST" categories and a selection of "non-ST" categories, among the latter very probably the Dombo. The "ST" are also referred to as Adibasi or Roit, which points to their status as original inhabitants and cultivators. Previously most of the "non-ST" Desia were engaged in shifting cultivation (*podu*). They did not own permanent fields (*bera* or *poda*). The landless clients receive rice for their services from the village.

The present article is divided into two sections. The first is a general description of the main "non-ST" Desia categories and their position in the local hierarchy. Since I refer to "the Rona" or "the Gadaba" in

4. Hardenberg (1999) also found the opposition of *boro/sano* to be employed in the ritual context of the Jagannath cult in coastal Orissa. The "tribal" descendants of Jagannath, the "Daita," are classified in that way (ibid.: 56f). Due to ritual segmentation, according to the three main gods, they have an additional "middle" category. The same structure is found among the carpenters (ibid.: 89) and the temple- "inspectors" (ibid.: 129) of the cult.

general I talk of social categories and not of groups. They are briefly introduced with reference to their internal segmentation and their respective diet. Then a broad scheme of the hierarchical relations between the Desia categories is presented.

The second part contains a description and a preliminary analysis of relations between different Desia groups in the village I call Gudapada. Since not all major Desia categories are found in that village I will complement the data by others collected in the neighbourhood. The focus will be on collective economic, ritual and ideological relations between Gadaba and other Desia. Individual economic relations between households or individual ritual relations between healers and clients are not taken into account. It goes without saying that these "domains" can only be separated for analytical purposes and do not present themselves as such. The economy of a village is dependent on its collective rituals. The latter always include offerings (bhog) to the gods the village as a whole. Everyone has to participate but not on equal terms. The social and religious hierarchy of the whole therefore becomes apparent within the regular ritual activities.

2. The "Non-ST" Desia

2.1 Dombo

In almost every Desia village we find at least some houses of Dombo. In contrast to most other "non-ST" Desia they are — to some extent — mentioned in the literature on tribal Orissa. The Pano of Phulbani District who are like the Dombo of Koraput clients of their tribal (Kondh) patrons are described by Bailey (1960) and Niggemeyer (1964a, b). They refer to the change within the reciprocal relationship between Kondh and Pano and and conceive the symbiosis as a political and economic system.[5]

The few other scattered remarks in the literature on the Dombo or Pano are of a stereotype form and in general of a derogative kind. The clients are regarded as an "untouchable caste" that immigrated "later" into the hills: "The Doms or Dombos are a population of low caste Oriya-

5. As Bailey describes the numbers of masters and clients have to be well adjusted. Demographic changes may lead to a disturbance in the equilibrium. When the Pano outnumber their Kond patrons they find their place in the new "diversified economy" (Bailey, 1960: 141-147).

speaking plains people, who have gradually infiltrated into most parts of the Gadaba country," Führer-Haimendorf (1943: 151 Fn.1) unwisely states. Although Niggemeyer presents the Dombo in much the same way, he conjectures that the Pano live with the Kondh for "...a couple of hundred years" (1964a: 20; my translation). Similarly Boal writes that the "...Pans have occupied a peculiar position in relation to the tribes-people of Orissa since the days of pre-history" (1982: 2). But in opposition to their "enchanted" tribal patrons the Pano or Dombo are represented as a rather secular and exploitative type because of their position as traders and money-lenders (Niggemeyer, 1964a: 17; 1964b: 411f). For Elwin the Dombo are "...degraded missionaries of a lofty faith" (1950: 21), whereas Somasundaram portrays them as part of the "...criminal population of the district who form the untouchable bulk in the society" (1949: 38). This distorted picture of a substantial part of the tribal society has since long been criticised by Pfeffer (1983: 90).

The Dombo of Lamtaput Block, called "Goren" by the Gadaba, do not comply with these stereotypes. They are neither economically better off than the Adibasi, nor do they exploit the cultivators. Gadaba say that there used to be much theft of domestic animals in the past and that Dombo were generally involved. Although they do have a bad reputation and are said to steal and to cheat, I was unable to observe any such behaviour. It may be that the Dombo-Gadaba relationship has been different in the past as statements from Gadaba referring to their previous dependancy on the Dombo indicate. Or the situation in the Kondhmals has always been different from Koraput.

Apart from their disreputable status Dombo around Lamtaput are significant in at least four socio-economic aspects: as weavers, musicians, traders, and as *Barik*. In January (pous) the Dombo start weaving a type of strong white cloth which is traditionally required as part of the bridewealth among the Gadaba who marry their sons and daughters in the following month of the year. As soon as the rains begin in June (*landi*) this work is discontinued. Since mill cloth, available on the weekly markets, has to a great extend taken the place of the traditional garments, today onlya few Dombo perform their weaving activities. They still do so in Gudapada.

But the other duties of the Dombo have lost nothing of their relevance for their patrons. Maybe most prominent among them is their work as musicians. On occasions like marriage and death rituals, or at the important sacrificial offerings of the village to its gods, music of the

Dombo is indispensable, lest the gods "are sleeping and won't listen" or the life-cycle rituals won't be successful. Further, the circular dance of the Gadaba, excessively performed during the spring festival (*chait porbo*) and on countless other occasions, is impossible without this particular music. The different steps of the women follow the rhythm of the instruments, three drums and one wind instrument, a type of clarionet, which is called *moira* like the player. The *moira*, played endlessly by a circular breathing technique, produces a very specific sound and leads the performance. Whereas everybody may play the drums, the *moira* may only be played by a certain Dombo man, the leader of the band, and others are even not allowed to touch it.

The main source of Dombo income is through trade. Not surprisingly they have gained the local reputation of being calculating and cunning as a result. The cash crops the Gadaba produce, mainly oilseeds and some rice and millet, are not sold by themselves on the market. They either have already been sold to Dombo middlemen (*bepari*) in the village in advance or the latter take them to the weekly market (*hat*), where they resell it to businessmen from Jeypore or from the plains. Apart from all sorts of crops, Dombo also deal with cattle, buying cows in far away places and reselling them on the local market. Or they take care of a cow which is brought to the market by someone who does not want to sell it himself. The latter will fix a price above which it is up to the Dombo to make his profit. Some Dombo also work in the weekly market as *jaleri*, i.e. they intervene in ongoing deals about cattle and try to influence it in favour of the seller. A successful assistence will get them 20 to 50 rupees.

Neither weaving nor music or trading is done by the Dombo women. Together with their husbands they prepare yeast from a special root, branches of a bush and crushed rice. This is a necessary ingredient for the local beer (*pendum*) and is sold by the women at home as well as at the market.

Finally in every village where Dombo live, the *Barik* is recruited from among them. This is a secular office in the village, not necessarily hereditary. The *Barik* closely cooperates with the formal head of the village, the *Naik*, who is always chosen out of the dominant cultivator group. In every village affair *Barik* and *Naik* have to be consulted. The Barik acts as a messenger and intermediary inside and outside of the village. He calls the inhabitants for village meetings, collects rice (*potri chaul*) from every household for the sacred food (*tsoru*) at village rituals and money for the sacrificial animals which he hs the duty to buy. At marriage and death rituals he has the function of a general organiser and he also settles inter-village affairs. If a former native of the village, a "sister" has been abandoned by her husband elsewhere, the *Barik* is the first to visit the family in order to demand compensation payments. He is thus viewed as a central and at the same time marginal figure. His most obvious attribute is his moving about. Furthermore, his office contains a contradiction since it combines low status with a high influence. In the area around Lamtaput the senior or Boro Dombo are distinguished from the junior Kupia Dombo.[6] The latter are not allowed to play the *moira*. Like the Gadaba all Dombo eat beef and pork and drink liquor.

2.2 Sundi

The Sundi are the liquor distillers among the Desia. Nowadays almost everybody prepares hard liquor (*mod*) out of a variety of fruits and grains. Previously, Gadaba and other Desia did not know how to distil mod. They were only able to brew beer (*pendum*) out of rice and millet. For hard liquor they solely depended on the Sundi. This privilege had been given to the latter by the goddess Kali as the following story of the Sundi explains.

To destroy the demon (*osur*) Kali needed liquor. So she called *Sukmuni Rusi* and instructed him to create a Sundi. Out of his body's odor and sweat the first Sundi was created who immediately asked what he should do. "You will distil liquor" he was told by his creator who — on being requested — gave the first Sundi a companion by cutting the destiller into two parts of which one became male the other female. The Sundi were told to sell the liquor only at their homes, never at the weekly market, and never to drink liquor themselves lest they would be outcasted (*jati hebo*). They started their work and many people came to their house to buy liquor. Kali also came to the Sundi demanding some. The liquor she drank made her strong and fearless and finally enabled her to kill the demon.

As the myth explains liquor is the reason of their existence. Furthermore, liquor being considered as their mother, the consumption of liquor will therefore be regarded as incest among the Sundi and

6. A third Dombo category are the Basa Dombo who have an intermediate status between the Boro and Kotia Dombo. They are said to live in Andhra Pradesh.

severe misfortune would follow in such a case. The work of distillation is only done by males, while women sell the product. Whereas originally liquor has been produced from the mohua flower (*mul mod*) only, the Sundi now also prepare it from mangoes, tamarind, jackfruit and rice among other substances.

The story clearly reveals the relation between liquor and the sacred. Liquor came from the gods and — in almost every ritual — it is returned to them as an offering. Like Kali, the Desia ritual specialist (*Dissari*) drinks liquor before he goes to the cremation ground (*mosani*) at night to fight the evil spirits. By contrast, beer is never given to gods, since it belongs to the realm of the household. Beer is prepared in every Gadaba house for personal consumption. Together with liquor it is also offered to the dead (*duma*).

Among the Sundi we find four sub-categories. The Boldia are of highest status and considered as senior to the Mojaponto, the one in the "middle" (*moja*). Junior to them are the Kira Sundi and the Dhobi Sundi, the latter two being of equal status.[7] All categories wear the sacred thread (*poita*) and may wear the *tulsi* necklace (*tulsi mali*). Generally Sundi do not eat meat of chicken, pigs, cows or buffaloes, although some have recently started consuming poultry.

The Sundi take food only from within their own or a senior sub-category. They generally do not interdine with or accept cooked food from any other Desia category. Similarly they only marry within their own sub-category. All other marriages would result in *jati*, i.e. the exclusion from the community.

2.3 Rona

Among the "non-ST" Desia, the Rona are the only land-owning category.[8] Irrigated *bera* fields as well as dry *poda* land, sometimes in large numbers, belongs to Rona. They also consider themselves to be Roit (landowners) like the Gadaba. This is due to their former relationship to the king of Jeypore for whom they served as soldiers (*sipai*). Rono

7. This information has been provided by a member of the middle category, the Mojaponto. It may well be that the two lower groups have more to say on the hierarchy between them. Very probably they won't consider themselves to be equal.

8. Also other Desia categories like the Dombo, Goudo or Kamar may have small plots of land, which they have bought from the Roit recently on *banda* basis, i.e. the original documents (*patta*) stay with the Gadaba who may buy back the land later on.

means "war" or "warrior" I was told by an old informant. Some Rona stayed permanently close to the king as his army, others were only recruited in time of conflict. Besides the Boro Rona and the Sano Rona, the latter also being called Kotia, another Desia (not Rona) category, the Dulia, served the king in this way. Since the term Dulia is regarded as derogative they are nowadays known as Paik (infantry).

Apart from their military duties, many Rona were working as tax-collectors or *mutadar*[9] for the king. One *mutadar* was responsible to collect the tax (*sistu*) yearly from the villages und his responsability. The *mutadar* of Badigor, for example, collected tax in 48 villages, mainly in the Bondo-area, which now belongs to Malkangiri. This Kesebo Patro, still a legend in the area of Machkund, is said to have had twelve wives and to have harvested some seventy *gorsa*[10] of paddy from his fields in every year. As people say today, the *mutadar* were respected, feared and had some influence upon the king himself. The taxes collected in the villages were given to another office-holder, the *omin*, also sometimes a Rona, who handed it over to the king.

For their work as soldiers or tax-collectors the king provided them, sometimes generously, with land. In contemporary Desia society the Rona do not have any special occupation like the other "non-ST" categories mentioned here. They are mostly cultivators. The Rona are still highly respected, they — ideally — do not drink liquor. Previously they claim not to have eaten poultry. Even nowadays, no Rona would ever touch beef or pork. Unlike many other Desia, Rona do not bear their respective clans in their names. Instead they have different titles like Pujari, Paral, Patro, Dolpoti, Dora or Majhi among others.

2.4 Mali

Although the Gadaba lay out small gardens close to their houses and on their dry fields in the rainy season, they mainly depend upon the gardeners or Mali for their vegetables. The latter have little or no rice fields being the specialists for the raising of all types of vegetables in their big and beautiful gardens throughout the year. Therefore, we find Mali only where water is sufficiently available.

9. Bailey (1957: 178-85; 1960: 175-80) elaborates how the British introduced the administrative divisions (*mutha*) in the middle of the 19th century and how they changed the Oriya chiefs of the Kondmals (previously connected to the lowland Kingdoms) into *mutha*-headmen or *muthadar* (or *sirdar*, ibid., 1957: 182).

10. One *gorsa* are thirty *bastar*, one *bastar* about one hundred kg.

Both men and women are working in the gardens, but only men carry the products to three to four markets in a week, where usually women would sell it. If the men operate as salesmen they only do so in return for cash, whereas the women also take paddy and millet. After after the harvest in particular, barter is the dominating mode of exchange and Gadaba women are seen to move around with a little bags of paddy or millet for the exchange against cabbage or egg-plants. On the days the Mali do not go to the market they cater in nearby villages. On such occasions vegetables are only given for kind and never for cash. They also prepare and barter sweets out of puffed rice.

The women of the (senior) Boro Mali are easily distinguished from those of the (junior) Sano Mali, since the former wear only two golden nose rings in an asymmetrical manner while the latter, like most Desia women, wear nose rings on both sides as well as in the middle. Unlike their junior counterpart, Boro Mali neither eat poultry nor prepare *lodu*-sweets out of puffed rice. Boro and Sano Mali do not intermarry or interdine, even if both are engaged in the same type of work. All Mali wear the sacred thread and occasionally the *tulsi* necklace. Generally they do not eat beef or pork and abstain from liquor and beer.

2.5 Kamar

Almost like the omnipresent Dombo, one or two blacksmith or Kamar houses are found in most villages. They produce and repair tools and implements such as axes, ploughshares, spears-heads and arrows and different types of knifes. A Kamar is mainly working for the village in which he lives. People from many other villages without Kamar also come to his smithy (*kamarsal*). Furthermore the Kamar is selling his tools at the weekly market.

Beside these secular jobs, the Kamar also produces irongods (*luar maphru*), found in some Gadaba houses and also referred to as Durga. For such tasks he is always paid in cash. Very frequently a Kamar is asked to make *luar kuti*. The male *kuti* is more or less like a nail, the female *kuti* looks like a bullet with a very pointed end and is filled with "medicine" (*oso*). These *kutis* are used by the ritual specialist and healers (*Dissari*) for witchcraft, to spellbind spirits of the dead or certain demons. In order to keep them away from the houses of the living, *kuti* are driven into the thresholds, or into all four corners of the house and on paths.

There are three types of Kamar. The (*boro*) Kamar is of highest status, followed by the Lora and finally Kabadi of lowest status. Whereas the Boro Kamar would eat pork, the two lower segments would also consume beef.

2.6 Kumhar

Like the Sundi the Kumhar or potters are only found in some villages. They divide into the senior Chotu and the junior Korsa. Only Korsa eat poultry but, like Rona and Mali, both segments neither consume beef nor pork and all wear the sacred thread. Liquor is nowadays drunk by both, Korsa and Chotu, but only the former also drink in their houses. As far as their work is concerned there is no difference between Chotu and Korsa. Men of both produce a variety of earthen pots (*handi*). The latter vary in size from very small ones, used only in ritual contexts to feed the dead, to very big ones to store beer. A medium sized *handi* is needed on all occasions when the sacred food, called *tsoru*, is cooked during the ceremonies after birth, at marriage, after death and in the collective sacrifices of the village. Furthermore these pots are used for ceremonial baths in turmeric-water.

Large quantities of pots are required for marriage rituals, since bride and bridegroom are fed sacred food four to five times by different relatives.[11] For weddings five or seven pots are piled up around each pillar of the marriage baldachin by the Kumhar himself. Other rituals like the bato biba (literally "marriage on/with the path"), an elaborate ritual for previously sick children, require additional earthen instruments like a pair of small clay oxen.

Nowadays the Desia do not ordinarily cook in earthen pots, since long lasting metal ones (*noki*) are available at the market. The earthen pots are made out of red earth and sand. Only men do the work at the potter's wheel as well as the following step, the closing of the bottom of the vessel. This work is continued until the day before the weekly market. On that day all pots are piled in a heap, covered with grass and clay and fired. The next morning the men carry their products on their shoulders to the market, the pots skilfully arranged around the carrying

11. The *tsoru* (sacred food) is cooked by the groom's "brother's" and *tsorubai* ("*tsoru*-brothers"), a special reciprocal, collective and hereditary ritual relationship. Further the *mamu* ("MB"), the father of the bride and the mamu of the bridegroom (if not identical with the bride's father) prepare *tsoru* and feed the couple.

pole in such a way that it resembles a huge molecular model. During the rainy season their work is discontinued.

2.7 Goudo

Goudo are the herdsmen among the Desia, found in many villages. Three types of Goudo are differentiated. In the area around Lamtaput and Machkund the senior most Dongait Goudo are by far dominating numerically. In former times they are said to have performed certain functions for the king at the Dosra festival (in October), like fetching water and carrying the palanquin. They have always been herding the sheep and the cattle of the Roit. Normally the Goudo of a village divide the patrons of the different parts (*sahi*) of the settlement among themselves, one or two persons being responsible for the cattle, goats and sheep of one of the sides. In some villages where Goudo are not available the work of herding can be done by Roit families who then are also called "Goudo". Mostly poor families perform this task.

Whether Goudo or "Goudo," they will have to collect cattle, goats and sheep in any case in the morning take them outside of the village and herd them the whole day. Before dusk the Goudo bring the animals back to the village. From May when the paddy is planted in the fields up to harvest time in November/December the work of the Goudo is of great importance. Unattended animals can do great harm to the crops. If the herdsmen are inattentive and some cows do damage to the crops, the Goudo will have to pay a compensation. From January to April their work is in less demand since the cattle are allowed to eat the remains of the cereals on the fields. Apart from small intervals the Goudo are thus guarding the cattle throughout the year. The term "Goudo" stands for watchfulness and protectiveness like the "shepherd" in Western/ Christian cultures. When a daughter is given in marriage the group of the bridetakers are reminded to take care of the girl "like a Goudo"[12] and a semi-god protecting the animals of the forest is called *Bono Goudo* ("Goudo of the forest").

The middle category are the Mogda Goudo who have larger cattle flocks and exchange milk for paddy or cash. These people are not

12. But this has also another dimension. A girl given in marriage is regarded as a cow, as also becomes clear in the songs sung at these occasions. Further one of the cows given as brideprice (*jola*) is considered to be a virgin, bride or daughter itself. It is supposed to give milk and breed.

conspicuous since they usually stay in interior jungle villages so that their herds do not destroy the crops of neighbouring villages. Such interior places are hard to find in the Lamtaput area of today. The most junior Koslia Goudo are not found at all in the vicinity. The Dongait Goudo I talked to could not even say what type of work they would perform.

2.8 Hierarchy among the Desia

As has become apparent from this brief description every Desia category is internally segmented into hierarchical parts. The idiom in which this hierarchy is expressed is *boro/sano*. "Big" or "elder" Rona will not intermarry or interdine with their "small" or "younger" counterparts. They often — but not necessarily — perform different tasks, as is the case of the Rona, Goudo or Dombo. Some myths tell how all Desia (the number of the whole is 12) were born out of one womb, but others, through the idiom of beef consumption, clarify that hierarchy prevails between the different Desia categories.

When Desia talk about their communities (*jati*), i.e. engage in "*jati* talk" as they frequently and freely do, they generally do not mention "purity" or "impurity" (*sud, asud*), but again employ the "big"-"small" dichotomy. A Dombo may be less pure than a Gadaba, but he is definitely "junior" to him. Generally there is no desire among the people to present a clear-cut picture of the whole hierarchical system. But three levels may be distinguished within a general hierarchy.

At the top there are the categories of Rona, Kumar, Goudo, Mali and Sundi. As a sign of their high status all members of these categories (men and women) wear the sacred thread (*poita*) and may equally wear a *tulsi*-necklace. None of them is willing to consume beef or pork. Within the different categories the prohibition of chicken-meat may serve to distinguish sub-categories, as mentioned above. The hierarchical relations between the categories of the upper level are ambivalent. A Rona might claim that his group is *boro* in relation to the Mali of his village or *vice versa*. In general people say that they do not know who among the wearers of the *poita* is *boro* and who *sano*.

While the hierarchy within this level may be ambivalent, relationships between levels are very explicit. On the middle level we find the different "ST" or Roit categories: Gadaba, Parenga, Joria, Didaye and

Bondo. The Gadaba, internally divided into two segments,[13] think of the Bondo as their elder and of the Parenga and Kondh as their younger brothers.[14] They consider the Joria to be still junior and the Didaye to be of lowest status. The Gadaba accept cooked food from all of their brothers, although they are not quite sure about that concerning the Didaye, since the latter settle a little far off, they say. Intermarriage is also possible, though hardly ever practised, with members of all the other Adibasi categories (again the Didaye case is unclear). But a marriage with a junior category requires a special ritual of reintegration. In case a Gadaba would marry a Dombo women his whole family would loose the Gadaba status. While the husband remains of Dombo status his family (parents, siblings) can regain it through a certain ritual. They "buy" back their old status (*jati kiniba*). If a Gadaba marries a (junior) Parenga women, both can "buy" back *jati* and obtain Gadaba status.

Together with few other Desia categories like the Kolia, Gorua or Ghasia[15] the Dombo represent the most junior level. Like the Gadaba and other Adibasi the Dombo eat beef and consume liquor.

The Kamar position is somewhat ambivalent. They do not wear the poita and avoid beef but eat pork. Their status is *sano* in relation to the categories of the first level. Some Gadaba say that previously none of them had accepted food from a Kamar and that they are *sano* to the Gadaba. Nevertheless, today Gadaba men eat in the house of the Kamar, while women and children don't. Another fact would indicate a slightly higher status of the Kamar. Within the village of Gudapada the Kamar married a Gadaba girl. This resulted in the exclusion of the couple from their group in the village but mother and brother of the Kamar could "buy" back *jati*. The Gadaba say that the married couple and their children are no Gadaba and though the Kamar's wife is allowed to enter her parents house, she should not touch any cooking utensils. They are "stuck in between" (*mojire rohiba*), the Gadaba say.

---

13. The "senior" ,Gutob or Boro Gadaba and the "junior" Ollar or Sano Gadaba of the Lamtaput area frequently interdine and intermarry.
14. Führer-Haimendorf (1943, 161 Fn. 2) states the opposite: "The Gadabas sometimes describe the Bondos as San Gadabas (Small Gadabas)". Likewise does Pfeffer (1983: 91).
15. The Ghasia near Nandapur and the Kolai on the other side of the Machkund river in Andhra Pradesh are considered as *sano* in relation to the Dombo. Below them are only the most junior Gorua, who are said to collect leftovers (cups, pots and plates) from cremation grounds. In the Lamtaput area there are only very few villages in which Gorua live. These categories, which are numerically very small, have not been included here since so far not sufficient data has been collected.

Hence, on the normative level, like in the caste system of the plains, prohibition of interdining and intermarriage mark the borders between the categories. All of the above mentioned Desia categories are endogamous and only categories of lower status accept cooked food from higher ones. Marriage of a son or daughter with a group of a lower category results in *jati*,[16] the exclusion of the whole family from the community. While the son or daughter is permanently "lost" for the community the family can "buy" back its old status.

The actual behaviour is very much guided by these norms and ideas. For example, I never saw a Gadaba eating in a house of a Dombo and was frequently told never to do so myself. But in day-to-day interaction the relationship between the different Desia status groups is "liberal" and free of discrimination. No status difference would be discernible when watching a group of Goudo, Gadaba and Dombo chatting, drinking and slapping each other's backs. The status differences are accepted as a given fact. Although terms like "Harijan" or "SC" have been introduced, the Dombo or Goren will not feel insulted if called as such by the Gadaba.

As we now turn to the specific context of Gudapada village, it will be seen how the general hierarchy described so far takes on a different shape. The Gadaba as the founders of the village and landowners are opposed as patrons to all other Desia clients, whether the latter are high status Goudo or the lowly Dombo.

3. Economic, Ritual and Ideological Structures in Gudapada

3.1 Gudapada

Gudapada is situated about one kilometre from the small main road connecting Lamtaput to Machkund. With about 160 houses Gudapada is a big village and several groups of "non ST"-Desia are found here: Dombo (25 houses), Goudo (four houses) and Kamar (one house plus a widow). Besides, one young Sundi widow is living in the village. Another man is referred to as "Guru Sundi" by the villagers but he is not considered to be one of them by the Sundi, since he married a Gadaba women like his father did who had already been expelled from his Sundi group.

16. Several other types of transgressions result in exclusion (*jati*) for a Gadaba: e.g. if a Gadaba is beaten by a Dombo or if he does the work of a Dombo (plays the *moira* or prepares yeast for beer).

The rest of the village[17] is inhabited by Gadaba, most of them from the cobra clan who are considered to be the original settlers of the village. In every Gadaba[18] village this senior status is attributed to a single clan dominating numerically and endowed special ritual privileges and duties. The small groups of other clans in Gudapada are hereditary affines of the cobras. In the course of history they have changed their settlement for pragmatic reasons.

The dominant cobra clan is furthermore segmented into the agnatic groups of Sisa, Kirsani and Munduli. The Munduli group is numerically insignificant while Sisa and Kirsani represent the bulk of the village population. The two again subdivide into several groups which also recruit members by patrilineal descent but are completely irrelevant for affinal relations. They are therefore not "lineages" in the strict sense. But the local term might also be misleading, since Sisa and Kirsani as well as their segments are referred to as *kuda*. Thus on the village level *kuda* signifies local descent groups of different order. Generally *kuda* as a category relates to a secular or sacred tittle among all Gadaba. Sisa, Kirsani, Boronaik and Munduli are by far the most common (see Pfeffer 1997). Whereas the clan categories (*bonso*) regulate marriage and are exogamous, the *kuda*-categories are titles of status which displayed in the name of every Gadaba. On the village level *kuda* describes local groups and sometimes, to add up to the confusion, all groups of the village, be they Dombo, Goudo or Gadaba, agnates or affines are called by that term.

3.2 *Economic Relations*

3.2.1 The Pholoi or Birti System[19]

Pholoi or *birti* signifies the rewards given by the village to a group or person for its services rendered for one year. The intra-village economy is generally based on exchanges in kind and *pholoi* consists of paddy or millet. Sometimes however services are also rewarded in cash. Not only the Gadaba but all villagers are in favor of these services but only

17. Some 15 years ago three Rona families lived in Gudapada, but they have died or left the village.
18. The same holds for Parenga and probably for Joria and others as well.
19. The author is aware of the literature on the *jajmani* or *jejemani* (Bailey, 1960: 126) system. Among the Desia this term was not found. Later on the Desia situation will be put into the context of the general debate.

the Gadaba can be regarded as patrons in a strict sense, since they do not receive *pholoi*.

Everybody who is working for the village in a *pholoi* relationship does so for one year, from January (*pous*) onwards. This "turn" is called palli. It is always decided in November (*diali*) who among the *pholoi* receivers will be going for another *palli* and who will not. The service relationship can be dissolved from both sides, the patrons (the village) or the clients. It is in the same month, after the harvest, when *pholoi* is given to the clients.

Pholoi receivers are:
Goudo who herd the cattle of the village;
Kamar, preparing the iron tools;
Kumhar, providing the pots for rituals;
Moira, the Dombo musicians; and
the Barik of the village.

In Gudapada no Kumhar is found. This service is therefore performed by a potter from the nearby village of Mojaput. He receives *pholoi* on the same terms. Also, at the moment, no one among the Dombo knows how to play the *moira*. The musicians are called from another village whenever necessary and paid in cash as well as liquor and food. In this case they are not involved in the *pholoi* system as in other villages.

When the farmers are still working on their threshing grounds the clients make it a point to come in time and ask their *pholoi* share from everybody. Otherwise they go from house to house at a later date. In Gudapada the clients receive the following amounts of *pholoi*, if the harvest has been an average one, receiving much less in a bad year. The Kamar receives 15 *man*[20] of paddy (*dhan*) from each household.[21] The *Barik* receives one winnowing fan of paddy (*kulek dhan*) from each household. The Kumar of Mojaput gets one winnowing fan of paddy per household and one big basket (*dalek*) from the village as a whole (*matam*). If he works for individual households of Gudapada he takes only half of the usual price to be paid in cash.

---

20. One man is about 2.5 kg, one winnowing fan (*kulek*) contains about 4-5 *man*, depending on its size a basket (*dala*) holds 15 *man*, two dala are one *phuti* (ca. 75 kg), one *bastar* is about 100 kg.
21. Two "own" (*nijoro*) brothers normally give the *pholoi* together.

As far as the Goudo are concerned the situation is a little more complicated. Previously there have been three groups of Goudo for each of the three spatial partitions (*sahi*)[22] of Gudapada. A Gadaba of the village used to work as "Goudo" for the lower sahi, a Gadaba from a neighbouring village took care of the animals of the upper sahi and the Goudo of Gudapada were only responsible for the middle *sahi*. Now the two Gadaba "Goudo" have stopped their work and only the Goudo for the middle sahi are left. People of this sahi regard the Goudo as their "own" (*nijoro*), even if the latter are also working for the other houses. From every household the Goudo receive 15 man of paddy no matter how many cattle or goats they graze. In addition to the mentioned *pholoi* and along with it Kumhar, Barik and Goudo receive one winnowing fan of paddy from every household "to eat rice" (*bhat kaiba pai*).

Beside the yearly *pholoi* only the Goudo receive *bhatia* from their patrons twice a day. This term relates to cooked rice (*bhat*); two meals a day should be given to the Goudo. But since the Goudo do not accept cooked food from any of the other Desia groups of the village they receive husked rice (*chaul*) along with some chillies or onions which they collect in the evening. In case the work of herding is done by a Gadaba, he will accept cooked *bhatia* from everybody except the house of a Dombo. When those "Goudo" receive more cooked *bhatia* than they can eat, they redistribute it in their neighbourhood.

Generally Dombo musicians are also included in the *pholoi* system. In an affinally related village the musicians receive one winnowing fan of rice from each household for the services of the passed year. The payment is also due in November (*diali*). Among themselves the musicians distribute the *pholoi* in unequal terms emphasising the significance and status of the *Moira*. He takes three quarters of the rice (twelve anna) while the three drummers share the remaining quarter (four anna). In this village the ferryman (*gatual*) is also included in the *pholoi* system. He gets five bastar of paddy from the village and in return none of the villagers have to pay anything if they want to cross the Machkund river.

Since the Goudo also need the skill of the Kamar and the latter possibly the watchful eyes of the former and both require the services of the *Barik pholoi* receivers also give *pholoi* to other clients. Goudo

---

22. The *sahi* is a purely spatial division in Gudapada. One *sahi* may comprise Gadaba of different clans and *kuda* groups as well as any other Desia category.

and Kamar give *pholoi* to the Kumhar, the *Barik* to all three of them etc. But they also might agree not to give *pholoi* to each other.

3.2.2 Return of Manti

Pholoi receivers literally pay "respect" (*manti*[23]) to their Gadaba patrons. While the external Kumhar, to my knowledge, does not return a *manti*-gift all other clients contribute directly to *hundi sitlani*, which is the offering to "cool down the village goddess" at the beginning of November (*diali*). This ritual of appeasement of the earth goddess is a precondition of the harvest and therefore also one for the clients to receive *pholoi*. On such occasion the Goudo give a red or a white cock, the *Barik* the required liquor and every third year the Kamar provides the pig.[24] Only after the goddess is "cooled down" the harvest of the wet rice fields can begin without the fear of severe losses and the *pholoi* can be given. The Goudo give additional *manti* to their patrons. In January (*pous*) they provide them with two big pots of beer. This *manti* is extraordinary in so far as it is not meant to be consumed by gods, who do not drink beer; only the patrons drink it. Also, the beer is not given in November together with the other gifts but in January.

In November the above mentioned meeting takes place to decide whether or not the palli will be continued. The village head, the *Naik*, also has to contribute to *hundi sitlani*. But the five *man* of husked rice (*chaul*) he provides are not manti since he is not considered to be a client of the village. The secular heads and the sacred leaders of the village are always Gadaba. They do not receive *pholoi* for their services or return *manti*. They have been given land by the village a long time, maybe generations, ago. Another contribution to collective sacrifices which is not regarded as *manti* is the ox the *Barik* has to give for the *bhag puja* ("offering to the tiger") in August each year. For this he is paid back *sari kadi* by the village three months later. *Kadi* means "food" and "sari" probably indicates that it is once a year.[25] The *Barik* is provided with food once a year in return for the ox. *Sari kadi* consists of paddy (*dhan*); the given amount depends on the size and condition

23. Vide Gustafsson, 1989: 421.
24. He takes turns with the two major Gadaba *kuda* of Gudapada, the Sisa and the Kirsani. The *Moira* of the above mentioned neighbouring village has to return a cock to his village every second year to be sacrificed together with a buffalo to the god *boirobi*, also in November.
25. According to Gustafsson's dictionary (1989: 490) *saira bera* signifies a wet-rice field which yields one crop per year.

of the ox. In the year 2000 the *Barik* got back eleven *phuti* of rice as was decided in the village meeting.

3.2.3 The Right to Demand Piai

Besides their yearly payment all clients of the village have the right to "demand" (*mangiba*) *piai* twice a year at the time of *chait porbo* and *bandapan porbo*, the festivals in April and August. Goudo, Kamar and Kumhar go from house to house to collect a leaf bowl of husked rice together with some chillies and half or one Rupia. Millet is never given on these occasions. Although entitled to demand the Barik of Gudapada avoids to do so saying he would "feel shy/ashamed" (*laj lagiba*).

Thus, the *pholoi* system puts all Desia groups of the village in an exchange relationship which crosscuts the economic, kindhip and ritual spheres. For the services of the year the clients receive part of the produce of the year (*paddy* or *dhan*). In return for their obligatory *manti*-gifts for rituals they have the right to demand piai at village festivals. This *piai* always consists of "husked rice" (*chaul*) which means it already contains the labour of grinding done by the women. The gift of *chaul* instead of dhan may point to a different quality of the relation. *Chaul*, never *dhan*, is given on all occasions of formal visits between relatives, mostly in ritual contexts like a marriage or a death. Therefore, the exchange of *manti* and *piai* also emphasises a ritual relationship between patrons and clients whose services themselves are very much of a ritual nature, at least as far as *Barik*, *Moira* and Kumhar are concerned.

A conspicuous feature of the exchanges is the gift of "cooked" rice to the clients, which is in fact paddy. Kumhar, *Barik* and Goudo receive additional paddy to eat "cooked rice" (*bhat*), but only the latter get *bhatia*. Although the Goudo and Kumhar only accept uncooked rice from the Gadaba the terms indicate that it "should" be cooked. "Cooked rice" given to Goudo and Kumhar clients by the Gadaba implicates a junior status of the former and is a reversal of the usual relation. This would support the impression that the general or "abstract" tripartite hierarchy among the Desia as presented in the first section is modified

26. The fact that Gadaba accept beer from Goudo as extra *manti* is not in line with their senior status the gift of *bhatia* suggests. Beer (not liquor) is closely connected to status and generally not accepted from junior groups. It might be that the beer is not regarded as official part of *manti* but given rather informally. The time when it is handed over (January) would support this view.

in the context of the village, where the people of the land are ideally the seniors of all others.[26]

3.3 Ritual Relations

The description in the previous paragraph presents the multiple and asymmetrical economic relations between Gadaba and the other Desia groups of Gudapada. Although the services of the pholoi system are for the benefit of the whole village the Gadaba generally are not *pholoi* receivers but landowners who give pholoi to the other Desia groups, the landless clients. In the context of village sacrifices we find the same asymmetry. Here the Gadaba — to be more precise: the Gadaba from the original cobra clan — act as mediators between the inhabitants of the village and the gods. They perform the worship and the actual killing of the sacrificial animals for the benefit and in the name of the whole village. Thus, in the terminology of Hubert and Mauss (1964: 9f) they act as sacrificers for the whole village, the sacrifier.

For the Desia the village is a most sacred entity. In order to guarantee fertility and well-being of humans, animals and land the gods in and around a village have to be regularly appeased by appropriate offerings (bhog). All gifts to the gods contain rice (husked and cooked), liquor and animals. Generally gods are differentiated by what they eat, but for all collective rituals blood sacrifices are necessary. Beside the ritual killing of animals the aspect of commensality of humans and gods is central. All Desia participate in these ritual activities but to a different degree, as will be seen.

In the following section I first want to describe how different Desia groups or persons are involved in sacrificial activities called *biru* by the Desia. Second, the basic structure of the three main festivals of the annual ritual cycle will be sketched. Furthermore, one sacrifice will be taken as an example for a closer look at the modalities of killing, cooking, distribution and consumption. The structure of the ritual communicates certain statements on values, in the sense of Dumont (1980, 1986), with regard to hierarchy. In a preliminary way, the last paragraph will therefore deal with the ideological relations between Gadaba and the other Desia as expressed in ritual action.

For all sacrifices at the village level the Pujari or sacrificer is of utmost importance. In the language of *boro* and *sano*, he is the most "senior" man of the village in general. This Gadaba is always a member of the local Sisa group or *kuda*. He also has to be of the cobra clan or *bonso*. His slightly junior twin is the ritual cook called *Randari* (*randiba* means "to cook"). Although the latter is also a cobra and therefore a "brother," he must be of the other big Gadaba group of Gudapada, the Kirsani. These two are performing all village sacrifices and are nearest to the gods in a spatial as well as in a spiritual way.

The actual date, time and sometimes also the personnel of rituals have to be found by an astrologer from outside of the village, the *Boro Dissari*. He is not only from the outside but also an outsider in another sense, because he mostly is from a different Desia category. In the case of Gudapada he is an old Rona and his family has served this village for several generations. In another Gadaba village he is a Joria of a rather remote place. It seems to be a general pattern that the *Boro Dissari's* "bigness" mainly lies in his "outsideness". Before every mayor festival a delegation from Gudapada visits the *Boro Dissari* for his advice and knowledge and once a year, before the spring festival (*chait porbo*), the villagers come in larger numbers and honor him with a feast in his own house. Under normal circumstances he does not directly participate in the sacrifices of the village. But about three years ago he was called by the Gudapada villagers. Due to ritual transgressions the village goddess (*hundi*) had become angry or "loose"[27] (*dil heigola*) and many people died during that time. He thereupon installed another stone inside the stone construction of the goddess and performed a sacrifice together with the village Pujari and Randari.

At the regular collective sacrifices all Desia have to contribute financially for the sacrificial animal, if this is not provided by any special person or group as mentioned above. In case a cow or an ox is sacrificed, the Goudo will not give any money. But on all occasions every household of the village has to give *potri chaul*, i.e. a handful of husked rice which is cooked as sacred food (*tsoru*) at the shrine by the *Randari*.

Money as well as rice is collected by the *Barik* who also has the duty to buy the animals on the weekly market. Rice, liquor and animals are taken to the shrine by the him even through, being a Dombo, the *Barik* himself is not allowed to come close to it. According to his position as a mediator of news, money or rice, he is also responsible for the proper distribution of meat to all households after the sacrifice, although such an office might not really be very obvious, the actual sacrifice being a rather noisy and controversial affair.

27. Vide Gustafsson, 1989: 228.

The killing, cooking, offering and worship is done by the Pujari and the Randari in the first place. But all others may worship the deity and get ritual rice (*arkot*) pressed against their forehead (get *tika*) as a sign of participation and blessing. Likewise all Desia men of Gudapada receive parts of the sacrificial animal in raw and/or cooked form.

Other Desia are more directly involved in specific situations. In the context of *bolani biru*, which is done several times a year, the old Goudo of the village does the worship together with *Pujari* and *Randari*. The Kumhar of Soilpada village have the duty to clean the space in front of the shrines of that village with cowdung, while the Gadaba do the actual sacrifice. Like many other Desia, the Rona of Badigor sacrifice a buffalo for the god *boirobi* every alternate year. While the Rona *Pujari* leads the worship the actual killing is done by Gadaba of a neighbouring village who receive the head for their services. Since the Rona do not eat the flesh, the Dombo of the village take the buffalo's body.

3.3.1 Main Festivals and Their Structure

All the gods of the village are provided with offerings in a regular rhythm which should never be altered. The shrines or places of sacrifice are sometimes solid stone constructions like the one of the village goddess or *hundi*. *Hundi* is the only divine being (except the house gods) residing inside the confines of the village. Her this shrine differs from all others because it is completely covered up looking like a small stone-igloo, the entrance being closed with stone plates. Inside, two stones covered with mud represent the goddess who is thus generally hidden from the views of humans. The round structure is encircled by a stone boundary.

Other gods outside the village in the hills are also represented by stones, but their shrines are open and simply consist of one or several stone boundaries separating the sacred stones and trees. Paths leading away from the village are also often places of sacrifices. The most powerful god outside the village is called "big house" (*boro gor, moro dien*, G), *gumang* or *pat kanda*. This god is sheltered in a small house at the foot of the hill. Again the only visible sign of the gods are plain stones.

These sacred places are worshipped by the villagers at three main festivals (*porbo*) in November (*diali*), April (*chait*) and August (*bandapan*), named after the respective months, e.g. *diali porbo* etc.

Although these festivals are of a very different character they have a similar structure as far as rituals are concerned. They generally begin at a shrine outside the village, at the "big house" in the months of April and November (dry season) and at the *jakor* shrine in August (rainy season). About one week to ten days after this sacrifice or worship (*biru*) the "festival day" (*porbo din*) takes place. It always starts with the *hundi biru* in the morning at the central village shrine. None of the villagers eat anything for the whole day and all are busy with preparations which vary according to the festival. Always all houses are newly painted. In the afternoon every household head performs a *biru* at the sacred post (*doron deli*) of his house. Like every village has its hundi, every house has its *doron deli*, the Desia say. But while *hundi* is conceived as "mother," *doron deli* is regarded as male phallus. After the ritual members every Gadaba family — but not the other Desia — initially feed the dead on the cremation ground before sitting together eating the sacred food (*tsoru*) cooked in the inner room of the house (*gondi dien,* G).

It has been mentioned previously that gods demand a variety of sacrificial animals. Red or black he-goats are offered at the "big house" along with white cocks, an ox and a pig alternate at the *jakor* shrine. Pigs are equally given to *hundi* at *diali porbo* in addition to red (small) chicken. For *doron deli* cocks are given at every festival: red and black in *chait porbo*, only red at other occasions. Every alternate year every household sacrifices a he-goat. The sarcalisation is done first at the *doron deli*, then the animal is led out of the house and killed on the path leading to the "big house".

Not only the gods but also different Desia have a different diet as has been described before. All Desia can eat from the meat of the goat killed at the "big house," while Goudo and Kamar of Gudapada will not eat from the ox given to *jakor*. In every Desia house we find the sacred pillar in a separate room, but since Rona, Boro Mali, Sundi and Kumhar do not eat poultry, they sacrifice ducks and/or a bird called parua for *doron deli* instead of the cock. Such an adaptation, however, would not be possible at the village level. Nowadays some Desia have abandoned beef but nobody would think of giving a goat to *jakor* in the place of his cows or oxen.

3.3.2 Sacrifice at the "Big House" in Chait Porbo

So far the description of the ritual system and the participation of the different Desia groups has been of a rather general kind. In order to understand thc ritual relationships between Gadaba and other Desia of Gudapada a more detailed account of one ritual context is necessary. Therefore I will now give an example of the *biru* at the "big house" as it is celebrated for the spring festival *chait porbo*. My focus is mainly on the aspects of division, distribution and commensality among the groups of the village, i.e. the "social" aspect. This emphasis should not imply any priority of the relations betwccn groups of the village over those entertained between humans and gods, or between gods, as expressed in the sacrifice. As Howell rightly points out :

> "Whatever else the act of sacrificing may or may not do, it seems save to assert that it acknowledges that the living and the dead, spirits and deities all belong to a single community" (Howell, 1996: 2).

All relations are "social" and have to be taken into consideration without arbitrarily selecting some while omitting others.[28] In order to highlight relations between different social groups of Gudapada only a part of the total system can be presented here.

The shrine is located at the foot of a hill very close to the wet rice fields. Before noon the Gadaba gather there to clean and prepare the area. Goudo and Kamar may also lend a hand, but not the Dombo who are only allowed to face the shrine standing in the rice field. *Pujari* and *Randari* together with the sacrificer (always from the Sisa group) of the goat then invocc the god who shows his acceptance of the offering through the animal eating rice.

By the stroke of the axe the animal is divided into two parts, head (*mundo*) and trunk (*gondi*). This distinction is of major importance for all Desia village-sacrifices and part of the "sacrificial language".[29] After the blood is collected in an earthen pot a small piece of meat is cut off from the throat (*sok*) and the head is then placed in front of the most sacred stone inside the shrine. The body of the animal is then opened and closed again with a few stitches after the liver has been taken out.

---

28. This claim is strongly put forward by the students of Dumont like de Coppet and others in their studies of exchange systems (1994: 3).
29. In the festival month of April each of the two Dombo segments of Gudapada also perform own sacrifices wherein the rest of the village does not participate. The heads of the sacrificial animals are only eaten by the subgroup, but the Dombo "cross-invite" each other for the consumption of the trunk.

A tiny bit of liver is roasted together with the part of the throat and offered with cooked rice (from the *potri chaul*) to the gods. This gift to the gods called *betisong* is first offered by *Pujari*, *Randari* and sacrificer and afterwards by all others, agnates and affines.

After worshipping the gods the animal's head is again divided into head (*mundo*) and neck (*gala*). Together with blood and part of the liver the head is cooked by the *Randari* in a new earthen pot in the immediate vicinity of the shrine. Further away the neck and rice (not *potri chaul*) are prepared on a different fire. Again some metres away the trunk is cut up into pieces and equally distributed on leaves for all village households who have contributed. The *Barik* is responsible that nobody will be forgotten, but others also take care. When the trunk has been divided and placed upon more than a hundred different leaves, the raw portions of the meat are taken away from the shrine, but they do not enter the village.

Although all village sacrifices submit to the pattern of division into head and neck the question "who eats what" is handled differently in diverse ritual contexts. As Durkheim (1968: 56) points out, the unseen sacred becomes "visible" through the rules which protect and separate it from the profane by regulating the latter. The fact that more prohibitions pertain to some village rituals and less to others relates to their different degree of sacredness. Together with the sacrifices at the *hundi* and *jakor* shrine the proceedings at the "big house" are the "strictest" in this sense. The Desia would not say that they are more sacred, but formulate it in their usual idiom: they are *boro*.

At the "big house" only Gadaba of the original cobra clan are eligible to eat the head cooked by the *Randari* as sacred food or *tsoru*. Their affines are sitting further away from the shrine and consume the neck they have prepared after the head-eaters had started. One leaf-bowl of this is also given to the *Barik* who sits at the very far end. The neck cooked by the affines is also referred to as *sano tsoru*.[30] Either *tsoru* can only be eaten by ritually married men or unmarried boys. A man living together with a woman without proper marriage or living apart

30. The author could observe and participate in the sacrifice at the "big house" thrice. The *Barik* did not participate in the *sano tsoru* on every occasion and it is unclear if he should do so. But his position at the very edge of the sacred area is very much in line with his general character as a mediator between different groups, as a marginal and at the same time central figure. How he is placed reflects this inherent contradiction of the *Barik*, low status and high office.

from his ritually married wife may not eat *tsoru*.[31] Before performing a sacrifice and participating in *tsoru* one should have fasted. This rule is loosely adhered to in other contexts, but no one would dare to eat *tsoru* at the "big house" after he has eaten rice.

On the other side of the rice fields, hundred meters away from the village boundary, the body (*gondi*) has been cooked under the shade of jackfruit trees. The *gondi*-eaters are all men of Gudapada: Dombo, Goudo, Kamar and the remaining Gadaba, who are not eligible for *tsoru*. *Gondi*-meat is prepared, cooked and consumed on the sub-group level. Therefore villagers gather around some 15 fireplaces. The Sisa have their different fireplaces close together, so do the Kirsani and the "upper" Dombo sit under a different tree than their "lower" segment. Thus the social structure of Gudapada is neatly laid out in the pattern of division and commensality. But the situation among the *gondi*-eaters is not that static. The number of fireplaces may vary over the years due to conflicts within groups. A Gadaba would never sit with Dombo or Goudo, but a tiger affine may join some segment of the cobra group or one Dombo group splits up and cooks on separate fireplaces. Hence this part of the ritual leaves some room for "agency," while this is not the case as far as *tsoru* is concerned.

Later the Gadaba *tsoru*-eaters return from the shrine and join the Desia *gondi*-eaters to enter the village together. *Pujari*, *Randari*, the *Sisa* sacrificer and the two Naik, all from the cobra clan, are taken on the shoulders of their Gadaba affines and other Desia and carried into the village in a procession.

3.3.3 Ideological Relations between Gadaba and other Desia

In his deconstruction of the debate on "totemism" Lévi-Strauss comes to see "totemistic phenomena" not necessarily as a matter of religion. They rather represented "...a particular illustration of certain modes of thought" (1991: 104). Thus it is a question of intellect or of understanding (ibid.). If the relation between animals (or generally *nature*) are used to represent social relationships (or *culture*) it is because they are "good to think" (ibid.: 89).

31. An immaculate ritual status is a precondition for participation in *tsoru* at the "big house". I observed that Gadaba with extra-marital relationships or those that have been "'utcasted" previously (but re-entered), stay away from the *tsoru* at the "big house". But they join in at less sacred shrines.

The same intellectual technique we find to be employed among the Desia of Koraput. Categories of nature are utilised to distinguish categories of society as can be seen in the system of clans or *bonso* (Pfeffer, 1997) and likewise in the way gods (*maphru*) and spirits of the dead (*duma*) are distinguished by the sacrificial animals given to them. These aspects have only briefly been mentioned and cannot be elaborated in this paper. But it has been pointed out in the last paragraph how specific social categories were related to certain parts of the sacrificial animal in the context of the "big house".

Another notion that has to be added is that of hierarchy. When talking about head, neck and trunk of the goat in the given ritual context we see, following Lévi-Strauss, that they are not only "good to eat" and connected to the level of behaviour or norms. Instead they refer to a system of ideas related to social morphology. Like in famous the case of the right and the left hand (Hertz, 1960) the categories of *boro* and *sano* do not form a "distinctive opposition," but are "value-ideas" as Dumont points out (e.g. 1980: 20; 1986: 248-252, chap. 8).[32] Right and *boro* are not only different from left and sano, they are superior. Their superiority derives out of a different relation to the whole :

> "Right and left, having a different relation to the body (a right relation and a left relaticn, so to speak) are different in themselves. [...] Being different parts of a whole, right and left differ in value as well as in nature, for the relation between part and whole is hierarchical, and a different relation means here a different place in the hierarchy" (ibid.: 248, original emphasis).

The division, distribution and consumption in the ritual context of the "big house" makes statements on values, i.e. on hierarchical relationships. This is communicated in different codes of spatial distance, temporal sequence and in the idiom of the victim's body. The latter is divided into head, neck and trunk. Because the head has a different relation to the whole body, "...it has a different place in the hierarchy" (ibid.), it is *boro*. Therefore the head, not the neck and least the trunk, is fit to represent the whole, as the ritual structure shows.

After the goat is decapitated, meat of the undivided head, liver and *tsoru*-rice (made from *potri chaul*) are first offered to the gods. Then

---

32. "Distinctive" vs. "hierarchical" opposition is one point of dissent between Needham (1980, 1987) and Dumont (1986). This controversy cannot be elaborated here.

the head is divided into opposites, head and neck. *Boro tsoru* (head) and *sano tsoru* (neck) are cooked by agnates and affines respectively. Only the members of the cobra group are fit to share the head with the gods after the latter have eaten. When, long ago, Gudapada was founded the founders of the cobra clan established the divine relations, so they are the only ones who can maintain them. Their affines who later settled in the village are Gadaba but also non-agnates or "others". They eat the neck, which was previously part of the undivided head. Finally, the non-Gadaba may only consume the trunk of the victim.

If the goats body as a whole is divided into ranked parts, so is the village. Like the head the agnates have a different relation to the whole and are thus boro. By their relation to the sacred, their transcendent property, they are senior to all other village segments. The transcendental is not far away, it is the earth and the hills of and around the village.

But head and agnates are not only senior to neck and affines, they can represent the whole. They have a special relation to and incorporate their opposites. Dumont calls this hierarchical relation "encompassing of the contrary" (1980: 239f). First, the agnates represent the undifferentiated village as a whole in front of their gods and feed them with the undivided head and *tsoru*-rice they have prepared. They encompass their contrary, the affines or "non-agnates," as well as all other Desia or "non-Gadaba" of the village. They are different things at once: Desia, Gadaba and agnates.

In the next step, at a different level, they become differentiated and the hierarchical opposition between cobras and non-cobras, *boro* and *sano tsoru* becomes visible. What was one head and one group the moment before segments into opposites. The way Gadaba talk about *tsoru* also reveals its double nature. On the one hand they say the head together with the rice collected from the whole village is the only and proper *tsoru*, cooked by the *Randari* in a new pot. But on the other hand they refer to the neck as *sano tsoru* and oppose it to its senior counterpart.

This hierarchical relation is also expressed in a temporal sequence. The cobras, representing the whole, feed the gods first, then eat together (*Pujari* and *Randari* served first) and only after they have started, the affines may begin eating their *sano tsoru*. Likewise the spatial arrangement suggests this hierarchy. Members of the cobra group sit around the shrine (*Pujari* first, *Randari* second), the affines some metres away and the *Barik* on the very edge of the area.

While on the first level we find unity, distinction between cobras and non-cobras appears on the second. On the third ideological level a new opposition becomes explicit and the previous one disappears or becomes implicit. Here, Gadaba (agnates and non-agnates) as eater of *tsoru* (*boro*/head and *sano*/neck) oppose all other Desia as the eaters of non-*tsoru* or the trunk (*gondi*) of the sacrificial animal. Again the hierarchy also is expressed in the codes of distance and sequence. *Tsoru* should and is always eaten first, *gondi* later. Furthermore all Gadaba eat together in the vicinity of the god in a relatively small area. On the other side of the river several hundred metre away, in between shrine and village, the *gondi* is cooked and consumed.

The hierarchy between agnates and affines is again stressed in the last scene when the agnatic office-holders are carried back into the village on the back of their in-laws. Affines should perform this duty but I have seen other Desia (never agnates) doing it as well.

The structure can be illustrated as a "binary tree" which shows unity on the first and the hierarchical oppositions on secondary levels (see Hage, Harary, Milicic, 1995).

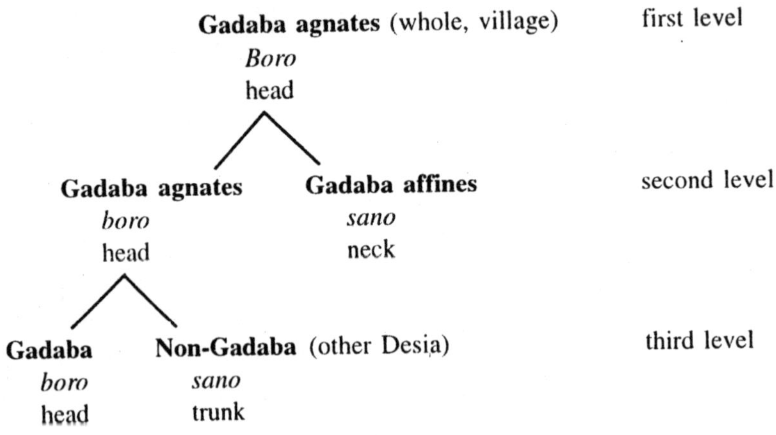

FIGURE 2.1: Hierarchical structure of the "big house" — sacrifice

As Pfeffer (1983: 120) states, seniority in middle India "...is always used as a synonym of the sacred, just as secular status will always imply a junior position". Thus the original cobra clan of the village is conceptualised as *boro*, which means senior and at the same time sacred in relation to all non-agnates who are relatively junior and secular or less sacred.

In a different context Pfeffer (1991, 2000) likewise points out the senior status of the agnatic principle in opposition to affinity. He interprets the exchange of "souls" (*duma*) between agnates in the great final death-ceremony of the Gadaba, called *gotr*, as a metaphysical type of marriage and superior or senior to the exchange of brides between affines.[33] In Gadaba marriage as in death rituals basically affinal and agnatic inter-village relations are at stake, not the village as a whole like in the here presented case.

The analysed sacrifice is a celebration of the village whose senior most (human) segment is in closest commensal relation to its gods. But all parts of this sacred entity are recognised, especially when the ritual structure of the whole festival (*chait porbo*) is taken into account. Then the village goddess (*hundi*), the house gods (*doron deli*) and the dead (*duma*) are also included. On an even broader analytical plain, all annual village rituals have to be compared, also in relation to the collectively celebrated *rites de passage*, like *gotr* and marriage. This could not be achieved in this paper and therefore analysis and interpretation can only be preliminary.

4. Conclusion

In the two sections of the paper relationships between Gadaba and other Desia have been described and analysed. It has become apparent that whatever may be their administrative label the "non-ST" are part of the specific Desia society which is quite homogeneous in its diversity.

First, attention has been drawn to relations within and between Desia categories. All Desia categories are internally divided into different hierarchically ordered segments, neither intermarrying nor interdining with one another. Further Desia categories themselves are ranked and it is suggested that the general hierarchy is tripartite. While status within levels may not be unambiguous as is the case among those wearing the *poita* (sacred thread), the hierarchy between levels is explicit. *Boro* and *sano* are the omnipresent expressions of seniority or status.

Secondly, the study of a concrete village setting reveals a modified picture of the hierarchy. The tripartite structure gives way to the opposition of senior Gadaba as patrons *vs.* their junior "non-ST" clients, be they *poita*-wearers or from the Dombo category. The general, "trans-village"

33. The hosts of a *gotr* provide their external clan-brothers with cows the latter prepare and eat during the ritual. To every group of "brothers" the hosts give half a cow, which is exactly cut in a longitudinal way. Although this is no sacrificial context, this might imply that there is no difference in status between "brothers".

hierarchy is also effective in the village, as can be judged from norms and behaviour of intermarriage and interdining. But the superior status of the Gadaba is expressed in economic and ritual relations of the village. "Land" in its economical and spiritual properties is the key to the senior status of the original clan in Gudapada. They maintain contact to the gods of the earth and hills and may therefore exploit the land. Not only the landholding Gadaba from the cobra clan, but the whole village is benefiting from the services of the clients who are rewarded with *pholoi* by the village. But unless Gadaba work as "Goudo" and are then called as such, they are never *pholoi* receivers. Acknowledging the senior and sacred status of the Gadaba agnates, clients take "cooked rice" and give "respect" or *manti* to the latter. These gifts are offered to the earth and village goddess (*hundi*) to appease her and make further cultivation possible. In return clients are allowed to demand *piai* (husked rice) on village festivals.

But clients do not only provide gifts to "cool down the village goddess" in November. In every collective ritual occasion the whole village participates. They jointly finance sacrificial animals and give *potri*-rice for the *tsoru*. Depending on the ritual context the "non-ST" Desia of Gudapada may share the head or trunk of the victim.

Patterns of division, distribution and consumption of sacrificial animals reveal the social morphology of the village and its intrinsic value. Thus seniority of the agnates as described in the "economic sphere" is also found in the ideology of the ritual system. Both domains (economic and ritual) are not separated but have to be considered together. In both cases the status of the agnates can only be understood with reference to the divine land or earth. Due to their specific metaphysical relation to the earth upon which all Desia depend, agnates of Gudapada occupy a superior position in the village. The value-idea of seniority always seems to point to this religious quality. In the sacrificial context of the "big house" seniority is displayed in the codes of the victims body, distance and sequence. In front of the gods the cobra clan represents the village as a whole and is several things at the same time: Agnates, Gadaba and Desia. On secondary levels hierarchical oppositions become visible. "Non-ST" Desia of Gudapada are very much part of the conceptual framework of the village, they find their place in a junior position and are encompassed by the senior status of the servants of the sacred soil.

REFERENCES

Bailey, F.G. 1957. *Caste and the Economic Frontier.* Manchester: Manchester University Press.

____. 1960. *Tribe, Caste, and Nation*. Manchester: Manchester University Press.

Barraud, C., D. de Coppet, A. Iteanu and R. Jamous. 1994. [1984] *Of Relations and the Dead. Four Societies Viewed from their Angle of their Exchanges.* Oxford: Berg.

Boal, B.M. 1982. *The Konds. Human Sacrifice and Religious Change*. Warminster: Aris & Phillips.

Dumont, L. 1980. *Homo Hierarchicus. The Caste System and its Implications*. Chicago & London: The University of Chicago Press.

____. 1986. *Essays on Individualism*. Chicago & London: The University of Chicago Press.

Durkheim, É. 1968 [1912]. *The Elementary Forms of Religious Life*. New York: The Free Press.

Elwin, V. 1950. *Bondo Highlander*. Bombay: Oxford University Press.

Fürer-Haimendorf, C.v. 1943. "Megalithic Rituals among the Gadabas and Bondos of Orissa," *Journal of the Asiatic Society of Bengal*, 9: 149-78.

Gustaffson, U. 1989. *An Adiwasi Oriya-Telegu-English Dictionary*. Mysore: Central Institute of Indian Languages.

Hage, P., F. Harary and B. Milicic. 1995. "Hierarchical Opposition," *Oceania*, 65 (4): 347-54.

Hardenberg, R. 1999. *Die Wiedergeburt der Götter. Ritual und Gesellschaft in Orissa*. Hamburg: Kovac.

Hertz, R. 1960 [1905/6]. *Death and the Right Hand*. London: Cohen & West.

Howell, S. 1996. "Introduction," in: S. Howell (ed.), *Sacrificing in Eastern Indonesia*. Leiden: CNWS Publications.

Hubert, H. & M. Mauss 1964 [1898]. *Sacrifice: Its Nature and Its Function*. Chicago: University of Chicago Press.

Lévi-Strauss, C. 1991 [1962]. *Totemism*. London: Merlin Press.

Needham, R. 1980. *Reconnaissances*. Toronto: University of Toronto Press.

____. 1987. *Counterpoints*. Berkeley, Los Angeles, London: University of California Press.

Niggemeyer, H. 1964a. *Kuttia Kondh. Dschungelbauern in Orissa*. München: Renner.

____. 1964b. "Kuttia Kond und Pano. Zur Stellung der verachteten Klassen in Indien," in: M. Schuster & H. Straube (eds.), *Festschrift für Ad. E. Jensen Teil 2*. München: Renner.

Pfeffer, G. 1983. "Generation and Marriage in Middle India: the Evolutionary Potential of 'Restricted Exchange'," *Contributions to Indian Sociology*, 17 (1): 87-121.

____. 1994. "Music in Context: Ethnography and Meaning," in *Ethnomusicology in the Context of other Sciences*. Beiträge zur Musikethnologie, 30. Eisenach: Wagner.

____. 1997. "The Scheduled Tribes of Middle India as a Unit: Problems of Internal and External Comparison," in G. Pfeffer D.K. Behera (eds.), *Contemporary*

Society Tribal Studies, Vol. 1. *Structure and Process*. New Delhi: Concept Publishing Company.

——. 2000. (in press) "A Ritual of Revival among the Gadaba of Koraput," in B. Schnepel & H. Kulke (eds.), *Jagannath Revisited: Studying Society, Religion and the State in Orissa*. New Delhi: Manohar.

Somasundaram, A.M. 1949. "A Note on the Gadabas of Koraput District," *Man in India*, 29 (1): 36-45.

THREE

THE JĀDOPAṬIĀS: Parasitic Charlatans or Benevolent Priests ?

HANS HADDERS

Budhesvar Citrakar told me: "we do not go [to perform our work] to the Bengali locality. We live with the Santal [*ādibāsī*] and we go to their locality"... "This is the work of our caste [*jāt*] ... this is our livelihood [*saṅgsār* cala]."

I inquired if they were Bengali. "Yes, we are Bengali and we are the priest [*thākur*[1]] of the Santal"... "We are two different groups. We are their priests [*thākur*]. We cannot intermarry with them. *Jādobābā*, they call us *bābā* , *Jādopaṭiā* and *thākur*".

I asked him in what way they were the priests [*thākur*] of the Santal. "We are the priest of the Santal because we do the "*cokhodān*". They do not have any Brahman [*bāman*]. They do not keep peace with the Brahman ... They had a Brahman. *Murmu* was their Brahman. *Murmu*[3] was their priest [*thākur*]. This has been rejected." I interjected: in their place you have come. "Aha, that is so".[4]

1. Thākur can have many meanings; a god, a deity, an idol or a lord, master or king. However, in this context the informant uses thākur interchangeable with the word Brahman or priest (Samsad, 1985: 373).
2. Bābā; father, ... a respectful title applied to ascetics (Samsad, 1985: 650).
3. Murmu is one of the major twelve clans (paris) of the Santals. This clan has got it's name from the totem of the clan, the murum jel, an antelope (see fn 24).
4. I will return to the fact that murmu has lost their authority as priest further on in this chapter.

In North-eastern India there exist a group of scroll painters and performers known as *Jādopaṭiās* or *paṭkars*. They occur in West Bengal as well as in the bordering areas of Bihar and Orissa. These male performers are of Bengali origin but operate mainly in the tribal villages where they show their scrolls in return for rice. As the Jādopaṭiās whom I met with mainly worked among the Santals my focus will remain on the interaction between the Jādopaṭiās and the Santals.[5]

The Santals belong to one of the many indigenous populations that inhabit the Indian subcontinent. They number approximately 5 million people and are scattered throughout the North Indian subcontinent, including Nepal and Bangladesh. The Santals speak Santali, a language that belongs to an Austro-Asiatic language family (Gautam, 1998: 14). The Jādopaṭiās generally live in the outskirts of the Santal village, or in close proximity to it. Their mother tongue is Bengali or Hindi, but they speak Santali with great ease.

The Jādopaṭiās also have another source of income, a ritual service they render in return for rice, as well other items and money. They eagerly await the news of any death that may have occurred in a Santal household. Some times later they visit that house and perform a mortuary ritual known as *cokhodān*. One of the central events of this ritual performance is the bestowal of eyesight to a pictorial representation of the deceased person. This picture is about the size of a hand. During the ritual invocations uttered by the Jādopaṭiā he puts a dot, representing the iris of the eye, in the blank eye space, with a pen. At the bottom of this picture are some representations of the remuneration that the Jādopaṭiā expects for his service. With the help of these actions the Jādopaṭiā claims to be able to assist the blind soul of the deceased person and render it a safe journey to heaven, so that it will turn into a benign ancestor instead of a haunting ghost. The Jādopaṭiā also claims that he has seen the dead one in his dreams during the night. The dead one has called him to the house of the bereaved relatives. When the Jādopaṭiā arrives at the house of the deceased he will relate things that the dead has told him, or he may speak as if he is the dead one himself. These and other

5. I wish to thank the "Institute for Comparative Research in Human culture" in Oslo for financial support of the 6 months of field research upon which this article is partly based. Many aspects touched on in this paper are discussed in more detail in my M.A. dissertation "The Gift Of The Eye" (2000, NTNU, Trondheim). The standard system of transliteration (as exemplified by Anderson, 1962) is followed with minor modification. Cokhodān is not transcribed "cakṣudān", which is the way it would be transcribed following the "sanskritised" manner. The reason for this is that I want to stay closer to the colloquial pronunciation of my informants.

ritual doings of the Jādopaṭiā are firmly planted in the religious world-view and ritual context of the Santal as well as Hindu society. However, this ritual event is not a compulsory part of the Santal funeral ritual cycle. When the Jādopaṭiā describes his practice and his role as a funerary priest, he borrows categories from the Hindu context and glosses his role with these categories. The Jādopaṭiā calls himself the *purohit, agradānī* or Brahman of the Santal.

How is it then that the Santal generally accepts the Jādopaṭiās visit, and complies with the Jādopaṭiā's demands when he performs his mortuary ritual act? Are the relationship between the Jādopaṭiā's and the Santals a parasitic one, rather than one of symbiosis? Many authors have described the Jādopaṭiā's practice as sheer exploitation of the Santal. W.G. Archer has characterised the Jādopaṭiā's role in the funeral context by calling him a funerary beggar (Archer, 1974: 335). J-B Faivre relates how the Jādopaṭiās try to impress and even threaten the Santal (Faivre, 1979: 111). Rosita de Selva, who perceive the Jādopaṭiās as "magicians", focus on the manipulatory aspects of *cokhodān* (de Silva, 1994). I can see the validity of all these views. However, in my exposition of the Jādopaṭiās I want to paint a broader picture of them and the mortuary ritual event in the light of a variety of contexts. Moreover, my view is that to be able to understand why the Jādopaṭiā is called the Brahman of the Santal, we have to conceptualise this statement as the Jādopaṭiā's discourse about himself. It is a statement by a professional about himself and the status of his guild. In that perspective it is of great interest to find out from what universe the Jādopaṭiā has borrowed his imagery.

How does the Jādopaṭiā anchor his claims that he is the Brahman (*thākur*) and the priest (*purohit*) of the Santal? He argues that the work (*kāj*) and service that he renders the Santal relatives after death can be equated with rites performed for the dead, and the service offered by other funeral priests after a death has occurred. Thus the Santal, his patron, is compared to the patron (*jajmān*)[6] of the Brahman and the *purohit*. The gifts (*dān*) the

6. Jajmān is a patron of a ritual specialist, especially of a Brahman priest (Parry 1994: xxiii). The Hindi (or Bengali) term jajmān derives from the Sanskrit term yajamāna, "patron of the sacrifice", for whom the priest performed the ritual. In parts of northern India, the term jajmān has been extended to cover "patron" in a more general sense (Fuller, 1989: 39). In the contexts discussed in this paper, the term jajmān refers to a relationship between patrons and artisan/priests prevalent in northern Indian villages, where payments or dues (paona) for a service rendered is paid in kind. These types of relationships are more or less formalised over time (Fruzzetti, 1982: 43). The description of the term jajmān, given here by me, mirrors my informants use of the term. For a discussion and a critique of anthropological understanding of the "jaimani system" see Fuller (ibid.: 33-63), and Parry (1994). In the later part of this paper I will return to the claim that the Santals are the jajmān of the Jādopaṭiās.

Santals give to the Jādopaṭiā are compared to the gifts that the Brahman and the purohit receive for his funerary work. In this manner the Jādopaṭiā borrows categories from the Hindu system and glosses his professional role with concepts from a Hindu context. I would like to illuminate these and other glosses made by the Jādopaṭiā by comparing these and other ethnographic data by H.H. Risley (1891) and J. Parry (1989/1994), collected in North India, that deals with funeral priests and Brahmans who perform mortuary rituals. Several of my Jādopaṭiā informants told me that the mortuary work they performed where agradān and that they where the *agradānī* priest of the Santals. In his ethnographic glossary "Tribes and Castes of Bengal"[7] (first published in 1891) H.H. Risley (1851-1911) gives us this exposition of the *agradānī*.

> *Agradāna, Agradāni, Agrasrāddhi*, a degraded sub-caste of Brahmans, ranking slightly above the Āchārji. They read mantras at the cremation of Brahmans and members of the Nava-Sākha, and take gifts (*dān*) at the first *srāddh*[8] on the eleventh or thirty-first day after death, and the subsequent monthly *srāddhas* for a year, after which time no more presents are given. Pure Brahmans will eat sweetmeats with the Agradāni, but not rice. In Bengal they bear the ironical designation of Mahā-Brāhman, Mahā-purohit, Mahā-srāddhi, Mahā-puttra, Marui-porā Brahman and in the rare instance when they have a smattering of Sanskrit, Pandit. In Behar they are called Mahā-Brāhman and Kāntāha. (Risley, vol. I, 1981: 11).

First of all it is important to notice that this type of Brahman is degraded. This fact reflects on the ironical titles that this Brahman has been given. The prefix Maha- means great (Samsad, 1985: 741). The ironical scorn of this epithet is obvious here. Further, Risley points out that the Maha-Brahman is known as *Kāntāha* in Bihar. *Kāntāha* or *kānthā* means thorn (ibid.. 189). This metaphor is also a proof of the contempt with which this type of Brahman is treated.[9] We are informed that this type of Brahman rarely knows any Sanskrit. If he does, it is this smattering of Sanskrit that would give him the

7. This work, useful as it may be, has to be read as sign of its time. Ronald Inden makes this comment. "Here in these tomes of alphabetised empiricism, then, is to be found what I would refer to as the hegemonic discourse on caste of the Anglo-French imperial formation." (Inden, 1990: 58).
8. Śrāddha "n. a respectful and well-wishing offering to the manes ..." (Samsad, 1985: 838).
9. Parry (see further below) also notes this derogatory meaning of the title kānthā (Parry, 1994: 76).

venerated title of "Pandit", usually reserved for those Brahmans who are respected for their command over this language of the Hindu holy scriptures. Risley has listed Maha-puttra as another title given to this Brahman. The translation of "puttra" given in Samsad Bengali-English dictionary is son (Samsad, 1985: 573). However, I suspect that Risley could have made a miss-transcription of *pātra*; vessel or a minister (ibid.: 559). Maha-patra, then, could be the great vessel. "In the drama of death the Funeral-priest is a vessel for the rancorous greed of the ghost. Worshiped as the deceased, he is dressed in the dead man's clothes, is made to wear his spectacles or clutch his walking stick, and is fed his favourite foods." (Parry, 1994: 76). Secondly, we also notice in Risley's account of the agradānī, the gifts (*dān*) that the Brahman is given and accept in connection with his role as the funeral priest. The concept of gift in this context is important. This is a point that I will return to further on in this paper. To get a more detailed description of this kind of funeral Brahman I will utilise some more of Jonathan P. Parry's ethnographic data from his book "Death in Banaras" (1994). In this book Parry exposes material that is based on his fieldwork done in the North Indian city Banaras over the last fifteen years (ibid.: xix). In chapter three, named "Shares and Chicanery" (ibid.: 75-118), Parry describes the division of mortuary labour between various groups of occupational specialists, who earn their living on and around the burning *ghāts*. One of the groups of mortuary workers that Parry introduces in this chapter is the Mahabrahman.

> At death the soul becomes a disembodied ghost or *pret*, a hungry and malevolent state dangerous to the survivors. On the twelfth day after death a rite is performed which enables the deceased to rejoin his ancestors and become an ancestor (*pitr*) himself. The Mahabrahman Funeral-priest presides over the ritual addressed to the ghost during the first eleven days after death, and accepts on behalf of the ghost the gifts intended for it (ibid.: 75-76).

The fact that the Mahabrahman accepts gifts on behalf of the ghost of the deceased is of great importance here. One of the major roles of this type of priest is to atone for the sins of the dead one by accepting these gifts. Thus the Mahabrahman will have to "digest" this sin and serve as a kind of medium or vehicle for the transmission of the moral filth of his patron. The performance of this task is often seen as a defiling activity (ibid.: 123).[10] It is also of interest to note that these Brahmans who have close communication with the *pret* or ghost - are in many contexts treated much like untouchables. They are "described as *achhut* ('not to be touched')" (ibid.: 77). "The

Mahabrahman is regarded with a mixture of fear and contempt" (ibid.: 78). In addition, that the Mahabrahman is associated with death and the polluting corpse in general also ads to his ambiguous status.

> The Mahabrahman's presence is, however, essential. He confers salvation, and allows the soul to "swim across" to the other world. For the successful conclusion of the rites he must be satisfied with the gifts offered. ... Without his blessing the deceased will remain in limbo of pret-hood to plague his family with misfortune and further bereavement... (ibid.:79).

The rational involved in the Hindu context referred to in the citation by Parry above is an important part of the parcel of ideas that the Jādopaṭiā invoke when they refer to themselves as the Brahmans of the Santals. In the Hindu context, described by Parry, the "true gift" (*dān*) is voluntary donation made without any ostentation or expectations of this-worldly return (ibid.: 120). However, this kind of calculation does not exclude the notion of reciprocity (as envisaged by Mauss 1990 [1925]), in relation to the gifts given to the funeral priest, in the case of the Jādopaṭiās and the Santals. Even if the giver of a gift is not supposed to expect any this-worldly returns, he certainly expects that the fulfilment of his filial duties will be rewarded by a successful "ferrying across" of his mane into the next world. He also hopes that the work performed by the funeral priest will result in a pacification of any kind of sin, inauspicious force, or evil influence that could plague the deceased or the relatives otherwise.

The Jādopaṭiās I talked to claimed that the all the sins of the deceased Santals would be reduced via the performance of *cokhodān*. This kind of statement has several implications. It connects the doings of the Jādopaṭiā with the judgement and punishments meted out by Yama in hell.[11] It also introduces the Hindu concepts of "sin" (*pāp*). The concept of "sin" is connected to the law of cause and effect (*karma*), and are intimately tied

10. Parry comments that the word pāp [sin] and doṣ [fault] are used for sin in this context. But the most common term for sin is the Hindi word "prāyashchitt". This term stands for expiation or atonement of sin. However, Parry also underlines that the term "prāyashchitt" also, in colloquial use, by the Banaras sacred specialists, has the additional sense of the 'sin' which is expiated, and is used interchangeably with pāp and doṣ (Parry, 1994: 281, n 3). My Jādopaṭiā informants used the Bengali prāyashchitt as a term for the action of purification from "sin" (*pāp*), or as a general purification from something inauspicious. Because they perform this act of expiation they claim to have a status of some kind of funeral priest or Brahman (see further on page 12 ff).
11. The theme of king Yama and the punishments in hell is one of the major themes on the scrolls of the Jādopaṭiā that he displays in the Santal village.

up with the Hindu eschatological notions of reincarnation (*samsāra*) and liberation (*mokṣa*). How does the Santal make sense of this allusion to 'sins' of their deceased relatives?

> Death is the privileged subject of faith, since death is a problematic theme, poorly defined for the Santal who lack a proper eschatology. This problematic theme is, so to speak taken over by the Hindu thinking, through the mediation of the jadu patua [Jādopaṭiā] who paint the picture of the Santal dead, as well as concepts related to "ethics," such as the notion of merit or fault, modalities of the karma, theory of individual fate (Carrin-Bouez, 1986: 181. English translation by Philippe Maincon).

It is important to keep in mind that, among the Santal society in question, as well as in Hindu society, there are many parallel ideas and theories about the destiny of the "life principle" or a soul, and afterlife in general. One of the reasons for this, in Hindu society, is the wealth of textual sources as well as an abundance of ideas from different periods of time.

> Here, as in most other cases, Hindu practice and belief does not simply follow from a logical extension of one basic idea but of a plurality of basic notions from which, quite logically but not always in mutually compatible fashion, specific beliefs and practices flow (Klostermaier, 1989: 162).

In the article "The After-Life in Indian Tribal Belief," Fürer-Haimendorf (1953) gives us some clear examples of the trend mentioned by Klostermaier above.

> Many a Hindu of today believes that a dead man's *jiv* ["life principle"] manifests itself in the crows which eat the food offerings put down at the cremation-ground, and if no crow touched the food it is taken a sign that the Departed is angry or distressed. At the same time he believes that the *jiv* must go before Yama's court of judgement, and if able to show sufficient accumulated merit or *karma*, will be admitted to the company of the sainted dead or *pitri*. Yet he also believes that a dead man may be reborn in a grandchild; and besides holding all these apparently inconsistent beliefs, he acknowledges his duty to perform for his deceased father a series of rites, known as *sraddha*, which are aimed at providing and sustaining a new, ethereal body for the departed (Fürer-Haimendorf, 1953: 47).

Hindu and Santal society have probably imposed mutual influence on one another when it comes to the understanding of soul-concepts and their eschatological belief (Fürer-Haimendorf, 1953: 44). Some regional facets of this extremely complex issue of co-existing models and variations in practice are reflected in the discourses and doings of the Jādopaṭiā.[12]

At this point it has become evident to the reader that the distinction I make between "Hindu society"/"Hindu context" *versus* "Santal society"/ "Santal context" rely on an abstraction undertaken for the sake of clarification.

The Degraded Priest Placed in the Santal Context

In what follows I will illustrate how the Jādopaṭiās plant themselves firmly within one of the most pivotal institutions of the Santals, the *Karam binti*; connected with the "story of the creation". The recitation of such *Karam bintis* are compulsory at a number of life-cycle rituals among the Santals such as *Caco chatiar*, the ritual purification and initiation of children as persons of the Santal society, and at the time of the performance of the Santal mortuary rituals (Bodding, 1942; Archer, 1974).[13]

The narrative that I include below is a mythological narrative by *Rām Bilās Citrakar*, one of my Jādopaṭiā informants. In this myth he relates how the Jādopaṭiā got their professional role as funeral priest in the Santal community. At the time of recording this myth the *Rām Bilās* introduced himself (in Bengali) with these words; "I am the purohit and thākur of the Santal. By reading and knowing the Santal scriptures and the tradition of Santal ancestors (*hapram*) I do the expiation (*prāyaṣciṭṭa*) work (*kāj*) for them". Having said this he told me the name of his Jādopaṭiā teacher (*guru*), as well as the name of his Santal teachers (*karam gurus*[14]) who had taught him his trade and the traditions of the Santals.

12. A penetration of this grand issue of origin of the notion of karma is far beyond the scope of this thesis. However, for an extensive discussion the origin of Karmic Eschatology in the Indian setting see; Erik Af Edholm, 1988 and Fürer-Haimendorf, 1953.
13. In the context I refer to here, the Santal person is conceived as the relational identity of any Santal, as a member of the Santal society [i.e. its cultural representation, referred to by Mauss as personnage (Parkin, 1992:220)]. I do not wish to enter into an epistemological discussion of the category of an individual in the Santal society. That is beyond the scope and focus of this paper.
14. Karam guru is a Santal who knows the karam binti, the oral tradition of the Santals and their ancestors. This tradition has gradually transformed into written texts, like in the case of the material collected by Skrefsrud from the Karam guru Kolean (the source referred to in fn 11, below).

"*Maran Buru*" created the world, seven girls and seven boys.[15] Later on *Maran Buru* saw that these people in the world had multiplied into large numbers - Who will protect these people? The wealth and possessions of the people will be mischievously taken away by thieves. For this reason *Maran Buru* thought: who is going to protect these people? For this purpose he made two animals, each with four legs. However, *Maran Buru*, the creator, could give them life, but to do *cokhodān* [gift of eyesight] was the duty of *Kāl Bhairab. Kāl Bhairab* means: from the lineage of Shiva. One of Shiva's names is *Kāl Bhairab.*[16] He used to do *cokhodān* - Who will protect the people of *Cae Campa Gar*[17] during the night? For this reason I have created some animals. Now *Kāl Bhairab* will give them eyesight [*cokhodān*]. *Maran Buru* sent his sepoy [beng. *sipāhi*; soldier/messenger] to fetch *Kāl Bhairab*, but the sepoy could not find him. The sepoy returned and said: - *Maran Buru, Kāl Bhairab* is not in his house. One day passed thus. The second day *Maran Buru* asked the sepoy to go and fetch him again. The sepoy did not find him in his house. In this manner six days past, but the sepoy did not find *Kāl Bhairab* in his house. *Maran Buru* became angry and said: - Today six days has passed since I gave life to the animals. They passed six days in difficulties. Why does not their eyes open! Where has *Kāl Bhairab* gone? For all the creatures that I give life, I have allotted the task of *cokhodān* to *Kāl Bhairab.* Why doesn't he come? Today six days has passed. Werever you find him, bring him here. The sepoy said: - Werever he is residing I will search, catch hold of him and bring him here. The sepoy went, but did not find *Kāl Bhairab* at first. He had gone fishing. There he found him. The sepoy said: you have to come, this is the order of *Maran Buru.* You have to leave whatever task you are doing and go to him. He has created two animals, and six days has passed without their eyes opening. Who will do *cokhodān*? That is your work. I will go said *Kāl Bhairab*. He and the sepoy quickly went from that place to *Maran Buru. Maran Buru* angrily told *Kāl Bhairab*: - six days has passed and these animals have had a difficult time. Why couldn't you come? Give them *cokhodān*! Thus *Kāl Bhairab* gave them *cokhodān*. This is the cause of the six days that pass before dogs open their eyes. Because *Kāl Bhairab* delayed

15. This starting point is a variation of the creation myth of the Santals. See "The ancestor's Story" in "Traditions and Institutions of The Santals" (Bodding, 1942: 3 ff).
16. Kāl Bhairab is a "terrible" form of Shiva. This is an interesting claim that may induce fear and respect with the Santals.
17. According to the Santal myth this was one of the main original dwelling places of the Santals (ibid.: 10).

his work for six days. When dogs have puppies it takes six days before their eyes open. Because of *Kāl Bhairab's* negligence *Maran Buru* gave him a curse - Why did you delay your work? Your lineage will start from *Ainto* and *Jainto*. They will go to the Santal in *Cae Campa Gar*, to "eat" [digest] the sin of their dead ones. *Kāl Bhairab* said: - do not cast such a curse on me! I have done a big mistake ... *Maran Buru* said: - you cannot avoid this curse. Why did you delay the *cokhodān*? *Kāl Bhairab* said: - well, be it so then. I have sinned.

When the people of *Cae Campa Gar* became too many, one of the eight girls became pregnant, and gave birth to *Madho Sin*.[18] *Madho Sin* started oppression and tyranny in *Cae Campa Gar*. He spread fear among the Santals. *Maran Buru* told the Santals: - do not stay here any longer. Your *dharma*[19] will be destroyed here. In the midst of the night they prepared twelve carts to bring the people, and escape from there ... *Maran Buru* saw the big waves on the gaṅgā river that was full of water. He thought to himself: - if the people of *Cae Campa* will be stopped by this river *Madho Sin* will kill them all. *Maran Buru* said: - listen! The river will dry up. But for this to happen you have to undertake a worship [*pūjā*]. He said: - look here; to enable you to cross you have to fast and worship. Then they sacrificed a brown fowl to *Jaher Era* and *Gossain Era* so that they would grant their wish and make the river dry up so that the twelve carts could pass ... Like *Maran Buru* had said, so it happened and the river dried up at one place and there was enough space for the Santal people to cross over with their twelve carts. When *Madho Sin* reached the shore of the river the big waves stopped him from crossing ... This was due to the might of the bonga, the divinities to whom the sacrifice was given by the Santals. Madho

18. At this point the narrator integrate his main theme into one of the themes in the Santal myth. Madho Sin was an illegitimate child. A result of an affair between a Santal girl and a Hindu (a young man of the "king") who threatened to kill her if she revealed the fact that he was the father of the child. The mother left this child in the jungle. Some girls of the kisku clan found the child and adopted it. The kisku people kept the secret. Madho Sin grew up and became intelligent and clever and the king gave him office. However, when Madho Sin demanded a Santal wife, none was offered, because the Santals did not know to which clan the bastard belonged. The Santals where afraid of having their daughters ravished and secretly prepared to escape from the land of Cae Campa (see Bodding, 1942: 21). According to Campbell, "Madhosin is said to have been the person who first broke up the unity of the Santal people" (Campbell, 1988: 498).
19. Dharma: refer to religion in a widesense. It can also stand for truth and justice.
20. Jaher than (the sacred grove) is the place where the Santals worship three of their main divinities; Maran Buru, Moreko-Turuiko and Jaher Era. Here these divinities are said to reside in three Sarjom trees (shorea robusta or Sal) (Troisi, 1978: 81-82).

Sin saw that the Santals had passed and understood that he could not catch them. *Maran Buru* said [to the Santals], look here, - however, first of all you have to do worship at the *jaher than.*[20] That one is called spring festival [*baha porob*]. If these divinities had not assisted you today you would have been killed by *Madho Sin*. Their [the Santals] dharma would have been destroyed. That is why *jaher* worship [*pūjā*] became their major worship. At the *jaher than* they worship and sacrifice a brown fowl. *Maran Buru* said: listen! - you have come out from here. Then your dharma could be destroyed. Who knows what will happen? Who can tell? The one who will perform the worship [*naeke thākur*] will be *Murmu thākur*, *Sada Murmu* and *Nij Murmu.*[21] He will do the worship. He will fast and make a ring out of copper and iron. This one he will wear. The day he will worship he will take it of and place it in the tree of the *jaher than*. There he will do the worship. *Jaher Era* will come there. That is the goddess Durga of Hindu religion [*dharma*]. They call *Durga pūjā* for *Jaher Era*. If you do not place that ring there you cannot do the *Durga* or *Jaher Era* worship there. That is why, also today, that the ones who do *naeke* worship at the *jaher than*, wear that ring. They fast and wear the ring. Then they install[22] the ring, place it in the tree and worship. Many days passed, one after another. Then the people of *Cae Campa Gar* had become manifold. *Maran Buru* told himself: - I will go once more and see in what condition these people are living. *Maran Buru* saw that they had built many houses. But they where drinking alcohol. They ate cows meat. The *naeke*[23] *thākur* slowly destroyed the *dharma* and *karma*. They have lost the power of earlier times. One day a cow died. They went and ate it. The *naeke* ate it all. At that time the *naeke* was a priest [*paitā*[24]] a Brahmin type of priest. That has fallen out of practice.[25] *Maran Buru* found out about this bad state of affairs. They could not continue to do worship.

21. Nij means original (here, original clan). "The original sept from which the sub-septs of all Santal septs have been derived." (Campbell, 1988: 551). Nij Murmu is the first of the Murmu sub-clans from which all the other Murmu sub-clans have originated.
22. Install it (sthāpan) by consecrating the place of worship.
23. Among the Santals the naeke is in charge of conducting religious sacrifice to the bon gas. However, here the narrator refers to Murmu thākur. See further on in the text.
24. "The holy thread slung over the shoulder in the fashion of a cross-belt by upper-caste Hindus, especially Brahmans...(Samsad, 1985: 524). Here paitā means Brahman priest.
25. The narrator means that the naeke priest (bāman; i.e. the Murmu thākur) has lost his position due to drinking alcohol and eating cows meat (a Hindu point of view). In fact, the Santals look on the rice beer (handia) as a compulsory offering to some of their deities. They also drink rice beer at the time of worship, festivals and social gatherings. Concerning the consumption of cow's meat; Santals eat cow's meat, but see further on page 10 about the Murmu sub-clan status.

Thus *Maran Buru* went there quickly and told them; - listen! Do not touch me! You have destroyed the *dharma*. You cannot continue to be priests [*thākur*]. The *naeke thākur* will continue to do worship, but at the weddings he will not do the priestly work any longer. At the time of weddings the *babne* will play the part of the *thākur* or the *bāman*. The older *babne*, that is, the older son-in-law.[26] *Maran Buru* said that the older son-in-law should become *bāman*. In the midst of the wedding, in the end when they have presented the turmeric cloth, than this older son-in-law will be the *bāman*. The *Murmu thākur* thought to himself: - what is *Maran Buru* saying? -What will be the solution for this? The *naeke* will fast, use the ring, take it of at the *jaher than* and do the worship. Thereafter if the *Murmu thākur* will go, we have been cursed. When your mother or father will die, the people of the lineage of *Kāl Bhairab* will come and do the expiation [*prāyaścitta*]. *Ainto* and *Jainto* are there, *Kāl Bhairab* is long dead. The descendants of *Ainto* and *Jainto* will come. After a death has occurred they will come there and collect what has become defiled: plates and pots, clothes and money. And they will give *jībdān*.[27] Mother and father will pass the river [*vaitaranī*[28]]. Before one used to give a cow as *jībdān*, they give goats and some will present a fowl for the crossing. If they give *jībdan* to the descendants of *Kāl Bhairab*, to the *jādo*, than their mother and father will cross over the *vaitaranī* river. Thus they will not suffer in hell. *Maran Buru* said: listen! You should heed the *ojhā*[29] *guru*. Without him you have no doctor. He can perform the *jhāṛ phuk*[30] against the evil. ... The *jādos* will come. To them you have to give something, otherwise, mother and father, those who have died, will not be able to cross over. The Santals [*ādivāsī*] then thought to themselves:

---

26. "...best man. The Santal word is the same which they use for a brahman (babre), generally a relative, especially a brother-in-law" (Bodding, 1942: 44).
27. The gift (dān) of life performed via the act of a sacrifice (usually a fowl). Jib "n. an animal, a creature, an organism; life; a corporeal or embodied soul; a living being; a soul of a living dead being... (Samsad, 1985: 352).
28. Vaitaranī literally means "she who crosses over". It is the name of a horrid river that one has to cross to come to heaven according to the Hindu eschatology. It is also the name given to the cow that one needs for this crossing (Filippi, 1996: 111). I shall return to this point later on in this chapter.
29. "Ojha. A medicine man, a charm doctor, an exorcist, a diviner" (Campbell, 1988: 564).
30. "n. exorcising of evil spirit by uttering charms and incantations" (Samsad, 1985: 362). The Bengali words Jhār means to brush and phuk means to blow. This type of healing is performed by brushing the body of the patient with the hands, an object (a feather of the Adjutant bird or a peacock, or straw of sirom, Andropogon muricatus, or saparom, Nyctanthus arbor-tristis, L.) or blowing on it, while uttering the charms. Bodding suggests that this practice involves hypnotism as well (Bodding, 1986: 14 [1925]).

should we call *Maran Buru*? - Do not call him! Their [the *Jādopaṭiās*] lineage have been cursed. They will come around on their own accord. They will consult the scriptures [*śāstra*], the house [*ghar*] will be purified ... Having said this *Maran Buru* went on his way. When the people of *Cae Campa Gar* became so many, to many, they lost their customs and rules. The older brother-in-law became *thākur, bāman*. The *naeke* was the *Murmu*. They used to do the worship at the *jaher than*. Many things have changed since then. Hembrom, *Tudu* and *Soren* have taken the role of *naeke* instead of *Murmu*. However, earlier the creator *Maran Buru* has said that except for *Murmu* there was no other *naeke*. But this has changed.

The discourse about the priests in the Santal context, presented by *Rām Bilās* above is a good example of the *Jādopaṭiās* eclectic use of a broad spectrum of ideas and elements from various contexts. With the aim of presenting himself as a worthy priest of the Santals, *Rām Bilās* utilises an amalgam of mixed ideas that blur into each other. At the time of recording this myth I asked *Rām Bilās* if there were any reason for the *Murmu* clans loss of priest status. He said that there is one and continued his narrative.

"Before there was one type of *Murmu*. When they became to many, this type was divided into many groups—*Sada Murmu*, *Bitol Murmu*, *Obor Murmu*. Think about this: - if there is no *Sada Murmu*, there will be no Brahman. But now any caste [*jāt*] can fast, keeping the *dharma* [the precepts of the religious law]. On that day one will fast and get shaved by the barber [*nāpit*]. Having been shaved one fast and then one can perform the worship properly. That worship will be proper. However, *Maran Buru* has cursed the *jādo* of *Kāl Bhairab's* lineage so that they will live from begging, showing scrolls and the gifts of the dead [*maṛār dān*] of the Santals".

When *Rām Bilās* had completed his narrative he told me from what written source he had got it. Thus he gave this myth extra authority. "This was from the *Hapram phuti*[31] story, by the author, servicer *Hasdak*. He wrote it in 1991. I got it from him."

Before I proceed I will make a few comments concerning the narrative by *Rām Bilās* included above. He has made a great point about *Murmu* clan, the Brahman (*thākur*) of the Santals, and their loss of priestly status. Let

31. Hapram = Santali; the ancestors. Puthi = Bengali; book. This is the same type of oral account that Skrefsrud collected from the Karam guru Kolean in 1871, and later wrote down in the form of a book (Traditions and Institutions of the Santals, Bodding, 1942).

32. Gausdal belonged to the Lutheran Santal mission and spent about forty years with the Santals. He has founded a large part of his book "The Santal Khûts" on ethnographic data collected by Bodding and Skrefsrud, the famous Norwegian missionaries.

us compare his statements with the data included in Gausdal's[32] account about the Santal clans, which includes many illuminating statements by informants recorded by Bodding (Gausdal, 1960). First we will look at one account of how the first *Murmu* sub-clan got their totem and how highly they regarded the same.

> When the first boy and girl met, their first boy died when he had grown up; and on his burial place a beautiful *karam* tree (Adina cordifolia) grew up. A female *murum jel* [Nilgae antelope[33]] ate of the tree and became heavy with child and gave birth to a boy, and that boy went about hunting. One day a hunting party caught the boy, and they gave him the *khût* name *Nij Murmu*." (Told by an old Santal near Kearabani, 1940) (Gausdal, 1960: 53-4).
>
> If at a hunt a *Murmu jel* should come our way, we let it pass by; we do not shoot at it. And those who agreed to eat the *murum* meat is outcasted. ... When they hear that a *murum* has been killed, they perform sacrificial cleansing as if a person were dead. If a sosam [a female *murum*] has been killed and there was a calf in her, they also perform the last rites, as when a member of the family has departed." (Paika Murmu of Kodam, near Mohuopaharia, 1949) (ibid.: 54).

Further we will see how the *Murmu* clan was perceived as the Brahman of the Santals and some accounts of how they lost that status.

> The present-day Santals speak about their forefathers as having had a "golden age" when they were in a country called *Champa,* and there the *Murmu* folk were the priests of the community, and therefore even today they are called *Thakur Murmu* (ibid.: 53).
>
> I found Phogra Haram of Jugya and asked him if he could tell me about their *khût* and he said: 'Under the Capakia fig tree *Pilchu Haram*[34] gave us this name, and we are the original *khût.* When we were in *Champa* we were the priests for all the people, just like Brahmins, and everybody showed us respect. The worship of the Bongas, the fasting etc. was entirely in our hands, and other persons could not do it like us, even the *Bongas* - so they say - were agreeable to us. We therefore took precedence everywhere. But since we have come out

33. Nilgae (Hindi; nilgāi); lit. blue cow (Boselaphus tragocamelus) the largest of the Asiatic antelopes. The flesh of this "blue cow" is not to be consumed by Hindus. Among the Hindus the killing of this animal generally results in religious sanctions.
34. Pilchu Haram was the first man according to the Santal myth of creation.

> of that country all our honour has gone (ibid.: 54).
>
> They were originally *Nij Murmu*, but when they once ate flesh of a *murmu jel* they were separated. ... I asked Baka and Cunda of Simra about this *khût,* and they said: They tell that in the old days we ate flesh from the *murum jel*, and so we were outcasted, otherwise we were *Nij Murmu* (ibid.: 54).

In the work "Studies In Santal Medicine & Connected Folklore" (Bodding, 1986), Bodding has recorded a great variety of meat that the Santals eat. In fact they eat meat of most of the animals, snakes, reptiles, fishes and fowls in their habitat, including cow's meat. However, they do not eat any kind of monkeys, vultures, horses, parakeets or the *jalo* falcon. Here Bodding notes that the Nilgae (*murmu*) is taboo to people of the *Murmu* clan (ibid.: 478-84).

> The Santals have no objections to eating the meat of cows and bullocks, in fact they relish it, but owing to the landlords and their Hindu neighbours they have to exercise restraint, and they will mostly go about obtaining, preparing and eating it at night. Bullocks may be sacrificed. The writer once came across a large number of Santals who had cut up a couple of cattle who had died from some disease. He tried to warn them not to eat such meat; but they had no fear of anything happening to them; and so far as is known no harm came to them (ibid.: 478).

It is obvious that *Rām Bilās*, in his narrative myth above, has had plenty of material from the Santal mythology and worldview to his disposal, from which he could elaborate the presented picture of the degraded Santal Brahman; the *Murmu thākur*. With this discourse he strives to justify his own position as the Brahman of the Santals. I have heard similar discourses from other Jādopaṭiās.

Crossing the River

Rām Bilās mentioned how they help the dead Santals to cross over the *baitaranī* river. As I have noted earlier *baitaranī* literally means "she who crosses over" or "she who makes one cross over" (Filippi, 1996: 111). In other words, *baitaranī* can be the name of the cow presented for the purpose of crossing, as well as the name of the river to be crossed. "*Vaitaranī* is also the name of the river of blood and excrements that, at the southern extremity of the human world, marks the boundary line with the kingdom of the god *Yama* (ibid.: 112). In Benares it is still usual to present a cow (or the partial/full cost of one) to the funeral Brahman to enact this crossing (see Parry, 1994: 173 and Justice, 1997: 166). Parry describes how the Mahabrahman leads this enacted crossing, which is executed over a dug out trench, filled with water and red powder (suggesting blood), representing the awful *baitaranī* river. Both Parry and Justice point out that this bloody river is also a metaphor for the birth passage of a child (Parry, 1996: 200).

> The Vaitarani is, at one level, a metaphor for the body. Falling into the Vaitarani River is falling into the womb and taking rebirth; successfully crossing the Vaitarani is achieving *moksha* [salvation] (Justice, 1997: 165).
>
> Most everybody at the Muktibhavan agreed that giving a cow before death helped the soul to cross the Vaitarani river, which by extension of the metaphor, means avoiding rebirth (Justice, 1997: 166).
>
> *Vaitarani* is brought into the old man's room, and her tail is held mightily in his right hand. He then consigns the gift to the brahmana. Up until recently, the dying man held on to the cow's tail with all his strength, in order to be pulled along for a few metres (Filippi, 1996: 112).

I have seen several illustrations of the *baitaranī* river and cow in scrolls made by the *Jādopaṭiās* and shown to the Santals. This topic does not appear as the theme of an entire scroll. It usually figures in a single register as an additional theme to the major theme of the scroll in question. Two of the scrolls I have collected contain such single registers with themes of a "river crossing". The first one shows a number of people swimming in a river next to a cow. Budhesvar Citrakar, who made the scroll gave the following comment (in Bengali) to this scene: "These ones cross the *baitaranī* river. The righteous have crossed over. The sinners swim and sink". The second example depicts a man who holds on to a cow by the tail with his right hand. Next to this man stands a man with a large axe, raised in the air, ready to strike. *Rājen* Citrakar, who made this scroll, gave the following comment (in

35. Kapil gāi: literally means a brown or tawny coloured cow. It also means a wishing cow. In other words a cow which can grant wishes (Samsad, 1985: 176). The Jādopaṭiā points out that this cow is slain by a blow on the neck with the axe (santali; kutam, lit. to strike with axe or a hammer). "Sacrifice to bongas are performed by beheading the sacrificial animal, whilst to the hapramko [the ancestor] it is always done by a stroke of an axe-head on the neck" (Bodding, 1986: 17). Kutam dangra, lit. "felled bullock", is a sacrifice to the Ancestors, performed due to a vow, after a grant has been favoured [here, the crossing] (Bodding, 1925: 228, fn 2).

Bengali) to this scene: "This one is crossing the *baitaranī* river. When crossing the *baitaranī* river, the righteous people went on their way. The righteous people crossed over and left. This one was a big sinner. He tried to cross several times, but could not do so. He was stuck in the river. Therefore he was brought to hell [*jampuri*] to be punished. That is the cow [*kapil gāi*[35]]. This cow will be sacrificed so that this sinner can cross over the river." In this last description there is an interesting overlap of idioms and ideas. On the one hand the sacrifice of the cow is executed for the expiation of the sinners sin. On the other the sacrifice is destined for the ancestors. In the Santal context it is not uncommon to slaughter a cow in the name of the ancestors, at the time of the bhandan, the final funeral ritual (Archer, 1974: 337). In the Hindu context, where cow-slaughter is a great sin, the cow is presented as a gift to the Brahmin. In *Rājen's* narrative these various ideas blur into each other.

The Jādopaṭiā as a Brahman

At this time I would like to stop and reflect about some of the facts and factors that enable an association between the *Jādopaṭiā* and the Brahman. The French Anthropologist Rosita de Selva (De Selva, 1994) tries to find reasons for how the *Jādopaṭiā* is related to a Brahman by consulting some Indological and ethnographic textual sources. In her article "Forcing, the Funerary Role of the *Jādu Paṭuā,* Painter-Magician" she has a chapter with the heading "The *jādu paṭuā* and the brahman." In the beginning of this chapter she establishes an association between the *Jādopaṭiā* and Brahman with reference to the term "*cakṣudān*" or "the gift of the eye." De Selva claims that this term corresponds to the Sanskrit nayanamilan, "the opening of the eye." "This word refers to a precise Hindu context: it stands for the Brahman's gesture during the Hindu ritual of "installation" (beng. *pratiṣṭhā karā*) of the divinity, at the location and for the time where it will be asked to exercise its power" (De Selva, 1994: 49, English translation by Philippe Maincon). The term *nayanamilan* is also used to designate the sequence of the rite of which this gesture is a part. This rite is practised in the whole of India. At this point de Selva lets us know that this rite has been described and commented in several treatises in Sanskrit and that it is well known to Indologists. She also comments that this rite is old but still regularly practised, and that it is easy to observe, in contrast to the "gift of the eye" of the *Jādopaṭiā*, which is difficult to observe. The gesture can be practised on an idol in a permanent public temple, or on one that is manufactured at the time of a given celebration (ibid.: 49). In the latter case this image will be immersed in a river or a tank (beng. *Bisarjan*, Samsad, 1985: 678). De Selva comments that such images are (in the latter case) made of clay, but it could also be a painting. Further she points out that it is said that the eyes of these images do not see. This faculty has to be activated by a Brahman during the rite of "*cakṣudān*". It is only after this act has been executed by the Brahman that the rite can start (de Selva, 1994: 49-50). In this respect de Selva supports her claims on data from Renou (1947, I: 572-73), Talwar (1979:106-7) and Ostör (1980) (ibid.: 50, n.10). I agree that these sets of associations produce a plausible picture of how we can associate the *Jādopaṭiā* with the Brahamn on a general theoretical plain. However, these corresponding data seem to be far from the particularities of the field, and the discourses and doings of the *Jādopaṭiā* themselves. As far as these discourses are concerned, de Selva utilises the statements that *Basudev Citrakar* makes, cited from an article by J-B Faivre (Faivre, 1979) about the *Jādopaṭiā* as a Brahman. She recognises that the *Jādopaṭiā* can be associated with the Brahman that officiates at the funerary rites of the Hindus. De Selva also notes that the gifts that the Hindu funeral Brahman receives in this context are with few exceptions the same as the *Jādopaṭiā* presents on the picture of the dead, and claim from the Santal. However, de Selva does not go out of her way to look for examples of other funerary priest, Brahmans and specialists in contemporary ethnography, but finds them mainly in indological texts.[36] At this point in her article de Selva asks herself how one can establish a relationship between the iris applied by a Brahman on an image of a divinity and the one that the *Jādopaṭiā* applies on the picture of the dead (ibid.: 53). In fact, once *Rām Bilās Citrakar* used the word installation (beng. *pratiṣṭhā karā*), when he talked about *cokhodān* ("the gift of the eye") that they, the *Jādopaṭiās*, themselves do on the picture of the dead. In his discourse about his practice, he himself (like a native creative "anthropologist") made the analogy between his practice and the one of the Brahman installing a deity! However, below I will include some more common statements, made by the *Jādopaṭiāi* met, concerning their professional role.

36. de Selva thus takes a position where she leaves herself open to being criticised for a potential reification and essentialisation of the idea of the Brahman portrayed in this literature. She refers to Toffin, 1990: 137 (an analysis cast in a Dumontian mould), and Kane, 1974: II, 843 (dealing with the Dharmaśāstras) to show the types of presents that the Brahman receives for his funerary service (de Selva, 1994: 53).

37. " n. a calendar, an almanac, an ephemeris (Samsad, 1985: 553)." Ephemeris ... a table giving the future positions of the planets, comet, or satellite during a specified period (Collins, 1988: 372).

One of my *Jādopaṭiā* informants once compared the picture of the dead (*mṛtyu paṭ*) with the calendar or the ephemeris (*pañji*[37]) of the Brahman. Thus linking the use of this picture to the art of astrology utilised by Brahmans and funeral priests. One *Jādopaṭiā* told me the following about the picture of the dead (*mṛtyu paṭ*) that is used at the time of *cokhodān*: "This picture is called *agradān*. Just like in the Hindu religion [*dharma*] where those who do *agradānī* make effigies in wood. With these the Brahman [*bāman*] do the expiation [*prāyaścita*]. In the same manner we have to make a *agradānī* picture in the name of the deceased for that purpose".[38] The Bengali shopkeeper, on whose verandah some of my *Jādopaṭiā* informants resided regularly, gave me a similar account. He said that the *Jādopaṭiā* are the gurus or Brahmans (*bāman*) of the Santal. "They utilise astrology to judge and estimate the sin [*pāp*] of the Santal and the cost of the expiation. The Santals give them gifts for this purpose." This man's father told me that the *Jādopaṭiā* exorcise ghosts (*bhut chāṛāy*) for the Santals. In the book "Hindu Manners, Customs and Ceremonies" (first published in 1816) Abbé Dubois recorded that if a death occurs in the last five of the twenty-seven constellations it is very inauspicious for the relatives of the dead one. The house must be carefully purified by a *purohit* (priest) and a meal plus presents must be offered to the Brahmans. If a death occurs on a Saturday; it is a hundred to one that another member of the same household will die before the year has passed. The only way to prevent this from happening is to sacrifice a living animal, such as a ram, a he-goat or a fowl as a burnt offering (Dubois, 1996: 564, the fourth impression).

"Bad" Death

The Santals believe that *Thākur* has measured out the length of each individual life. At the same time misfortune, disease and death is believed to be the result of the displeasure and maliciousness of *bongas* and witches (*dān*).

They acknowledge natural causes of illness [and death]; they cannot avoid seeing effect and immediate cause; as a rule they can also see the material nature of a disease [and death]. But there is always a suspicion that

38. My Bengali father-in-law's mother told me that the Brahman (bāman) consults the constellations of the planets at the time of the death. This will enable the Brahman to estimate the sin of that person as well as inauspiciousness generated by those constellations. On the basis of these calculations the agradānī Brahman can make a wooden effigy which along with the many gifts presented to him at that time will effectuate the expiation. Such wooden sculptures are planted next to the funeral ground (śaśān) of her native village were I have seen them myself.

the natural cause is not the original one, but that evil influence are at work in the first instance (Bodding, 1986: 2).

Evil *boṇgas* and witches are said to "eat" people. Witches, more specifically eat the liver of people and thus cause illness or death (ibid.: 1,7). "*Boṅgas* and witches know how to 'eat'; they do not know how to make well" (ibid.: 3). Children who have not been made full members of the Santal community by the initiation *caco chatiar* will become ghosts (*bhüt*) and will not transform into ancestors. Women who die in childbirth or pregnancy can turn into dangerous ghost (*curin*) (Bodding, 1923: 73, fn 1). Likewise, the stillborn child will turn into a ghosts (*bhüt*). The witches are always female (Bodding, 1929: 40). "The Santals are mortally afraid of a certain class of women, believing that after death they are always on the watch for men. They are supposed to lick their victims to death, filing off the flesh with their rough tongues" (Cole, 1878: 274).

Another force to reckon with is *Yama*, the king of death himself. "*Jom raj* or *raja* is the regent of the netherworld. The word is the Skr. For *Yamarāja*, the idea being very hazy with the Santals" (Bodding, 1929: 95, fn 3). The Santals also conceive of the netherworld as a prison-house were the dead one is imprisoned behind the large door, guarded by the assistants of *Yama* (Bodding, 1942: 187). The underworld (*norok disom*) is full of dangerous animals such as snakes, insects, crocodiles and the likes (Gautam, 1977: 149). Gautam states that his Santal informants told him that "Those who follow the Santal tribal customs and fulfil their obligations of clan and lineage bonga worship and offer the sacrifices go to heaven. Those who are against exogamy and tribal endogamy go to hell (ibid.: 149). Troisi states that the main object of the Santal's funerary rites is twofold. One objective is to rid the living survivors of the death pollution and the malicious influence of the potentially dangerous spirit of the deceased and other evil powers. The other is to release the departed spirit from the underworld and help it to unite with the ancestors (Troisi, 1978: 196-7).

We have seen that every status/state transition in the life cycle of the Santal is fraught with danger of various kinds. This calls for apt attention and participation, of the Santal community, as well as, assistance from various ritual specialists, such as the *ojhā* and the *Jādopaṭiā*. As we have seen earlier, the *Jādopaṭiā* often attributes these bad influences to the concept of "sin" (*pāp*). Further, Carrin-Bouez points out that the Santals generally lack a concept of "sin" connected with a system of "ethic" ideals like those of the Hindus (Carrin-Bouez 1986: 181). Irrespective of how these malicious forces are attributed (i.e. either as "sin" or "pollution"), the Santals feel the need for a purification to pacify these dangers. In this connection I would like to point out that Parry underlines the following find from his own research in the Hindu context in Banaras: "my own evidence overwhelmingly suggests that notions of 'sin' and 'pollution' commonly shade seamlessly into each other, and that both are a source of misfortune" (Parry, 1994: 136).

The Santal as a Client/Patron

How does the Santal percieve the *Jādopaṭiā* claim that the Santal is his *jajmān*? Among all the Bengali authors who have written about the *Jādopaṭiā*, M. K. Gautam and Sankar Sen Gupta differ from the rest in their more positive description of the relationship between the *Jādopaṭiā* and the Santals. The folklorist Sankar Sen Gupta presents an interesting picture of this kind of scroll-painter in Purulia district of Bengal, where they are known as "*pattikars*" or *paṭkars*.

> The *pattikars* in the district of Purulia call themselves as *patua* Brahmin. They have their *jajmans* in the manner the Brahmins have their clients. No one is allowed to disturb other's clients. These *patuas* are not as neglected in their society as the Hindu or Musalman *patuas*, rather they have a dignified position. A Santal, a Bhumij and the type of people think that the *pattikar* has some supernatural power and he himself too claims so at the time of painting the Supreme God Marang Buru. When a *patua* comes to his clients a *Majhi Haram* or the village chief will always oblige him with a *dhuti* [a loin cloth] and a *Pargana Haram* or the chief of a few villages will offer him more than a *dhuti*. [Sen Gupta, 1973: 49. Data supplied by P. P. Mahato (see ibid.: 47)].

Sen Gupta (above) and Gautam characterises the relationship as *friendly* (Gautam, 1977: 38). In contrast to high cast Hindus and landowners, considered as outsiders by the Santals, the *Jādopaṭiā* are described as one among the many groups of low cast artisans and service rendering professionals (like for example the barber), who coexist in symbiosis with the Santals. Gautam has categorised these groups as "Santal cognates." The Santals embrace these groups into their history and tradition. Thus, Gautam relates that the *Jādopaṭiā*, like these other service rendering groups, receive customary dues (*paona*) at the time of feasts, festivals and harvest, in the common manner of a priest-client/patron relationship (i.e. *jajmān*) (ibid.: 148). It is interesting to note that the *Jādopaṭiā* have been described to achieve such a status among the Santals in other areas of Bengal as well. Daniel Rycroft relates the existence of such symbiosis between the scroll painters (*paṭkars*) and the tribal people of the Purulia district of West Bengal (Rycroft, 1996). However, non of the Santals who I inquired about this matter acknowledged a "*jajmāni*-relationship" between themselves and the *Jādopaṭiās*. In contrast, the *Jādopaṭiās* who frequented the villages of these Santals questioned, adamantly claimed such a "*jajmāni*-relationship" with the Santals of those areas. "Certainly they are our *jajmān*. Our grandfathers and great-grand-fathers have visited these areas ..." Budhesvar Citrakar told me. He also explained that other *Jādopaṭiās* from other villages than his own would not venture into his territory. Budhesvar's statements rather describe the pragmatic organisation of the funerary market of the *Jādopaṭiās* than a formalised "*jajmāni*-relationship." One possible reason why some scroll painters have developed a closer tie with their patron might be that these scroll painters live in close proximity to these patrons. The majority of Santals with whom I talked to live far away from the villages of the *Jādopaṭiās* who visit these Santals.

From the data presented above it becomes clearer how the *Jādopaṭiā* can find a foundation for his claims of being the Brahman of the Santals. In the eyes of the Santals the *Jādopaṭiā* is definitely regarded as some kind of priest with special powers. Mildred Archer noted how the *Jādopaṭiā* is treated with respect and received accordingly in the Santal households: "On arriving at the house, he would be politely welcomed, given a cot to sit on and supplied with tobacco... " (Archer, 1977: 16). I have also observed how the *Jādopaṭiās* are received with respect, offered a seat and tobacco[39] whenever they make a call at a Santal household. Sudhansu Kumar Ray gives the following characterisation of the *Jādopaṭiā* as a priest-painter with undisputed authority.

> A Jadu-*patua* is an undisputed authority on the semi-magical mortuary rites of the deceased. He knows how a man is put to death by a *pisacha*, an evil spirit ... It is he who can lead the dead bodily from this world to heaven - an act for which he himself is ritually capable (Sudhansu Kumar Ray, 1961: 54).

Many of the Santals I talked to claimed that the *Jādopaṭiā* had been with them from "the beginning of time." The myths delivered by the *Jādopaṭiā*

---

39. It is a common practice among santals and Jādopaṭiās to chew tobacco. A piece of a tobacco leaf and some lime is put in the hollow of the hand. This is thoroughly mixed by grinding it with the thumb and a generous pinch is than thrown into the mouth to be chewed. To offer or ask for tobacco is an invitation to stop and have a talk.

of how the first *Jādopaṭiā* got his role as a painter-priest among the Santals also places the beginning of this relationship in primordial time. To be enable a better understanding of why the Santals accept the *Jādopaṭiās* and their work we have to take another look at the character of their relationship. Is it a relationship made of exploitation and parasitism, or is one of friendly coexistence and symbiosis?

"*Horo-Mitan*" the Friend of Man

> The discursive reifications of caste [and tribes], intimately tied at their genesis to the politics of colonial rule, later became the foundation of much anthropological and historical writing on Indian society (Raheja, 1996: 508).

Advocating the concept "*Horo-Mitan*" (lit. "Man-Friend") P. P. Mahato, research officer at the Anthropological Survey of India, Calcutta, has made an attempt to give us a concept with which we can describe the friendly and symbiotic relationship that exist among the "indigenous tribal" (the *kheroals* or *Hor*) and the peasants and "folk-artisan" groups of Jharkhand[40] (Rycroft, 1996: 96). The "*Horo-Mitan*" society is visualised as rooted in the pre-colonial condition, and the effort to write or rewrite its history is associated with the project of the so called Subaltern Studies, undertaken and advocated by Ranajit Guha (1982) and others.[41] Thus, one can say that Mahato's project is part of the "decolonisation" of cultural identities in Jharkhand. Since the 1930s a political strife for autonomy, known as the "Jharkhand Movement," has united several tribes under the common name *ādibāsī,* "aboriginals" (Andersen, 1999: 41). Without going into any detail about this political movement I like to underline that the non-tribal groups, designated as *mitan* above, have united with the *ādibāsī* in the struggle against the oppression from the "outsiders." Who are these enemies conceived as 'outsiders'?

In opposition to the dyad "*Horo-Mitan*" stands the dyad "*Hor-Diku.*" In his Santal Dictionary Bodding writes: "*deko*, n. A Hindu or Bengali (of

---

40. Jharkhand now exists as a political entity recognised by the Indian government. Geographically Jharkhand region is situated mainly in the Chotanagpur plateau, with an extension into Santal Parganas (Kelkar and Nathan 1992: 21). The name Jharkhand, which means "forested area" is an old Mogul name of this region that covered the bordering area of the present states of West Bengal, Bihar, Orissa, and Madhya Pradesh (Andersen, 1999: 42).
41. In the light of an "Orientalist" type of critique, the Subaltern Studies is an example of how the colonised speak back in a postcolonial situation (confer Inden, 1986, 1990). Guha follows a Gramscian line of theory, and utilises the term "subaltern," coined by Gramsci, as a heading for the strife to write the histories of the "subalterns".

the better class, not low-caste Hindus as e.g. *Doms, Bauris, Haḍis* ..." (Bodding, 1934: 69). The term *diku* is a term with a derogatory slant to it. With its pejorative associations, *diku* has been applied by the Santals to groups of oppressors such as moneylenders, rajas, landowners and landlord's servants (Guha, 1992: 281-2). The strong derogatory associations of this term also has its history in the tribal peasant insurgency (*hul*) against the British Colonialist rule in eastern India in the year 1855, and its aftermath's (ibid.: 111, 281). However, the term *diku* is also used in a more neutral general sense to designate any non-autochthon such as Hindu, Muslim, European or any foreigner (ibid.: 281). The dichotomy of diku, an oppressor verses *mitan*, an ally or a friend, is not absolute. Relationships between the Santals and other groups should rather be conceptualised as placed along an axis stretched between relationships of close affinity characterised by symbiosis, and relationships of distance characterised by parasitism. As far as the *Jādopaṭiās* are concerned, in this context, they can be included in the "*Horo-Mitan*" type of society. Statements made by informants show that this inclusion is supported by their own mutual acceptance of each other. As I have mentioned earlier in my text, Gautam describes the relationship between the *Jādopaṭiās* and the Santals as friendly (Gautam, 1977: 38). He categorises *Jādopaṭiās* along with other scheduled caste[42] such as Paharia, *Māhli, Mal, Pāl, Tūri, Dom, Tānti* and others. Gautam calls these groups "Santal cognates" in opposition to high caste Hindus, which he simply designates as Hindus. The latter are characterised by the Santals as *dikus* (ibid.: 38-9). This type of conceptualisation, made by Gautam, is comparable with Mahato's "*Horo-Mitan*" versus "*Hor-diku.*" Concerning the Santal attitudes to the "Santal cognates" Gautam includes this statement by a Santal teacher.

> These groups, except the Paharia, immigrated to the Santal Parganas with us. They were brought in by the Santal for their help. Since then along with us they have also suffered the ups and downs of life (ibid.: 38).

Further, Gautam relates how the friendly relations described above are based on mutual respect and rendering of mutual socio-economic assistance.

42. Scheduled (listed) castes is an official designation used by the Indian government, parallel to the designation scheduled tribes. In a move of 'protective discrimination' the groups labelled thus are considered "backward classes" and are given safeguards in various areas for their "social welfare" (Devalle, 1980: 22). Rājen Citrakar told me that he was entitled to such subsidies because of his status as a member of a scheduled caste. However, as far as I know, the Jādopaṭiās are not listed as a schedule caste by the Anthropological Survey of India (confer K. S. Singh, 1995). Nevertheless, in practice it is quite possible that the Jādopaṭiās get such subsidies all the same.

In opposition to this the relationships with the *dikus*, or the high caste Hindus, the "outsiders", are based more on economic transactions and not on a sense of common welfare (ibid.: 38). Gautam also notes that there are intermediary groups that fall in between these two categories mentioned above. These intermediary groups try to be as neutral as possible (ibid.: 38). Kelkar and Nathan (1992) also describe a symbiotic relationship existing between "*ādibāsīs*" and the artisan and service castes. These authors make some interesting comments that apply to the *Jādopaṭiās*.

> For the past few hundred years the adivasis of this area [i.e. Jharkhand] have lived in a symbiotic relationship with various artisan and service castes, referred to as *sadans* [non-tribal castes], who now constitute upto 50 per cent of the population. In many revolts in the area, the *sadans* too participated in large numbers (ibid.: 21).

Once when I recorded an interview with *Rām Bilās* Citrakar in his village in Santal Parganas, he requested me to turn on the tape-recorder once more, so that he could include a final message. When I did so *Rām Bilās* explained why the name of this forested area was Jharkhand. Finally he included his passionate support for the cause of the "Jharkhand movement".

Why Do the Santals Comply?

Time has come to take stock and ponder over the various perspectives of the *Jādopaṭiās* and *cokhodān* presented in the text above. In order to do so we shall return to one of the major questions posed in the initial part of my article. Why do the Santals comply with the demands of the *Jādopaṭiās* at the time of the performance of the mortuary ritual event known as *cokhodān*?

To cast some further light on this issue I would like to expose some comparable data from an Anthropological study of funeral priests operating in a Hindu context at Gaya on the Ganges. In one of the chapters in the ethnography "The Sacred Complex In Hindu Gaya" (Vidyarthi, 1961) the author analyses the motives given by his informants for having the last rites performed by the rapacious funeral priest at Gaya. Vidyarthi comments that in most cases the sacrificers had several objectives. The most common purpose given for the observance was to heed religious and social duties, such as that of the son towards his father, and the duties towards the ancestors. One of the major motivating forces for observance was thus a feeling of filial piety, sentiments of love and attachment, and above all, the consciousness of the social and religious duty to one's father and progenitors (ibid.: 43). The second set of objectives presented by Vidyarthi can be understood as motivated by fear. The belief in spirits and the dread for the potentially malignant ghosts of the dead, motivated sacrificers to undertake the rituals, and to be generous towards the funeral priests. Finally, related to the other motives above, Vidyarthi states that the sacrificers believe that the welfare and the prosperity of the family partly depend upon the blessing of the manes. Thus the sacrifice to the manes is of great importance (ibid.: 43-45). Complex ideas and rituals from diverse levels of various traditions are invoked and resonated in the ritual complex at Gaya. The motivations involved in the context described above, are strikingly reminiscent of the kind of motivations that may influence the Santals to comply with the *Jādopaṭiās* demands at the time of *cokhodān*. Furthermore, Vidyarthi describes a type of possession that is widespread in the villages of Bihar.

> On the eleventh day of the death ritual, a Kantaha (sometimes known as a lower form of Brahman), who is invited to represent the dead, is said to be possessed by the spirit of the dead. The statements that he makes are believed to be coming from the dead (ibid.: 47).

The practice by the funeral priests occurring in a Hindu context, described by Vidyarthi in the citation above is similar to some of the mediumistic actions performed by the *Jādopaṭiās* at the time of *cokhodān*.[43]

I have illustrated how the creative *Jādopaṭiās* improvise with the many cultural elements available to them as possible ingredients in a ritual event known as *cokhodān*. We have seen how the *Jādopaṭiās* navigation through the different discourses on death reveal contradictions and paradoxes. Many authors who have described the *Jādopaṭiās* have characterised them as charlatans or exploiters of the Santals. Why have the *Jādopaṭiās* been described in such unfavourable terms? As we have seen there are plenty of other funerary priests in India that could be labelled with similarly derogatory designations as "manipulating magicians" or "funerary vultures" who prey on the bereaved relatives. The undertakers of our own society may also qualify for a characterisation in equally unflattering terms. It is easy to understand that the line between empathetic advice and calculated exploitation is precariously thin in the professional life of the undertaker. It is also obvious that a composed and experienced undertaker holds an advantageous position

43. It is important to note that among the Santals or the Soras this type of possession is a common occurrence (Elwin, 1955; Carrin-Bouez, 1986; Vitebsky, 1993). In contrast in the Hindu context described by Vidyarthi and Parry, where it is less known, it nevertheless do occur (Vidyarthi, 1961: 47, Parry, 1994).

of power in relation to a relative suddenly struck by grief, due to an unexpected loss of kin. However, I believe that it is important to view the work of any funerary priest of undertaker with a number of wide angled lenses.

In is not difficult to see how the funeral priests, as well as the *Jādopaṭiās*, have created a favourable vantage point from which they have various ways of orchestrating their ritual play in their own favour. As my Santal friend *Sona* told me: "They [the *Jādopaṭiās*] have entered into the very psychology [*sic*] of the Santal mind." It is thus partly through their empathetic skill and their extensive knowledge of the Santal worldview that the *Jādopaṭiās* are able to make the Santals comply. However, although it is obvious that the Santals are manipulated by the *Jādopaṭiās*, it is also true that the Santals comply of their own accord.[44]

To summarise, I like to underline that the material I have presented in this article expose several different incentives that operate together as potential forces utilised by the *Jādopaṭiās* to influence the Santal to comply with their demands. Following Bloch and Parry (1982: 6, 1989) in their approach to mortuary rituals and the morality of various types of exchange, I see it fit to conceive the various incentives, operating at the time of *cokhodān* through a sociological analysis as well as a symbolical one. In other words, it is possible to perceive the *Jādopaṭiās* as a pragmatic professional operating within a world of potentially meaningful symbolic material, where practical considerations must be understood in relation to potential cultural imperatives. Utilising this perspective I hope to have shown that the question posed in the heading to this article is framed in a faulty mode.

44. I have also heard of rare instances of non-compliance. In these cases young Santal men might make fun of a visiting Jādopaṭiā, or scare him away with the threat of a thrashing.

REFERENCES

Anderson, J. D. 1962. *A Manual Of The Bengali Language*. New York: Frederick Ungar Publishing Co.

Andersen, P. 1998. Ethnicity, Ritual Integration and Literature as Illustrated by the Karam Ritual among the Santals. Unpublished Ph.D.-thesis. Institute of History of Religion, University of Copenhagen.

Archer, M. 1977. *Indian Popular Painting in the Indian Office Library*. London: Her Majesty's Stationery Office by The Alden Press.

Archer, W. G. 1974. *The Hill of Flutes. Life, Love and Poetry in Tribal India: A Portrait of the Santals*. London: G. Allen & Unwin.

Bloch, M. and J. P. Parry. 1982. "Introduction: Death and the Regeneration of Life," (pp. 1-44) in M. Bloch and J. Parry (eds.) *Death & the Regeneration of Life*. Cambridge: Cambridge University Press.

____. (eds.). 1989. *Money and the Morality of Exchange*. Cambridge: Cambridge University Press.

Bodding, P.O. 1923. "Santal Folklore," (pp. 41-119) in S. Konow & O. Solberg (eds.), *Indian And Central-Asian Miscellanies*. Oslo: A.W. Brøggers Boktrykkeri A/S, 1921-1940.

____. 1925. *Santal Folk Tales*. Serie B: skrifter II; vol. I, Oslo: Instituttet For Sammenlignende Kulturforskning.

____. 1929, *Santal Folk Tales*. Serie B: Skrifter XIV; vol. III, Oslo: Instituttet For Sammenlignende Kulturforskning.

____. 1932-36. *A Santal Dictionary*. 5 Vols., Oslo: Det Norske Videnskaps-Akademi.

____. 1986. Studies In Santal Medicine & Connected Folklore. Calcutta: The Asiatic Society.

____. 1994. *Traditions and Institutions of the Santals*. New Delhi: Bahumukhi Prakashan (First published 1942. Oslo: Oslo Ethnographical Museum Bulletin: 6.).

Campbell, A. 1899. *A Santali-English Dictionary*. Pokhuria, Manbhum, India.

Carrin-Bouez, M. 1986. La Fleur Et L´os, Symbolisme et rituel chez les Santal. Paris: Éd. de l`lÉcole des hautes études en sciences sociales.

Cole, F.T. 1878. "Santal Ideas of the Future," *The Indian Antiquary, Bombay*, 5: 273-4.

Dasgupta, B. (ed.). 1985. *Samsad Bengali English Dictionary* [Revised & Enlarged Second Edition]. Calcutta: Nabajiban Press.

Devalle, S. 1980. *Multi-Ethnicity in India: The Adivasi Peasants of Chota Nagpur and Santal Parganas*. IWGIA Document 41. Copenhagen.

Dubois, Abbe J.A. 1996. *Hindu Manners, Customs And Ceremonies*. Calcutta: Pupa & Co.

Edholm, E. A. 1988. "The Colours of the Soul and the Origin of Karmic Eschatology," (pp. 95-111) in C. Cederroth *et al.* (eds.), *On the Meaning of Death; Essays on Mortuary Rituals and Eschatological Beliefs*. Uppsala: Almqvist & Wiksell International.

Elwin, V. 1955. *The Religion of an Indian Tribe*. Bombay: Geofferey Cumberelge, Oxford University Press.

Evans-Pritchard, E. E. 1937. *Witchcraft, Oracles and Magic among the Azande*. Oxford: Clarendon Press.

Faivre, J-B. and U. Chakroborty. 1980. "Rouleaux peints des chitrakars ou jadupatuas des Santal Parganas. Etat du Bihar (Inde)," *Objets et mondes*, 20 (3): 111-122.

Filippi, G.G. 1996. *Mṛtyu, Concept Of Death In Indian Traditions*. New Delhi: D.K. Printworld (P) Ltd.

Fruzzetti, L. M. 1982. *The Gift of a Virgin, Women, Marriage, and Ritual in a Bengali Society*. Delhi: Oxford University Press.

Fuller J. F. 1989. "Misconceiving the Grain Heap," (pp. 33-63) in M. Bloch and J. Parry (eds.), *Money and the Morality of Exchange*. Cambridge: Cambridge University Press.

Fürer-Haimendorf, C. Von 1953. "The After-Life in Indian Tribal Belief," *The Journal of the Royal Anthropological Institute*, 83: 37-49.

Gausdal, J. 1960. *The Santal Khûts, Contribution To Animistic Research.* Institutet For Sammenlignende Kulturforskning. Serie B: Skrifter L, Oslo: H. Aschehoug & CO. (W. Nygaard).

Gautam, M. K. 1977. *In Search of an Identity: A Case of the Santal of northern India.* Leiden.

____. 1998. "Tribal Material Culture, The Santal of Northern India," *IIAS Newsletter,* 15 (Winter): 14.

Guha, R. 1992. *Elementary Aspects of Peasant Insurgency in Colonial India.* Delhi: Oxford University Press.

Hadders, H. 2000. *The Gift of the Eye.* Forthcoming. Trondheim Occasional Papers. In Social Anthropology. Trondheim: Tapir.

Inden, R. 1986. "Orientalist Construction of India." *Modern Asian Studies,* 20: 401-446.

____. 1990. *Imagining India.* Oxford and Cambridge, Mass.: Basil Blackwell, Inc.

Justice, C. 1997. *Dying the Good Death. The Pilgrimage to Die in India's Holy City.* New York: State University of New York Press.

Kane, P. V. 1974. *History of Dharmasastra.* Poona: Bhandarkar Oriental Research Institute.

Kelkar, G & D. Nathan 1991. *Gender and Tribe, Women, Land and Forest in Jharkhand.* New Delhi: Kali for Women.

Klostermaier, K. K. 1989. *A Survey of Hinduism.* New Delhi: Munshiram Manoharlal.

Macphail, R. M. (ed.) 1988. *Campbell's Santali-English Dictionary.* Calcutta: Firma KLM Private Ltd.

Mahapatra, S. 1986. *Modernisation and Ritual, Identity and Change in Santal Society.* Calcutta: Oxford University Press.

Mauss, M. 1990. *The Gift: The Form and Reason for Exchange in Archaic Societies.* Routledge.

McLeod, W.T. & P. Hanks. 1988. *The Collins Concise Dictionary of the English Language.* London: Guild Publishing.

McLeod, W.T. & P. Hanks 1988. *The Collins Concise Dictionary of the English Language.* London: Guild Publishing.

Ostör, A. 1980. *The Play of the Gods.* Chicago: Chicago University Press.

Parkin, R. 1992. *The Munda of Central India: An Account of their Social Organisation.* Delhi: Oxford University Press.

Parry J.P. 1994. *Death in Banaras.* Cambridge: Cambridge University Press.

Raheja, G. G. 1996. "Caste, Colonialism, and the Speech of the Colonized: Entextualisation and Disciplinary Control in India," *American Ethnologist,* 23 (3): 494-513.

Ray, S.K. 1961. *The Ritual Art of the Bratas of Bengal.* Calcutta: Firma K.L. Mukhopadhyay.

Renou, L. & J. Filliozat. 1947. *L'Inde classique,* Tome I. Paris: Payot.

Risley, H.H. 1981. *Tribes and Castes of Bengal.* Calcutta: Firma K.L. Mukhopadhyay.

Rycroft, J.D. 1996. "Born from the Soil: Indigenous Mural Aesthetic of Kheroals in Jharkand, Eastern India," *South Asian Studies,* 12: 68-81.

Selva, R. De. 1994. "Contraindre Ou Le Rôle Funèbre Du Jādu Paṭuā, Peintre-Magicien (Bengale, Inde)," *Le duil et ses rites III, Systèmes de pensée en Afrique noir,* 13: 43-87.

Sen Gupta, S. *et al.* 1973. *The Patas and Patuas of Bengal.* Calcutta: Indian Publications.

Singh, K. S. 1995. *The Scheduled Caste. Anthropological Survey of India.* Delhi, Bombay, Calcutta, Madras: Oxford University Press.

Talwar, K. & K. Krishna. 1979. *Indian Pigments Painting on Cloth.* Ahmedabad (Historic textiles of India at the Calico Museum, vol. 3).

Toffin, G. 1990. "Hiérarchie et idéologie du don dans le mond indien," *L'Homme*, 114, 30 (2): 130-142.

Troisi, J. 1978. *Tribal Religion. Religious Beliefs and Practices among the Santals.* New Delhi: Manohar.

Vidyarthi, L. P. 1961. *The Sacred Complex in Hindu Gaya.* Bombay: Asia Publishing House.

Vitebsky, P. 1993. *Dialogues With the Dead: The Discussion of Mortality among the Sora of Eastern India.* Cambridge: Cambridge University Press.

FOUR

BEYOND THE "TRIBAL" MIND-SET: Studying Non-Bengali Peoples in Bangladesh and West Bengal[1]

WILLEM VAN SCHENDEL AND ELLEN BAL[2]

Bengal is usually seen as a culture area dominated by a single language, Bengali, and shaped by a shared history. The overwhelming majority of the 200-odd million people living in Bengal identify themselves as Bengalis. But Bengal was cut in two in 1947. This has led to different political developments and new regional identities in the two halves, and the two Bengals can be seen as "Siamese twins who have been separated and have asserted their individuality".[3] Much research on the bisected region has focused on what this has meant for Bengali culture, self-identification and social arrangements.

This chapter, however, deals with the "other peoples of Bengal," by which we mean the non-Bengali inhabitants of Bangladesh and West Bengal. Not all inhabitants of the two Bengals consider themselves as

1. This is an adapted translation of Willem van Schendel and Ellen Bal, 'Bhumika: Name Ki Eshe Jay?' in: Willem van Schendel and Ellen Bal (eds.), *Banglar Bohujati: Bangali Chhara Banglar Onnanyo Jatir Proshongo* (Calcutta: International Centre for Bengal Studies, 1998), 7-25. Contributors to this volume are Andre Beteille, Robbins Burling, Binay Bhusan Chaudhuri, Ranajit Das Gupta, Swapan Dasgupta, Prasanta Tripura and Willem van Schendel.
2. University of Amsterdam and Erasmus University Rotterdam, respectively. The authors can be contacted at vanschendel@pscw.uva.nl
3. Sekhar Bandyopadhyay, Abhijit Dasgupta and Willem van Schendel, 'Introduction,' in: Sekhar Bandyopadhyay, Abhijit Dasgupta and Willem van Schendel (eds.), *Bengal Communities, Development and States* (New Delhi: Manohar Publications, 1994/Dhaka: University Press Limited, 1995), 3.

Bengalis or are regarded as such by others. Although most of these people do speak Bengali as a second language, they clearly set themselves apart by different mother tongues, distinct cultures, and different historical experiences. They are strangely absent from contemporary accounts of the recent history of Bengal. We feel that this is not just an unfortunate oversight, a case of small and scattered groups of people not being noticed by social scientists concentrating on the mainstream of society. On the contrary, we feel that it is a fateful omission with far-reaching political consequences. The histories and experiences of non-Bengali peoples have been marginalised in the dominant accounts because they disturb the nationalist presumptions which inform the bulk of social science writing on the two Bengals today. Such presumptions have had a host of negative practical effects for non-Bengali people: from a neglect of their languages in education to a refusal to accept their systems of land ownership as legitimate, and from folkloristic exploitation in search of tourism to exposure to targeted state violence. In short, non-Bengali people have become second-rate citizens in both Bangladesh and West Bengal, and social scientists have done far too little to expose this.

This paper is concerned with groups of people who are generally referred to as tribes, upojatis, adivasis, etc.[4] We shall see that these peoples share many problems, whether they live in Bangladesh or West Bengal. More is known about the situation in West Bengal because considerably more research has been done there. A serious problem with the literature, however, is the absence of a satisfactory theoretical framework. We feel that it is an urgent task to review the concepts, which continue to frame research on these groups till today. This short note is meant merely to signal the problem.

1. Tribes as a Colonial Heritage

It has been argued that colonial attempts to classify and rank the people of South Asia into various categories have had a great impact on processes of identity formation in the subcontinent. A number of authors have demonstrated that endeavours to (re-)define South Asian society along religious and caste lines have deeply influenced the self-perception

4. There are, of course, several other non-Bengali groups in Bengal, especially immigrant groups (e.g. the stranded Pakistanis (or "Biharis") of Bangladesh, and various large non-Bengali communities in Calcutta). These fall outside the scope of this article.

of indigenous social groups, and have led to the articulation of community identities.[5] Eighteenth-century Orientalists, the argument goes, derived their ideas about the Indian subcontinent from the study of texts which were explicated by pandits and scholars of the Hindu scriptures. They did not sufficiently question the relationship between these written texts and the actual situation of individuals or groups. This resulted in the picture of a timeless, static and highly fragmented society.[6] In the course of the nineteenth century, British administrators became increasingly aware that this picture could no longer be sustained. And a close reading of their works reveals something much more complex and colourful than a uniform colonial discourse about a "primitive caste-dominated society".[7]

In order to rule British India efficiently, a great deal of effort was expended in collecting socio-economic and anthropological data about its population. At first, it was individual British officers of the East India Company who collected information on population, economy, agriculture, land and history. Later, these activities were institutionalised and formalised, resulting in censuses, surveys, and gazetteers.[8] There was more to this project than the bureaucratic desire for systematic data. The colonialist endeavour must also be seen in the light of intellectual developments in nineteenth-century Europe. First, colonial rule found a strong basis in Social Darwinist theories, which justified colonisation (and slavery) by pointing to "racial" biological differences and the

---

5. See for example: Bernard S. Cohn, "The Census, Social Structure and Objectification in South Asia," in his *An Anthropologist among Historians and Other Essays* (Delhi etc: Oxford University Press, 1987), 224-254; Lucy Carroll, "Colonial Perceptions of Indian Society and the Emergence of Caste(s) Associations," *Journal of Asian Studies*, 37: 2 (February 1978), 233-250; G.S. Ghurye, *Caste and Race in India* (Bombay: Popular Prakashan Private Limited, 1979 [1932]); Sekhar Bandyopadhyay, "Caste in the Perception of the Raj: A Note on the Evolution of Colonial Sociology of Bengal," *Bengal Past & Present*, 104 (1985), 56-80; Bandyopadhyay, Dasgupta and Van Schendel, "Introduction," 1-16; Swaraj Basu, "The Colonial State and the Indigenous Society: The Creation of the Rajbansi Identity in Bengal," in: Bandyopadhyay, Dasgupta and Van Schendel (eds.), *Bengal*, 43-64.
6. Bernard S. Cohn, "Notes on the History of the Study of Indian Society and Culture," in: Milton Singer and Bernard S. Cohn (eds.), *Structure and Change in Indian Society* (Chicago: Aldine Publishing Company, 1968), 3-28.
7. Cf. Susan Bayly, "Caste and 'Race' in the Colonial Ethnography of India," in: Peter Robb (ed.), *The Concept of Race in South Asia* (Delhi, etc: Oxford Press, 1995), 167.
8. Cohn, 'The Census.'

"natural" supremacy of one race over all others.[9] On top of this, a number of administrators felt that they were contributing to scientific development back home. "Social evolutionist" theories were based on the belief that the world's population could be divided according to the stage of civilisation, which they had attained. In these theories Europeans were assumed to represent the most advanced and civilised section of mankind.

In South Asia, such concepts of race came to be expressed in terms of the presumed moral and political distinctions between the so-called Aryan and non-Aryan races.[10] In the nineteenth century, the terms "race" and "tribe" were applied widely to various South Asian communities and (sub-)castes, but in the first four decades of the twentieth century academic anthropologists narrowed the focus of these terms down to the so-called tribal population."[11]

In the course of the twentieth century, the social categorisation and resulting "caste view" of society presented by colonial administrators and researchers came under close scrutiny. It was criticised as being a view, which distorted and exceptionalised South Asian realities. By contrast, the categorisation underlying the perception of "tribal" peoples has remained remarkably unassailed. This persistent "tribalist discourse" is characterised by a persistent dichotomisation between the observed Other ("tribals") and the observing Self.

Of course, one may question the need to change concepts which have been used for a long time and are now widely accepted. What is in a name anyway? What is wrong with designating certain people as "tribals" or, to use a more modern variant, "indigenous peoples"? Our argument is that there is indeed a serious need to reconsider all current designations for the peoples examined in this paper, because each designation starts from a distinction between "normal humans" (the observing Self) and "special humans" (the observed Other). This results in boundary-stressing designations such as civilised *vs*. primitive, mature

9. See e.g. Jan Breman (ed.), *Imperial Monkey Business. Racial Supremacy in Social Darwinist Theory and Colonial Practice* (Amsterdam: VU University Press, 1990); Albert Memmi, *The Colonizer and the Colonized* (London: Earthscan Publications, 1990 [1957]); Ashis Nandy, *The Intimate Enemy. Loss and Recovery of Self under Colonialism* (Delhi etc: Oxford University Press, 1990 [1983]); Edward W. Said, *Orientalism* (New York: Vintage Books, 1979).

10. Bayly, "Caste and 'Race'," 168.

11. Cf. Cohn, "Note on the History."

vs. naive or childlike, and modern *vs*. tribal or indigenous. Such categories seriously hamper research because they blinker a researcher, limit her or his capacity for empathy, foster paternalist attitudes, and lead to unrealistic models of society.

A crucial aspect of this is the assumption that all people designated as "tribal" or "indigenous" somehow share basic political, social, economic, and cultural characteristics with each other, enabling scholars and policy-makers to group them all together into a single category. But the essence of what tribal or indigenous might mean remains highly elusive, and therefore undefined. This makes the category a catch-all for all groups considered to be distant from the "observing Self": it is a category which explains more about the categoriser than about the categorised.

This is not to say that a shared designation cannot generate a sense of belonging to a large (even worldwide) category of "like-minded" people. As we shall see, the category that was once imposed on people considered as "tribal" came to structure parallel experiences of marginalisation and discrimination among them, and was often appropriated by them as a badge of identity. Today numerous non-Bengali people in the two Bengals do in fact refer to themselves as tribal. Let us have a look at the various terms, which are in use today. In the process we shall demonstrate that they are all much more ambiguous than their everyday use may suggest.

1.1. "Tribe"

The English term "tribe" or "tribal" was first introduced in Bengal by the British colonial administration and foreign anthropologists. Since then the word has become more or less incorporated into the Bengali language. This can be explained by the fact that most research about the people who are thought to fall into the category have been published in English. In the case of West Bengal, the adoption of the administrative category of "Scheduled Tribes" by the Indian Government shortly after 1947 has further contributed to its general use.

As pointed out before, it is interesting to note that nineteenth-century authors did not apply the word as strictly as we do nowadays. At times it was also used to denote ("semi-Hinduised") castes or sub-castes. In the course of the twentieth century its use narrowed down to the people who are still referred to as tribal. Many scholars have pointed to the fact that the term "tribe" in itself is highly problematic.[12] There is not one single satisfying definition at hand, which suits the South Asian situation. People generally understand who are "tribes" and who are not well enough. Yet when they are asked to describe what a tribe actually means the picture, which is presented rarely corresponds with the real situation. So-called "tribal characteristics" such as being primitive, isolated, simple, undeveloped, believers in local religions, or having specific tribal political and economic arrangements rarely make any sense. And as we have seen, the term "tribe" retains its strongly evolutionist connotations. It refers to people in the "archaic stage of development" and implies an image of "primitive" man as opposed to "civilised" man. Tribals are thus seen as "inferior races".[13]

Finally, while some authors argue that "tribe" was essentially a colonial construct, a colonial category, others feel that this is not quite consistent with the ideas about tribe in the earlier anthropological writings.[14] Whether a colonial construct or not, its relevance did not, however, dissolve with the end of colonialism. Much contemporary research shows remarkable similarities with colonial ethnography. It has been remarked that these studies are not only written in a style, which is reminiscent of colonial ethnography, but also from a functionalist or even evolutionist perspective.[15]

Despite the many problems with the term "tribe," the word has been given new meanings. As indicated above, for some of the peoples to whom it applies it has become part of their self-identification. For example, the Rabhas of North Bengal are proud of being "tribal". They

12. Researchers who have contributed to the discussion about the validity of the term tribe are e.g. M.H. Fried, *The Nation of Tribe* (Menlo Park, Cal.: Cummings Publishing Company, 1975) and M. Sahlins, *Tribesmen* (Englewood Cliffs, N.J.: Prentice Hall, 1968). For contributions relating to Bengal, see e.g. André Béteille, "The Definition of Tribe," in: Romesh Thapar (ed.), *Tribe, Caste and Religion in India* (Delhi: Macmillan, 1977), 7-14; and the debate between Susana B.C. Devalle, *Discourses of Ethnicity. Culture and Protest in Jharkhand* (New Delhi, etc: Sage Publications, 1992); and Binay Bhushan Chaudhuri, "The Myth of the Tribe? The Question Reconsidered," *The Calcutta Historical Journal* 16.1 (1994), 125-156.
13. David Hardiman, *The Coming of the Devi: Adivasi Assertion in Western India* (Delhi, etc: Oxford University Press, 1995), 14.
14. See e.g. Devalle, *Discourses of Ethnicity;* Chaudhuri, "The Myth of the Tribe?" 125-156 (with special reference to: 132-134); and B.G. Karlsson, *Contested Belonging. An Indigenous People's Struggle for Forest and Identity in Sub-Himalayan Bengal* (Lund: Department of Sociology, Lund University, 1997).
15. Karlsson, *Contested Belonging,* 44-45.

actually prefer the word "tribe" over "adivasi".[16] However, other groups or communities resent the word and insist on being called "indigenous people" or "adivasi" instead. We shall see that similar problems arise with practically all concepts or words in use.

1.2. "Scheduled Tribes"

The Partition of 1947 and the subsequent division of Bengal marked the beginning of a distinct political development in each part. West Bengal has obviously been influenced greatly by India's national policies. In post-colonial India, special national and state policies were formalised in the Constitution to "uplift" the "backward tribes". The post-colonial state showed the same systematising urge that its colonial precursor had displayed. In order to identify the people who qualified for preferential treatment, an extensive list was prepared of all "tribes." The people concerned have been referred to as *Scheduled Tribes* (ST) ever since.[17] In 1952 the Commissioner for Scheduled Castes and Tribes admitted that no uniform test to classify the "Scheduled Tribes" had been developed. Difficulties were experienced in determining which tribe was to be included in or excluded from the schedule of tribes. Nevertheless, the Commissioner did feel that three features were common to all tribal people: (a) they had a tribal origin, (b) they had a primitive way of life and habitation in remote and less easily accessible areas, and (c) they showed general backwardness in all respects.[18] The tautological nature of catchwords such as "tribal origin", "primitive" and "backwardness" to define "tribes" will be clear from the foregoing.

Not all so-called tribes were actually included in the category of "Scheduled Tribes". Only those whose primitiveness, backwardness and isolation made them deserving were selected for special treatment. This resulted in the curious situation that people belonging to the same group but living in more than one state of the Indian Union were included in the schedule in one state but not in the other. A similar problem arose with the so-called "criminal tribes" or "denotified tribes."

---

16. Karlsson, *Contested Belonging,* 47.
17. These same policies have been applied to the "Untouchables," "Harijans" or "Dalits," who have henceforth been addressed as Scheduled Castes (SC). Numerous publications about the Indian reservation policies have been published since then. For an extensive account see Marc Galanter, *Competing Equalities. Law and the Backward Classes in India* (Delhi etc.: Oxford University Press, 1984).
18. *Report of the Commissioner for SC & ST.* Vol.1 (New Delhi: 1952), 11.

In some states these were included in the category of Scheduled Tribes but in other states they were not. In West Bengal the designation Scheduled Tribe has gained enormous socio-economic and political importance because of the special facilities, which are provided for people who are included.

In East Pakistan (and present-day Bangladesh) the state never bothered to collect systematic information on the "tribal" population and never developed formalised policies regarding 'backward' groups. As a result, the term "tribe" remained vaguely defined in political discourse. Therefore, "Scheduled Tribe" is a term with purely West Bengal connotations; it has no currency in Bangladesh.

1.3. "Indigenous Peoples" and "Aborigines"

A third English term which has gained popularity in both English and Bengali is "indigenous peoples". This expression has become particularly popular in Bengal since 1993, the United Nations Year for Indigenous Peoples. The term has gained a great relevance for the people concerned because it links them to a large number of peoples all over the world, and provides them with a sense of shared identity which exceeds local, regional or national boundaries. In a way, the term is very similar to the old concept of "aborigines" or "aboriginal tribes," introduced by the British during the colonial period. The connotations and the social and political implications, however, differ greatly. The British used the term aborigines to distinguish so-called primitive peoples from the "modern Indian," with the underlying assumption that aborigines belonged to older, less advanced strata of population who had somehow failed to keep up with progress. The category did not just include people known as tribes today but also different castes, which were seen as having assimilated to some extent to the surrounding Hindu culture. The term "indigenous peoples" shares with "aborigines" the idea of early settlement but points to the old rights to land and other resources flowing from that early settlement. In this way, "indigenous people" has become a marker of emancipation and empowerment, and it provides a basis for a worldwide network of organisation and action.

"Indigenous peoples" was a clear concept in the Americas, where it was developed and first gained currency: the Amerindian population was indeed indigenous compared to the later immigrants from Europe, Africa and Asia. In South Asia, the concept is less clear, as recent immigration from other continents is not the issue, and the idea of indigeneity is contested. Nevertheless, theories of historical settlement continue to surface. Recently, in India the status of indigenous people has also been claimed for Dalits on the strength of the argument that Dalits were the original inhabitants of South Asia, and are a distinct people with their own culture.[19] In Bangladesh it is often argued, without much historical evidence, that so-called tribal people are no more indigenous to the country than Bengalis. In fact, the dominant discourse often reverses the positions by claiming that Bengalis are the truly indigenous people of Bangladesh and others, such as Garos, Santals, Tripuras, or Koches, are immigrants and therefore cannot claim to be indigenous to Bangladesh. All this points to the need for much more serious research into historical patterns of settlement on the regional level in Bengal than is presently available.[20] But it also points to the fact that the term "indigenous" itself is a bit of a red herring: surely it is not the status of earliest settlers but that of resisting being socially and culturally marginalised which has come to dominate conceptions of indigenous peoples.

1.4. "Adivasi"

"Adivasi" is a common term in both Bengali and English. It gained popularity in pre-Independence India and continued to be used in India after 1947. It is a recent term which probably originates from the Chhota Nagpur region in Bihar in the 1930s and was popularised at a wider level in the 1940s.[21] In Bangladesh, however, the term has not been popular until quite recently. Adivasi, coined from the Sanskrit *adi* (meaning "beginning" or "of earliest times") and *vasi* (meaning "residents of"), is a close translation of "aborigine." It also incorporates the idea that the adivasis are the original inhabitants of South Asia. G.S. Ghurye argues that because many of the so-called aboriginal tribes have come to their present habitat from somewhere else in South Asia, they cannot be considered autochthonous to their present home. Nevertheless, he adds that although they may not belong to exactly the same area, which

19. Ruth Manorama, "The Situation of Dalit Women," *Indigenous Affairs* 2 (1995), 4-7.
20. See e.g. Samaren Roy, *The Roots of Bengali Culture* (Calcutta: Firma KLM, 1981 [1961]); Krishnapada Goswami, *Place Names of Bengal* (Calcutta: Jnan Prakasan, n.d. [1984]).
21. Hardiman, *The Coming of the Devi*, 13.

they are now occupying, they still are the autochthones of South Asia. And to this extent they can be called adivasis or aborigines.[22]

David Hardiman, who prefers the term adivasi to tribe, acknowledges that there have been so many migrations in and out of the region that no particular group can have genuine grounds for making such a claim. Yet the term adivasi relates to a particular historical development, which generated a shared spirit of resistance that incorporated a consciousness of the adivasi against the outsider. Hardiman defines adivasis as:

> "groups which have shared a common fate in the past century and from this are evolved a collective identity of being adivasi".[23]

This definition shows that "adivasi" is by now primarily a political category rather than a cultural one. Taken in this way, the "observed Other" has rejected the passive role allocated to her or him and adopted the role of an self-conscious actor on the social stage.

1.5. "Upojati" and "Shomproday"

Perhaps the best-known term for non-Bengali groups in Bengal is "upojati". This word from the Bengali language is, however, increasingly being rejected by the peoples concerned. They argue that upojati is a derogatory term, which suggests that they are of a lower order than the Bengalis, who form a "jati" or nation, whereas an upojati is a mere sub-nation.[24] Upojati has connotations similar to the English word "tribe". Upojatis are perceived as uncivilised, less developed, and innocent peoples who live more or less isolated from the "mainstream" of "civilised" Bengali society.

Some writers have substituted "upojati" by "shomproday," which is usually translated into English as "community".[25] Although at face value this term seems to be a neutral one, it has become a key term in debates about Hindu-Muslim relations in Bengal (as in shamprodayika, or communalism), and this makes it less suitable as a term distinguishing non-Bengalis in Bengal.

22. G.S. Ghurye, *The Scheduled Tribes* (Bombay: Popular Prakashan, 1963 [3rd. edition]), 11-12.
23. Hardiman, *The Coming of the Devi*, 15-16.
24. Cf. Anu Mohammad, "Problems of Nation and the State: Parbotyo Chattogram," in: Subir Bhaumik, Meghna Guhathakurta and Sabyasachi Basu Ray Chaudhury (eds.), *Living on the Edge: Essays on the Chittagong Hill Tracts* (Calcutta: South Asia Forum for Human Rights/Calcutta Research Group, 1997), 1-16.
25. E.g. Subhas Jengcham, *Bangladesher Garo Shomproday* (Dhaka: Bangla Academy, 1994).

1.6. "Pahari"

In recent times, attempts have been made by non-Bengali inhabitants of Bengal to forge terms, which are non-pejorative and at the same time create a larger category than individual ethnic groups. These attempts, particularly in Bangladesh, have led to important new debates, which are still far from having been resolved. Two terms in particular have been influential, if ambiguous: "Pahari" and "Jumma".

Pahari (or Paharia) refers to both "tribes" in general and people who live in hills or mountains. It has been argued that the name was originally given by plains people to their hill-dwelling neighbours in the Rajmahal Hills in Bihar.[26] In Bangladesh, Pahari (or Paharia) is also used to refer to one specific community in Northwestern Bangladesh. "Pahari" is thus a term, which has once been imposed by others on the basis of environmental aspects. The peoples referred to have different designations for themselves, and yet hill people have utilised the term "pahari" to forge a common identity and distinguish themselves from plains people.

Doubtlessly, "pahari" is an ambiguous term because it suggests that a shared habitat implies shared experience and identity. This may be true for certain experiences and certain identity aspects at certain times, but can certainly not be posited as a general rule. The term "pahari" also suggests that there is some connection between non-Bengali identity and living in the hills, which is easily disproved if we look at groups such as the Rakhaing (Rahkain), plains Garos and Rabhas, and indeed the many hill-dwelling Bengalis.

1.7. "Jumma"

The final term which we discuss is "Jumma". *Jhum* refers to a particular type of cultivation, and Jhumia (in the Chittagonian dialect and the Chakma language: "Jumma") to the cultivators. In the 1970s, Jumma was appropriated by the regional political party of the Chittagong Hill Tracts, the JSS (Jana Sanghati Samiti), to refer to all inhabitants of the Chittagong Hill Tracts. Jumma has become a tool for distinguishing the inhabitants of the hill regions of southeastern Bangladesh from Bengali

26. Stephen G. Gomes, "The Paharias in Bangladesh: A Case Study of Assimilation and Identification with Policy Implications," in: Mahmud Shah Qureshi (ed.), *Tribal Cultures in Bangladesh* (Rajshahi: Institute of Bangladesh Studies, 1984), 140. Stephen G. Gomes, *The Paharias: A Glimpse of Tribal Life in North Western Bangladesh* (Dhaka: Caritas, 1988).

settlers in that area. Therefore the term refers to a shared experience of marginalisation, exploitation and militarisation, and to a social or solidarity movement. It embraces groups of various linguistic, cultural and religious backgrounds.[27]

2. The Importance of the "Other Groups" for the Study of Bangladesh and West Bengal

This brief sketch of the terminology in which discussions on non-Bengali groups in Bengal has been couched points to the following conclusions.

2.1. Terminology

There is now no broadly accepted term in either Bengali or English to refer to these groups. Further thinking about terminology and its implications is of crucial importance for the innovation of a field of inquiry in Bengal which has been remarkably stagnant for a long time. This requires three lines of inquiry. First, we need historical research into the changing meanings and uses of the various terms outlined above among academics, journalists, civil servants and politicians. Second, we need detailed knowledge of how different groups of non-Bengali people in the two halves of Bengal have identified themselves and how their self-identifications have been transforming, especially in recent decades. And third, it is necessary to break out of the parochialism of South Asian studies when we are dealing with issues of terminology. Many of the terms mentioned in the foregoing pages have a much wider currency than the South Asian subcontinent and have been analysed in sophisticated ways by specialists working on other regions of the world. These insights can greatly enrich discussions on the "other peoples" of Bengal.

2.2. Practical Consequences

Terms refer not only to ways of thinking but also to ways of acting. Dominant views of "tribal" people in Bengal have had devastating

27. See Willem van Schendel, "The Invention of the 'Jummas': State Formation and Ethnicity in Southeastern Bangladesh," *Modern Asian Studies*, 26:1 (1992), 95-128. Reprinted in: R.H. Barnes, Andrew Gray and Benedict Kingsbury (eds.), *Indigenous Peoples of Asia* (Ann Arbor, Mich.: Association for Asian Studies, 1995), 121-144.

practical effects on the lives of these people. The idea that they are somehow lagging behind Bengalis in civilisation is connected with associations of hills, forests and other "wild" and marginal places. Just as colonial and post-colonial ruling elites have considered such places as in need of being conquered by civilisation and development, so they have considered "tribal" people as being in need of "uplift" and improvement, not as full-fledged citizens but as wards in need of refinement on lines set out for them by ruling elites.

This view has opened the gates for a whole range of exploitations of the "other people" of Bengal. Generally speaking, such exploitations have been more brutal in Bangladesh than in West Bengal because West Bengal became part of a huge multi-cultural state whereas since 1971 Bangladeshis have been encouraged to think of their society as mono-cultural.

Economically, non-Bengali peoples of Bengal have often not been accepted as owners of their own resources. Local systems of land rights have been disregarded, land encroachment by outsiders condoned and at times encouraged, and representation in courts of justice made difficult. The same has happened with other resources, such as fishing rights and common property resources. Forests have been made state property and their inhabitants sent away on the unfounded assumption that their activities were detrimental to the environment. In many cases, the state has presided over severe environmental degradation of these forests, especially through injudicious (and usually illegal) timber and bamboo extraction. Similarly, development activities by the state and foreign donors have often been presented as being in the interest of "tribal" people whereas in fact they led frequently to population displacement, economic marginalisation and few if any local benefits. The Kaptai hydroelectric project in the Chittagong Hill Tracts (Bangladesh) is the best studied of these. Economically, the "other peoples" of Bengal have been in decline over a long period, and many of them have joined the underclass of the underemployed wage-dependent.

Politically, exploitation has taken various forms. "Other peoples" in Bengal have been used as vote banks for Bengali-dominated political parties, and they have acted as foot soldiers in armed political confrontations as diverse as the Naxalbari uprising and the Bangladesh Liberation War, generally without getting either recognition or political spoils. In East Pakistan/Bangladesh, in particular, control of "other peoples" has been made easy by the effective political tool of branding them as agents of a foreign power (= India) or agents of un-Islamic forces (especially applied to Christian groups). By invoking a threat to national integrity, it has been relatively easy to mobilise Bengali public opinion against any "tribal" movement and to silence legitimate concerns about human rights abuses.[28]

Culturally, exploitation has taken the form of making cultural difference harmless by turning it into something decorative and traditional. Thus sanitised "exotic" cultures of "other peoples" are served up as folkloristic amusement to Bengali audiences and prospective foreign tourists. In this way, various de-contextualised "tribal" dances are incorporated into the pretty self-image of the nation as presented on film, television and the stage, and in the printed media. Here "tribal" women, associated in the minds of the audience with wildness and uncivilised abandon, are put on titillating display. This folkloristic and erotic exploitation contrasts sharply with the discouragement which cultural pluralism receives otherwise, particularly with regard to languages in education and administration.[29]

In short, for various forms of exploitation of "other peoples" in Bengal to stop we need an overhaul of the dominant mindset regarding these groups. It is here that social scientists should act as pioneers.

2.3. A New Discussion

It is clear now that what used to be a discussion about people whose own voices were not heard or disregarded has now become a discussion in which these very voices demand centre stage but are still largely

28. See e.g. Harikishore Chakma, Tapash Chakma, Preyasi Dewan and Mahfuz Ullah, Bara Parang: *The Tale of the Developmental Refugees of the Chittagong Hill Tracts* (Dhaka: Centre for Sustainable Development, 1995); Chittagong Hill Tracts Commission, *Life is Not Ours: Land and Human Rights in the Chittagong Hill Tracts, Bangladesh* (Copenhagen/Amsterdam: International Work Group on Indigenous Affairs (IWGIA)/ Organising Committee Chittagong Hill Tracts Campaign, 1991). *Update* 1 (1992); *Update* 2 (1994); *Update* 3 (1997); *Update* 4 (2000).
29. See Willem van Schendel, Wolfgang Mey and Aditya Kumar Dewan, *The Chittagong Hill Tracts: Living in a Borderland* (Bangkok: White Lotus, 2000/Dhaka: University Press Limited, 2000).
30. See Willem van Schendel, "Who Speaks for the Nation? Nationalist Rhetoric and the Challenge of Cultural Pluralism in Bangladesh," in: Willem van Schendel and Erik-Jan Zürcher (eds.), *Identity Politics in Central Asia and the Muslim World* (London: I.B. Tauris, 2000); Willem van Schendel, "Bengalis, Bangladeshis and Others: Chakma Visions of a Pluralist Bangladesh," in: Rounaq Jahan (ed.), Bangladesh: Promise and Performance (Dhaka: University Press Limited, 2000), 65-105.

disregarded by the intellectual and political establishments of Bangladesh and West Bengal.[30] In Bengal we observe the remnants of an old debate, which used to be concerned with cultural essences, evolutionary stages and boundaries between observer and observed, being overtaken by a new debate, which is concerned with issues of cultural hegemony, nationalist myths, citizenship, power and self-determination. The former debate is still well entrenched in academia whereas the latter is spreading rapidly in political associations and non-government organisations (NGOs). It is important and rewarding to explore the dimensions highlighted by the new debate and to study the new uses to which old social categories are being put. Social scientists have almost completely ignored the fact that old categories such as "Rabha" or "Garo" have taken on new meanings to those who identify with them. These transformations have come about in the interplay of group rethinking, state intervention, NGO activity, and new media and transport facilities. They have created a highly significant and powerful discourse among the "other peoples" of Bengal, which needs to be taken seriously.[31]

2.4. A Comparative Perspective

Studies of the "other groups" of Bengal need to take account of the social categories, which these groups themselves employ (or employed) to make sense of the world in which they live. To this end a more sophisticated historical-anthropological perspective and methodology needs to be developed. This can be done only by taking discussions on Bengal and its "other people" beyond the regional confines and linking them up to the rich debates on indigenous peoples all over the world. Discussions on land rights in Australia, ethnocide in Ecuador, the social effects of hydro-electric projects in Norway, biodiversity in Brazil, and the concept of indigenous peoples in Asia are highly relevant for a better understanding of the "other groups" in Bengal.[32]

---

31. See Ellen Bal, Yasuhiro Takami and Johannes Sandgren, *Manderangni Jagring: Images of the Garos in Bangladesh* (Dhaka: University Press Limited, 1999); and Ellen Bal, *'They Ask if We Eat Frogs': Social Boundaries, Ethnic Categorisation, and the Garo People of Bangladesh* (Delft: Eburon, 2000).
32. A good introduction to these issues in Asia is R.H. Barnes, Andrew Gray and Benedict Kingsbury (eds.), *Indigenous Peoples of Asia* (Ann Arbor, Michigan: Association for Asian Studies, 1995). A series of excellent reports on the situation of indigenous populations worldwide are the IWGIA Documents, published by the International Work Group on Indigenous Affairs (IWGIA) in Copenhagen, Denmark.

Finally, the importance of this work is not confined to a better understanding of how smaller ethnic groups form, survive or disappear in modern society. The insights go much further: serious study of the "other peoples" of Bengal inevitably leads to a much better understanding of how social life in Bangladesh and West Bengal in general is organised and how it transforms over time. It will lead especially to a reconsideration of existing ideas about the relationship between states and citizens in this part of the world, and of notions such as development, democracy and legitimacy. After all, it is in their treatment of smaller groups that societies show their priorities, their norms for the application of power and governance, their quest for participation and consent, and their blueprint for the future.

REFERENCES

Bal, Ellen. 2000. *'They Ask if We Eat Frogs': Social Boundaries, Ethnic Categorisation, and the Garo People of Bangladesh*. Delft: Eburon.

Bal, Ellen.,Yasuhiro Takami and Johannes Sandgren. 1999. *Manderangni Jagring: Images of the Garos in Bangladesh*. Dhaka: University Press Limited.

Bandyopadhyay, Sekhar. 1985. "Caste in the Perception of the Raj: A Note on the Evolution of Colonial Sociology of Bengal," *Bengal Past & Present*, 104: 56-80.

Bandyopadhyay, Sekhar, Abhijit Dasgupta and Willem van Schendel. 1994-95. "Introduction," (pp. 1-16) in Sekhar Bandyopadhyay, Abhijit Dasgupta and Willem van Schendel (eds.), *op.cit.*

Bandyopadhyay, Sekhar, Abhijit Dasgupta and Willem van Schendel (eds.). 1994/1995. *Bengal. Communities, Development and States*. New Delhi: Manohar Publications / Dhaka: University Press Limited.

Barnes, R.H., Andrew Gray and Benedict Kingsbury (eds.). 1995. *Indigenous Peoples of Asia*. Ann Arbor, Mich.: Association for Asian Studies.

Basu, Swaraj. 1994-95. "The Colonial State and the Indigenous Society: The Creation of the Rajbansi Identity in Bengal," (pp. 43-64) in Bandyopadhyay, Dasgupta and Van Schendel (eds.), *op.cit.*

Bayly, Susan. 1995. "Caste and 'Race' in the Colonial Ethnography of India," (pp.165-218) in Peter Robb (ed.), *The Concept of Race in South Asia*. Delhi, etc: Oxford Press.

Béteille, André. 1977. "The Definition of Tribe," (pp. 7-14) in Romesh Thapar (ed.), op.cit.

Bhaumik, Subir, Meghna Guhathakurta and Sabyasachi Basu Ray Chaudhury (eds.). 1997. *Living on the Edge: Essays on the Chittagong Hill Tracts*. Calcutta: South Asia Forum for Human Rights/Calcutta Research Group.

Breman, Jan (ed.). 1990. *Imperial Monkey Business. Racial Supremacy in Social Darwinist Theory and Colonial Practice*. Amsterdam: VU University Press.

Carroll, Lucy, "Colonial Perceptions of Indian Society and the Emergence of Caste(s) Associations," *Journal of Asian Studies*, 37:2 (February 1978), 233-250.

Chakma, Harikishore, Tapash Chakma, Preyasi Dewan and Mahfuz Ullah. 1995. *Bara Parang: The Tale of the Developmental Refugees of the Chittagong Hill Tracts*. Dhaka: Centre for Sustainable Development.

Chaudhuri, Binay Bhushan. 1994. "The Myth of the Tribe? The Question Reconsidered," *The Calcutta Historical Journal* 16 (1): 125-156.

Chittagong Hill Tracts Commission. 1991. *Life is not Ours: Land and Human Rights in the Chittagong Hill Tracts, Bangladesh*. Copenhagen/Amsterdam: International Work Group on Indigenous Affairs (IWGIA)/ Organising Committee Chittagong Hill Tracts Campaign, 1991. Update 1 (1992); Update 2 (1994); Update 3 (1997); Update 4 (2000).

Cohn, Bernard S. 1968. "Notes on the History of the Study of Indian Society and Culture," (pp. 3-28) in Milton Singer and Bernard S. Cohn (eds.), *op.cit.*

____. 1978. "The Census, Social Structure and Objectification in South Asia," (pp. 224-254) in Bernard S. Cohn (ed.), *An Anthropologist among Historians and Other Essays.* Delhi etc: Oxford University Press.

Devalle, Susana B.C. 1992. *Discourses of Ethnicity. Culture and Protest in Jharkhand.* New Delhi, etc: Sage Publications.

Fried, M.H. 1975. *The Notion of Tribe*. Menlo Park, Cal.: Cummings Publishing Company.

Galanter, Marc. 1984. *Competing Equalities. Law and the Backward Classes in India*. Delhi, etc.: Oxford University Press.

Ghurye, G.S. 1963 [3rd. edition]. *The Scheduled Tribes*. Bombay: Popular Prakashan Private Limited.

____. 1979 [1932]. *Caste and Race in India.* Bombay: Popular Prakashan Private Limited.

Gomes, Stephen G. 1984. "The Paharias in Bangladesh: A Case Study of Assimilation and Identification with Policy Implications," (pp. 135-157) in Mahmud Shah Qureshi (ed.), *op.cit.*

____. 1988. *The Paharias: A Glimpse of Tribal Life in North Western Bangladesh.* Dhaka: Caritas.

Goswami, Krishnapada. n.d. [1984]. *Place Names of Bengal*. Calcutta: Jnan Prakasan.

Hardiman, David. 1995. *The Coming of the Devi: Adivasi Assertion in Western India*. Delhi, etc: Oxford University Press.

Jahan, Rounaq (ed.). 2000. *Bangladesh: Promise and Performance*. Dhaka: University Press Limited.

Jengcham, Subhas. 1994. *Bangladesher Garo Shomproday.* Dhaka: Bangla Academy.

Karlsson, B.G. 1997. *Contested Belonging. An Indigenous People's Struggle for Forest and Identity in Sub-Himalayan Bengal.* Lund: Department of Sociology, Lund University.

Manorama, Ruth. 1995. "The Situation of Dalit Women," *Indigenous Affairs*, 2: 4-7.

Memmi, Albert. 1990 [1957]. *The Colonizer and the Colonized.* London: Earthscan Publications.

Mohammad, Anu. 1997. "Problems of Nation and the State: Parbotyo Chattogram," (pp. 1-16) in Subir Bhaumik, Meghna Guhathakurta and Sabyasachi Basu Ray Chaudhury (eds.), *op.cit.*

Nandy, Ashis. 1990 [1983]. *The Intimate Enemy. Loss and Recovery of Self under Colonialism.* Delhi etc: Oxford University Press.

Qureshi, Mahmud Shah (ed.). 1984. *Tribal Cultures in Bangladesh.* Rajshahi: Institute of Bangladesh Studies.

Report of the Commissioner for SC & ST. Vol.1. 1952. New Delhi.

Robb, Peter (ed.). 1995. *The Concept of Race in South Asia.* Delhi, etc: Oxford Press.

Roy, Samaren. 1981 [1961] *The Roots of Bengali Culture.* Calcutta: Firma KLM.

Sahlins, M. 1968. *Tribesmen.* Englewood Cliffs, N.J.: Prentice Hall.

Said, Edward W. 1979. *Orientalism.* New York: Vintage Books.

Singer, Milton, and Bernard S. Cohn (eds.). 1968. *Structure and Change in Indian Society.* Chicago: Aldine Publishing Company.

Thapar, Romesh (ed.). 1977. *Tribe, Caste and Religion in India.* Delhi: Macmillan.

Van Schendel, Willem. 1992. "The Invention of the 'Jummas': State Formation and Ethnicity in Southeastern Bangladesh," *Modern Asian Studies*, 26 (1): 95-128. Reprinted in R.H. Barnes, Andrew Gray and Benedict Kingsbury (eds.), *op.cit.*

____. 2000. "Who Speaks for the Nation? Nationalist Rhetoric and the Challenge of Cultural Pluralism in Bangladesh," in Willem van Schendel and Erik-Jan Zürcher (eds.), *op.cit.*

____. 2000. "Bengalis, Bangladeshis and Others: Chakma Visions of a Pluralist Bangladesh," (pp. 65-105) n Rounaq Jahan (ed.), *op.cit.*

Van Schendel, Willem, Wolfgang Mey and Aditya Kumar Dewan. 2000. *The Chittagong Hill Tracts: Living in a Borderland.* Bangkok: White Lotus / Dhaka: University Press Limited).

Van Schendel, Willem, and Ellen Bal (eds.). 1998. *Banglar Bohujati: Bangali Chhara Banglar Onnanyo Jatir Proshongo.* Calcutta: International Centre for Bengal Studies.

____. 1998. "Bhumika: Name Ki Eshe Jay?" (pp.7-25) in Willem van Schendel and Ellen Bal (eds.), *op.cit.*

Van Schendel, Willem, and Erik-Jan Zürcher (eds.). 2000. *Identity Politics in Central Asia and the Muslim World.* London: I.B Tauris.

FIVE

THE SANTAL CONCEPTION OF TIME

MARINE CARRIN

The Santals call themselves *hor hopon,* children of men, which refer to Santal identity and opposes to the category to *diku* - outsiders and foreigners.[1] But at the same time, Santals see themselves as members of the Santal *samaj*, "society," and the formulation of Santal identity is rooted in the consciousness of a distinctive past. This past which is expressed in narrative implies - as Bloch argues for the Zafinary - the combination of two kinds of past: the semantic past which organised talking about time and the episodic past which is conveyed through the autobiographical memory. Bloch (1998) defines the semantic memory as the memory which aims at organizing and transmitting knowledge, while the autobiographical memory tends to evoke events which are tinged with emotion. Bloch criticizes Sahlins who in Islands of History (1985, chap.2) shows that two kinds of past are associated with Hawaii and Fiji history: one kind of past is dominated by heroes and gods and another kind which has been greatly influenced by the memory of the nineteenth century. Bloch argues against Sahlins that these two kinds of past are not so different, showing that the Zafinary of Madagascar construct time in very complex ways. Indeed the Zafinary have a variety of narrative ways for "evoking the past and representing the passage of time, some are oral and some are written. One image may dominate in one context and another in another context" (Bloch, 1998: 110).

1. The concept of diku relates to two different categories: the Marang Diku "big foreigners" alludes the upper castes who are seen as oppressive while the Hurin Diku or "small foreigners" labels groups who share the same socio-economic conditions than the Santals.

In different social and political contexts, Santals act as members of a "scheduled tribe," or as "adivasis". The term *adivasi* which refers to those who were the original inhabitants and relate to land and forest rights has been forged around 1915 by Christian Munda and Oraon students who were proposing this term to fight discrimination against the "tribes." Later on, in 1953, when *adivasi* resistance to assimilation became more assertive, a tribal party Jharkhand was formed under the leadership of a Munda leader, Jaipal Singh. The term Jharkhand from *jhar*, "sacred grove" and *khand*, "country" was chosen to express the territorial claims of the Munda groups. These three terms Santal, adivasi, or Jharkhandis are used in different kinds of contexts to assert group identity. While the term santal from *saont* "grove" is used in daily conversation, the villagers rather prefer to call themselves *hor hopon* whenever they want to talk about Tradition colon, a Bengali word which is used to reinvent the *heritage of the past* and has been influenced by the introduction of literacy in Santal society.

This introduction aims at suggesting that the Santals have complex representations of time which range from present to historical consciousness. I argue that Santal categories of time reflect a Santal way of life and imply a choice of values which crystallize around the concept of *raskau*, "pleasure, good time". Still this conceptualisation shows how Santals concentrate on their activities without indulging in capitalisation of time or money. Time is shared by all, and to claim more time (or more wealth) means to go against egalitarian values.[2]

How the Santal Talk about Time

The alternance of day and night is thought with reference to the position of the sun: they say the sun rises *ber rakap'* whenever the coq sings (*sim rakap'*) but the night falls at sunset (*ber hasur*). Two meals rhythm the day, the first one *baskeak'* is made of leftovers from the previous day, and rice cakes are made out of cold rice. The housewife is cooking in the evening (*ayub'*) a more complete meal (*bela kedok'*) which includes rice and vegetable curry, as well as some fish or meat curry when they can afford it. When rice is plentiful, a third meal may be taken at three o'clock in the afternoon, *tikin*. Women go to the fields

2. Anti-social elements are suspected to worship secretly kombro bonga ko "thieves deities" who steal grain on other villagers threshing-floor and give it to their devotees.

to bring this meal to their husbands. More globally, the threat of starvation shapes the Santal conception of time, and whenever a Santal meets a kin or a friend from another village he asks about *suk and duk*, the good and bad news which evokes meeting relatives at fairs and markets and asking for what is happening in other villages while smoking tobacco together. In the same way Santals, as good agriculturists, talk about *sukal* "a good season" in opposition to *akal* "a bad season".

Evening (*ayub*) is the time where cattle returns to the cowshed, and children are put to bed is *gitic' jokhec*,' a time when grandmother is singing *japit' seren,* lullabies. This is the time when crows and bats make a tremendous noise in the trees and when deities (*bongas*) follow human beings into the village street. It is becoming dark, (*nut*) but still we hear the voices of working women coming from the cookery. They walk carrying their working tools on their heads while old widows whisper against young women, accusing them of following lovers in order to get some "pocket money." Just before it gets dark, old men sitting on the verandah scrutinise the sky in order to study the strange dance of the vultures (*gidi*). These birds are considered as negative omen, such as bad crops. Then comes the dark, *nutat*', the time when snakes (*bin*) are seen. Santal men talk about village affairs and the last meal is eaten before going to sleep. The days where the moon is full (*purnima*) Santal boys and girls met at the village *akra* dancing-ground and dance and sing until late in the night, playing the drum (*tumdak'*). *Tala ninda*, midnight, is the time when witches (*dain*) are roaming, seated on their magical vehicles (*pathri*), darting arrows at the doors of the houses of their victims. It is during night that witches are supposed to play with their tiger pets or initiate sexually a *gupi kora*, a herdsman they have induced to follow them. When it is full night witches throw the germs of disease at the doors of their victims' houses while *ojhas* witch-finders will try, later on, to localize them at dawn when they engage in exorcism on behalf of their customers.

The end of the night corresponds to the time where *bongas*, Santal deities, try their best to attract their victims in the other world. For example, a man gets up and goes to urinate at the back of his house, where a female deity takes the seductive form (*rup*) of a girl and makes love to him. But to enjoy sex with a bonga sometimes ends tragically as the deity tries by all means to attract her lover near a pond where the latter will loose his *umul*, shadow, if, by chance, his image is reflected in the water.

Santals identify themselves with trees and particularly value the branches of sal trees (*Shorea Robusta, L*).[3] Branches of sal are also used to notify time as the number of leaves indicates the number of days before a meeting. Such signs are used to fix an auspicious event, such as a hunt-meeting. Thus, the number of leaves may indicate the number of days before the *bitlaha* is to be celebrated, a ceremony of exclusion of the culprits in cases of incest or sexual commerce with outsiders (Archer, 1989: 555).[4]

Work and Seasons

Santals call *raban din*, cold days, the time from Aghar November-December to the month of *Phagun*, February-March. The first crop is reapened by the end of *Pus* January, just before the new year. This is the time to arrange the marriages (*bapla*), which will be celebrated a month later. After the winter crop, everybody repair their tools and visit their friends. The Santal year is marked by a number of festivals. Baha is a fertility ritual but it is also the time when possessed oracles go to fetch *mohua* flowers in the forest, and before this rite nobody is allowed to pluck the wild fruits and flowers as taboos are reinforced. Without entering into the description of the ritual, we may just note that the *mohua* flowers are distributed by the village priest (*naeke*) to the mature women as a token of fertility. Coming soon after Baha *bonga*, the spring hunt marks a time for rest, when everybody gets some leisure from the field. It is a time when men go from market to market gambling in cock-fighting and drinking rice-beer with kin (*pera*).[5] It is the time for repairing the mud houses, which have to be consolidated before the heavy rains. The intense heat *seton* lasts from *Baisakh*, April-May, to *Jeth*, May-June. It is the time of sowing, and later on, of transplanting the *paddi* seedlings. Lentils and other cereals are also sown in May and ripen in January. *Bhador*, July-August, is dry, and the animals get emaciated since grazing is poor. Then the rainy season *japut*' comes,

---

3. The symbolism of the branch conveys the idea of generation. During the migrations, the Santal chief was showing the branch to call his clan men to follow him. See Carrin (to be published).
4. I have argued elsewhere that to have a sexual relationship with a foreigner (a *diku*, a Hindu) or to be incestuous means to pollute the tribe. The categories of being too close or too far define ethnic closure (Carrin, 1991).
5. In the creation myth, Maran Buru, the tribal god shows the first pair of siblings how to brew rice-beer.

a term which means to "cover with one's hands" and alludes to the gesture of villagers when they try to protect themselves from the heavy rain. The rainy season lasts during *Dasâe*, August-September, and is the time when *ojhas*, witch-doctors and healers, go with their disciples to beg from village to village during a week. This is a ritual wandering which is experienced as a mystic and initiatary voyage in the sky.[6]

Festivals rhythm the year, most important among them the cattle festival *Sohrae* (litt; elder sister) and *Baha* the spring fesival which marks the Santal new year. The end of the year is celebrated by a festival during which villagers drink rice-beer and eat rice cakes with kin and friends, while they do not forget to dedicate offerings to the ancestors *hapramko* who reside in the ancestral shed of the house (*bhitar*).

This rather idyllic[7] ethnography represents the way the ethnographer learns to listen to Santals talking about time. The cycle here is framed, as we have seen, by the agrarian routine. But the individual also has to respect the engagements he has towards his clanic deities (*abge*) and his house-deities, *orak'bongas*. He has to respect the time he himself has fixed to sacrifice to his clanic and household deities, and which corresponds to a periodicity fixed by the family tradition and transmitted from father to son.[8] A householder should go, every two or four years, with his agnates to sacrifice a he-goat in a barren field. Whenever the time approaches the head of the family tends to get nervous as he has no way to postpone the sacrifice, on the pain of being exposed to the wrath of the *abge bonga*. If he must postpone the sacrifice he will find, by divination, some evil sign that one household member, sooner or later, will get sick. Such a concern is a secret that the elder males may share but which they do not disclose in front of women. In case of disease, they rather consult an *ojha*, a medecine-man, who will generally urge them to go to the barren field to perform the missed sacrifice.

---

6. The ritual wandering is a mystic voyage which prepares the future ojha to get possessed (rumok') as the guru is supposed to dismembers and remembers his body in the sky. When the novice gets down on earth, he is both male and female. Feminity confers to the ojha the healer's sensitivity.
7. I have not taken into account here the fact that many Santals are casual workers in urban centres and in this case they have to adjust both "modern" time and village time. Workers have often protested in order to get leaves to attend village festivals.
8. Some clans members sacrifice every two three years to their abge bonga, or clanic deity. Orak'bonga ko are worshipped every three or four years. But in both cases, these rituals are sometimes postponed for economic reasons.

In case of illness, the head of the family will make the promise of sacrificing a chicken (*sim agom*) later on, when the sick has recovered. The promise is symbolised by a bundle of *sal* leaves,[9] which are abandoned once the sacrifice has been made.

To the concern for work which rhythmes the succession of days and nights there corresponds another time which progressively unveils the activities of the *bongas*. For example, when it is three o'clock (*tekin*) in the afternoon, the deities are sitting in the cotton tree or in the *pipal*, ficus, and the herdsmen must learn to avoid resting under these trees at this particular time. But during the full night, the picture is quite different, beause some individuals such as witches leave in their bed another human form (*rup*) while they themselves go to the secret meeting of the witches. Similarly, the men who tend to get seduced by a *bonga* at night are often individuals who feel nostalgic about love. To get seduced by a *bonga* is both exciting and dangerous as it implies exploring another world, the entrance of which is signalled by inauspicious time. Those who transgress the rules against resting under certain trees in the early afternoon may be seduced by *bongas* and will then experience other times as well as other places. Then, some men forget the time when they should offer sacrifices to their clanic deities. Housewives, too, may forget to propitiate their husbands' ancestors.

The idea that the memory of ritual duty fails is recurrent in the Santal mind and becomes an obsession: men get trapped in their daily routine and forget that they are watched by the *bongas*. This careless attitude may perhaps be explained by the rather discontinuous time which is suggested by Santal mythology.

Mythic Time

The Santal creation myth tells us how Maran Buru, the tribal God created the world but Thakur, the Hindu God, destroyed his work by sending a fire-rain over the world. Finally, the two gods negotiate, and Thakur decides to create the world a second time. For that purpose, Thakur saves a couple of wild geese who have laid their eggs at the surface of the ocean. Later, a pair of siblings are born from these eggs and they copulate. From them twelve couples are born to found the twelve original Santal clans. In this creation myth Maran Buru appears

9. Sal leaves symbolise the ancestors.

like a good father who teaches his children how to brew rice-beer and even induces them to drink and to forget, through *maya*, that "they were brother and sister". In the creation myth incest has a positive function, but later on, Thakur introduces order into the world when he decides to organize the society into castes and communities (*jati* and *samaj*).[10]

Without entering into that long story it is enough here to state that Santals resist the division of the world into communities (Carrin-Bouez, 1985). For that purpose Thakur prepares many leaf-cups containing different kinds of food. Those who come first will choose their regime. The Santals, who are strong since they work hard, win the race and choose the cow meat, which they consider the best food. This implies resistance, expressed by the Santals' refusal to consider themeselves inferior from eating beef. The cow is not just their food, but also important as a sacrificial animal.

Another myth, the story of the bastard traces some links between Santals and Hindus. The myth first passes in rapid review the migrations of the Santals, telling us how first they went from Hihiṛi Pipiri to Khoj Kaman, then to Sasanbeda Jarpi and Kaende until they finally setlled in Cae Campa in Hazaribagh. The first *raja* was called Dharapnaran and lived in Campanagar but there was also a *pargana*, named Mandhwa who was the son of a Hindu father, a son of the king, and a Santal or a Birhor girl (according to different versions). Finally, Mandhwa told the king he was his grandson and got half of the kingdom. He thus changed his name into Mandho Singh. Later on, the ancestors went to a Buru *beret* (the summit of a mountain) but they did not yet have festivals at the time. Mandho saw and fell for a Hembrom girl but he could not get her as the Santals ancestors considered him a bastard. Mandho Singh wanted to take her by force. Fearing Mandho Singh's soldiers, the ancestors fled in the night shutting the main gate of their village. During five days and five nights they fled until they reached the Damodar river. Mandho Singh was following them, so they prayed in order to stop the flow of water in the river. Their wow was excused and so they crossed the river. On the other side, the ancestors fulfilled their wow and killed a white fowl in the name of Maran Buru (Big Mountain), who later became the chief of the *bongas*. A little later the ancestors performed the first marriages and established villages. Then

10. Santal texts criticise the concept of jati but accept the concept of *samaj* one could translate by society. *Samaj* implies the idea of ethnic and social consciousness.

they tied bullocks and cows to posts and sacrificed them. There are several episodes where Mandho Singh is trying to find them. The clan elders discuss whether their *bongas* can save them since Mandho Singh is a Hindu. One ancestor from the Copear clan is telling "we have seven umbrellas full of bongas." So the ancestors tell him to go ahead and "open the doors". They escape from the land of the Ojoe river, which is ill omened, and establish themselves at the Sikhar boundary in the Sonaboi Upland. In other narratives, the Santals admit that cow-eating may be seen as impure, and decide to manipulate the very idea of impurity in order to drive away Mandho Singh. Consequently they tie cowhides to their village doors and Mandho Singh, feeling disgusted, flees away with some Santals, who thus betray their brothers. The traitors end up in Chotanagpur where they sell their services to the Munda petty chiefs.

Mythical time is construed in projecting events, such as the deeds of ancestors in particular places, such as sacred hills, or rivers, which then become highly emblematic in Santal poetry.

The World of the Bongas

Dreaming of another world inhabited by *bongas* is experienced by some of my Santal informants as living another emotional life, in parallel to the cyclical routine. The experience is described as emotional and positive by *ojhas* or priests and deviners who master the relationship thay have with a Santal *bonga* (Carrin-Bouez, 1986). On the contrary, the same experience is lived as a luring into dark illusion by those women or men who become the *bongas*' victims. Santals have a strong relationship to their *bongas*. During their whole life but particularly before marriage, the bongas try to impinge in Santal affairs. The *bongas*, it is thought, try to get closer to human beings, taking the guise of the other sex. The theme of the *bonga* lover is a favourite with the Santals as they feel that bongas get closer to their minds than human beings. Except Santal *ojhas* who sometimes boast of their romantic encounters with bongas, other people are rather discrete on the subject. We learn about the world of the *bongas* through narratives: the world of the bongas is symmetrical to the world of men. *Bongas* eat like men but there both men and women have long hair. They wear clothes like us. Snakes are their seats but the snakes do not harm them. Their feet are turned backwards. When you go into their land you get down by a crack in the earth. But *bongas*, boys and girls, come and bathe in tanks and pools in the world of men. This kind of description insists on symmetry between the world of the *bongas* and this world. But nothing is said about time even if it is striking that men and *bongas* live in different worlds.[11] This time difference appears at the eschatological level where it is assumed that men will become *bongas* three generations after their life, provided that their funerals have been performed. But in narratives, *bongas* appear to react more quickly than men as if their mind was made of fire. They seem particularly eager to trap human beings whenever the later ones transgress rules or forget their promises *Bongas*, then, appear as threatening, invisible forces generally identified too late by the humans who, normally, have not noticed their presence (Carrin, 1996). A well-known example is a woman who is walking by night between two villages when she meets a *bonga* and asks him for tobacco, a gesture which is not very proper at night for a woman. The *bonga's* laconic words imply an immediate threat: "you will soon dance" and three days after, the woman vomits blood and dies. In other accounts, humans forget that they have made a vow to the *bongas*, who then irrupt in the world to chatise them.[12]

How People Mature

If a pregnant woman goes near a *bonga*, the deity is enraged and the child will be born prematurely. Pregnancy, then, is a time when taboos concerning places and food as well as rules of commensality are reinforced. Birth itself pollutes the *bongas* and this pollution ends with the first haircut and name-giving ceremony. As a general rule, Santal boys and girls become gradually aware of family duties. From the age of five or six boys and girls make themselves useful herding the goats. Boys learn to shoot birds and to place nets in rivulets and backwaters. Girls follow their grandmothers in the forest to collect fallen branches which are used as fuel. Boys learn how to repair fences in the vegetable garden (*burge*) behind the house, while girls learn to sweep the courtyard and carry water on their head, following their mothers.

The Santal child learns about time as he takes the animals to the field early in the morning and brings them back with his grandfather

11. Another main difference implies that men live in a world of scarcity while *bongas* enjoy wealth and all sorts of food. Still *bongas* are insatiable.

12. Bongas are perverse as they induce men to transgress taboos.

(*gorom baba*). Santal mothers do not breast-feed their children at regular intervals, they rather comply with the demand of the child. *Nunu gidra* means the time of breast-feeding which may last until the child is two years old, and *sidup*' means the time when the baby learns to sit. *Janam chatiar* corresponds to the first shaving and name-giving ceremony. This ritual aims at introducing the child to the tribe and to place him under the *bongas* as he is given the clanic deities of his father. This time is ritualised, and the parents invite the headman, the village priests as well as kin and friends to ceremonially include the child in their clan (*kili*). On this occasion a guru enumerates the mythic places where the ancestors were living and evokes the impurity of birth which after the ritual comes to an end.

Children gradually learn to share their meals with the adults and become conscious of the commensality rule which start to apply when a child is eight, a time where *caco chatia*, a confirmation entrance into the society (*samaj*), must be performed if it has been postponed for economic reasons. During that ritual, a guru recites santal myths about the deeds of the ancestors. From then on, the boy is included in his father's commensality circle (*kond*) and the girl is able to clean the *bhitar*, the corner of the house which is dedicated to the ancestors. Both become closer to the *bongas* and this degree of closeness is a rite a passage in itself.

Marriage (*bapla*) unites two families, according to the rules of endogamy of the tribe and clan exogamy. Nowadays, it is frequent to find marriages within the same clan but not in the same sub-clan.[13] There exists several marriage forms but here I shall stress how marriage concerns time symbolism. During the marriage ceremony, the spouses are sprinkled with *tulsi* water in order to bestow fertility on them. This ritual aspersion is supposed to strenghthen the power of their "bones" which is important to make a child. Bone symbolizes continuity in time, as *ji* the life principle is thought to reside in the bone of the crane. A child is made when Thakur gives life *jiu* to a piece of bone and the flesh (*jel*) that grows around it. This insistance on bone symbolism seems to indicate that the Santals, like the Kachin, conceptualize conception from the "bone" which is definitely a male substance. In many metaphors, bone is seen as equivalent to stone which symbolizes male body parts such as the chest. Still, the feminine part, the flower (*baha*: uterus) is

13. Clan: *paris*; sub-clan *khunt*.

important, too, even if flowers are associated with ephemeral qualities (Carrin-Bouez, 1986).

Death, too, is a time when the agnates must offer libations of rice-beer to the bones of the deceased in order to "nourish" them and thus ensure the continuation of the lineage. There is a time after death when kin of the deceased are in debt (*dharua*) towards the *bongas* as they go through the different phases of the funeral which conclude with the immersion of the dead in the Damodar river. The liminal time from death till cremation is dangerous as the bongas are polluted. People who die suddenly may turn into *bongas* or witches (Carrin, 1996, 1997). According to a similar idea, women who die before marriage become *jugini*, a Hinduised kind of malevolent spirits who haunt the cremation ground. Those who die in pregnancy become *curin*, malevolent deities who cause harm to babies. *Bongas* or *bhuts* attack to provoke a sudden death which inspires fear. Equally fearful is the witch (*dain*) who "eats" her victims slowly. The slow action of witches emphasizes their mysterious power, as they are supposed to attack their victims by throwing magical darts at them or by burying a hair belonging to the victim under the hearth of the kitchen.

Hana Puri

Besides the grief experienced at the time of death there is the knowledge of a sudden crisis occurring in the departed person's house and in the village. Death might be seen as a victory of the malevolent deities against the major *bongas* who reside in the village and who are concerned with Santal welfare. According to Santal ideas, the deceased seems to have failed in his main duty "to belong to the living," like the branch of a tree. The villagers know that the departed spirit may be outraged as he is deprived of his kin's affection. The tree mataphor is related to time in several ways: Santals count generations by saplings.

Death implies a distance which at first is experienced through spatial metaphors, the departed has gone "to fetch salt" (*bulun agui lagit'*) which used to evoke a distant journey taking many days. Through the different stages of the funerals the deceased will become an ancestor and later on a *bonga*, a process which may take three generations but can be shortened by hastening the funeral cycle. The living may be possessed by the departed and learn to read his footprints (*panja*) in the ashes of the hearth. After the washing of the flower bones (some weeks, a year or even some years after death in case of financial difficulties) the soul of the departed person is removed from his temporary "shell."[14] The dead go to Hana Puri,[15] the other world, a place where they sometimes suffer from their past mistakes. For example, a lazy man will be stuck in his stool in Hana Puri while a glutton will be forced to eat. It may be possible to read some Christian influence into these terms of punishment, but we find also narratives which describe the world of death as a labour camp. There, men and women must work ceaselessly under the custody of terrible chowkidars. But they stay indefinitely in this camp which evokes colonial labour and from which there is no escape (Carrin, 1993). Even the idea of becoming a *bonga* is forgotten. Still, as the stock of human beings is limited, the inmates are forced to build new human beings out of the stock of bones of the deceased. Time has no place in this process as nobody seems to know who decides about new births. This seems to be an innovation in Santal eschatology, which generally assert that Thakur, the Hinduised god is granting every individual a determined span of life. Thakur's intervention here represents a Hindu strategy to impinge in Santal affairs, and Santals sometimes say that Thakur has invented death and boundaries, as he is also held responsible for the power of zamindars who have harassed the Santals. Before the coming of Thakur there was a golden age, when death and boundaries did not exist, say my informants. Thakur - whose name after all also means landlord - evokes the colonial time where Santals had to work for the Sahibs and their Hindu intermediaries. Thakur is also connected with Kali yuga which for the Santals means the time of being in debt (*rin*)[16] and of being subjected to forced labour as they get dispossessed of their lands. For all these reasons, Hana Puri is associated with a time of servitude. In some other stories, Jom Raja a Santal version of the Hindu god Yama appears with his terrible messengers; The punition of Jom Raja is sometimes justified but does not imply the concept of *Karma*. When a witch or a thief has committed a bad action he receives retribution for it later, but the idea of several lives (*karma*) is not generally implied.

---

14. The Santals do not have megaliths like the Mundas or the Hos. Traditions seem to imply that they used to bury their dead under slab-stones in a remote past. The chest of the elder son is called "maran buru" big stone, a metaphor which also alludes to the name of the creation god Maran Buru.
15. Hana Puri is located "beyond the human regard," *parom n'el.*
16. Rin means a long term debt which implies the payment of a high interest. Panca is a short-time loan taken on grain which does not implies a big interest.

When Time and Space Get Entangled

The slow effect of evil thought might also be attributed to the *bongas* or to *bad thoughts towards kin.* A typical example is the story of a woman who had tried to throw her husband in a well. When, in the evening, she sees him coming back she says to herself - "if it is him, if he is not dead, O Sin Bonga, I will die myself!" The husband understands, but keeps silent. Later on, as a grandfather he tells the story to his grandchildren. The woman, who is sitting under a cotton-tree, screams: *riri* ! as the possessed (*rum ko*) do; then she dies. The husband thinks: "by telling the story I made the oath (*kiria*) come true". Here, the woman takes an oath in front of Sin *Bonga*, the Sun god. To be effective the logic implies that Sin *Bonga* punishes, in due time, the woman who has herself asked for punishment.

The woman who takes the oath evokes the witch who sometimes takes vengeance on her kin. Witches, like malevolent *bongas*, are able to transcend time as well as space boundaries. For example, witches "are dancing at the five corners of the world" and invocations sung by the ojhas tell us that "while dancing witches have forgotten to die." Moreover witches and malevolent bongas are bestowed with supernatural qualities which are sometimes described as strange physical features: for example, witches and *bongas* have feet turned backward and both indulge in cannibalism. These anomalies are reflected in their sexual life as they may ape their victims but are unable to procreate. So transcending time allows witches and malevolent *bongas* to be excessive beings, which have no rest and roam from place to place (Carrin, 1996). Similarly, the magical land of Kamarupa which is located in Assam is associated with the magic powers of Kamru guru, the *ojhas*' guru. *Ojhas* who have a *bonga* lover sometimes visit that land to get magical powers before returning to the world. These magical powers include the ability to fly in the air and to restore the dead to life. But unlike witches and yogis, the witch-doctors may be able to use their powers in a positive way, becoming famous healers. Unlike witches they are not getting their powers through hate but by loving a female *bonga*. This last point conveys the idea that for Santals, the quest for power is often illusory unless it is used in a positive way. Transcending time and space, then, is sometimes dangerous. The yogi or even the ojha is invested with feminine sensitivity as he is bestowed with matted hair (*joto*) which is associated with fire and evokes the ascetic flame of the Hindu god Siva.

Thus mystical powers to transcend time and sometimes space are linked to physical characteristics which transform the *ojha*, the witch, the *bonga* or the *yogi*, giving them a fantastic appearance. In opposition to these mythical beings, ordinary men refer to their body to measure length as if the human body was the centre of a world which could be mastered.

This description of situations where time and space are entangled suggests that Santals try to place the inner time, projecting its different modalities in different countries, Hana Puri the land of the dead, the *bonga* world, the land of Kamru the magician. For the anthropologists these three worlds may be seen as different modalities of time. Hana Puri is viewed as a looking-glass world where the dead reap the results of their actions while the *bonga* world is a world which mirrors human life. From an eschatological point of view, Hana Puri is an intermediate world where souls of the departed souls rest before becoming bongas, thus implying that the world transforms itself into Hana Puri for the dead, then finally makes room for the *bonga* world. One is born into this world, dies to go to Hana Puri, and ultimately to the *bonga* world. But while ordinary men do not trespass these boundaries, witches, for example, live in this world and have a foot in the *bonga* world. In a similar way, *ojhas* have one foot in this world and another one in the bonga world or in the land of Kamru guru. If a succession of worlds is proposed to the ordinary man after his death, the individual might try to find his own way by trying to get supernatural powers.

From Autobiographical Time to Historical Time

I have argued that ordinary Santals evoke work and pleasure as an objective alternance but refer to an inner time which may be defined as the time for intimacy with the *bongas*. To long for a *bonga* lover means to "burn" time as everybody will become a *bonga* one day. Nevertheless, ordinary men talk of the good old days as the memory of their youth. For men these memories are associated with hunting in the forest, where they learnt how to behave towards elders and to feel both friendship and competition. For women this memory is linked with going with a friend to pluck flowers and to dig tubers in the forest. For both sexes, the forest is the place of pleasant memories, such as illicit love, before it is tinged with fear of *bongas*. When a Santal talks about an event in the family, he often tries to locate it by referring to a village event: "my mother fell ill on the eve of Sohrae, the cattle festival". On other occasions, my informants were talking of a particular family event but tried to relate it to a seasonal occupation.

Family events are encompassed by seasonal activities or rituals in a way which suggest that Santals are eager to dissolve the subjective dimension of the family by ritualising it. Does this process apply to history? The Santal sense of history is focused, first, on myths and, second, on the nineteenth century, rather as Sahlins (1985) notes for Hawaii. The transformations imposed by colonialism were different in nature and scale to the changes the Santals had experienced in the past. Thus, the introduction of individual ownership by the permanent settlement of 1770, was important since it resulted later in the alienation of adivasi lands and the migration of Santals to clear jungles or work as contract labour. Migration during the colonial period produced a split of their clanic system as they spread over a large territory to work in indigo factories, or in building railways. They were recruited to clear the jungles of the Rajmahal Hills and other regions around 1850. Displaced from their original homeland in Chotanagpur (Hazaribagh) the Santals were exposed to the exactions of the zamindars and money-lenders (*mahajuns*), a situation which produced the Santal rebellion of 1855. The rebellion, led by two charismatic leaders Sidhu and Kanhu had a strong ethnic overtone as the leaders promised to recover for the Santals their old kingdom of Champa, whose location was uncertain, but whose existence was proved by royal symbols, such as the umbrella, the turban, or the elephant granted to the leaders by Thakur - the foreign Hindu god - in their religious visions. Legitimating the chiefs Thakur symbolised the power of the dikus, the outsiders whose power was thought useful. The Santal insurrection as well as the Birsaïte movement of 1895, expressed agrarian and social claims but also contained a symbolic dimension. We see from Santal texts, written by witnesses of the Hul, that the chiefs were not exempts of critics. They were accused of being despotic and greedy, and of indulging in self-aggrandizement. A woman even stresses how Sidhu and Kanhu were prone to accuse of witchcraft the women who did not accept their sexual advances, a point that is also stressed by R. Guha (1983). Despite these criticisms and the lack of coherence in the chiefs' strategy, they did construct the Santal myth of a lost kingdom. More precisely, they managed to map out a dream of autonomy wrapped in the imagery of a Santal *raj*. To be effective, this myth must also offer another future, as Santals often take for granted that their history starts in 1855.

The time of the Hul marks a break in Santal thought as they suddenly feel the need to produce a historical consciousness, to be able to chase the *dikus* (outsiders) who exploit them but also to build a Santal identity. Reinventing Tradition, Santal narratives imagine how the degraded landscape was once a luxurious forest, sheltering a hidden kingdom.

Kali Yuga or the Time of Disenchantment

After the Santal rebellion (1855) various missionary societies established themselves in the present Santal Parganas and participated in the colonial penetration by developing infrastructures such as schools. Nevertheless, the Scandinavian missionaries who came to the Santal Parganas in 1867, wanted to create not just an independant Church among the Santals but a National one, considering the Santals a nation in the Herderian sense (Carrin and Tambs-Lyche, 1998). The missionaries had an impact on the different judicial reforms which were implemented in order to protect the Santals from outsiders. But the missionaries also collaborated with the colonial state to exercise pressure on the Santals, demanding the British, for example, to prohibit the sale of alcohol, or asking the police to arrest the Kherwars, who were Santals engaged in a Hinduised reform movement active from 1870. From the Santal point of view, the time since the rebellion is seen as Kali yuga, a time when the rule of the Sahibs prevails and make the dream of a Santal *raj* impossible. It is also a time when the forest is lost and the landscape becomes marked by industrialisation. The missionaries unconsciously pursue their own utopia when they invent Santalistan, a Santal territory where the centre is occupied by the Mission headquarters in Dumka and where Heathens surround the Christianised Nankar district. When the missionaries create an evangelical community in Assam around 1880, they create in fact a colony of the "old country" and name the newly founded Santal villages after themselves, Börresenpur, Carolinepur, etc. as explorers used to do when discovering unknown islands.

The orientalism of the Scandinavian missionaries was oriented towards the figure of the noble savage and probably contributed to reinforce Santal identity in mapping out Santalistan.[17] But when the

17. Santalistan the Santal country was isolated from the rest of the Jungle Mahals as for the missionaries the Santals were a "nation". See Carrin and Tambs-Lyche, 1998.

missionaries try to give the Santals a history (*Itihas*), we find the Christian text books conveying some notions of Greek and Latin antiquity to Santal children. Ancient Romc or Athens were seen as Heathen countries, opposed to the Holy Land as the teaching of history was oriented towards understanding of the Bible. This understanding was rooted in the Missionaries' own background, so Santal periodicals such as *Pera Hor* published information about Scandinavian pietism, centred around Hauge[18] and other religious figures of nineteenth century Scandinavia.

From the point of view of historical knowledge, the Santals were suddenly face to face with the contradictions of the Scandinavian Churches. Fortunately, the missionaries also wanted to know about Santal culture, probably to facilitate conversion and avoid a complete schism with the unconverted Santals. Introducing the roman script among the converts, as they needed the cooperation of the Santals to translate the Scriptures,[19] the missionaries induced native teachers to collect Santal traditions.

The idea of storing tribal knowledge aimed at transforming Santal Heathen beliefs and ritual into a folklore that children could learn at school. Thus the tribal gods would be desacralised and Santals would slowly forget the tribal deities (*bongas*) and embrace Christianity.

Space and Time Rediscovered: Ethnic Closure

The missionaries stimulated the Santals to "reinvent" their traditions by asking Santal teachers to collect stories, beliefs and customs in order to document their publication of Santal folklore.[20] Accepting this challenge, the Santal teachers, who were often converts, produced a huge collection of texts collected from many different informants ranking from school teachers to Heathen chiefs, or illiterate men and women. Still, these texts reflect a range of knowledge and emotions which escaped the missionary's attention. These narratives describe Santal traditions but at the same time, they deplore the blurred memory of a

18. Hans Nielsen Hauge was the main figure of the Norwegian religious revival in the early 19th century.
19. The translation of the Evangiles that Skrefsrud, the founder of the mission started around 1880 was only published by his successor P.O. Bodding in 1906 (Hodne, 1966: 225-227).
20. After Bodding's death, these manuscripts have been donated to the University Library in Oslo. See S. Soren (1999) for the index of the archives.

forgotten kingdom, or they express regret to see how the twelve original clans split into more than one hundred and sixty sub-clans when the Santals moved in order to clear jungles of the Jungle Mahals. Some texts deplore the alteration of kinship ties and the difficulty of finding good friends. Without entering into a description of change in Santal culture let us note that the narrators avoid stigmatisation and look at the diverse cultural influences which have pervaded the tribal culture as an "encounter". One text,which I feel is central, is called "why it is necessary to know about the belief of one's neighbours". Here, the Santal narrators distance themselves from the religion of their Hindu neighbours, seen as oppressors, and assert that understanding the gods of the *dikus* may help in fighting them. In other words, they try to understand the symbolical logic of Hindu power in order to resist the better to exploitation. The Santal ability to grasp the logic of their neighbours enables them to parody Hindu custom as well as missionary attachment to money.

The reinvention of tradition - as T. Ranger has shown for the Tswana (1993) - emphasises tribal culture but this does not imply that economics is unimportant in tribal life. On the contrary, the Santals criticise the zamindars and money-lenders in 1855 and 1861, and also reproach the missionaries for enriching themselves from taking school fees around 1880. But Christianity also allowed Santals to stress that any man may consider himself entitled to equal rights with any other. The Christian ethos here has merged with Santal egalitarian ideas such as the management of land in the traditional economy where the headman (*manjhi*) annually distributed fields from the commons to households of the village. Still, Christianity, was contradicting the authority of the clan (*paris*) to control employment within tribal society. By opening new links to employment, the Mission placed the Santals in a new market. The widening of social space through migrations, education and urbanisation produced a deepening of historical consciousness which ultimately led to the creation of the Jharkhand party in 1953. But with the development of a Santal elite, the egalitarian tribal society was divided on communal lines and notions of caste and class were creeping in.

The Making of a Jharkhandi

How should we characterize the Jharkand party's use of history? The common memory of a shared experience of exploitation has brought different Munda group to join the Jharkhand which functions today as a rallying symbol even if it has split into various parties proposing different strategies of resistance. Religious differences also contributed to split some of the pan-tribalist efforts which were emerging in the 1920s. Reformist movements such as the Saph Hor, who were very active in the Indian Freedom Movement of 1943-44 in some areas, as well as movements resulting from the creation of state boundaries - for example when Mayurbhanj became part of the State of Orissa[21] - created for the Santals as well as for the other Munda groups *specific histories influenced by local events and conflicts*. These local histories are influenced by ethnic closure but are also shaped by events in the different states. The socio-economic conditions of Santals may differ drastically from one State to another, explained, sometimes, by the different policies the states have implemented towards the adivasi. In Birbhum in 1981, for example, I noted that the ties of solidarity of Santals with Naxalite peasants and intellectuals in the sixtees were still reflected in the way they are seen today by the dominant population. Such a solidarity was more difficult to achieve in Mayurbhanj where I worked in 1978-80. Listening to stories about the splits in Jharkhand, one feels that factionalism often results from the pressure of local factors. Certainly, the creation of the Jharkhand Party was an important step to resist exploitation (Carrin, in *press*).

But how can a Jharkhandi mobilize history to sustain his fight, when the historical consciousness is rooted in belonging to a society affected by *memocide* as Sammoddar (1998) notes, studying the Judicial records of the Jungle Mahals. Over some twenty years, I have met Santals of different regions who were affected by this historical *memocide*. Working on reformist movements such as Sarna Dhrom in 1978-81 I felt that one major preoccupation of the Santals and Hos was to heal a wounded memory. In Santal village theatre, the plot of the play seemed often to be turned on something forgotten, whether a ritual or a local event, which needed to be revived.

Jharkhandi rituals incorporate significant events such as the murder of important Jharkhandis in their history. Ritualizing the event, they transform it into Historical knowledge. Jharkhandi commemorations

21. The Santals rebelled against the idea of being transfered to another state as it implied schooling in Oriya and other difficulties for them. The revolt was repressed but today, they still commemorate the death of their fellows which is seen as a symbol of "martyrdom".

tend to unify the local histories which divide the Munda groups, as V. Damodaran (*in press*) notes from attending a Jharkhandi Sarhul *puja* in Ranchi in 1992. She feels it has become an important urban event to be compared to the Muslim celebrations in towns like Lucknow.

Still, the party cannot alone weave a new meaningful time to transcend the cleavages of local histories. The Santals who started to reinvent their tradition in the nineteenth century show the importance of literacy and writing for producing historical consciousness. The development of literacy, and the advancement of *adivasi* literature and art may thus challenge the memocide that tribal societies, and subaltern groups more generally, have suffered. Adivasi leaders realise that they are the main assertive voices of a unified history of Jharkhand to harmonise the various conceptualisations of time.

When the anthropologist wants to describe other people's times, she may freeze time and reify it through ethnographic description. I have tried to show how an inner emotional experience of intimacy with the tribal deities was shaping Santal time, otherwise fixed by daily routine and agricultural seasons. But the Santals, who are good epicureans and like to experience the intensity of the present, also want to remember the good old days associated with the golden age, the forest, hunting and gathering, and solidarity with clan members, kin and friends. While mythic time shows the influence of Hindu elements such as the figure of Thakur epitomizing dominance and boundaries, historical time seems to have appeared in the nineteeth century. Even so, parallel times do exist in Santal tradition, as when myths tell us how the Santals refused Hindu influence. But as Santal narratives succeeded in reinventing tradition the Santals were able to think of strategies for survival.

REFERENCES

Archer, W. 1984. *Tribal Law and Justice. A Report on the Santal.* New Delhi: Concept Publishing Company.

Bayly, S. 1995. "Caste and Race in Colonial Ethnography," (pp. 165-218) in P. Robb (ed.), *The Concept of Race in South Asia.* Delhi: Oxford University Press.

Bodding, P.O. 1925-1929. Santal Folk Tales. 3 vols. Oslo: Aschehoug.

____. 1932-1936. *A Santal Dictionary.* 5 vols. Oslo: i kommisjon hos Jacob Dybwad.

Bloch, M. 1998. *How We Think They Think. Anthropological Approaches to Cognition, Memory and Literacy.* Colorado: Westview Press.

Carrin, M. 1993. "From Forest to Factory: The Santal Conception of Labour," (pp. 150-158) in P. Robb (ed.), *Dalit Movements*. New Delhi: Oxford.

____. 1996a. "Des récits tenus pour réels, les bonga, alibi du désir," *Traditions Orales dans le Monde Indien, Etudes réunies* par C.Champion, Purusartha, 18: 367-381.

____. 1996b. "Celles qui sont sorties du regard," Histoires de sorcières en pays santal, Autres mondes, numéro coordonné par G.Calame-Griaule *et al*., *Cahiers de Littérature Orale*, 39-40: 157-174.

____. 1997. *Enfants de la Déesse Dévotion et Prêtrise féminines au Bengale,* Paris Editions du CNRS et Maison des Sciences de l'Homme.

____. (in press). "A Tradition of Resistance: the Santal Case," paper presented at the seminar on Indigenous People: The Trajectory of a Concept, Uppsala, April 2000.

Carrin, M. and H. Tambs-Lyche. 1998. "Une église nationale pour les Santal: du romantisme scandinave à l'orthodoxie luthérienne," (en collaboration avec H.Tambs-Lyche)
Archives des Sciences Sociales des Religions, 103 "Le christianisme en Inde," études réunies par C.Clémentin-Ojha, juillet-septembre, 1998: 99-127.

Carrin-Bouez, M. 1985. "L'inégalité bien partagée ou l'impureté comme mythe chez les Santal," (pp. 71-104) *Cahiers de Littérature Orale*, 17, numéro coordonné par M. Carrin *Mythe et Histoire*.

____. 1986. *La fleur et l'os: symbolisme et rituel chez les Santal*. Paris: EHESS (Cahiers de l'Homme, 26).

Damodar, V. (in press). "History, Landscape and Indigeniety in Chotanagpur, 1850-1980," paper presented at the Conference on Indigenous Peoples: The Trajectory of a Concept. Uppsala, April 2000.

Guha, R. 1983. *Elementary Aspects of Peasant Insurgency in Colonial India*. Delhi: Oxford University Press.

Hodne, O. 1966. *L.O. Skrefsrud: Missionary and Social Reformer among the Santals of the Santal Parganas*. Oslo: Land og Kirke.

Ranger, T. 1993. "The Invention of Tradition Revisited: The Case of Colonial Africa," in T. Ranger and O. Vaughan (eds.), *Legitimacy and the State in Twentieth Century Africa*, Houndmills: Macmillan.

Sahlins, M. 1985. *Islands of History*. Chicago: Chicago University Press.

Samaddar, R. 1998. *Memory Identity Power Politics in the Jungle Mahals 1890-1950*. London: Sangam.

Soren, S. 1999. *Santalia. Catàlogue of Santali Manuscripts in Oslo Compiled by Santosh K. Soren*. Copenhagen: NIAS.

SIX

LAMENTING THE LOSS OF FOREST SONGS:
Songs of an "Assimilated" Tribes

MARGARET TRAWICK

We know that grief at the loss of a life is often streaked with rage.[1] We rage against a loved one lost to death for leaving us; we rage against ourselves for letting her go; we rage against those we believe killed our loved one; we may even rage against God for consigning His gentlest creatures to pain and death so wantonly and unfairly.

In the Christian tradition, rage against God is not encouraged. After all, what good could such rage do? God holds all the aces, and He makes all the rules. If we question God or rebel against Him, we follow that radical angel Satan, and off to the fiery pit we go, to suffer forever the heat of that pit and the darkness, the bodily torments of fever and hunger, the quarrelsome neighbours, the smell of stale urine, the rats. If we want to retire in the afterlife to a more salubrious place, our safest bet is to praise God for His love and mercy, assume that His actions are all for the best, and hope that He will reward our devotion by letting us join Him in heaven when we die.

In the Hindu tradition,[2] by contrast, rage against God has a venerable history, indeed it is one of many established (though by no means failsafe) means for gaining the power to overcome death and to break

1. Rosaldo, 1984.
2. Throughout this paper, I use the admittedly problematic words "Hindu" and "Hinduism" to refer to ideas, sentiments and activities associated with deities originating in South Asia.

down the walls separating God from oneself. Rage against God is a legitimate means of expressing one's passionate and consuming love (*bhakti*) for God. It is a means of showing God to himself as the dependent, amoral baby that he is. It is a means of showing God that he needs us more than we need him, and finally, it is a means of bringing God under the control of those of us who love him despite all his cruelty and imperfections.[3]

In Hindu myth there are some demons whose hatred of God is so obsessive, pure and intense that it has the same effect as desire-driven meditation upon His form: it dissolves the boundaries between the heart of God and the heart of the one attacking Him, and leads at last to these hearts' union. Behind the notion of fierce and angry love as a legitimate path to union with God lies a realisation on the part of Hindus that basic human emotions are powerful forces within our souls: so powerful that used rightly they may open any door for us, especially doors behind which other souls are hiding, God's own formidable soul not excluded. Desire and anger give us sentient creatures strength and courage. Without them we are merely objects; we submit to the fate imposed upon us however it may be. But armed with desire and anger we may change things; we may even pierce the well-fortified hearts of those who rule our world.

Expressions of commingled grief, desire and rage directed against more powerful others are not only found in ancient poetry; they are common still in the normal discourse of ordinary Hindu villagers. The more powerful others against whom villagers vent their rage may be gods or they may be people: the two are not mutually exclusive categories in Hindu thought. I have seen a young man on the death of his father furiously shatter the clay image of the family deity, the image embodying all the ancestral spirits, including the spirit of the father himself. The young man performed this act of destruction in grief at the death of the father he loved, and in rage that when the father's land was divided among the sons, he, the youngest son, got nothing. I have seen a farmer, whose tiny rain-dependent field of grain was withered by drought, curse the beautiful clear blue sky, curse also the successful large landholders of the village whose irrigated fields were flourishing, and cry out in a mixture of mockery, anger, desire and sorrow a plea to the goddess of rain: "Wife of my older brother, you bring my older brother your sweet

3. Shulman, 1993: 57-62.

body's water. Why won't you quench my thirst in the same way?" The curses and pleas were in a song the old man sang while watering his field by hand.

The wife of this old farmer — her name was Niilammaa — was a specialist in funeral laments. Niilammaa's name meant "blue (or dark) woman" after the dark goddess of the earth and rain her people worshipped. The laments that she and others sang were sometimes called niilappaadal "blue (or dark) songs". They were also, and more frequently, referred to as aayira paaddu, "crying songs," because the singers wept as they sang. Such songs, with every breath drawn through a sob, had a form that was easy to recognise; they could not be mistaken for anything but laments. However, these laments were not only sung at funerals, and their topic was not only death. A crying song could be performed whenever the singer felt grieved — in particular, whenever she felt wronged — and its topic could be any lamentable event in the singer's life. Often a crying song would create an equation between death and an event that would normally be thought of as death's antithesis. For instance, woman singers would often lament their marriage as though for them marriage was equal to death. They sang of their being cut off from the vine of their family prematurely, of the wasteful destruction of their fine rich bodies, of their sense that the sun was setting on their lives, of their feeling that they had reached the end of their road.

The parallels drawn in these women's laments between the auspicious and the inauspicious, between death and life, were more than responses to death. They were also questions, challenges thrown at life. Overtly addressed to the dead and departed ("mother who bore me, the distant land you have gone to is beyond my searching . . . ") they were covertly addressed to the living close at hand. There was anger in them, anger simultaneously at the law of God and at the law of men, for in the Hindu world, these two laws are one. Thus in one lament, Yama the god of death was called oorakaaratteevam, the "biased god," because he unfairly cut some off from life before they had reached fulfilment, while letting others survive. The temple of Paramasivam (the great god Siva) was said in another lament to be, for the singer, like the temple of Yama, the god of death. Paramasivam is one of the great and high Hindu gods; he is purity, fertility and eroticism all rolled into one: his very name means "the most auspicious". But for the singer of this lament, this most high god was a god of death, because the singer, being a member of an untouchable caste, was excluded from the precincts of his temple. He too was a biased god, an unfair one. Comparing him with Yama, the singer challenged Siva, and brought him down.

Parallels were likewise drawn in laments between the beginning of life and its end. Niilammaa sang a lullaby in the form of a lament, showing that even the birth of a healthy beloved boy baby could be a cause for grief, if because of his caste the baby was destined all his life to be denied access to the good that was rightfully his.

In Tamil Nadu women of untouchable castes were specialists in lament for two reasons. First, it was the socially prescribed role of untouchable castes, their "traditional occupation," precisely to deal with lamentable aspects of life, especially death, to keep the pollution of death and related bad things from tainting higher caste people. Niilamma's caste, the Paraiyars, got their name from the parai, the skin drum they were required to beat during funeral processions, to announce death's presence. Paraiyars were also the ones to dispense with the carcasses of cattle and to prepare the corpses of human beings for burial. It made sense, therefore, for them also to be the singers of death.

The second reason that untouchable women were and are good at singing laments is just that in their own lives they have much to lament about, being not only female, but also for the most part poor, and stationed at the bottom of the caste system, where they bear the weight of considerable oppression and abuse. They are used to seeing the bad side of things and it makes sense for them to sing of it and to cry out against it. What is interesting and encouraging from the point of view of a democratically inclined outsider. Is that these singers are evidently not expected to pretty things up; they are not expected to pretend that their life is a happy one and that they are contented with it. At the same time they are not expected to pretend that they themselves are ugly or foolish or evil, so that they deserve their unhappy fate. They pour their anger at the world into their laments at the same time as they build their sense of self-esteem from within them. Thus, much of the content of crying songs consists in a kind of self-ornamentation. The singer of a lament addresses her song plaintively to another, to her departed mother, for instance, but always she sings of herself. It is her own loss, her own fate she bemoans, and not the fate of another. "I am ripe fruit, mother," she sings, "I've been left in the sun to dry. I am unbeaten gold that they have beaten and carried away". Though she does not represent her situation as pleasing, the singer works hard to make her song fine poetry, to make it beautiful. Through the artistry of her anger, she keeps her sense of herself whole and intact.

I have written about Tamil Paraiyar women's laments extensively in another paper,[4] so I will say no more about them here. I give this summary description of them because they form an important part of the context of what is to follow. I hope they will make this story more comprehensible, and my own argument more credible.

In the place where I worked,[5] Paraiyars were the most numerous and powerful of the untouchable castes. Though most of them were landless laborers, they had organised themselves politically, had achieved some major successes in improving their economic situation, and had high hopes for their children's future. Bodily they were healthy and strong. Other low castes were not so fortunate. For instance, there was the group of people called Villis, "bowmen," or Kaaddukkaaranka, "people of the forest/wasteland" (the term kaadu carries both meanings). In my village there was just one family of them, camped out across the pond from the village school. They were called bowmen and people of the wasteland because, my landowning host told me, they had once been hunters living in the forest. Now, however, they carried no bows. Nor did they work in the fields — perhaps the Paraiyars kept them away; I never learned. Instead, they performed a number of other services for their patrons, the village landholders. They acted as night watchmen for the orchards; they gathered wild honey; they captured and dispensed with poisonous snakes; they captured rats infesting the fields and houses and ate them.

My host's wife's sister said that the Villis of this place were dirty compared to the Villis of her home village back in the mountains, and indeed to me also they looked ragged, sick and unhappy. They were by far the poorest people in this village full of poor people.

A certain ghostly-romantic mystique was attached to the Villis. They had a secret potion, my host told me, which they rubbed on their hands when they went to catch a poisonous snake; it would keep the snake from biting. The snakes they caught lived only in taaram flowers (a big white flower with a strong scent and spiky leaves — a favorite of the goddess in her form as a lone and angry woman). These snakes were the cobra (nallappaampu) and the Russell's viper (viriyampaampu). The

4. Trawick [Egnor], 1986.

5. The fieldwork upon which this essay is based was done in a village of Tamil Nadu, near the town of Chingleput, in 1980.

former was always female and the latter always male, my host believed (who was not a close observer of poisonous snakes), and when they mated they twined in a helix upwards. Anyone who watched them mating would not escape alive. But Villis had a certain power over them, my host said. Also Villis knew how to gather wild honey without being stung. They were suited to be guardians of the orchards because demons haunted the orchards at night and no one else was willing to go there then. The Villis were also not monogamous, my host told me, smiling. The head of the family of Villis in this village was an eighty-year-old woman who was on her sixth or seventh husband. He was about thirty or forty. As for the food the Villis consumed, well . . . their diet was their own choice, my host said.

I stored all this information away, planning to go talk with the Villis themselves sometime. Then one day a granddaughter of Niilammaa's, a young woman of about sixteen, came up to me and asked me if I would like to hear a "Villi song". I said sure. She began a song of a kind I had never heard before. The words were simple: "Want kaara flowers, Kanniyammaa? Want kaara fruits, Kanniyammaa?"- (The kaara vine grows in uncultivated areas. Kanniyammaa is the name of the village goddess.) Whereas most of the Tamil songs I had heard had a moderate or slow tempo, and were sung (when they were done by women) in a thin childish soprano, this song had a fast, difficult syncopated rhythm, and was delivered in a powerful percussive alto that struck me as almost Jazzy. I liked it, but at the end of a few lines the singer ran out of breath, burst into giggles, and ran away. That afternoon I went to the Villi camp to find out more about their songs.

They would sing only at night. The forty-year-old man whose name was Little Boy needed a fire over which to tune his drum. All of the Villis were there around the fire — about eight of them, including the children. It was the rainy season; they all had coughs. Little Boy would sing as he played his drum. It was an unnatural situation for them. I was there, and so was my host, their patron, the person upon whose good will their living depended. They were nervous and uncomfortable. What did we want?

It's okay, I said. Whatever you feel like doing is fine. Try to pretend we're not here. (Children giggle. Adults quickly hush them up.) Or maybe I could come another night; there's no hurry, I said. No, said one of the women. You're here now. It just takes us time to warm up. Little Boy started, beating his drum slowly, singing quietly, words that I couldn't hear, sentence fragments, groans, pauses, sniffs, chuckles, occasional spoken narrative. The steady drumbeat stopped, then started again, a beat at a time. The old woman told him, "Lift it up and sing it". She started to sing herself. He picked up the tune and sang it loudly. His song drifted back into moans. The old woman tried to help again, giving him a tune. He shouted the tune then paused. She sang some more. He picked it up and then dropped off, singing "Tell me how it goes, woman," as though this were part of the song. This went on for a while. They paused. "Do you know any other songs? Songs about Kanniyamma?" I asked, trying to be helpful. The old woman tried to teach Little Boy some more; they alternated back and forth. "Would you like to rest a bit?" I asked, feeling embarrassed for them. They passed the songs and the conversation around among themselves. "Let's sing all the songs we don't know," one of the women suggested. "I'll sing," said another. "No," said the first. "Okay, go ahead". She began a song about the Chief Minister of Tamil Nadu. "No, not that," said Little Boy, "She knows all about that. Kids, you sing". "The kids don't know any songs". "Try singing about Kanniyammaa," I suggested again, "about kaara flowers and kaara fruits".

"What is this kaara flower kaara fruit stuff?" one asked. "We don't know any songs like that". "The one about the onan vine, that's about Kanniyammaa," said another. "Okay, do that." She began again, and Little Boy picked up the rhythm with his drum. It was the same fast, syncopated rhythm that I had first heard from Niilamaa's granddaughter. This singer's voice was shrill and harsh, but she kept the beat and her words were clear: Friends playing ball, girlfriends playing ball, to my forest who has come running? Find an onan vine, friends playing ball, girlfriends playing ball. Tie up his hands and feet, girls. Make him stand — stop him. Here was an interesting song. Was it the goddess Kanniyammaa speaking? Was she a goddess of the forest? The village goddess named Kanniyammaa had no connection that I knew of with forests. Was this a different Kanniyammaa? Was there some old custom in which girls would chase boys through the forest and capture them and tie them up with vines and torment them in some delightful fashion? The name Kanniyammaa means virgin-woman. I thought of Diana. Romantic sylvan images frolicked through my mind.

As soon as the song was over, Little Boy said, "Now let the kids sing". One child volunteered to sing, started, then changed her mind. I praised the song about the vine that had just been performed and asked the singer to do more. Little Boy was nonplussed. "Let this woman sing her woman's songs," he said. For the rest of the evening, "this woman" did most of the rest of the singing. I learned a little about her during that time, mainly through her songs and her delivery of them, and I learned a little about her thoughts. I believe that she probably composed some of the songs she sang, as many of the people in this village composed their own songs. Each singer that I knew in the village there had a unique repertoire, and a few songs that were uniquely her own. Songs were often very personal in nature, that is, they expressed the feelings of the singer about her own life and her relations with others. A number of communities in South India have well-developed traditions of composing personal songs to comment upon emotionally significant events in the singers' lives. Among the Toda, for instance, every man, woman and child used to compose such songs. Emeneau (1970) recorded thousands of them. Thus I believe that Little Boy was telling me the truth when I asked him about the origin of the songs that were sung to me by the Villis that night, and he replied very emphatically, "We ourselves! We ourselves created them all!"

The main singer's name, it turned out, was Kanniyammaa, after the goddess. It was hard for me to guess her age. They said she was in her twenties, but she looked older. She was quite thin. Her style of singing was fast, intense, and loud and her voice was like a steel wire pulled very tight. I imagine it took a great output of energy to sing the way she did. After the third song she asked for me to turn off the tape recorder and wait a while until she caught her breath. One of the other women said, "She isn't well, so she sings haltingly. Her breath runs out". One of the children said quietly, "Blood will come". Often throughout the night, Kanniyammaa would finish a song with a gasp, and sometimes a curse. It did not occur to me to make her stop singing, since I liked her songs so much. Only a few days later did my host explain to me that Kanniyamma really was very sick; she had tuberculosis. The songs that Kanniyammaa sang for me were basically of two types. First, there were the songs she sang about the goddess Kanniyammaa, and about other, unnamed goddesses and young women, possibly all of them forms of this one goddess, goddess of the forest and of virgins. Then there were songs of social commentary, songs about the changing world. Most of the songs of this latter type were sad, some of them deeply so, some of them also very clearly angry. Taken as a whole, the corpus of songs left to us by Kanniyammaa the woman portrays the death of Kanniyammaa the goddess, and laments this death — the death of the forest, the death of a better form of womanhood, the death of a way of life. At the same time it tells of the birth of a new way of life and new values, values the singer does not like and cannot fully accept. Among the songs concerning Kanniyammaa the goddess, a number of them simply describe images and acts associated with her, images and acts of a world that no longer is. The first song Kanniyammaa sang is a song of this type. Maybe sometime in the past girls played ball in the woods and attacked men who came there and tied them up with vines, but this does not happen anymore.

Other songs in Kanniyammaa's corpus reveal other details of this world where the virgin-goddess reigned (henceforth songs will be numbered according to the order in which they were performed):

2.

On the mountain the rain falls;
 the water from the mountain runs down.
At the edge of the river waits a virgin girl.
 For the flower garden's watchman to pick a flower,
how many days will it take?
 A plantain tree is in the wagon,
in the girl's hair is a taaram flower.
 He is coming into the scent of the flower, mother.
He will give a gift.

Until very recently, many lower castes in South India paid brideprice at weddings. Now, in imitation of higher castes, who in turn imitate North Indian trends, lower castes are paying dowry, a custom which devalues women (you have to pay the other family to take your girl) and which many people abhor, though they feel compelled to adopt it. The song above is about the older custom, and about the sexual power of a young girl, which by itself is enough to attract a suitor. Having been drawn into "the scent of the flower," he will pay a price in order to marry its wearer. The plantain tree in the wagon is being taken to build a wedding platform (they make them out of these trees). The taaram flower appears in many other women's songs, narratives, and ceremonies in South India. This is the flower said to harbor poisonous snakes, the one signifying lone, independent and aggressive femininity. My host told me that "only Villis" use this flower at weddings, at the weddings of higher caste people, it is forbidden.

Kanniyamma's songs, like many other Tamil songs, are spare and evocative. When there is a story to be told, they do not tell the whole of it, but depend upon a few key images to make the listener feel their meaning. As in the séance songs described by Feld (1982), the indirection of Tamil songs, especially laments, is in itself a powerful emotional device — suggesting but not stating the truth, it gives the feeling of something hidden, something just out of reach, something tormentingly present in memory but unable to be touched, like the spirit of a dead kinsman, or a way of life lost. I have argued elsewhere (Egnor, 1986) that indirection also protects the singer of critical messages against vengeful abuse. If her message is questioned, she may always say, I didn't mean that.

Paronomasia has similar uses. Several singers in Kanniyammaa's village started songs about secret sexual liaisons with the word eerinaa which means both "if the lake" and "if one mounted". Such songs would then go on to celebrate (or bemoan) a lakeside tryst in which the woman "mounted" the man's "tree". Kanniyammaa started one of her songs in this way, but this song is not about a tryst. Rather it is about a goddess of serpents living in an anthill at the edge of a village called "Woman Mounted". In this song, it is suggested that there is a place where a woman is on top. Recall that Kanniyammaa's people, the Villis, now live as the village snake catchers. Poisonous snakes are a sacred animal for many people in India; their association with anthills and with female divinity is ancient and well known.

7.

Say lake, the mounted lake bank,
        woman mounted, at the edge of Woman Mounted
a great tree, mother, at the great tree's base,
        an anthill whose flesh is swollen. Like the anthill,
the king of serpents, a woman king,
        the woman king of serpents has
a great snake as her protector, so they say.
        Say lake, the mounted lake bank,
woman mounted, at the edge of Woman Mounted,
        an anthill whose flesh is swollen. Like the anthill,
the king of serpents,
        a woman king.

None of the songs given above can be taken, by itself, as a lament. Each of them describes an event or a condition upon which the singer offers no comment but which we may safely assume she does not find lamentable. I would argue here, however, that taken as a whole, Kanniyammaa's performance of that evening was indeed a lament, albeit a loosely constructed one, of which each individual song, including each of the three above, formed a part.

In the tightly constructed Paraiyar laments that I recorded in Kanniyammaa's village, a number of conventions were common. One very commonly employed convention was to contrast a happy condition of the past with a sorrowful condition of the present. For instance,

> I was born in a conch shell, o mother who bore me,
>   and I ruled the ocean.
> He took my conch shell, mother,
>   and made me a beggar.

Or again,

> For me, clumps and clumps of eggplants,
>   o older sister born with me,
> they fruit for us on the vine.
>   With no one to hold and embrace us,
> we rot on the vine, mother.

A related convention in Paraiyar laments consisted in the listing of a series of diminishing conditions, representing or paralleling the diminishment of the singer's own state. For instance,

> On top of a ten-story house …
>   We were paddy drying in the sun …
> On top of an eight-story house …
>   We were sesame drying in the sun …

Or again,

> For me, four hundred cars would come …
>   They would set out a four-legged chair for me …
> For me three hundred cars would come …
>   They would set out a three-legged stool for me …

Or again,
I made feed for the elephant ...
    And the elephant-keeper struck me with a stone ...
I made feed for the horse ...
    And the horseman threw stones ...

Now let us consider the eighth and ninth songs in Kanniyammaa's performance, which make use of both of these conventions:

8.

Lifting one foot and dancing, [repeat]
    what will Lord Murugan do? [repeat 3 times]
In one hand, a holy skull,
    in one hand, an angry fire, they say. [repeat 3 times]
What will Lord Murugan do? [repeat 3 times]
    Lifting one foot, what dance will he do?
In one hand, a drum and an ankle bracelet,
    in one hand, a holy skull, they say.
In one hand, an ankle bracelet,
    in one hand, a skull, they say.

Lord Murugan is a charming young boy, god of war and of masculine beauty. His tokens are the spear and the peacock. In this song, he assumes the characteristics of his father, Lord Siva, the dancer, in the latter's form as destroyer of the universe. In contrast with songs sung earlier in the performance about the domain of Kanniyammaa, songs describing happy states of the past, this song about the actions of Siva-Murugan suggests that destruction of the world is near at hand.

9.

Could it be a crow that's calling, girl,
    in my two forests?
Could it be Maayammaa's doing, girl?
    Maayammaa goes there.
The gods dance on the south street.

Could it be a blackbird calling, girl,
in my two forests?
Could it be Maayaa's doing, girl?
Maayamma goes there.
The gods dance on the south street.

Could it be a sparrow calling, girl,
in my two forests?
Could it be Maayaa's doing, girl?
Mayammaaa goes there.
The gods dance on the south street.

I offer here some observations which may help to explain this deceptively simple song. First, there is an echo of the line in Song #1, " . . . Who has come running to my forest, girlfriends?" But the echo is ominous. The crow is an inauspicious bird, a carrion-eater, bird of hunger, winter and death (Trawick, 1990).

Second, south is the direction of cremation grounds, of ghosts, and of the temple of Yama, god of death. For that reason, "good" gods and their temples are not usually situated on the south side of a village or a town. But in this song, the gods are dancing on that side, and we have just had a song about Murugan's performing a dance of destruction. The direction south is often mentioned in Tamil laments, precisely because of its association with death.

Third, the crow, the blackbird, and the sparrow form a series of descending (successively smaller) items, similar to the descending series' found in laments. Crows are sometimes mentioned in Paraiyar laments, as in the line, "Not even a female crow will eat what I cook". The blackbird and the sparrow are similarly considered birds of no account.

Fourth, Maayaa can mean darkness, magic, or illusion. Maayamma is also a name of the dark goddess after whom many low caste people name their daughters (other names for her are Niilammaa and Karuppaayi; all three names translate roughly as "dark woman").

I cannot say what the "basic meaning" of this song is, if indeed it has one. It forms a contrast, or an answer, to some of the songs surrounding it. Darkness, decline, and death in the forest of the goddess are surely suggested. It could also be that the singer is making derogatory reference to the color of her own face and the sound of her own song. Perhaps she does feel like just a crow cawing in the woods. Perhaps through self-derision she protects herself. The twelfth song in Kanniyammaa's presentation is addressed to a powerful woman of a different kind. She is not adorned with flowers, she is adorned with jewels. All the creatures are drawn to her. The direction she is associated with is the West. The tune addressed to her is bright and dancing, but the message is ambiguous:

12.

There a chaste woman is singing hymns.
She presses down on the cause sin
[Paava kaaranam patittiraal]
There a chaste woman is singing hymns.
She presses down on the cause of sin..
Pearls and great jewels and workmanship glitter.
Pearls and great jewels and workmanship glitter.
When one sees you, desire takes hold.
When one sees you, desire takes hold.
All the species of water animals
are gathered in crowds and crowds,
are leaning in armies and armies.
When they see you, desire takes hold.
When they see you, desire takes hold.
All the species of forest animals
are leaning in crowds and crowds,
are leaning in armies and armies and armies.
When they see you, desire takes hold.
When they see you, desire takes hold.
When one sees the West, it seems very far away.
It comes bearing thunder and lightning.
When one sees the West, it seems very far away.
It comes bearing thunder and lightning.
When one sees you . . .

Here the song suddenly ended. "Your breath?" I asked. "Her breath," said Little Boy quietly.

The last song that Kanniyammaa sang about young girls and flowers seems to me to be self-explanatory:

15.

The roses and jasmine
bought just yesterday
have faded in the box.
To gather them up
in their hair and wear them
are no divine young girls,
not a single one to be found.

I have said above that Kanniyammaa sang two kinds of songs, the first kind having to do with goddesses and young girls and women, the second kind having to do with changes in the world. It should be clear at this point that songs of the first kind are not really separate from songs of the second kind. The songs about goddesses and womanhood seem to be songs of longing, anxiety, desire, doubt and confusion — all these and other feelings consequent upon change. With the changes in the world, something is dying. This death is signalled by the war gods' dance, the crow's call, the flowers fading. What is dying is the kind of being that the singer is named for, her "identity" we would call it, her way of life, her self. It seems clear that there is grief and mourning in her songs for this loss. I have also said above that it is part of the ordinary discourse of Hindu villagers to express rage against more powerful others. A more old-fashioned way of putting this would be to say that such expressions of rage are part of tradition. In many Tamil villages, including the one I worked in, there was and is a tradition of lower caste women going from house to house during certain festival times and singing songs before the homes of the wealthy, which songs were intended both to flatter and to shame the wealthy into treating their wards with more respect and paying them better. No punches are pulled in these songs. Here is an example from colonial days:

The white man sits idly on his porch;
he doesn't know any Tamil;
he has a mistress in every corner.
Piss into his pot, girl;
pour it into his rosy red mouth;
clap your hands, girls,
clap your hands.

Other songs are more subtle but very astute and stinging; there are quite a few about state-level politics and about money. I see this tradition of critical song-delivery in Tamil villages as being similar in some ways to the Holi festival in north India. During this festival, for one day, the oppressed are able to get back at their oppressors — sweeper women, for instance, are permitted to dump buckets of buffalo urine on the heads of their landlords and to beat them with cudgels. Ethnographers portray the Holi festival as a day of communitas and light-hearted camaraderie among people ordinarily separated by hard social boundaries, but the violence that occurs on that day strikes me as something a bit other than light-hearted; or rather, the sweepers' hearts may be lightened in the Ilongot sense (Rosaldo, 1984) by thrashing their landlords, but I doubt that they carry out their revenge in what we would call a light-hearted manner.

I would suggest here that Tamil village women get their revenge and so lighten their hearts not through the strength of their arms but through the strength of their songs. And just as north Indian sweeper women reportedly spend weeks in training, building up their biceps for the day when they will get to use them against the people they hate, so Tamil women pour much creative energy into the composition and delivery of their biting verbal art.

Now Kanniyammaa happened to be one who was very good at composing and delivering this kind of song. The night she performed before me, she sang three of them in a row, followed by a fourth towards the end of her performance. At first she was hesitant. Neither she nor anyone else there was sure "what I wanted". She sang her first songs, none of them critical except in that they portrayed with longing a lost past to which the present compared unfavorably. Then she stopped for breath. There were long uncomfortable minutes during which more discussion occurred on the topic of what there was left to sing, and a few of the other adults began singing weakly then tapered off. Then without warning Kanniyammaa's voice stabbed the darkness and the others fell instantly silent. This happened again and again throughout the evening. Each song came out suddenly, fully formed, as though Kanniyammaa was drawing it all together inside her mind, gathering tension, before letting it go. She sang with a feverish energy, loudly and powerfully, while Little Boy followed her beat with his drum.

Of her three critical songs, the words of the first were least pointed, the words of the second were more so, and the words of the third were sharp and direct. The first song began with the names of the Chief Minister of Tamil Nadu, who was also a popular movie star, and of this movie star's comic sidekick:

4.

M.G.R. is acting,
    Baalayyaa is laughing
all the little children
    are going to school.
When they go to school, lady,
    please teach their lessons well.
All the big children
    are in the first grade.
When they're in the first grade, sir,
    please teach their lessons well.

The irony of this song lies in the fact that the Villis were camped across the pond from the village school, where they could see all the children coming and going, but they were far too poor to send their own children there. Tamil people of all walks of life nowadays see schooling as the one usable ticket to a secure life. For those who own no property, schooling is especially precious. The reference to the Chief Minister M.G. Ramachandran is perhaps to point out his role in social reform including attempts to institute universal childhood education. The Villis can observe such reforms, but are not assisted by them.

5.

Make a kolam, lady, make a kolam out of rice.
    Make a kolam, lady, hide this kolam, lady.
Who made this one here?
    Saccakkaa made this one here.
Make a kolam, lady.
    Who made this one here?
Saccakkaa made this one here.
    Hide the kolam, lady; sprinkle water, lady.
Make a kolam, lady; make a kolam out of millet.
    Who made this one here?
Rukmani made this one here.
    Make a kolam, lady. Hide this kolam, lady.

Little Boy started this song, then Kanniyammaa took over. Her voice was higher, louder and slириller than before, almost a shriek, and she sang the song frantically and breathlessly. The words of the song, by contrast, seem empty and mechanical. A kolam is a design drawn by high-caste women on the thresholds of their houses every morning, to indicate that their household is in an auspicious condition. Usually they make the kolam out of chalk powder, but sometimes, they make it out of rice flour. The next morning, they erase the kolam of the day before by sweeping it away and sprinkling water over the spot. The designs can be quite beautiful and ornate, especially on holy days such as Pongal (celebrating the turning of the sun). When there has been a recent death in the house, no kolam is drawn on the threshold.

One can only guess whether there is some kind of hidden meaning in this song. The contrast between the rich and the poor is suggested by the move in the song from rice flour to millet flour. Rice is much preferred to millet, and here is another example of the movement from good to not-so good, from greater to lesser, so common in the songs that I collected.

The song shows a kind of frantic rush to make one kolam and hide another. It also suggests competition between ladies of different households over who can make the best kolam. I think the song may be a comment upon respectable ladies' concern with keeping up appearances, to the extent of carefully hiding unlovely events that may be going on inside the household. This practice may also be called "traditional" in the sense that it has been going on for a long time, and also in the sense that respectable people are expected to do it. There is a Tamil saying, "Every house has its threshold," which was explained to me at another time in another town by a respectable (and very kind and good) woman that every household has secrets it must keep from the outside world. Of course, the Villis in Kanniyamma's and my host's village did not even have a house, much less could they afford to use rice flour or millet flour (both food substances) to decorate their non-existent thresholds. They lived in the open, and scarcely could afford clothing enough to hide (or decorate) their own bodies.

The song that followed strengthened my feeling that Kanniyammaa was pointing, through her songs, to contrasts between the poor and the well-to-do, and to the sometimes cruel hypocrisy of the latter.

6.

Cousin, cousin, what town is this?
    Wind-like cousin, it's Chingleput.
Cousin, cousin, what do they dish out here?
    Wind-like cousin, they dish out big rats.
Cousin, cousin, what town is this?
    Wind-like cousin, Pukkatturai Reddiars.
Cousin, cousin, what do they dish out?
    Wind-like cousin, they dish out big rats.

This song was not sung but rather screamed out. Kanniyammaa finished in exhaustion and said to me, "Mother, stop the tape-recorder," which I did. Chingleput is the name of the district in which we lived; Pukkatturai is the name of the village; Reddiars are the dominant caste in the village, the caste to which my host and his family belonged. This song was unambiguously aimed at them.

My host at first tried to deflect the song's message. He could not believe that Kanniyammaa had said of his family, "They dish out big rats (peruccaali pooduvaanka)". He thought she must have said, "They serve nice gifts (paricu alli pooduvaamka)". But my own ears told me that Kanniyamaa had definitely said the word for "big rat," not the words for "serving gifts". It was all clearly recorded on the cassette, which we listened to repeatedly. Still my host insisted that his interpretation must be right, until his wife's sister reminded him (while I looked on) that just a few days before, the Villis had been called to the house to capture a rat that lived there. Their pay had been the body of the rat itself — as usual.

My host flinched at this divulgence. It was a terrible insult to suggest that this purity-conscious vegetarian family, that prided itself on its generosity, "served" its visitors rats to eat. The stinging part was, it was true. Moreover the song made it clear that the Villis did not choose to eat rats. The fact was that they had no choice.

As times change, so do Indian castes, adjusting to new conditions. Like other forms of life, castes work with what they have, taking specialisations developed for the performance of outmoded functions, and using them to adapt to new times and to create new niches for themselves. Some hit upon success. Brahmans, the traditional literati, become lawyers and civil servants. Mercantile castes ride the winds of the world economy. Leatherworkers build shoe factories; toddy-tappers establish chains of liquor stores; masons unionise.

But in this changed world what could the Villis do, who once had been hunter-gatherers? Now incorporated into the village economy, their foraging skills were put to use of a sort. Instead of hunting forest animals, now they hunted vermin.

Urban and agrarian foraging is a vital activity in modern South India. For many people with little money, wild foods form an important dietary supplement. Niilammaa and her family, for instance, ate crabs and snails from the fields. The high castes, who ranked everybody minutely according to what foods they would eat, despised people who ate such things as crabs and snails, but then, crab meat is a healthy food and not really so bad tasting. Rat meat, however, is a different matter. Villis themselves described it as foul and tough; nobody else that I knew in the village-would touch it. Further, rats carry many diseases harmful to humans. As catchers and eaters of rats, Villis had been given a niche in the agrarian environment, but they knew they were not thriving on it. If things failed to change, the one family of Villis in Pukkatturai was likely to perish bodily, as it had already perished culturally. Kanniyammaa's song seemed to be trying to communicate this point.

The term of address used in the song above is macci, which means female crosscousin. The song is in the form of a question-and-answer dialogue. The questions all begin macci macci, "cousin cousin". The answers all begin kaattaam macci, "wind-like cousin," or "cousin whose form is wind". When we listened to the tape later, I asked my host what this term "wind-like cousin" might mean. Hc said he did not know. A clue, however, lies in a comment that one of the Villi women made after Kanniyammaa began singing. It would be good if the singer's macci were here, the woman said, because that macci was the one who knew best how to sing. But then, she added, that macci was dead and gone (cettuppoccee).

Now in Tamil Nadu, the spirits of the dead, as well as the possessing spirits of some deities, are often said to take the form of wind. They wander about like the wind, restlessly and erratically, longing for a stable home, a flesh-and-blood body in which to find shelter, comfort and peace. The spirit of a dead person is thought to have the form of wind because it is the breath or wind (uyir, muccu) whose presence signals the presence of life in a body, and whose absence means that life is gone. My guess, then, is that the call kaattaam macci addresses the singer's dead cross-cousin, whose only voice now is the voice of the wind, and the song incorporating this term is an internalised dialogue between the singer herself and the spirit of this cousin. The spirit is asking the singer where she is and what there is to eat and the singer is answering. Perhaps there is a suggestion, in the pointed reference to rats, of a link between the "serving" of this food and the cousin's death. Perhaps, also, there is some intentional irony in Kanniyammaa's calling her dead cousin "wind," as though to comment upon the relation between wind and life, and the shortness of life that her own shortness of wind so acutely forebodes.

Song # 12, translated above, was the fourth critical song that Kanniyammaa sang that night. The song was addressed to me. I know this because Little Boy said so, quietly but audibly, after the song was over. Kanyamma sang this one, also, after some hesitation. As before, there was a lull, and some conversation back and forth on the matter of what to sing next. Then my host, who by that time had taken on (at least externally) some of my sympathetic spirit, and who had a fairly clear idea of what I would find interesting, said to Kanniyammaa, "Sing some more about what goes on in this village. Sing about the people in the village. You know the way you sang about Reddiars? Sing some more of those kinds of songs". Kanniyamma paused, then the song burst out of her fully armed.

On the surface, the song appears to be mostly ingratiating flattery, but in fact it embarrassed me mightily, for the woman described in the song was definitely not me or not as I saw myself, anyway. For I was neither beautiful nor bejewelled, I always tied my sari wrong, and was usually sweaty, dusty, and tired. I was not religious, and could not bring myself to pretend to be so. Although I wore no jewelry, and back home was just a lowly untenured assistant professor, I had considerably more money than the richest man in the village, which also a cause of embarrassment to me. I tried to be generous to the poor, but my relationship to "sin" and its "cause" (paavakkaaranam) was quite ambiguous. Just as thunder and lightning coming from the far away West must have been perceived as fearsomely powerful, and capable of boding great good or great ill, so perhaps, to my chagrin, I was perceived, although I just wanted to be a normal person there and melt into the everyday life of the village. Wherever I went, children crowded around me, laughing. Perhaps these were the "forest animals ... leaning in crowds and crowds," to which the song referred.

The main refrain of the song was, "When they see you, desire takes hold," and this charge made me very uncomfortable indeed. Desire is a problem more than a blessing, especially if one desires the wrong things. Children in the village desired expensive goods; they desired to be like the people they saw in the movies. The parents complained about the children being consumed with desire; families were being destroyed because of it. My presence certainly did not help.

Women in Tamil Nadu mock and criticise each other for looking too good. For a woman "to show (another woman's) beauty," aval araku kaadda, means for her to shame the other woman publicly and verbally. I with my white skin was an easy target for such abuse. I tried in vain to disguise myself by dressing like a Tamil woman, even though I could not behave like one. I do not know whether Kanniyammaa intended to shame me, but she had just shamed my host, who was my good friend, and therefore I do not think it impossible that she had decided to "dish out" the same to me.

Kanniyammaa sang only two songs about herself that night — that is, songs in the first person singular. These songs have a number of traits in common with the formal laments that people of that village called "crying songs" (oppaari or "comparisons" in formal Tamil): first, they are songs of grief and loss. Second, they contrast a happy past with an unhappy present (hence the name oppaari). Third, they implicitly question the wisdom and justice of ruling powers. And fourth, they focus on the self of the singer: the words for "I" and "me" are repeated again and again. The singer's own sorrow is the topic of these songs.

Kanniyammaa's songs differ from formal laments in that she does not weep as she sings them; the tempo is fast and energetic rather than slow; and more importantly still, in these two songs she sings about what she does or will do rather than about what has happened to her, and the powers she challenges are not specifically the powers of gods, of senior kinsmen, or of village landholders, but rather, the powers of the West — the powers of technology and of money.

These songs are not in any way what we might call conclusive. They do not call for revolution or offer any clear answers to the problems they raise. Nor do they move from a clear beginning to a clear ending. Rather, they are cyclic, reflective, and open-ended. In my view, they are the most beautiful songs of Kanniyammaal's corpus.

The first song is about gifts given to the singer by her maamaa, her mother's brother (or in some uses of this term, her male cross-cousin).

In songs of this village, women sang to or about their maamaa as a gentle, protective lover, not "higher" than the singer but equal to her. Here Kanniyammaa sings about modern gifts, bought for cash: a "glass" (kannaadi — could be a mirror or could be eyeglasses) and a bar of soap. Both of these things are luxury items and status symbols that poor people in India generally cannot afford. The singer is uncomfortable with these modern forms of beautification and contrasts them with flowers she could fetch from the forest and wear. The song is addressed to a friend called Valli, which name means "vine" and evokes the slender willowy grace of a young girl. Valli is also the name of a forest-dwelling girl of mythology who was abducted by the god Murugan after he spied her from heaven and fell in love with her.

3.

My maamaa gave me a glass that
    makes my body shiver, and my
heart pines, Valli, my heart
    goes out to him. My
maamaa gave me a glass that
    makes my body shiver, and my
heart pines, Valli, my heart
    goes out to him.

Climbing the jasmine trees, I
    brought him some jasmine flowers, and my
heart pines, Valli, my heart
    goes out to him.
Climbing the jasmine trees, I
    brought him some jasmine flowers, and my
heart pines, Valli, my heart
    goes out to him. My
maamaa gave me a soap that
    makes my body shiver, and my
heart pines, Valli, my heart
    goes out to him. My
maamaa gave me a soap that
    makes my body shiver, and my
heart pines, Valli, my heart
    goes out to him.

The second song is about various methods of communicating with God. The singer prefers silent and solitary meditation, but the village is celebrating by setting off noisy fireworks, which the singer does not like and which she cannot understand. She tries to escape to the forest, but this proves of no avail. The singer's maamaa tells her to go to a mountain top, and at that place burn camphor and break coconuts. Camphor and coconuts are "traditional" worship offerings, which get a god's attention as it were, and establish communication with him. The singer takes her maamaa's advice and goes to the mountaintop, where she gets a better view of the fireworks, as well as of other distant and beckoning things. On the mountaintop she also has the opportunity to meditate in silence, and there she must choose what to do.

Fireworks, or in general any objects that explode noisily, are called vedi. The word "vedikkai" means "explosion"; it also means "show," in the sense of a loud, bright, attention-getting display; it also means "joke" in the sense of something which causes people to explode in noisy laughter, suddenly showing their bright teeth. The word teriyile means "not see" as well as "not know" and "not understand". Vedikkai teriyile can therefore mean either "(I) can't see the show," or "(I) don't get the joke." Kanniyammaa's song plays on the two meanings of this phrase.

11.

I will close my eyes myself
    and I will seek the Lord, I
will close my eyes myself
    and I will seek the Lord, I
want to go to the flowery forest but —
    bang! boom! — the rockets explode. When I
go to the flowery forest —
    angl boom! — the rockets explode. When
they explode with a bang! boom! —
    I don't see the joke, maamaa. When
they explode with a bang! boom!
    I don't see the joke, maamaa. If
you don't see the joke, girl,
    climb to the top of the mountain, girl. If
you don't see the joke, girl,
    climb to the top of the mountain, girl. When

you climb to the top of the mountain,
    get some camphor and take it with you, girl. When
you climb to the top of the mountain,
    get some camphor and take it with you, girl. When
you take the camphor with you,
    facing forward, burn it, girl. When
you take the camphor with you,
    facing forward, burn it, girl.

Look! There goes the train, but
    I don't have a bit of money, maamaa.
Look! There goes the train, but
    I don't have a bit of money, maamaa.
So what if you have no money,
    I will give it — climb up, girl.
So what if you have no money,
    I will give it — climb up, girl.

Bang! Boom! The rockets explode.
    The rockets go far into the sky.
Bang! Boom! The rockets explode.
    The rockets go far into the sky.
What if they go into the sky?
    I can see the joke now, maamaa.
What if they go into the sky?
    I can see the joke now, maamaa.
So what if you see the joke now?
    Get a coconut, little girl.
So what if you see the joke now?
    Get a coconut, little girl.
When you've got the coconut,
    Facing forward, break it, girl.
When you've got the coconut,
    Facing forward, break it, girl.

I will close my eyes myself
    and I will seek the Lord, I
will close my eyes myself
    and I will seek the Lord, I

want to go to the flowery forest, mother,
    when I seek the Lord, I
want to go to the flowery forest, mother,
    when I seek the Lord. When I
go to the flowery forest,
    I can see the joke, maamaa, when I
go to the flowery forest,
    I can see the joke, maamaa.
So what if you see the joke, girl,
    go and get some camphor, girl.
So what if you see the joke, girl,
    go and get some camphor, girl.
When you've gone and got the camphor,
    facing forward, burn it, girl.
When you've gone and got the camphor,
    facing forward, burn it, girl.

REFERENCES

Emeneau, Murray B. 1970. *Toda Songs*. Oxford: Clarendon Press.

Feld, Steven. 1982. *Sound and Sentiment: Birds, Weeping, Poetics and Song in Kaluli Expression*. Philadelphia: University of Pennsylvania Press.

Rosaldo, Renato I. 1984. "Grief and a Headhunter's Rage: On the Cultural Force of Emotions," (pp.178-195) in Stuart Plattner and Edward Bruner (eds.), *Text, Play and Story: The Construction and Reconstruction of Self and Society*. 1983 Proceedings of the American Ethnological Society. Washington, D.C.: The American Ethnological Society.

Shulman, David. 1992. *The Hungry God: Hindu Tales of Filicide and Devotion*. Chicago: University of Chicago Press.

Trawick Egnor, Margaret. 1986. Internal Iconicity in Paraiyar "Crying Songs," (pp. 294-344) in Stuart Blackburn and A.K. Ramanuian (eds.), *Another Harmony: New Essays on the Folklore of India*. Berkeley, CA: University of California Press.

____. 1990. "Untouchability and the Fear of Death in a Tamil Song," (pp. 186-206) in Catherine Lutz and Lila Abu-Lughod (eds.), *Affecting Discourse: Language and the Politics of Emotion*. Cambridge: Cambridge University Press.

SEVEN

TOWNSMEN, TENANTS AND TRIBES: War, Wildness and Wilderness in the Traditional Politics of Western India

HARALD TAMBS-LYCHE

Wildness

"Thinking about the centrality of wildness," says Ajay Skaria in the preface to his thought-provoking book on the Dangs of South Gujarat, "may have implications for understanding eighteenth- and early-nineteenth-century India" (1999: ix). He then goes on to stress that the prevalence of "raids and similar activities" in mainstream politics of Western India, during that period, turned on "a particular kind of political power, one that put wildness at its centre" (ibid.: x). Rather than viewing these activities in terms of "chaos and decline" we should, if I read Skaria correctly, see them as part of a process of dynamic change. Later, however, with the establishment of the colonial order, such "wild" politics are pushed to the periphery, with which they then become identified: "wildness" becomes a quality associated with "tribes".

I agree so far: seen in this way, "wildness" is certainly a central feature of the traditional political system of Western India. In writing about Saurashtra (Tambs-Lyche, 1997), I try to describe the rise and fall of the political system closely associated with the term Rajput, gradually taking form from the beginning of the Middle Ages and flourishing roughly from the sixteenth to the eighteenth century. There was a distinctive culture around the Dangi raids, says Skaria, "and they were often celebrated for enacting a particular kind of masculine wildness"

(1999: x). My first point, then, is that this would seem to me true of many cultural figures of the warrior, and that it applies perfectly to Rajputs in their heyday as well as to Marathas, Kolis, or Muslim mercenaries. These figures, surely, are not culturally identical, but they share certain traits which were, I think, intrinsic to warrior identities wherever war was celebrated as heroic masculinity: in this sense, I would hold, much of what Dumezil (1969) says of the epic heroes of the Nordic as well as Indian myths is equally true of Western India at the period we are discussing here.

It may be well to recall briefly some of these traits. The heroic warrior is, of course, "wild": his courage in battle is often depicted as a kind of rage, and in Western India this rage was often sustained by opium, stressing that the warrior had to leave ordinary norms of behaviour behind, when he went to battle. This is certainly part of the old custom of donning ochre garbs, like a renouncer: the warrior, like the *sanyasi*; should be dead to society in order to face his own, likely, death. The fear that the warrior inspires, stems from this wildness. Tactics like the burning of villages and the rape of women are not just strategic moves but clearly meant to sustain this kind of fear. War, then, is wild. But the warrior, as seen by Dumezil, is also transgressive in another way. As war threatens order, so the warrior's prestige and power threatens authority and hierarchy. We must of course keep in mind here, that the strictly hierarchical order of armies is, relatively speaking, a modern phenomenon. While not denying that some Rajput generals were great strategists, the typical unit of the kind of politics I shall discuss here is closer to the fighting band.

Are Tribes Wild?

My main criticism of Skaria's book, then, is simply that, in spite of the introductory remarks I have quoted, he has constructed his book around an opposition between the "wild" Dangis, living in the hills, and an implicitly "civilised" Hindu society of the plains. There is a reference, here, to the work of Pierre Clastres (1993). I would distribute the opposition differently, between "wild" warriors and raiders, and, at the other pole, such "civilised" groups as the Banias and Brahmins of the towns. Between them we find a number of possible transformations or combinations, like "peaceful peasants" who arm themselves and go on raid in a changing political situation, or the "criminal" Koli as constructed by Kennedy, the police officer (1906) — who till their fields peacefully by day only to go raiding at night. In this, I do not mean to imply that Western India, at the time, was a particularly "uncivilised" region: it was, however, at the times and places discussed here, an unruly place where physical power and self-defence were important factors for survival.

This brings me to the problem of "tribe". The danger I see here, in Skaria's approach, lies in associating "wildness" with "wilderness," i.e. with tribes. He does, indeed, underline this link, which would seem manifest when tribesmen in the Dangs speak of themselves as "jangli". If I am right, however, "wildness" should rather be associated with most kinds of political domination as such — until visible force can be replaced with more subtle forms of dominance, such as — we feel — is mostly the case today. In these terms, there is no need for "tribal" or indigenous peoples to be "wild," unless, as the reader may well remark, such wildness is effectively part of a cultural strategy of retaining control over a particular area. The Sami of Northern Scandinavia, to take an example, are certainly eager to be seen as an indigenous people, and in that sense may well be called "tribal": they are certainly not "wild" in Skaria's sense. And then, they have no real tradition of warfare either.

The relevance of my point, here, for tribal studies is this: We should be wary of identifying "tribal" culture with particular attitudes and assumptions, especially about "wildness" since such a perception marries too readily with popular stereotypes about "tribes". Such identification is as problematic as identifying tribes with particular levels of evolution. Does a Santal or a Sami cease to be tribal when he has become a coalminer, an engineer or a university professor? Similar problems arise with sophisticated distinctions in terms of social structure, such as the well-known definition of tribe by F.G. Bailey (1961). Nor is it at all my point here to deny the cultural specificness of Indian tribal populations or to imply, as C. Bates (1995) seems to do, that the category of tribe is a colonial invention with little foundation in pre-colonial society.

What I shall do here, is basically to deal with some aspects of dominance, resistance and the culture of conflict in pre-colonial and early colonial Gujarat. In this context, I shall try to show, tribes do not stand out as a separate kind of community. At the same time, however, I hope to show that "caste" is a rather unsatisfactory category for describing the many "turns and twists" of the precolonial political order.

Gujarat is, even today, a region where "tribals" are few and difficult to identify: only in the Dangs and certain other districts of South Gujarat do we find a concentrated population of "scheduled tribes". I shall try to show, then, why traditional politics did not, indeed, produce any consistent distinction of this kind. But in doing so, I wish to stress the particularities of the region — as of any other region. One such particularity, too obvious to be missed, is the lack of any group of speakers of languages other than Indo-European, at least in recent times. To say that distinctions between "caste" and "tribe" are blurred in Gujarat does not mean, therefore, that the same is true of other regions. I shall return to these questions in my conclusion.

Early Rajput State Formation: The Tribe-King Alliance (ca.800-1100 A.D.)

It is generally accepted, today, that today's Rajputs stem from various communities that gradually merged into a "caste". I have myself dealt with the matter at length (1997). Among the many important contributions I would like to stress that of Kolff (1991) who, precisely, stresses the warrior element in the emergence of the Rajputs.

I shall not, here, deal with the rise of the Gujarat kingdom. By the end of the first millennium A.D. it was an established centre of power, controlling trade, with Cambay as its main port. In relation to this centre, Saurashtra was a periphery. We know, however, something about two minor states of the peninsula at this period.

Most important of these was the kingdom of the Chudasamas at Junagadh. Thanks to several myths concerning these kings as well as the Goddess Khodiyar, we have some idea of the power structure of this state. The earliest myth tells how the founder of the dynasty found the ruins of an old fort (*juna gadh*) hidden in the jungle. The foundation of the dynasty is traditionally placed in 875 A.D. This is not so unlikely as it may sound, since the Uparkot, the fortress of Junagadh, certainly has antecedents going back to the days of Ashoka. Of greater interest to us are the myths concerning the king Naughan, who is said to have mounted the throne in 1030 A.D. His father had been killed when the Gujarat king attacked and conquered his kingdom. The prince, the myth tells us, was saved by a maid-servant of the queen, who took the boy to a chief of the Ahir tribe, clearly described as pastoralists at the time, living in the forests to the South. Briefly, the myth then tells the story of how the Ahir chief outwits the governor placed at Junagadh by the Gujarat king, and succeeds in placing Naughan on the throne. The role of the tribe is marked by the chief's daughter placing the *tika* on the king's forehead, and we are told that this gesture was repeated for as long as the Chudasamas — often called the Ahirani Ranis — ruled in Junagadh (Tambs-Lyche, 1991, 1997; Amarji, 1882; Mehta, 1978; Solanki, n.d.).

The structure of the Chudasama state, then, seems to have been an alliance between a small royal clan — later to be classified as Rajputs — and the Ahir tribe. The latter, now an agricultural caste but still remembering its pastoral antecedents, is now the dominant caste of large parts of Junagadh District. From 1470 when the Gujarat Sultan Muhammad Begada conquered Junagadh, and until independence, the Ahirs were subjected to Zamindars, but they still formed the bulk of the agriculturalists.

A similar type of alliance between tribe and king would have seemed to characterise the Jethwa kingdom of Porbandar. Here, our material is more scanty, but the Mers, whose antecedents are unknown but who are today the dominant caste of much of the former state's area, occupied a similar position here to that of the Ahirs of Junagadh. They, too, possessed the privilege of placing the *tika* on the king's forehead during his inthronation (Tambs-Lyche, 1997: 35-36; Trivedi, 1961: 106).

Yet another example of the same type is found on the Eastern boundary of the old Gujarat kingdom, in Mewar. Here, the founder of the dynasty is said to be one Guha, named so because his mother, a queen from Saurashtra, took refuge in a cave when she learnt that her husband's kingdom hed been taken by the enemy. "Guha grew up in a forested area populated by the members of the Bhil tribe," Harlan tells us. "Enormously popular, he was eventually elected king of the Bhils at Idar (also in Gujarat). He was officially invested with royal authority when a Bhil cut his own finger and with his blood applied to Guha's brow the red mark (*tika*) of sovereignty" (1991: 27-28). This ceremony, still practiced at Udaipur until the end of the Mewar state, clearly marks an alliance between the Bhil tribe and the royal house. Tod and the royal records of Mewar place this event in the fifth century, a date accepted by Harlan. I suspect this to be too early.[1]

1. Several of Tod's dates seem to me too early. I suspect that the bards were guilty of lengthening their genealogies to add to their prestige. Such lengthening would be difficult when applied to generations well remembered, so I suspect that brothers in the great-grandfather's generation were periodically reconstructed into father and son. This would probably allow for the addition of say, one in four generations, lengthening the time-span by about a third. By this reckoning, Guha might have lived at around the late 8th century, which corresponds with important changes in Gujarat due to the fail of the Vallabhi kingdom. I stress, however, that this is purely a hypothesis based on conjecture.

What I feel to be important here, is the existence at this early period of several kingdoms having ostensibly a similar structure of tribe-king alliance, a type of structure well documented, at a much later date, from inland Orissa (Eschmann, Kulke and Tripathi, 1975). It would seem that we have here a polity typical of the periphery of stronger states, a fairly standardised Indian form of secondary state-formation.[2] The point here is that this polity marries the legitimacy of kingdom to the military prowess — or, if you like, the "wildness" — of the tribe, so that the latter serves to protect a peaceful population concentrated in the capital and other towns.

In Junagadh, this population included the Nagar Brahmins, whose presence in the Vallabhi kingdom is also attested. They were, even then, urban landholders. Much later, we learn that the family of Narsinh Mehta, the poet, who were Nagars, moved from Talaja to Junagadh in the early fifteenth century (Sivapriyananda, 1985: 4-5), a period when the region around Talaja was controlled by "tribal" Kolis. As I have argued elsewhere, trade and other urban activities then needed the defence of the city walls and an alliance with those who controlled the countryside (Tambs-Lyche, 1998). This type of situation is excellently described by Sharma (1977: 2-3) with regard to the formation of the Rathod clan from the defensive alliance the traders of Pali, in Marwar, made with their forefathers.

Rajput Vassals on the Periphery of the Gujarat Kingdom (from 1100 A.D.)

A very different type of Rajput polity emerges from the story of the formation of the Jhala clan of Rajputs in Northwestern Saurashtra. Here, the prince Harpal, a refugee from Sindh, is received at the court of the Solanki ruler of Gujarat. The myth of his encounter with Shakti Mata, the minor goddess come to earth to seek a human husband, has been told elsewhere (Tambs-Lyche, 1996, 1997: 42-43; Maine, 1921). We are then told how the king, grateful for the miracles that Harpal has wrought with his divine wife's assistance, promises the young warrior "the right to all the villages on whose gate he can tie a garland in one single night" (Tambs-Lyche, 1997: 43). Helped by his wife's supernatural powers he

2. For this concept, see Krader 1968. My perspective on Rajput state-formation also borrows heavily from Fox, 1971.

succeeds in thus "marking" two thousand villages, of which five hundred are then returned to the Solanki queen as a gesture of friendship and ritual brotherhood.

Exaggerations apart, it seems clear that Harpal founds the Jhala clan by holding in fief an important domain on the Western fringes of the Gujarat kingdom. Shakti Devi is said to have died in 1115 A.D. (Maine, 1921: 28), so these events may be placed towards the end of the eleventh century. This pattern, of course, was to become another common form of the Rajput domain — a front-line chief, who by his fierceness controlled the borderlands too distant, or too unruly, for the king to control himself. The many changes of "capital" during the early centuries of Jhala rule attest, I think, to the lack of stability in the region. The Jhalas are also important in being the first attested case of generational segmentation among the Rajputs of the region: Harpal's chiefdom was divided among his sons (Tambs-Lyche, 1997: 43-44).

We may wonder whether this early domain of the Jhalas should be characterised as a "tribal" formation or a caste society. Most probably, the bulk of the local population, then as later, were Kolis, a group of communities we shall return to shortly. But while the Jhalas, and probably other groups of which we have no knowledge, were certainly chiefs at the time, the various chiefs had not yet been merged into a common set of Rajput norms and customs. Several indices point to the gradual growth of this "Rajput culture" and the concomitant formation of a Rajput caste. I have dealt with this elsewhere (Tambs-Lyche, 1996; 1997: 46-48, 60-68, 194-96, etc.) and shall not deal with that question here. Let me just state that the process is gradual, and that the emergence of the particular status of the Charan bards and genealogists is, in my view, an integral part of the process. Thus, by the turn of the millennium, the groups that are to become Rajputs are still very close, in one way or another, to the tribal world — in alliance with them, or forming domains not so different from that of the Dangi Bhils described by Skaria. Five hundred years later, the Rajputs have become an aristocracy whose links to the tribal world survive mainly on the symbolical level.

The Periphery of the Gujarat Sultanate (15th Century)

But even by this time, Rajputs were far from controlling all of Western India, even beyond the reaches of the Gujarat Sultanate. Both these state-formations had to deal with a significant periphery beyond their effective control. Much of this periphery was controlled by the various populations known as Kolis, while particular regions were in the hands of other communities, such as the Kathi of Central Saurashtra. It is an open question whether these regions should be called "tribal"; they were certainly characterised by minor chiefdoms rather than states, and they were certainly defended by their "wildness".

I shall first look at some of the problems facing the Sultan of Gujarat, Mahmoud Begada, who ruled from 1459 to 1511 A.D. He, of course, conquered and annexed the Sorath (Junagadh) kingdom, in 1470. This does not really concern us here, but we may note that Chaube makes a referene to "pirates" on the coast of Sorath as one of several reasons for the conquest (1975: 46), and that, having conquered Junagadh, Mahmoud found that the roads from Ahmedabad to the conquered territory were "infested with robbers" (1975: 61). Another point is even more pertinent here. Around 1460, Mahmoud had asked Ra Mandalik of Junagadh "to chastise Dudo Gohil of Arthila who had been ravaging the border districts of the Gujarat kingdom" (Chaube, 1975: 43). The Gohil Rajputs had arrived in the Northern part of the present district of Bhavnagar during the 13th century, and they were relatively active and expanding at this time. Dudo's niece Kunta was, in fact, married to Mandalik and Dudo was supposed to be tributary to him. Yet Mandalik now marched against him, defeated and killed him. Chaube feels that this expedition, which lost Mandalik the support of the Gohils, had been arranged by Mahmoud precisely to weaken the alliances and the political base of his future adversary (ibid.: 44). If this is correct, we see here how the periphery called for an active and deliberate policy in Mahmoud Begada's time — and also, how raiding remained a problem in spite of the consolidated power of the centre.

More precise is the reference to the Rathods of Dwarka, who ruled a population of Vaghers known for piracy then and afterwards. Indeed, according to some sources piracy and robbery were the main sources of revenue to the temple of Ranchod (Krishna) at Dwarka.[3] Wildness, then, was apparently an integral part of the social and cultural order of Okhamandal — the country surrounding Dwarka. Mahmoud's particular excuse for attacking Dwarka came when the ship of the merchant,

3. I am dealing with this matter in Tambs-Lyche, forthcoming. The main source for this particular infomation is the account of James Macmurdo, who participated in a military expedition to Dwarka in 180X (Ghosh, 1977).

Maulana Mahmud Samarqandi, was taken by the pirates, who also detained his wife at the island of Shankhodara (or Beyt) at the inlet of the gulf of Kacch. Mahmoud himself managed to reach the capital of Gujarat with his two small children and appealed to the Sultan for help. Thus, Mahmoud Begada attacked and plundered Dwarka in 1473, while the Rathod ruler Bhim Raja took refuge on the island of Beyt. Mahmoud did not have the naval strength, at first, to attack across the sound, but then the Sultan got his ships together and finally conquered the island (Chaube, 1975: 68-71).

The Gujarat Sultan had now conquered the main states of Saurashtra and other chiefs had accepted submission to the sultanate. Yet soon after his return, Mahmoud Begada had to deal with pirates operating from the western coast of the Gulf of Cambay. He sent a fleet to Gogha, and is said to have been succesful in suppressing piracy (Chaube, 1975: 72). This area, we should note, is later described as a stronghold of Kolis. We have already suggested that the unstable political situation here may be one explanation for the move of Narsibh Mehta's family from Talaja to Junagadh in the early fifteenth century. The area, evidently, still gave trouble to the centralised order of Gujarat around 1475. It was to contiue to do so later. Though the Gohil Rajputs were active in the area as well as the Kathis and Kolis, they only succeeded in forming a really stable, centralised state there on the foundation of Bhavnagar in 1723.

The Sultan next turned his attention to the Rajput state of Champaner in the southeast. Again, Chaube's comments are significant: "....its conquest was necessary because it had been a place of refuge for the recalcitrant chiefs of the Sultanate" (1975: 73-74). In 1470, we are told, Jayasinha of Champaner assisted "disaffected people of Baroda and Dhaboi" in their revolt against the Sultanate. In 1473, Mahmoud "sent detachments to ravage the country of Champaner" (Chaube, 1975: 75). The tactique of raids was not a monopoly of the hillmen! Similar tactics were repeated in 1482, but now Jayasinha retaliated — and Mahmoud Begada had a welcome excuse for his full-scale attack on Champaner. In spite of recalcitrant support from Malwa Champaner fell in November 1484 (Chaube, 1975: 77-84).

When Mahmoud Begada attacked Sirohi in 1487, the reason was, as for Dwarka, disturbances in trade. A party of merchants bringing four hundred horses for the sultanate had been robbed close to Mount Abu. Chaube feels that this robbery did not have the support of the Sirohi raja, so that we are again faced with an instance of lack of control (Chaube, 1975: 84-85).

Forbes' remarks on the last years of the Gujarat sultanate probably hold some truth: "(the) powerful Rajpoot chiefs, who had maintained their lands and much of their independence against all the encroachments of the dynasty of Ahmedabad had, of course, little to fear from the fragments of its shattered power, and the wild aboriginal tribes began again to break forth like a fire which had been restrained, indeed, by superincumbent weight, but had never yet been extinguished" (1878/1973: 299).

Even in the undisputed heyday of the Gujarat sultanate, then, there were "tribal" peripheries were raids, piracy, robbery and a show of "wildness" represented a real problem for the centralised state. At this time, most of the surrounding Rajput rulers played this mixed game of raids on the central territory at one time, submission and alliance with the central state to suppress other "robbers" at another. The difference, here, between centre and periphery is not so much in the tactics of raiding and pillage, destruction and exaction of "tribute," as in the scale of operations, the size of the area controlled and the degree of control exercised over it. These differences can and have been construed, it is true, as an opposition between "civilisation" and "wilderness," but I would submit that the continuity in political patterns is more significant than the breaks.

1500-1700 A.D.: Kolis, Kathis and the Rajput Great Tradition

The Gujarat sultanate went through a severe crisis in the second half of the 16th century, which culminated in Akbar's conquest of Gujarat (1573). From the point of view of the periphery, however, the inclusion of Gujarat in the Mughal empire mainly meant that one strong, centralised state-formation was replaced by another. Rajasthan as well as Saurashtra remained peripheries to the empire in political and strategic terms, though alliances between the Rajasthan states and the Mughals strengthened the hands of both in dealing with the periphery.

To the West of the Jhala country another Rajput clan, the Jadejas, had been carving out their own territory from about the 13th century onwards. Here, an important step in state-formation was made when Jam Raval founded the port and city of Navanagar (later Jamnagar) in 1540. This state now became the leading force in Rajput politics of the peninsula until the 18th century, when Bhavnagar was founded as an important rival. Navanagar owed much of its success to its expanding trade with Oman and East Africa (Tambs-Lyche 1997: 69-72). This secondary centre now engaged in political expansion southwards, where its main opponents were the Kathis. Smaller states segmented from the senior state of Navanagar to base themselves in areas conquered from the Kathis.

Raval himself faced an alliance of several states and "tribal" communities. They were, first, the Jethwa Rajputs — the state which later became Porbandar, whose agricultural population came mainly from the Mer community, as mentioned above — and which was also to use troops of Rabari pastoralists for its defence against the Jadejas. Then there were the Vala Rajputs, of whose domains we know little since practically nothing was left of them in British times. The Vadhels, the pirate lords of Okhamandal (Dwarka) who had been chastised by Mahmoud Begada, were now fully active again. Finally; there were the Kathis, who were to be the main losers as the Rajput states of Saurashtra expanded from the 16th to the 18th centuries. Sources also mention the Dedas, driven eastwards towards Jhala territory: in spite of the name I suspect they were among the various populations usually called Kolis. I shall deal with them later, since southeastern Saurashtra and Northern Gujarat — where Kolis were dominant — remained as yet outside the sphere of Rajput expansion. There, Kolis seem to have had their own chiefdoms, but we know very little about them.

The opponents of Jam Raval, then, would seem to have been a mixture of minor states, chiefdoms and "tribes," subsisting by different degrees of "wildness" and warlike qualities. Raval would have been as "wild" as them, I feel, until his domain was stabilised and he could promote his chiefdom towards real statehood by founding a city. Very soon after, merchant communities, such as the Jains, came to settle within the town walls (Banks, 1992).

Of these opponents, the Kathis are central to my argument here. We do not know when they settled in Saurashtra,[4] but all sources agree that

4. There are several opinions here. Enthoven (1921) concluded that there were two main waves of immigration: around 800 and around 1500 A.D. Wilberforce-Bell opines that they came "about the eleventh century", and notes that they served at that time in the Junagadh army (1916: 67). Certainly there are several references to them from then onwards. Wilberforce-Bell also notes that "the last of the race in Kacch were driven out by Jam Abda, in the fifteenth century" (*ibid.*).

they came from Sindh by way of Kacch. It seems clear that the Kathi chiefdoms were more loosely structured than their Rajput opponents,[5] and so lost out to them. We shall return to them later.

Their "wildness" is especially clear from the succeeding period, the 18th and early 19th century, when numbers of Kathi chiefs became outlaws trying to regain the domains that were lost to them during the simultaneous expansion of the larger states of Junagadh, Jamnagar and Bhavnagar in the 18th century (Tambs-Lyche, forthcoming a; 1997: 275-90, etc.).

The typical Kathi tactic was the raid — ranging from very modest cattle raids[6] to the sacking and plundering of quite important towns. But Rajputs engaged in the same type of tactics — several wars between erstwhile "states" were occasioned by cattle raids, and one great internecine strife among the various Jhala chiefs is said to have had for its origin the theft of a single goat (Forbes, 1878/1973: 410-12). What I refer to as "wildness" here, then, is a particular ethic found among Rajputs as well as other populations of the periphery: manliness was proved by a willingness to fight on the occasion of the slightest insult. The word "wildness" is apt here, for it seems clear that fierce reactions to any insult formed part of what we may call psychological defence: trust in political neighbours was scarce and security rested on the fear of retaliation. Yet, since fear is an unmanly feeling, it seems to have been equally important to tease the opponent continuously.

It is important, here, to stress the continuity of fierceness and use of violence from the smallest-scale level to that of the state. As I have stressed elsewhere (*forthcoming*) there is no difference here, in principle, between the outlaw and the king. Kings might be more reticent in going to war than minor chiefs in planning a raid, but this would seem to have been a question of weighing costs and consequences, rather than any distinction of a moral nature. This morality of "wildness" only changes

5. Wilberforce-Bell and Forbes agree on the relative incapacity of the Kathis to build durable states. One point often cited is the absence, among them, of primogeniture. Among the Kathis, several brothers or other close kin shared authority. As an anthropologist I should note that this arrangement might well be as solid as the recurrent conflicts over succession in the Rajput states. To be frank, the matter has never been properly studied, yet the historical fact remains, that Rajputs encroached on Kathi territory and that the latter's states often lost wars against Rajputs in spite of the undisputed reputation of the Kathis for fierceness and courage.
6. We may recall, here, the importance Sontheimer (1993) gives to cattle raids in his work on inland Maharashtra.

towards the middle of the 19th century through increasing British influence.

At the battle of Bhuchar Mori, in 1591, a confederation of Saurashtra chiefs led by the Jam of Navanagar lost to a Mughal force (Wilberforce-Bell, 1916: 108-109). Formally, Saurashtra remained under Mughal suzerainty until the mid-18th century. This dependence certainly affected the larger states of the periphery, such as Junagadh[7] and Jamnagar, but less so the periphery's periphery, which I have been dealing with here. Gradually, though mutual raiding was common, the larger states of the periphery increased their control over the minor chiefdoms, but the process was far from uniform or unilineal.

Marathas, Rajputs, Kolis and Kathis: 18th Century Contests

The replacement of Mughal authority by the Marathas, in the early 18th century, has been represented as a lapse into chaos and disorder.[8] The raids (*mulkgiri*) by which the Marathas collected tribute in their peripheral provinces are well known. In Saurashtra, as elsewhere, they met resistance, occasionally successful. But the change from late Mughal times was not radical. First, Mughal authority had already suffered a long and gradual decline: secondly, while the Mughal viceroys interfered in the affairs of larger states they were hardly able to keep up with the quarrels of petty chiefs. Rather, in Saurashtra, the decline of Mughal power helped the emergence of the larger peripheral states. Junagadh, Jamnagar and Bhavnagar,[9] and a few others, largely succeeded in retaining their autonomy in the face of Maratha incursions, but at the cost of minor chiefs and more or less "independent" villages. The Kathis and the Kolis, closer to a "tribal" order than the Rajputs, suffered at the hands of the more efficient state-formations of the latter and of the Muslim state of Junagadh. Thus the contraction of the area under Kathi control, in the middle of the peninsula, accelerated during this century. But here I shall deal more fully with the Koli territory stretching along Saurashtra's east coast, from Bhavnagar to Mahuva.

7. Junagadh declared itself independent of the Mughals in 1748.
8. This view has been challenged elsewhere. Thus, Ray (19xx) analyzes thoroughly the situation in the hinterland of the port of Cambay, and concludes that there was no such "lapse into chaos", in spite of the exactions and the tribute which the Marathas demanded from the Nawab of that state.
9. Bhavnagar, from about the foundation of that city in 1723, was a newcomer to the power games of Saurashtra.

As noted, this area seems to have been dominated by Kolis, probably since at least the early fifteenth century. When the Gohil chief Sejuk first arrived there in the thirteenth century, he was granted twelve villages by the Junagadh ruler to protect the country from "the Kant Bhils" (Forbes, 1878/1973: 239). Sejuk's daughter married prince Khengar of Junagadh, an alliance since repeated, probably several times. The Vala Rajputs then held Vala (Vallabhipur) and Talaja (ibid.: 240), but we also hear of Dhan Mer, a Koli chief of Dhandhuka. Then Ebhal Vala is killed and his lands conquered by the alliance between Dhan Mer and Ranji, the Gohil chief who had become Dhan's son-in-law (ibid.: 244-45).

At this time the Gohils were still "wild". Mokheraji, Ranji's son, was "rendering himself the terror of the surrounding country," says Forbes. He conquered the port of Ghogha and the island of Piram from the Bareia Kolis (ibid.: 247-48). Probably he was something like a pirate: this was certainly what Muhammad Tughlaq thought, when he in his turn attacked Ghogha, killed Mokheraji and destroyed the fortress that the latter had built on Piram. This was in 1347 A.D. (Wilberforce-Bell, 1916: 73). Mahmoud Begada, as we have seen, later had to deal with "piracy" on the same coast. The pirates are thought to have been Kolis.

In the 16th century, the Kathis overran the small chiefdom of the Gohil Noghanji. They later took Vala and killed his senior kinsman who had tried to help him. Noghanji sought the aid of the Bareia Koli chief Rajo, whose daughter he married. The Kolis helped retake his chiefdom, while the main Kathi adversary was lured to attend a marriage at Jamnagar, where Noghanji, helped by the Jam, killed him by stratagem (Forbes, 1878/1973: 350-51). We see here how Kathi, Koli and Rajput — ranging from village chief to head of an important state — take part in the same political game.

By the time that Akheraji ruled in Bhavnagar, Talaja was a stronghold of the Koli "pirates". In 1771 Bhavnagar allied itself with the British to "suppress piracy," and Talaja was taken by a combined force, in which Junagadh also participated. The town was offered to Akheraji, but he refused it, as it lay well beyond his lines of control at the time. But these lines were pushed forward continuously by his successor Wakhatsinhji, who was able to buy Talaja from the Nawab of Cambay in 1780. The "suppression of piracy" in this area was, in effect, the dispossession of the Koli petty chiefdoms in favour of a relatively modern, organised state.

Bhavnagar had, in fact, spent most of the 18th century extending its dominion towards the south and west, finally taking Mahuva in 1784. This southern area, like the hilly ground to the west, was Kathi territory, but the central area of the state — with Ghogha, Trapaj and Talaja — had belonged to the Kolis. We have considerable information on the wars against the Kathis, but very little on the campaigns against the Kolis, except for the Talaja affair. It would seem that the conquest was gradual and that the old Koli chiefs, rather than being chased from their domains, were "Rajputised". Now, apparently, these families of "Garasia Rajputs" still form the village elite (Tambs-Lyche, 1992: 72; *forthcoming* b).

The Kolis of North Gujarat represent a different case, for they were not conquered nor rajputised until the British froze the political domains in the early 19th century. The territory in question corresponds largely to an intermediate zone between what used to be the heartland of the old Gujarat kingdom, and, to the west, the present domains of the Jhalas. These were the areas in which the latter first established their fief, and would seem to have a Koli population continuous with that of the Jhala territory. The Koli chiefdoms here, therefore, correspond to a belt from which the Jhalas were chased by the forces of the Gujarat sultanate, which in its turn did not bother to establish Zamindari dominion over the rather poor territories in question. But it is clear that the area was long considered unstable and that the Koli chiefs were engaged, quite frequently, in raids and robbery both during Mogul times and later.

It would be an exaggeration to use the term "tribal" for the various Koli and Kathi territories that subsisted till the 18th century. But they were certainly peripheries, they were certainly the source of raids and disorder in neighbouring, more centralised territories, and they were certainly subject to the morality of "wildness" that we have discussed above.

1800-1850: Insurrection or Return to the Old Order: the Early 19th Century

The Kathis have acquired, says Wilberforce-Bell, "great reputation from their plundering forays" (1916: 68). This is a typical statement, and the Kathis were duly classified as a "criminal tribe" during British times.

It was, above all, their raids on Bhavnagar territory in the early 19th century that earned them the name. They were prominent among the *baharvatiya* — outlaws — of this period. Typically, the Kathi rulers of Jetpur, a well-administered and successful little state, were seen as "reformed Kathis".

The outlaws were, most of the time, rulers or landowners who had lost (or claimed they had lost) their lands due to the settlement of Col. Walker in 1806-07, when the British tried to "freeze" the political situation. I have dealt with some of these cases elsewhere (1997: 279, 290-91: *forthcoming*). The most interesting here is the settlement of 1824. The British, this time, had helped Bhavnagar against the Kathis, and had captured the principal "outlaws". They had, however, handed them over to Wajesinhji of Bhavnagar, in whose territory the "crimes" had been committed. The raja, however, only kept the captives for a while, then sent them back to their villages: later he returned, too, the hostages they had sent for their security. The British were not content. Clearly, the ruler was dealing honourably with political opponents whose claims he acknowledged though he did not accept them: while the British thought in terms of law, order and punishment. The strategies incumbent on "wildness" were being transferred from the domain of politics to that of crime (Tambs-Lyche, 1997: 291; *forthcoming* a).

Events of 1857-58

It has often been said that Gujarat remained relatively peaceful during the great conflicts of 1857-58. As Dharaiya (1970) shows conclusively, peace was relative indeed. The most important revolt of these years was that of the Vaghers of Okhamandal, around Dwarka, whom we have already met when Mahmoud Begada attacked them. In 1857 they were formally subject to the Gaekwar of Baroda, but they rose in January, 1858, probably inspired by the events elsewhere. For details of the rebellion I refer to Dharaiya (1970: 118-30) and to my earlier short account of it (1997: 291-93). Here it is sufficient to say that it was relatively successful, and the British ony succeeded in repressing it by October, 1859.

More relevant to our purpose here are two other details: it seems that piracy and robbery, if we choose to call it so, traditionally furnished important incomes for the temple of Ranchod (Krishna) at Dwarka (Ghosh, 1977: xxx). It is also striking how the temple and the political order built around it were defended by their situation in the "wilderness" — Okhamandal means, in fact, the "bad" or "difficult" country (Meghani, 1928, xxx; Tambs-Lyche, *forthcoming* a). Here, an important place of pilgrimage finds it place in the context of "wildness" as a central part of the political order.

Among other places of unrest during 1857-58 we may note the country around peripheral Rajput states such as Idar and Rajpipla. Both may be seen as "mountain fortresses" which had largely been successful in maintaining their independence from the Gujarat kingdom and sultanate, and (at least in real, if not in formal terms) from the Mughals. At Rajpipla it was mainly the Muslim sipais (called Vilayatis in Gujarat) who gave trouble (Dharaiya, 1970: 58). This may be thought outside the scope of this paper but it should be noted that the way for such soldiers to revolt (often because of arrears in their pay) was to start looting, destroying law and order — in other words, frightening the people by their soldier's "wildness".

The chief of Mandetti, formally a vassal of Idar, refused to pay the arrears of his tribute and declared himself independent. The chief, Surajmal, "threatened to loot the territories and to encourage the rebels" (Dharaiya, 1970: 43). Attacked by the British, he took to the hills and resisted for a long time: his rebellion lasted from March, 1858 to about the end of the year. It should be noted that Surajmal made good use of the old tactics of withdrawing with his men into the hills where it was difficult to follow them. Perhaps it should be noted that Surajmal had a strong detachment of Bhils in his force (ibid.: 42-52).

A third locus of rebellion was peripheral villages with a strong location, such as Canaria, in the ravines of the Mahi, which belonged to the Gaekwar. Ram Shanker, the Thanedar, had protested against the injunction to hand over all arms to the Government as "they were surrounded by enmical regions with armed population" (Dharaiya, 1970: 83). The British seem to have been highly aware of the strategic location of the village, for they burnt it completely and ordered the population to settle on the plain nearby. This, like Dubara, burnt at about the same time, was a Koli village. In Dubara, however, only the Koli portion was burnt. Dharaiya does not say so, but it seems clear that we are here dealing with villages located "outside the law" whose inhabitants were among the excuses for dubbing the Kolis a "criminal caste".

Kolis also rebelled in several villages in the North of Gujarat, where, as we have seen, they had remained outside Rajput dominance. This, too, was considered a "wild" and loosely controlled region.

Scattered Incidences of Peripheral Revolt: 1860-1953

In 1872, a band of Kolis attacked Junagadh "with the idea of restoring the dynasty... of the Chudasama Ras" (Wilberforce-Bell, 1916: 238). They came from Chichod and other villages near the boundary between Gondal and Junagadh State in Saurashtra. These Kolis, the Mahias, were later seen as Rajputs. They came originally from Marwar, however, where their ancestors had apparently belonged to the Mena "tribe". They had fought their way, over several generations, down to their present area by way of Wankaner, which they are also supposed to have held for a while. Sometime around 1800 — at a time when Junagadh was weakened by long wars, they had settled in their present area, and "taxed" the surrounding countryside by raids. In 1867, they had revolted, clearly in protest against the encroachment of larger states — notably Gondal — on their territory.[10] But the Junagadh raid brought them a lot of trouble. They were made to pay a special tax since they were now deemed unacceptable for military service by the British. In 1882 they left their villages and went into outlawry, the case being finally settled only in 1888 (Wilberforce-Bell, 1916: 238-39; Tambs-Lyche, 1997: 293-94). Though their villages were "very much in the interior," wildness was getting harder to sustain in Saurashtra in the second half of the nineteenth century.

The last group in the peninsula to remain "wild" in this sense, was probably the Mianas. They lived on dry and infertile lands by the Rann of Kacch, where the ruler of Malia, a minor Rajput state, had invited them around 1730. He needed them to fight his brother, the ruler of Morvi, from whom he was trying to gain independence. He, clearly, wanted to exploit the "wildness" of the Mianas as a deterrent force. He succeeded, but then had to contend with Miana raids both on his own villages and those of his neighbours, who tended to hold him responsible. But neither he nor they could succeed against the Mianas, entrenched in their inaccessible hamlets, until the various states got together, and with British support "brought them to order" in 1903 (Tambs-Lyche, 1997: 294; Village Monograph No., 16: 10).

10. This encroachment partly took the form of settling Kanbi immigrants in their villages. The Kanbis were clearly regarded as less "wild" by the Gondal rulers. Today the Kanbis have become the majority caste in the area (Tambs-Lyche, 1997: 293-94; Village Monograph No. 8).

In general, the "cuture of wildness" had now ceased to be acceptable in the political game. Yet in 1949-52, the old tradition of outlawry was revived in protest against the land reforms and the disbanding of the princely states (Thorner, 1956: 43; Tambs-Lyche, 1997: 307).

Traditional Political Systems and the Category of Tribe

The argument I have tried, here, to underpin by scattered and necessarily sketchy evidence, is the following. "Wildness" is not a particularity of tribals but was, in Western India at any rate, an integral part of the political order. Warriors were wild, because wildness frightened the enemy, and sometimes, when circumstances so warranted, even those who depended on the warriors' force. The "civilised" order of the modern army was yet to be invented[11] — though acts of chivalry might soften the blow of the warriors' might. I am not sure, either, that this observation would not be as valid for other parts of the world, as it is of India.

The colonial period certainly saw the British trying to establish a distinction between their own, disciplined and civilised army, and the barbarian ways of their opponents. How far they succeeded in this, and how far the distinction venges on myth, is not our subject here.

But the realisation that wildness is a quality of the warrior, rather than the tribal, certainly tends to reduce the pertinence of distinguishing between "caste" and "tribe" — or better, between those "inside" or "outside" the caste system, when dealing with the political history of Western India. I have tried to show that there is rather a continuum, where at one end centralised power achieves control over towns and surrounding villages and succeed in maintaining the peace to a high degree, while at the other end we have peripheries where every adult man carried arms for self-defence and would be a potential warrior if the situation called for his participation. Between these extremes there is no hard and fast line, as the hold that centres have over the periphery increases or wanes, and as densely populated plains give way to hills, forests and other scarcely populated and relatively inaccessible areas. Variations over time and space, then, determine whether wildness is the monopoly of a specialised warrior class or the common heritage of the male population.

---

11. This idea of an orderly and civilized army is, of course, not always the rule even now, as recent wars in Bosnia or in parts of Africa show.

But if this analysis of wildness in politics blurs the line between "tribe" and "caste," this does not mean that the identities of these various communities can be seen as sudden constructs of the colonial mind — or any other modern mind for that matter. What is equally striking, when we look at the political history of Western India, is precisely the degree to which we can identify communities over long spans of time. This continuity should of course not be confused with permanence. We have seen, for example, how members of the Mena "tribe" of Marwar come to Saurashtra, to forge themselves a new name — the Mahias — and to be identified, at first, with the very loose and accommodating category "Koli" before gaining at least local acceptance as "Rajputs". Historical events, then, clearly change identities, sometimes merging them with others, sometimes forging new ones: but there is always some identity to start with, and always some identification (or several ones at a time) which are used at any given point in the process.

The point about the distinction between "tribe" and "caste," then, is not whether we may find an objective reference for it but what we want to say by making the distinction at any given time. The relative lack of "scheduled tribes" in Gujarat is, I would hold, above all the effect of an historical process where the various states treated different communities as allies or enemies, more or less useful or dangerous, as the case might be. The dichotomy between "insiders" and "outsiders" to the caste system only made sense to those who identified strongly with the latter, as Brahmins often have done, whether they wrote classical literature ages ago or advised the British colonial regime. The dichotomies perceived and used by the groups themselves, similarly, would reflect their own view of their own position in the multitude of communities we find in India.

But yet another lesson emerges from the sketch of "wildness" in the history of Western India, as presented here. We have seen numbers of peripheral communities, imperfectly integrated both in the political system as viewed from the centre and in the "caste system" as seen from a brahminical point of view. Viewed from these angles — though not necessarily from their own — their position was ambiguous. The colonial order and the present tendency to view the caste system as an all-compassing order means that the tribe-caste distinction, which once and for all stamped the "tribes" as outsiders, has gained a new significance.

REFERENCES

Amarji, R.1882. *Tarikh-i-Sorath.* Bombay: Education Society's Press.

Bailey, F.G. 1961. " 'Tribe' and 'Caste' in India," *Contributions to Indian Sociology,* 5: 7-19.

Banks, M. 1992. *Organizing Jainism in India and England.* Oxford: Clarendon.

Bates, C. 1995. "Lost Innocents and the Loss of Innocence," in R.H. Barnes, A. Gray and B.Kingsbury (eds.), *Indigenous Peoples of Asia.* Ann Arbor: American Association for Asian Studies.

Chaube, J.1975. *History of Gujarat Kingdom,* 1458-1537. Delhi: Munshiram Manoharlal.

Clastres, P. 1993. *Society against the State*. New York: Zone Books.

Dharaiya, R.K. 1970. *Gujarat in 1857*. Ahmedabad: Gujarat University.

Dumezil, G. 1969. *Heur et malheur du guerrier*. Paris

Enthoven, R.E. 1920/21/22. *Tribes and Castes of Bombay*, I-III. Reprint 1973: New Delhi: Cosmos.

Eschmann, A-C, H. Kulke and G.C. Tripathi. 1975. *The Cult of Jagannath and the Regional Tradition of Orissa*. Delhi: Manohar.

Forbes, A.K. 1878 (1973). *Ras Mala. Hindu Annals of Western India.* Delhi: Heritage.

Fox, R.G. 1971. *Kin, Clan, Raja, Rule: State-Hinterland Relations in Preindustrial India*. Berkeley: University of California Press.

Ghosh, S.C. 1977. *The Peninsula of Gujarat in the Early Nineteenth Century*. New Delhi: Sterling.

Harlan, L. 1991. *Religion and Rajput Women. The Ethic of Protection in Contemporary Narratives*. Berkeley: University of California Press.

Kennedy, M. 1906. *Criminal Classes in the Bombay Presidency*. Bombay: *Times of India Press*.

Kolff, D. 1991. *Naukar, Rajput and Sepoy.* Cambridge: Cambridge University Press.

Krader, L. 1968. *Formation of the State*. Englewood Cliffs: Prentice-Hall.

Mayne, H. 1921. *History of the Dhrangadhra State*. Calcutta: Thacker, Spink & Co.

Meghani, Jh. 1928. *Sorathi Baharvatiyo, 2*. Ahmedabad: Gurjar Grantharatna Karyalaya.

Mehta, R.R. 1978. *Shri Khodiyarmata Akhyan* (in Gujarati). Surat: Shri Harihara Pushtakalaya.

Ray, A. 1992. "Cambay and its Hinterland: Early Eighteenth Century," in I. Banga (ed.), *Ports and their Hinterland in India, 1700-1950*. Delhi: Manohar.

Sivapriyananda. 1985. "Introduction," in Swami Mahadevananda (transl.): *Devotional Songs of Narsi Mehta*. Delhi: Motilal Banarsidass.

Sharma, G.D. 1977. *Rajput Polity*. Delhi: Manohar.

Skaria, A. 1999. *Hybrid Histories. Forests, Frontiers and Wilderness in Western India*. Delhi etc.: Oxford University Press.

Solanki, P. (n.d.). *Jay Khodiyar Akhyan* (in Gujarati). Ahmedabad: Mahavir Book Depot.

Sontheimer, G.D. 1993. *Pastoral Deities in Western India*. Delhi etc: Oxford University Press.

Tambs-Lyche, H. 1991. "Le roi et les enfants de la déesse," *Cahiers de la Littérature Orale*, 29: 61-85.

____. 1992. *Power and Devotion: Religion and Society in Saurashtra* (2 vols). Bergen: University of Bergen.

____. 1996. "Réflexions sur les mythes de fondation des royaumes Rajput," in N. Revel and C. Champion (eds.), *Les littératures de voix: les épopées. Les rites de fondation*. Paris: Centre de Recherche sur l'Oralité /INALCO: 37-54.

____. 1997. *Power, Profit and Poetry. Traditional Society in Kathiawar, Western India*. Delhi: Manohar.

____. 1997. "The Urbanity of Non-Violence: Reflections on the Specificity of Urban Religion in Western India," Paper for the Conference of the International Association of Sociologists of Religion, Toulouse.

____. forthcoming a. "Les baharvatiya (hors-la-loi) au Saurashtra," in V. Bouiller and D. Leblanc (eds.), *Héros régionaux, héros nationaux. Le figure du héros en Inde*. (provisional title). Paris.

____. forthcoming b. *The Good Country: Individual, Situation and Society in Saurashtra.* India. Delhi: Manohar.

Thorner, D. 1956. *The Agrarian Prospect in India*. Delhi: University Press.

Trivedi, H.B. 1961. *The Mers of Saurashtra.* Baroda: M.S. University.

Village Monograph no. 8: Chichod in 1961 Census of India, Vol. V, part VI. Ahmedabad: Director of Census Operations.

Village Monograph no. 16: Kajarda in 1961 Census of India, Vol. V, part VI. Ahmedabad: Director of Census Operations.

Wilberforce-Bell, H. 1916. *A History of Kathiawad from the Earliest Times*. London: Heinemann.

EIGHT

THE STRUCTURE OF MIDDLE INDIAN TRIBAL SOCIETY COMPARED

GEORG PFEFFER

1. Social Structure

The term "social structure" has been widely used in sociology indicating interrelated patterns of social roles, social strata and social classes of a given society. A role would normally refer to a bundle of social customs and norms, or behavioural expectations and demands, a stratum to a higher or lower income group and a class to the relative control of the means of production. In his factory, a technician would play his role. According to his income, he might be placed in the lower-middle stratum of society, while selling his labour power, he would belong to the wage-earning class.

These technical instruments of sociology have proved their use in "Western" or "Westernised" societies where the bureaucracy of the state is responsible for ordered interaction within a framework of a formal legal system. Thus a German is registered immediately after his or her birth, exposed to baptism and various vaccinations at infancy, made to participate in the routine of a kindergarten, and automatically enrolled in the school for the suitable age. A man is later called to the armed forces or to substitute health services. Males or females find their type of work on account of their specialised and certified professional training. Marriage without state sanction is illegal, but if commenced by the verdict of a court, implies access to major tax benefits, housing mortgages, and insurance rebates. A home is rented in a written contract or bought by a permanent entry into the official "book of the ground". Standard taxes for the state and the religious community are drawn from every bank account to which the employer is regularly transferring the weekly or monthly income. All jobs necessarily go together with insurance of health, old age and employment and guaranteed retirement at a fixed age, when a home for senior citizens would be booked in advance. Illness and death are always documented by elaborate reports of physicians and hospitals. No burial or cremation is allowed without the death certificate of a qualified doctor and at the site provided by the government. The individual is thus guided by innumerable registrations — ranging from the bankers' reports on his or her credibility to those of the central traffic archives on his or her conduct of a vehicle. Human existence has been tailored for the benefit of the individual in legal situations and even in the *spare* time, a person is bound by contracts to travel agencies or television stations. The structure of such a societal set-up contains elaborate formal links within a bureaucracy as well as informal methods of circumvention or tactical exploitation of such public pressure for the individual's gain.

The "Western" legal-bureaucratic order,[1] however, does not suffice in regulating the complex Indian social system of caste and nepotism. Here children find schools, adults find work and the old or the ill find consideration through their family, peer and neighbourhood ties. Birth and death certificates may be issued at times, but — not being essential — their entries need not be reliable. Individuals and families are guided throughout their existence by their larger community of the neighbourhood and the local subcaste, the region, the sect, and the religious centre, all of which will vary greatly in the second largest country of the world, but will refer to collectively ascribed and not individually achieved status.

In the rather transparent small-scale world of tribal middle India the standard instruments of Western sociology are even less effective. When discussing the tribal "social structure" of such a face-to-face society, textbook-sets of social roles, social strata and social classes evaporate. Other instruments of analysis are required, since other concepts govern. Cultural traits being relative, such alternative concepts must relate to those devised and observed by the tribal people themselves.

---

1. The ideal type of legitimacy for this type of rule has been devised by M. Weber (1956).

Perhaps the sociological paradigm of "social structure" was developed by the anthropologist Radcliffe-Brown for whom it included "all social relations of person to person". It was to discern the "differentiation of individuals and of classes by their social role" as generalised "in actually existing concrete reality" (1952: 191-92). Taking this British structuralist approach into consideration, Lévi-Strauss went on to develop it further by deviating from the basic "concreteness" of his Anglo-Saxon predecessors. His interest in "lived-in" social orders — or objective social reality — was limited, when compared to his focus upon "thought-of" orders which "cannot be checked against the experience to which they refer, since they are one and the same thing as experience". The "thought-of" orders are those of myth and religion. The only way to study them is "in their relationships with the other types of "lived-in" orders" (1953: 548).

Following Lévi-Strauss we would thus have to take the ordered social relations of concrete reality into account but subordinate them to the meta-model which — because of contradictions at the lower level — may never have existed empirically. Its mechanical implications, however, have been responsible for the concrete and incomplete forms allowing us to recur to the superior or pure model of ideas. In tribal middle India — the society to be discussed here — we are likely to find diverse and partial relational patterns of the "lived-in" order making sense only when linked to the "thought-of" order. The necessarily partial empirical signs will require logical completion at a level beyond the concrete on the ground.

Problem and solution of the discrepancy between the empirical and the ideal may be illustrated by an example of the marriage rules of the Oraon or Khurukh tribe. Roy (1915: 352) mentions a "bar to marriage" for three generations between the members of two local lineages involved in an affinal union, and this restriction is irrespective of clan membership. During my own visits to Khurukh villages, I was informed in everyday language of the custom called "bilateral cross-cousin marriage" in anthropological jargon. Among the tribes of the immediate Khurukh neighbourhood, I found Munda with the "three generation bar" and Kharia practicing "cross-cousin marriage". Other Kharia told me of a proscription on intermarriage in adjoining generations. The "lived-in" models of behaviour appeared to be very different from one group to the other.

In a more general sense — relating the ideas involved in these concrete rules and actions — the norm of so-called "bilateral cross-cousin marriage" would initially have to be translated from its individualistic ego-centrism to the general idea that marriage relations involving two sides were of the collective and permanent kind and were reconfirmed from one generation to the next. This diachronic quality of affinity, not intelligible to most Western minds, may be retained by the two sides immediately after marriage in the previous generation in the form of mutual giving and taking of brides, or this first reciprocal link may serve as a *sign* of affinal mutuality for one or more generations beyond those joined in intermarriage. This *sign* will then have to be renewed in later generations, lest the reciprocity of the two sides be forgotten.

All the marriage rules mentioned, i.e. immediate repetition or the interval of one or three generations, will imply the same message: The gift of a bride is the appropriate reciprocation for such an initial transfer, and intermarriage is a relationship beyond time as a limiting factor. The diachronic nature of affinity is communicated in the "thought-of" model of Khurukh, Munda and Kharia, and since a bride must be given for a bride, the model may be qualified as "elementary" and called "restricted exchange" (Lévi-Strauss, 1969: 29f). In following the French school, my article on the social structure of the tribes will therefore consider the contrast of social orders on the ground and their non-empirical logical completion.

2. The People

Perhaps some 100 million — or ten crores — of people belong to the tribal world of middle India situated in the vast territory between the Ganges in the north and the Godavari in the south, the deserts of Rajasthan in the west and the Bay of Bengal in the east. Compared to the Hindus and Muslims of the plains, the tribal people are a minority, but wherever the landscape is hilly and forested, they still form the major section of the population. In some states, such as Orissa, they make up about half of the population and inhabit two-thirds of the territory. The boundaries of tribal units never coincide with provincial borders. Thus the Gond are a major tribe in Orissa, Andhra Pradesh, Maharashtra and Madhya Pradesh. Similarly the borders between Orissa and Bihar or West Bengal divide the major tribal groupings such as Santal, Bhumia and Munda of the region.

If the term "tribe" has become disreputable in Africa south of the

Sahara, it is without any negative connotations in India. For more than sixty years, the administration has applied the term *Scheduled Tribe* (*ST*) to some distinctive communities of the hills, and the name *Scheduled Caste* (*SC*) to other inhabitants of the tribal territory. More recently the technical expression *Other Backward Classes* (*OBC*) has been attached to yet another extended set of natives of the hilly region. The name of each one of these is listed in the governmental schedules. The administration has attempted to isolate single tribes or their parts as well as three different categories of indigenous people.

In Orissa at least, a fourth one furthermore distinguishes *Primitive Tribes*[3] (*PT*), i.e. groups named Juang, Hill-Bhuiyan, Hill Kharia, Mankirdia, Birhor, Lodha, Didayi, Saora, Lanjia Saora, Dongria Kondh, Kuttia Kondh and Bondo. In most of these cases, so-called "development agencies" under special officers of the provincial government demarcate the tribal territory and administrate special budgets earmarked for "tribal welfare".

The policy of isolating different administrative units of the tribal world has been followed by most of the anthropologists in the region. Concentrating on "tribes" in their research they have frequently equated them with the ST or PT of the hills, ignoring the vast population of interrelated SC and OBC. The following article will avoid this approach and use the term "tribe" to include all native inhabitants of the hills, i.e. those groups residing in the area at the time when the colonial power invaded it and began constructing roads and railways in the late 18th century. Since that time numerous plains-people have moved into the hills and become a dominant minority there. The enormous coal and mineral resources in areas like Chhota Nagpur have attracted major industries and transformed the landscape, just as vast hydro-electric projects have led to the mass evacuation and starvation of the local tribal population and benefited incoming plainsmen. In the course of my own work in Orissa, however, I have met a number of communities who had not suffered under such a radical impact and continued in their modest and autonomous ways.

Such conservative communities are growing paddy in the riverbeds with the help of ploughs and draft-animals. By the ancient technique of shifting cultivation (*podu*) they raise millet on the hill-slopes, just

2. Government of Orissa. 1994. *Tribal Education in Orissa in the Context of Education for All by 2000 AD*. Bhubaneswar: Tribal Welfare Department Publication.

as they obtain vegetables from their kitchen gardens and meat from their domestic animals. Generally they are considered "backward" by the plainsmen, but they are not poorer and their life expectancy is not shorter than that of their fellow tribal people in the slums of the industrial and irrigated region. In spite of their poverty, I would say,[3] they are leading a good life.

Bureaucracy has made some impact in all of the tribal areas. The ownership of land — traditionally resting with the local lineages — has been settled in the names of individuals during the last decades and money is gradually coming into use, where the landless clients used to barter tools, household goods, various services and dry fish for the crops of the fields. The forest officials have come to guard the Reserved Forest against its inhabitants of the last millennia and the police is imposing law and order where mutual checks and balances used to be self-understood. Perhaps even some schools have found students, so that the unemployed youths, socially disqualified from agricultural work by their formal education, have begun to wear what is known as "shirt/pant" and substitute the traditional dances by the exercises they have witnessed in urban cinemas.

But the bureaucratic impact is still superficial. The few achieved roles are outnumbered by the constitutional or ascribed ones, social strata are insignificant where nobody is wealthy and social classes coincide with traditional patron-client relations. The ST, OBC and PT have always been the owners of the soil, while the SC are their client-craftsmen, cattle-herders, petty traders, and creditors. Neither the landed patrons nor the articulate clients, acting as intermediaries with the plainspeople, are dominating the traditional symbiosis, even though the former are of higher status and the clients' perspective goes beyond the local setting. Nobody sells her or his labour-power within this tribal society. The lack of equality is not expressed in material terms. When discussing social structure, I shall therefore confine myself to the internal patterns rather than stressing the inroads of civilisation.

This procedure is unusual. I can very well understand, how my Indian colleagues, particularly those of a tribal background, thematise dominance rather than symbiosis, intrusions rather than coexistence. Much of the Indian anthropological literature on tribal society is problem-oriented. Monographs and articles on current affairs present a picture

3. Heralds of various civilisations would certainly not share my view.

of exploitation and corruption, hunger and alcoholism, displacement and transgressions of the strong against the weak. Outsiders like me will be less informed, however, whereas they might take certain principles into account which are noticeable as "family resemblance" throughout the tribal world, but which, for most visitors from the plains, are overshadowed by the impression of the tristes tropiques.[4] The principles relate to order of place and time constituting the social structure of the tribal world.

3. The Tribe

My article will not focus upon a single tribe, but deals with a middle Indian societal type I call "tribal". In fact, it may be asked legitimately, if an entity called "tribe" does carry a relevant meaning apart from the administrative convention. In case the answer is positive, the question remains, whether such a unit is a bounded substance or a reference to a wider mode of classification.

Having worked among the ST Gadaba for example, I found at closer inspection how the substantial boundaries of this concept were dissolving. The people associated with the name have been counted by the Census of India but they have never been unified as such for any particular action or purpose. Apart from the name, nothing special is uniting them. Their customs — such as major rituals — as well as their marriage networks tend to change about every 30 to 50 kilometres, so that the talk of a religious or an endogamous entity must be seen as meaningless formalism.

All people who call themselves Gadaba, however, agree on a binary opposition dividing the tribe into those called "senior" (*boro*) and "junior" (*sano*) "siblings". This tribe of southern Orissa displays the same features as the Kharia one of the north opposing Dhelki and Dudh Kharia. Intermarriage is formally barred for such moieties related in the language of consanguinity. Practically, however, no Gadaba would exaggerate these rules, so that weddings between "seniors" of higher status and "juniors" would happen at times. The members of the former half call themselves "Gutob" in their language of the Munda linguistic family, while the latter are the "Ollari" in their Dravidian tongue. In order to

4. This is the title of Lévi-Strauss' accounts of travelling though interior Brazil in the 1930s (Lévi-Strauss, 1976).

communicate with one another, they use a local dialect of Oriya, an Indo-European language. Tribal and linguistic boundaries frequently do not coincide, as noticed by Boas (1911) long ago and they are wide apart from one another in the present case. For British social anthropology, Edmund Leach (1954: 49) has stressed the same point half a century ago and ridiculed the "nonsense of the whole linguistic-historical argument" in his classic work on highland Burma. Perhaps one day this message will be heard in South Asian anthropology.[5]

Gadaba particularity is furthermore fading, if their status as Porja is taken into account. The term implies their peasant status[6] and their commonality with several other ST of the Porja type in opposition to such ST or OBC as Bhuiya, Bhatra or Rona[7] who understand themselves as the relative seniors demanding certain occasional services[8] from their Porja neighbours. All of them, seniors and juniors, unite as Desia or locals, and all share the same totemic exogamous categories. Thus intermarriage might exceptionally unite a Rona and a Gadaba, but never if the two are of the same totem. Either tribe is not bound by linguistic or other cultural criteria. Within an overall mode of classification, the various intermediary classes include that of the tribe. The latter term is in no way related to common action or particulars of individuals, except for their formal hierarchical opposition to other such classes. The tribe is a category not a group. It is also a paired category. Everywhere the Ho and Munda, the Kisan and Oraon, the Raj Gond and Gond or the Dora Kondh and Kondh are opposed as relative seniors and juniors.

Tribal names also indicate such a unifying order. The cultivators would call themselves "people of the earth" (e.g. Baiga, Bhumia, Bhuiya, Matia), "people of the hills" (e.g. Kui, Kuvi for the Kondh) or simply "people" (e.g. Horo for the Munda, Koitor for the Gond), whereas their

---

5. Contrary to this view, Parkin (1992) names people "the Munda," because they speak languages of the Munda family. They thus differ extremely from the ST everyone else calls "the Munda". Parkin goes so far as to provide "his" synthetic Munda with their own particular social organisation. Thus the "senior" Gadaba would belong to Parkin's "Munda," whereas the "junior" Gadaba would be excluded. Many other authors refer to "the Austrics" in middle India, as if these were social units and the reference to the - major - Austroasiatic language family of the - subordinate - Munda language family was in any way relevant for their social organisation.
6. The literal meaning of the Sanskrit word *praja* is "child" or "subject."
7. The term Rona refers to the royal Rajput title of Rana applied to the noblemen of western India.
8. Porja must, for example, bring firewood on festive occasions.

clients would be named according to their traditional craft (e.g. Dombo or weaver). British or Indian officials have, at times, misunderstood their tribal counterparts, e.g. Koya for Koitor, and eternalised the wrong name in official records, where these designations lead their own existence, acquiring genuineness after the tribal languages have died out. Names for "humans" imply permanent boundaries like those of species in our language. Thus the Munda would accept their neighbouring hill tribes as Horo in contrast to the Diku of the plains who are quite different types of beings just as the Europeans are yet another of the various "species". In our terms, they are those of another culture.

The political history of tribal India has rarely witnessed internal forms of government (see Sinha, 1962). Society is acephalous. No "chiefs" or "headmen" find obedience among neighbours, even though all of them have "elders" or individual positions called "big men" and "petty chiefs" in Sahlins' terminology (1963). Some groups may have also been tied to so-called "jungle kings," i.e. plainsmen ruling petty kingdoms, by nominal contributions delivered annually at dassera,[9] but such a link would — at least on the tribal side — be considered voluntary. They would not involve regular taxation or services. Only when the European colonial expansion reached the tribal area from the late 18th century onward, the society was "opened" in the sense that roads were built for the influx of information, commodities, and people.

4. African and Biblical Structures of the Unilineal Descent Groups

Even if this article will avoid the "concreteness" of the British tradition to stress the dialectical relationship between "lived-in" and "thought-of" models, it will — for the sake of clarification — have to be confronted with some issues of descent and descent groups in tribal India. The differences of the two schools are important, but have been exaggerated at times and in some fields as Dumont (1975) has shown.

British structural functionalism became famous on account of the analyses of African acephalous societies (Fortes & Evans-Pritchard 1940), and the detailed work on the structures of segmentary lineages. Fortes (1945, 1949a, 1953, 1969), in particular, offered seminal books and essays on the "dynamics of clanship" in the politico-jural domain

9. These royal rituals in Orissa have been analysed by Hardenberg (2000). See Glatzer and Braukämper in this volume.

as opposed to the "web of kinship" at the domestic level. Later efforts of cultural comparison revealed the limited utility of the "African model" in other regions of the world (Barnes, 1962). Moreover Leach (1961: 5) was to criticise the basic argument as tautologous and Kuper (1982) was to "de-construct" the entire lineage theory. The critique of Verdon (1982) dismissed the concept of lineage as such. Inspite of these elaborate discussions, two reasons call for a reconsideration: the critical debates have received little attention in India and several Indian peasant castes seem to follow the "African model" of descent, as Tiemann (1966) and Fox (1971) have shown for the Jat. But these do not belong to acephalous societies. Their "corporate character and local orientation" is historically rooted in kingdoms without proper "feudal" organisation, as the Stein (1975:76) has elaborated. Following this author we can see the Jat (or other) peasant lineage structures as the organisational backbone of a "segmentary state".

Anthropological jargon has termed unilineal descent groups as lineages and Fortes (1949b) has indicated different compositions of local groups representing the lineage. Segmentary lineages in the African context, e.g. those of the Tallensi or the Nuer, recruit their members according to the patrilineal rule, i.e. female and male descendents of a man belonged to his lineage. Through any new male member the lineage might branch into new units of subordinate status. This process of branching has been termed "fission" by the jargon. At the highest level of segmentation, the maximal lineage or "clan" would include numerous inclusive lineages at lower levels, created by fission, such as "major", "intermediary", "minor", and "minimal" lineages. Theoretically the clan would continue to become broader and ever more inclusive, whereas practically, with the general population remaining constant, all clans could not grow at the expense of one another, as the model would seem to imply. So in reality, larger lineages become clans on their own or are slimmed down by the process called "telescoping," and smaller lineages are united by what the jargon calls "fusion". The dynamics of the social whole are revealed by these trends towards fission and fusion.

The generational depth of the African maximal lineage would not normally exceed five or six generations and never pass the extreme of 13 or 14 levels of this kind. But the ruling and peasant castes of northern India are able to link the present to the past far beyond these limits within the unilineal descent group — thus unifying large corporate contemporary lineage confederations — since they can count on the expert services of specialist castes of genealogists. Both the African and the Indian methods of lineage segmentation rest on the rule of exogamy, prohibiting in-marriage at any segmentary level of the unilineal descent group.

The descent model of the Bible, however, today represented everywhere between Morocco on the Atlantic Ocean and the Northwest Frontier Province of Pakistan, is unaware of exogamy, practicing incest rules on an individual level only.[10] Thus all Pathans or Pashtun are seen as descendents of a single ancestor named Quais and local lineages marry within their ranks. Barth (1959), by reference to Pathan ethnography, has challenged Fortes' African model of segmentary opposition in a rather famous article, but he has failed to stress this basic difference of the Biblical structure, the lack of exogamy. I am not aware of other authors pointing towards the alternative causality implied by Middle Eastern endogamy, even if they (e.g. Peters, 1990: 90) discuss it at length. The highest level of this system, i.e. that of Adam and the Adamites in the Bible, was called conical clan by Sahlins (1968: 25). He described its structure in Polynesia (1954). Just in passing, yet another a comparable trait may thus be mentioned: Unlike the African or Indian peasant systems, Sahlins' Polynesian or Biblical lineages differentiate "senior" and "junior" segments[11] according to status. Otherwise different in many respects, the tribal descent group of middle India follows these *temporal* criteria as well.

Time is also the principle of classification in the paradigmatic Africanist studies. Relative age describes the relationship between lineages. Among the Nilotic Nuer, Evans-Pritchard has observed "ecological time" in one context of classification and "structural time" (1940: 100-8) in another. The latter is referring to patrilineages as well as the terminology of kinship and the age-sets of the Nuer. All three of these domains are relevant in middle Indian tribal societies. The structure of the unilineal descent groups will at once reveal the differences.

10. Lévi-Strauss (1969) has built his theory upon the basic premise of a collective type of incest tabu (i.e. the rule of exogamy) and ignored the Biblical model. Further analysis will reveal, however, that even the individual incest tabu of the Middle East carries far-reaching structural implications. The term was coined by Kirchhoff in lectures of 1935, first published in 1955, and made generally available in Fried's Readings in Anthropology II (pp. 260-70) of 1959.

11. Among the Biblical children of Israel, Ruben and his clan (just as Levi and Simeon), transgressing against the Lord's orders, lose the privileged seniority within the tribe in favour of Juda who, on becoming the founder of the senior clan, gives his name to the Jews.

The criteria of Nuer patrilineages can be best understood, if the link between two agnates or "brothers" is conceived as the line, upon which the system is grounded. Direct siblings or other living members of the patrilineage are horizontally connected by this line, because they are the descendents of the same father or forefather in the male line. The father of two siblings represents the lowest top of the triangular structure arising above the groundline of the siblings. Above him, the grandfather, great-grandfather and other forefathers of the male line make up successively higher summits of larger and ever more inclusive triangular structures, whereas the groundline of agnates continues to be extended horizontally towards cousins of the more distant degrees. Thus the lineage structure of the Africanist model implies a series of inclusive triangles, vertically connecting living descendents on the ground with ever-higher "fathers" or deceased individual ascendents. Evans-Pritchard's major thesis is stressing the synchronic aspect of the lineage pattern. The ancestor focus is in fact connecting the living members of the lineage. The pedigree is constructed and manipulated to express the graded relations of interacting groups on the ground.

5. Middle Indian Tribal Descent Categories

The comparative reference to African and Biblical models of the lineage structure was introduced only to stress the fundamental difference of the unilineal descent categories in tribal middle India. The latter, though classed patrilineal like the former, have very little in common with clans and lineages in Africa, the Middle East or Polynesia, just as they are quite different from the royal or peasant lineages of the Rajput or Jat castes or those of Brahmins in coastal Orissa. If the question of the fundamental difference between caste and tribal society should arise, the answer would have to point to the structure of descent concepts along with the usual references to the division of labour and ritual services and to government in the caste system. Whereas all of the north and central Indian castes and all of the middle Indian tribes include a man's male and female children in his unilineal descent group the structured whole of these patrilineal categories among the castes is worlds apart from the overall pattern of the tribes. Where lies the difference?

Patrilineal tribal descent categories, like those of the the Nilotic Nuer, employ criteria of time to order synchronic social relations, but they do so in a manner quite different from the inclusive triangles of the African tribes. Any kind of ancestor-focus is lacking in tribal middle India. The descent categories, named after plants and animals or other totemic objects of nature, regularly refer to a particular location or habitat. They are the code for patterns of biotopes inhabited by the hill-people and they govern ritual interaction, intermarriage, feuding and status.

The Gond may be taken as an initial example. We learn from Buradkar (1940: 268-9) that one of the biggest Indian ST, comprising a population of some five million people, is segmented into four "Phratric Totems," or totemic categories of a superior level, opposing porcupine, tiger, crane and tortoise in the author's local example of Chanda. My own fieldwork in the old districts of Phulbani, Kalahandi and Koraput of Orissa and in Bastar, Madhya Pradesh, revealed what Grigson (1938: 306-7) had indicated earlier: The totemic names may change over the vast territory inhabited by the Gond, but the pattern remains the same. I think, I understood the superior fourfold classification when I found local examples where Buradkar's crane was substituted by the totem of cuckoo and his porcupine by that of cobra. The sky-bound animals and the earth-bound creatures juxtaposed exogamous social categories, just as tiger (land-bound) stood in a binary opposition to tortoise (water-bound) for humans of this difference. Such negative opposition between the two categories was inseparable from the positive affinal link[12] — or non-opposition — each one of them had to the two other categories of the quartet.

The phratric arrangement of the Gond represents the superior level of descent categories. Each phratry would furthermore include a specified number of totemic categories at a subordinate level. If we follow Buradkar, the earth-bound category would be linked with the number seven, the sky-bound one with number five, the land-bound one with six and the water-bound with four.

In my own ethnographic work it became clear that these numbers referred to gods as well as totemic clans. Grigson (1938: 306f), von Fürer-Haimendorf (1956: 500), and Hajra (1970: 81f) indicate marriage prohibitions among the phratries which I would rather see as positive and permanent rules: Those of even numbers are bound to intermarry

12. The "thought-of model" would suggest alternating links, not found by me on the ground, and deciphered from the ethnographic literature only with difficulties.

with those of odd numbers. In the biotopic code this would make earth-bound clans marry either land- or water-bound ones — but never those of the sky. The hiatus between land and water would be eternal.

By far the most comprehensive ethnography of the Gond is offered by von Fürer-Haimendorf (1948). Just as Herrenschmidt (1966) later, he reveals the temporal order of the phratries, i.e. their birth-order which is linked to the relative status of seniority. Unfortunately these detailed ethnographic accounts are presented in a modest style without theoretical claims so that their principle relevance does not become transparent at first sight. If von Fürer-Haimendorf's vast mass of descriptive ethnography is interpreted properly, it should become clear that Gond myths and affinal links order status by reference to time. The relations between the phratries clans and totems, i.e. the syntagmatic chain as well as the paradigmatic association[13] of the totemic categories linking humans to habitats in a temporal sequence, would have delighted Durkheim and Mauss (1963) at the beginning of the 20th century.[14] The social structuring employs the language of time and space in order to juxtapose the fourfold phratric classification. The odd or even numbered lists of clans introduce different habitats in a sequence of seniority.

The principles of classification are the same in all other tribes. Thus among the Santal seven senior totems precede five junior ones and among the former, the swan (i.e. bound to water) is the senior most, narrowly followed by the antelope of the land. The two must not intermarry. They are followed by categories of the sky-bound and the earth-bound type, meant for intermarriage with the first two totems (Pfeffer, 1984). These very oppositions, linking the biotopic code with that of status, politics and food, have similarly been interpreted for the Kharia (Pfeffer, 1993) where "late-comers" among the clans are divorced from "early birds" and those who settle "upstream" privileged against the "downstream" categories, i.e. "earlier" and "later" categories of purification. Following the general trend in Chhota Nagpur, the Kharia's superordinate level is not of the fourfold Gondi type but orders nine clans in a three-by-three style, united by the common myth of creation.

For a night I was able to listen to a similar myth among the Dangria Kondh relating the story of how their clans, all named after plants, left

---

13. These basic concepts of structural analysis are, of course, taken from F. de Saussure (1959).

14. For reasons of space, I have deliberately avoided introducing these classics here.

the body of mother earth in a certain sequence. Like Hansdak (swan) and Murmu (antelope) of the Santal, a good number of the Dangria clans were classed within consanguinally related — i.e. mutually non-marriageable — units of threes and fours. My friend and student Albert Götzelmann has collected the Kuttia Kondh myth of origin and discovered the same pattern there:[15] the earth goddess has given birth to the seven Kuttia clans in a particular sequence, and the first, the Nondrukar, oppose the last, the Timaka, who were debarred from leaving the maternal body on the normal route and had to find an extra route south of the Godavari.

This pattern could be exemplified by several other tribes, but I should also refer to an embarrassing failure: Having visited the unified assemblage of Desia tribes in Koraput/Orissa regularly since 1980, I was unable to discover a creation myth. All of the people are aware of their eight clan categories, i.e. fish, cobra, cow, bear, leopard, monkey, vulture and sun, but the typical myth linking these totemic indicators of biotopes in a temporal order was not found until finally in February 2000 an interview revealed the the complex myth and the seniority of the tiger clan. People were not so fond of narrating their origin to outsiders because it involved certain episodes which may be viewed as precarious under present circumstances.

6. Lower Levels

The fascinating aspect of the Africanist lineage theory was the systematic transition of the domestic into the politico-jural domain, to use Fortes' terminology. The local conditions represented one of several similar levels included by the global concept. Every male child stood for a potential lineage, every household was a "minimal lineage," structured like the clan or "maximal lineage". The obvious question, therefore, would be directed towards the alternatives of tribal middle India. I begin once more by stressing the importance of affinity.

Tribal marriages may follow the bilateral "cross-cousin" rule or demand intervals of one or three[16] generations. The Sora[17] altogether

15. Personal communication A. Götzelmann. The interview was conducted by a group including R. Hardenberg, M. Hussain, P. Mohanty, U. Blindt and me.
16. Among the Dangria Kondh, I may have been directed towards the concept of an interval of seven generations, but ethnographic work was so difficult, that I cannot confirm this information of a tribe absolutely prohibiting the repetition of intermarriage within short spans.
17. Vitebski's (1993) wonderful book is concerned with the Sora.

lack lineages clans and phratries.[18] I have found their local (patrilineal) lines to be affinally connected to those of other villages in some regions by "cross-cousin" marriage and in others[19] by the same kind of bilateral exchange demanding an interval of three generations. Among the Ho of Singhbhum people mentioned to me the name "mandi chattu" for the cognates of these three generations. It literally meant "eaters from the same pot" and implied that those eating from the same pot should not intermarry, or that those relatives by marriage beyond the third generation were not longer acceptable for commensality[20] and thus became marriageable.

Albert Götzelmann's ethnography[21] of the Kuttia Kondh is offering a riddle, which may lead into the same direction. These people do not admit affinal unions between those local groups, remembered to have married in the past.[22] Furthermore, the senior-most Nondruka clan — as an exception[23] — will not observe the rule of exogamy but permit internal marriages. Within the clan, however, Nondruka lineages are exogamous preserving their separate identity by the worship of certain "lineage-stones" or *bicha baling*. Worshippers of the same stones never intermarry. For every generation, Götzelmann was told, the lineage is adding a stone to the sacred collection. My question then related to the number of stones, and the ethnographer had noticed amounts of ten or less, but certainly not a great numbers linking many generations. My guess would therefore relate the sacred stones of the local lineage to their affinal rules or see them as indicators of a certain time span within which intermarriage was prohibited. But the details will have to be clarified

Beyond the marriage rules two other criteria differentiate the local exogamous units within the major clans and phratries. The first one is an obvious reference to time. Everywhere the original settlers of a village obtain higher status than those of a later arrival. Roy (1912: 92f),

18. The only other tribes of middle India lacking these institutions seem to be the Saora Paharia and the Mal Paharia of the Rajmahal Hills.
19. The former was in the neighbourhood of G. Udayagiri, the latter uphill from Parlakimidi.
20. This should be understood for ritual occasions. All over the tribal area, ethnographers find it difficult to count the separate hearths and pots on formal occasions such as marriages and funeral rites.
21. Personal communication.
22. This was the information I received during a three-month stay at village Tuakola near Belgarh.
23. My own fieldwork was conducted in a village of the - exogamous - Saraka clan.

on account of his legal training, was perhaps the first to elaborate the *khuntkatti* system of the Munda privileging those families who originally cleared the jungle for the village. Apparently, the term *khunt* stands for the local line of settlers. Among the Santal everywhere the "real" or *nij khunt* is opposed to the *sada khunt* of everyone else (Gausdal, 1960: 51f).

The second measure to differentiate local groups is to differentiate ritual obligations. All cultivators of tribal villages — but not their clients — are united by different functions for the village as a whole and for each other on ritual occasions such as marriage and death. All members of a tribe are given one of a very limited number of titles, which refer to sacred or secular obligations at the local level and never beyond. Normally these titles would be Sancritic terms. Thus the Kuttia Kondh differentiate *jani* local lines from *majhi* ones, or "priests" from "headmen," but the actual priest or petty chief might belong to either hereditary section. The secular opinion-leader would be appointed by the village council, the sacred one "discovered" by the shaman of the locality. In the same manner, Kondh segments settling north of the Kuttia territory offer the titles of "Pradhan" and "Malik" even though they are quite unaware of the Arabic origin of the latter term. The Dangria Kondh villages use a fourfold ritual classification separating the *jani* and *pujari* on the sacred side from the *mandal* and *bismajhi* in the secular department (Nayak, 1989).

When the British came to Chhota Nagpur, they may have been negotiating with people who introduced themselves as "Munda," so the whole tribe was given this name. Technically this was only the title of secular leadership, opposed to that of the sacred *pahan*, assigned to the second status group of the village while, following the threefold classification so typical of Chhota Nagpur, the *manki* of the senior secular group is added.

7. Taxonomy

The separation of exogamous and endogamous groups at the local level is only provisional or a technical device to clarify the differences. In reality both types are inseparably intermingled very much in the polythetic style of the Plains Indians of North America.[24] But whereas innumerable

24. See for example Fletcher & La Flesche (1972).

publications try to reconstruct the North American past, very few professional anthropologists seem to be interested in the middle Indian present. The latter also offer an exceptional or unique mode of classification. This feature of Juang ethnography may inspire further research.

The source is McDougal's (1963) dissertation, reporting how the Juang unify alternating generations on certain occasions. An individual identifies her- or himself with the members of his grandparental and every other *even* generation of ascendents and descendents but never with the parental or any other *odd* one. In longish appendices, McDougal demonstrates how the Juang keep track of the opposition between odd and even inspite of the irregularities of the sequence in natural generations. In fact, five or six classificatory generations may live together in a single village. A little child may belong to the generation of the great-grandparents of her adult neighbours. The relevant point is that all Juang belong to either one of two opposed blocks containing members of alternating generations. Literally McDougal has noted:

> "These generation-sets are recognized by the Juang although they are not named, nor are there technical terms to describe them. This twofold division does not depend upon an Ego based reference: The two generation-sets have independent existence in relation to each other. In certain formal situations the two generation-sets contained in a village function as groups — not categories — to which differential rights and obligations are allocated" (1963: 141).

In passing we may notice that kinship-terms too (McDougal, 1963: 447-8) unite alternating generations, and within each generational level seniors and juniors are separated. Thus senior siblings are linked to the grandparental and junior siblings to the generation of grandchildren. In fact marriages are possible between partners classed as "grandparent" and "grandchild" provided the clan is different.

Other endogamous links on the local level are unnamed affinal relations permanently, bilaterally uniting the relatives of one hamlet with those of several other villages. Affinity always contains a diachronic quality. In a co-ordinated manner, the tribal categories of classification may be presented in the following taxonomy of Figure 8.1.

Exogamous categories

Totem (water : land :: senior : junior) = Biotope in mythical time
(several binary oppositions at tribal and intertribal level)

Title = intra-village segments named "priest" : "headman":: senior : junior
(binary opposition at village level)

Alternating generational block "odd" : "even" :: senior : junior
(binary opposition *within* the village; only among the Juang)

Endogamous categories

Tribal pair, e.g. Ho : Munda :: j
(binary opposition at the intertribal level)

Tribal moieties, e.g. Dhelki Kharia: Dudh Kharia :: senior : junior
(binary opposition at the tribal level)

Alternating generational block "odd" : "even" :: senior: junior
(binary opposition *between* villages *only* among the Juang)

Figure 8.1: Taxonomy of Tribal Middle Indian Categories

8. Conclusion

All tribal categories are structured by the time factor. While the unilineal descent group of the Nuer or Tallensi employs the classificatory instrument of generations to construct agnatic corporations, the north Indian royal or peasant lineage can even exceed the generational depth of the African constructs by the specialist services of the genealogist caste and can — just like the Biblical or Polynesian endogamous or conical clan — achieve the dimension of history.

By a radical contrast, the unilineal construct of the middle Indian tribes is able to avoid history by juxtaposing its totemic categories, e.g. earth-bound *vs.* sky-bound, or by references to space. Categories of time always oppose the senior and the junior in a relativistic fashion, determining status, i.e. precedence in relation to the whole, but not history. Mythical time enumerates and orders the parts of the whole without a start in the present.

Classifications of this type do not offer fixed boundaries. The tribe is never the most inclusive or endogamous category, but rather a category of a binary opposition within and including others of the same type. As is the case with totemic categories, its relative status is determined by seniority. The Dhelki Kharia, for example, are the seniors, because they are said to have reached their present habitat before the Dudh Kharia. Time and space, the categories of understanding, are social constructs (Durkheim, 1912: 9f).

Beyond such series of oppositions, local segments of tribal society are bound together by intermarriage, the dynamic or live aspect of the structure. Similarly in the field of ritual, all local networks of villages are involved in grand give-away feasts (Pfeffer, 2000) or total social facts which, as opposed to affinal give and take, represent the religious or "senior" aspect of the eternal reciprocal obligations that constitute social structure.

REFERENCES

Barnes, J.A. 1962. "African Models in the New Guinea Highlands," *Man*, 62 (1&2) Art. 2.

Barth, Frederik 1959. "Segmentary Opposition and the Theory of Games: A Study of Pathan Organisation," *Journal of the Royal Anthropological Institute*, 89 (1): 5-22

Boas, Franz, 1911. *The Mind of Primitive Man.* New York: Macmillan.

Buradkar, M.P. 1940. "Totemism among the Gonds," *Man in India*, 20 (3): 113-43 & 20 (4): 268-94.

Dumont, Louis. 1975. (transl. by M. and J. Douglas). "Preface to the French Edition of E.E. Evans-Pritchard's The Nuer," (pp. 328-42) in J.H.M. Beattie and R.G. Lienhardt (eds.), *Studies in Social Anthropology. Essays in Memory of E.E. Evans-Pritchard by his Former Oxford Colleagues.* Oxford: Clarendon.

Durkheim, Emile. 1912. *Les Formes élémentaires de la vie religieuse: le système totémique en Australie.* Paris: Alcan.

Durkheim, Emile and Marcel Mauss. 1963. (French orig. 1903). *Primitive Classification.* Translated and Introduced by Rodney Needham. Chicago: The University of Chicago Press.

Evans-Pritchard, E.E. 1940. *The Nuer. A Description of the Modes of Livelihood and Political Institutions of a Nilotic People.* Oxford: Oxford University Press.

Fletcher, Alice C. and Francis La Flesche. 1972. (org. ed. 1911). *The Omaha Tribe.* Lincoln: University of Nebraska Press.

Fortes, Meyer. 1945. *The Dynamics of Clanship among the Tallensi.* London: Oxford University Press

____. 1949a. *The Web of Kinship among the Tallensi. The Second Part of an Analysis of the Social Structure of a Trans-Volta Tribe.* Oxford: London University Press.

____. 1949b. "Time and Social Structure: An Ashanti Case Study," in M. Fortes (ed.), *Social Structure: Studies Presented to A.R. Radcliffe-Brown.* Oxford: Clarendon.

____. 1953. "The Structure of Unilineal Descent Groups," *American Anthropologist*, 55: 17-41.

____. 1969. *Kinship and the Social Order. The Legacy of Lewis Henry Morgan*. London: Routledge & Kegan Paul.

Fortes, Meyer and E.E. Evans-Pritchard. (eds.). 1940. *African Political Systems*. Oxford: Oxford University Press.

Fox, Richard. 1971. *Kin, Clan, Raja, and Rule*. Berkeley: University of California Press.

Fürer-Haimendorf, Christoph von. 1948. *The Raj Gonds of Adilabad*. London: Macmillan.

____. 1956. "The Descent-group System of the Raj Gonds," *Bulletin of the London School of Oriental Studies*, 18 (3): 499-51.

Gausdal, J.G. 1960. *The Santal Khuts*. Oslo: Aschehoug.

Government of Orissa. 1994. *Tribal Education in Orissa in the Context of Education for All by 2000 AD*. Bhubaneswar: Tribal Welfare Department Publication.

Grigson, W.V. 1938. *The Maria Gond of Bastar*. London: Oxford University Press.

Hajra, D. 1970. *The Dorla of Bastar*. Calcutta: Anthropological Survey of India.

Hardenberg, Roland. 2000. *Das rituelle Königtum in Puri (Orissa). Symbolische Analyse einer universalen Ordnung*. Berlin: Das Arabische Buch, Reihe Indus (in print).

Herrenschmidt, Olivier. 1966. *Le cycle de Lingal*. Paris: Unpubl. Dissertation.

Kirchhoff, Paul. 1959. The Principles of Clanship in Human Society," (pp. 260-70) in Morton H. Fried (ed.), *Readings in Anthropology II*.

Kuper, Adam. 1982. "Lineage Theory: A Critical Retrospect," *Annual Review of Anthropology*, 11: 71-95.

Leach, Edmund. 1954. *Political Systems of Highland Burma*. A Study of Kachin Social Structure. London: Athlone.

Lévi-Strauss, Claude 1953. "Social Structure," (pp. 524-53) in A.L. Kroeber (ed.), *Anthropology Today*. Chicago: The University of Chicago Press.

____. 1969. (2nd. ed.) (French first edition 1949). *The Elementary Structures of Kinship*. Boston: Beacon.

____. 1976 (French orig. 1955). *Tristes tropiques*. Harmondsworth: Penguin.

McDougal, Charles. 1963. The Social Structure of the Hill Juang. Unpubl. Diss. The University of New Mexico (University of Minnesota Microfilm).

Nayak, P.K. 1989. *Blood, Women and Territory*. An Analysis of Clan Feuds of Dangria Kondhs. New Delhi: Reliance Publishing House.

Parkin, Robert J. 1992. *The Munda of Central India. An Account of their Social Organisation*. Delhi: Oxford University Press.

Peters, Emrys L. 1990. *The Bedouin of Cyrenaica. Studies in Personal and Corporate Power*. Cambridge: Cambridge University Press.

Pfeffer, Georg. 1993. "Kharia Totemism," *Journal of the Indian Anthropological Society*, 28 (3): 221-28.

____.1984. "Santal Totemism," *South Asian Anthropologist*, 5 (1): 37-43.

____. 2000. "A Ritual of Revival among the Gadaba of Koraput," in H. Kulke and B. Schnepel (eds.), *Jagannath Revisited*. Delhi: Manohar.

Radcliffe-Brown, A.R. 1952. *Structure and Function in Primitive Society*. London: Routledge & Kegan Paul.

Roy, Sarat Chandra. 1912. *The Mundas and their Country*. Calcutta: Asia Publication.

____. 1915. The Oraons. Ranchi: Man in India Office.

Sahlins, Marshall D. 1954. Social Stratification in Polynesia: A Study of Adaptive Variation in Culture. Unpubl. Ph.D. Dissertation, Columbia University; Microfilm: University of Michigan Press, Ann Arbor.

____. 1963. "Poor Man, Rich Man, Big Man, Chief: Political Types in Melanesia and Polynesia," *Society and History*, 5: 285-303.

____. 1968. *Tribesmen*. Englewood Cliffs: Prentice Hall.

Saussure, F. de 1959. *Course in General Linguistics*. London: Owen.

Sinha, S.C. 1962. "State Formation and Rajput Myth in Tribal Central India," *Man in India*, 42: 35-80.

Stein, Burton. 1975. "The State and the Agrarian Order in Medieval South India: A Historiographical Critique," (pp. 64-91) in B. Stein (ed.), *Essays on South India*. New Delhi: Vikas.

Tiemann, Günter. 1968. "Begriff und Wert der Bruderschaft bei den Jat von Haryana in Nordindien," *Sociologus*, 18 (1): 35-45.

Verdon, Michael. 1982. "Where have all the Lineages Gone? Cattle and Descent among the Nuer," *American Anthropologist*, 84: 566-79.

Vitebsky, Piers 1993. *Dialogues with the Dead. The Discussion of Mortality among the Sora of Eastern India*. Cambridge: Cambridge University Press.

Weber, Max. 1956. *Wirtschaft und Gesellschaft*. Tübingen: Mohr.

NINE

THE SOCIAL STRUCTURE OF THE JĒNU KUṞUMBA: A South Indian Gatherer/Hunter Society

ULRICH DEMMER

The present article explores the social structure of the Jēnu Kuṛumba, a society of gatherer/hunters in South India. As is well known by now, foraging societies in India, as well as in many other parts of the world,[1] often do not exhibit the clear cut and well articulated spirit of systematic structure as it has been shown to exist among tribal cultures of Middle India (Pfeffer, 1982) or Nepal (Gaenszle this volume). Rather the social structures of foraging societies as the Palliyar (Gardner, 1966), the Maḷa Pandaram (Morris 1982), the Nayaka (Bird David, 1987) or the Jēnu Kuṛumba show a considerable degree of fluidity and flexibility — in fact to an extend that scholars have denied the very existence of a social structure at all among these groups. A second look, however, provided by more recent studies made clear, that structures of relationships do play a considerable role in South Indian foraging societies. Of course they do this to varying degrees but, as the present paper will disclose, at least among the Jēnu Kuṛumba structures of social relatedness are of paramount importance.

For these structures to become visible, however, the exploration of the rather fluid social structure of a foraging tribal community like the Jēnu Kuṛumba needs to pay close attention to the forms of lived social praxis, since it is predominantly, though not exclusively, in the various

1. Cf. Lee and DeVore, 1968 and Ingold, Riches and Woodburn, 1988, Vols. 1 and 2.

fields of social practices that relational structures are objectified. In what follows we will examine various fields of the relational fabric which, taken together, constitute this society.

The major part of the paper will deal with what could be called the internal structure of the community. Here we will look first into the structure of interpersonal relationships, i.e. the structure of kinship as it is relevant for sociality. We will ask how personal kinship relations are structured and we will outline the social resp. moral concepts which the Jēnu Kuṟumba employ in this process. This will be followed by an analysis of actual kinship structures in everyday as well as in ritual life. We will investigate the structure of camps organised for economic purposes: the foraging camps and their structure of kinship relations and we will analyse a further domain of praxis, namely the death ritual of the Jēnu Kuṟumba. To be sure, until not long ago religion and ritual were regarded as almost irrelevant for foraging societies in South India. Yet, more recent studies show that religion and ritual performances constitute an important part of the social life of these cultures.[2] This is in particular true for the Jēnu Kuṟumba who perform rituals in an elaborated manner. Accordingly, the present essay will examine more closely the structure of social relations as enacted in the performance of this ritual.

Finally the Jēnu Kuṟumba, like all the other above mentioned foraging groups in South India, are by no means isolated from the rest of Indian society. The concluding section of the paper will therefore examine the concepts that are used to structure the "outside world," i.e. the more encompassing regional society. In that section we will explore the social structure of the intertribal-system in the region and we will see how the Jēnu Kuṟumba situate themselves in this regional system of intertribal relationships.

It will become evident throughout the paper that the Jēnu Kuṟumba show a richness of social structure not anticipated so far for a "simple society" as theirs.

Habitat and Economic Background

The Jēnu Kuṟumba belong to the class of foraging cultures in South India that includes tribes as, to mention only the better studied groups, the Palliyar, the Mala Pandaram or the Nayaka. Among these the Jēnu

2. Cf. Bird-David, 1999 and forthc.; Demmer, 2000; Gardner, 1991; Morris, 1981.

Kuṟumba are, as the reports of the Census of India[3] publications show, the largest gatherer — hunter society, enumerating more than 15,000 people. The home range of the Jēnu Kuṟumba stretches along the western side of the ghat forests being parts of the states of Kerala, Tamil Nadu and Karnataka respectively. Linguistically the Jēnu Kuṟumba belong to the Dravidian language family and speak a language that is peculiar in many respects, though it is close to Kannada and to the Ālu Kuṟumba language.[5]

The Jēnu Kuṟumba of the present study live in the forest region of the northern Nilgiri Hills.[6] This area constitutes also the traditional foraging range of the people. In these forests they gather a variety of eatable tubers, fruits, berries and leaves for consumption. In addition they hunt minor animals, though hunting was never that important for their subsistence economy. Since the establishment of so called "Reserve Forest Areas" and the wildlife sanctuaries of Mudumalai and Bandipur in the middle of this century, however, the Jēnu Kuṟumba are no longer permitted to forage in these forest regions permanently. Instead they are forced to live in settlements at the periphery of the sanctuaries and Reserve Forest Areas. In the latter, however, they are entitled to gather the so-called "minor forest products", like honey, tamarind, treemoss, soapnuts, etc. and the Jēnu Kuṟumba are throughout the year engaged in gathering these "products" in the forest. For that purpose the Jēnu Kuṟumba form gathering camps moving through the Reserve Forest Areas. However, they return to the settlements, either as the whole camp or simply as single conjugal pairs, every three or five days, because outside of the forest the state government has established an institution that purchases their gathered products — a branch of the so-called "LAMP" — Societies.[7] But soon after selling their gathered products to the "Society" the Jēnu Kuṟumba return as quick as possible back into the forest and a further period of gathering begins. In terms of residence and locality then the Jēnu Kuṟumba can be said to continue their flexible

3. Cf. Census of India 1961: Vol. IX, Part V-B(1), Preface. Vol. XI, Part V-A. Vol.VII, Part V-A, p. 125 and Census of India 1971: Series 19, Part IX, p. 227; Series 9, Part II-C (I), p. 215.
4. In Tamil and Malayalam speaking areas the Jēnu Kuṟumba are also known as "Kattunayaka".
5. For the language of the Jēnu Kuṟumba cf. Gossel, n.d. For the language of Ālu Kuṟumba cf. Kapp, 1982.
6. For a detailed study of their socio-economic organisation, see Demmer, 1996.
7. LAMP translates as "Large Multipurpose Society". This institution is exclusively entitled to purchase the minor forest products.

foraging style of living. And this is also true with regard to their social structure.

Levels of Analysis: Individualistic Culture and Moral Community

Apart from their economy and the resulting fluid foraging pattern of continuous movements in and out of the forests, the Jēnu Kuṛumba share with all the above mentioned groups a set of societal features demarcating their peculiar social configuration as societies of the gatherer/hunter type.

On the most general level one can state that these cultures are not organised on the group or inter-group level of relatedness. As all studies concerned with the social order of South Indian gatherer-hunter societies show, these cultures have no lineages, no unilinear or agnatic descent groups that act or define themselves as corporate units, nor do we find clan- or moiety systems of organisation.[8] This pattern is further underlined by the fact that a model of well formed group organisation is also not articulated in indigenous discourses — neither in mythology nor in narratives or rituals do we find a representation of their society in these terms. All this holds true for the Jēnu Kuṛumba as well. In sum, then, one can say that the social order of these societies is obviously not framed in a group model of society and the social structures of these societies cannot be grasped in terms of such a model either. In fact, some of the above mentioned communities show an absence of societal structures to such an extent that quite early the foraging cultures of South India were termed "individualistic cultures".

This term was initially coined by Gardner (1966). It was intended to characterise the social system of the Palliyar and was later also taken up by Morris (1978) and Bird-David (1987). Faced with the above mentioned absence of "society" these authors tried to come to terms with the social systems of these cultures and the very term "individualistic culture" was referred to in order to indicate their typical features. Those features were variously described. Thus the Palliyar are characterised by "a low level of communication" (Gardner, 1966: 399), by the absence of "formalised bodies of knowledge" (ibid.: 398), by a stress on individual autonomy and a corresponding lack of cooperation (ibid.) and by the

8. On Hill Pandaram see Morris, 1982, on Palliyar cf. Gardner, 1966, on Nayaka see Bird-David, 1987 and on Jēnu Kuṛumba Demmer, 1996, 1997, 1999.

absence of any social structure "beyond the nuclear family" (ibid.). In a similar way Morris (1978) and Bird-David (1987) stressed the absence of cooperative units or social organisations beyond the nuclear family for the Mala Pandaram and the Nayaka. Bird-David (1987) too stated that among these cultures social relations are fragmentary to the extent that formal kinship patterns are of no importance for these societies. And in the case of the Mala Pandaram Morris found a "relative 'emptiness' of the kinship system as a guide to behavioral expectations between relatives" (1982: 136). In sum one can say that the model of "individualistic culture" was so promising because it suggested a type of society on the most simple level, society in it's *status nascendi*, so to say. Indeed Gardner, when he found that the Paliyar represented an individualistic culture, quoted Levi Strauss' famous expression where he spoke of a society "reduced to the point at which I found nothing but human beings" (1966: 399).

However, as attractive as this model of "individualistic culture" was, all authors were also aware that it left out the many indications of moral and kinship obligations that were described in their respective analysis. Thus Gardner describes a system of social control as well as a concept of solidarity where "primary bonds (brother-sister, sister-sister, parent-grown child) oblige a member of one nuclear family to extend aid to a member of another" (1966: 393). Among the Mala Pandaram Morris (1982: 157, 183) found the importance of affinal kinship ties for the formation of cooperative gathering groups, and finally Bird-David (1994, 1995) described the relevance of dyadic kin relationships among the Nayaka.

Therefore the present contributors to the debate on Indian foragers social system seem to agree that the model of individualistic culture yielded results mainly in the negative or in what Nurit Bird has recently called the "impression of social deficiency" (1987: 152). This impression, she continues, "is a logical corollary of analysis which dwells upon what hunter-gatherers do not have and do not do. Such an analysis in turn derives to a large extend from using the 'group model,' which is not wholly suitable for hunter-gatherers" (ibid.). As a consequence neither of the two levels of social analysis seem to provide an appropriate frame for the study of the South Indian foraging cultures. Indeed, as most recent studies suggest, it is neither the group level of organisation nor the level of the individual but rather the level of sociality where the social character of these foraging cultures becomes visible. Thus Bird-

David (1994) argues that sociality, defined as the level of immediate personal relatedness, is the most relevant starting point for the social analysis of the Nayaka. And in the present article too we will disclose, how the study of sociality, understood as *interpersonal* kinship relationships *in praxis*, is able to show central patterns of the social system of the Jēnu Kuṟumba.

Kinship and Morality

Since there are no lineages, unilinear or agnatic descent groups that act or define themselves as corporate units, the social order the Jēnu Kuṟumba is, as already mentioned, not framed in a group model of society, but rather in interpersonal terms of sociality. In fact, on the most extended level the Jēnu Kuṟumba are organised in a quasi endogamous network of relatives. As I have shown elsewhere in more detail this network is the result of a specific marriage pattern and embraces between 250 to 300 married people.[9] And since all of the members of this network are related with each other through narrow and extended kinship ties of filiation and marriage, one could speak of such a network as of a classificatory kindred.[10]

Relationships within the network, however, are not only based on kinship. Rather is sociality essentially based on a moral order? This implies first and foremost the idea that the conventions that people employ to structure their personal relations are directed by what Harre has called habitual schemes: "moral orders, local systems of obligation and duty with associated valuation criteria" (1990: 348). In fact, the Jēnu Kuṟumba understand themselves in terms of a moral community where relatedness is based on shared moral obligations. These moral conventions, though, are articulated in the idiom of kinship. It is therefore the kinship system that provides, along the line of filiative and affinal relationships, the "blue print," so to say, for morality and thus for reciprocity, for the flow of ritual gifts and contributions as well as for the legitimacy of everyday demands. In the following we will outline the most important features of this moral system of kinship. On the most abstract level the moral system of the Jēnu Kuṟumba is represented in the classificatory scheme of the kinship terminology, being of the common Dravidian pattern as shown in the figure below.

9. Cf. Demmer, 1996.

10. In contrast to Yalman's or Barnett's micro-castes the networks are not confined to genealogical kindred formations. Cf. Yalman, 1962 and Barnett, 1975.

ETTAN		*ACCI*	
APPAN	OVVE	MĀVAN	ATTE
AṄṄAN	AKKA	BĀVAN	ATTIGE
TAMMAN	TEṄGE	MAYIDAN	NĀDINI
MAṄAN	MAGA	AḶEN	SOJE
MŪMAṄAN		*MŪMAGA*	

Figure 9.1: The System of Terms

For this terminological system equations of kinship apply as in the list below:[11]

Ettan = FF, MF	Acci = MM, FM
Appan = F, FB	Māvan = MB, FZH, WF
Ovve = M, MZ	Atte = FZ, MBW, WM
Akka = eZ, FBeD, MZeD	Attige = MBeD, FZeD
Teṅge = yZ, FByD, MZyD	Nādini = MByD, FZyD
Aṇṇan = eB, FBeS, MZeS	Bāvan = MBeS, FZeS
Tamman = yB, FByS, MZyS	Mayidan = MbyS, FZyS
Maṅan = S, für Ego Δ = BS, für Ego 0= ZS	Aḷen = DH, für Ego Δ = ZS, für Ego 0= BS
Maga = D, für Ego Δ = BD, für Ego 0 = ZD	Soje = SW, für Ego 0 = BD, für Ego Δ = ZD
Mūmaṅan = DS, SS	Mūmaga = DD, SD

Figure 9.2 : The Terms and their Equations

If we further analyse this terminological system in terms of moral expectations and behavioral attitudes we can see that two domains of sociality arc cmbcddcd in the system, namely a domain of kin relations and a domain of affinal relations. Each domain, in turn, is made up of a limited number of dyadic relationships.

To be sure, this system of classification is relevant not only for the morality of personal behavior but it outlines also the direction for marriage relations. On the one hand, therefore, this scheme of oppositions expresses, as it does elsewhere in South India,[12] an associated pattern

11. Classificatory siblings or cross-cousins acquire their status of elder or younger to each other on the base of their actual relative age, for example *aṇṇan* = FBS [elder then Ego].
12. Cf. Dumont, 1983.

of cross-cousin (MBD/FZD) marriage, resulting in the network of the classificatory kindred.[13] In the context of the present article, however, we will focus in more detail on how the structure of the system is relevant with regard to specific moral concepts that people use to structure their interpersonal relations in the economic and in the ritual field of social praxis.

KIN DOMAIN		*AFFINAL DOMAIN*	
ovve	appan	māvan	atte
maga	maṅan	aḷen	soje
akka	aṇṇan	bāvan	attige
teṅge	tamman	mayidan	nādini

Figure 9.3 : Domains of Sociality

Moral Concepts of Kinship

Recent developments in social theory suggest that the social structure of a society can be seen as an active accomplishment of its members. This accomplishment, in turn, is the result of agents who structure social life through the application of social concepts and habitual schemes. Thus Bourdieu[14] and Ortner (1984), to take only the more prominent praxis theorists, argue that structures are based on habitual dispositions and cultural schemata. And Giddens too sees a reservoir of "mutual knowledge about rules and resources" enabling actors to generate structures and social patterns.[15] As a detailed structural analysis shows, this is also the case among the Jēnu Kuṛumba, where the structure of many fields of social life can be seen as being based on explicit social concepts. Among the Jēnu Kuṛumba, however, these concepts are embedded in the system of kinship.

The classificatory scheme of kinship as shown above represents an elaborate system of moral conventions. In other words, what is embedded in the terminological system is a moral system that defines the possible behavioral expectations and attitudes among the social actors. And it does so on at least two levels. One level is certainly the domain of

13. Cf. Demmer, 1996.
14. Cf. Bourdieu, 1987: 30, 108 pp. or 197 pp.
15. Cf. Giddens, 1979: 64 pp. 84.

dyadic kinship relationships. Thus we find, for example, the dyad *akka/tenge*, the dyad *aṇṇan/tamman* or the dyad *māvan/aḷen*. These dyadic sets constitute domains of sociality constrained by moral conventions — a set of certain attitudes with regard to everyday transactions and behavior (e.g. avoidance, joking, respect, sharing, reciprocity, etc.).[16] All dyadic sets are thus associated with specific expectations of behaviour between these relatives. On a second level, moreover, the system as a whole clearly separates kin and affinal relatives and thus differentiates two broad domains of sociality: a domain of affinity and a domain of agnatic-consanguine (kin) relationships.

If we focus on this latter level we can see that both domains are associated with a system of moral expectations which repeat the opposition between the two domains of kin and affines. In general the kin-domain is dominated by hierarchical and asymmetrical social expectations and attitudes. The affinal domain, in contrast, is dominated by egalitarian and symmetrical attitudes. Among affines the expectation of reciprocal support and help is appropriate. Thus expectations of sharing and the distribution of work and things prevail within circles of affines.

The most important social category in the affinal domain that is associated with a morality of sharing and support is constituted by relatives denoted with the term *bā-mayika*. This category encompasses a circle of relatives standing in relationships of marriage so that the term is equivalent to Dumont's application of affines.[17] In everyday life it is in particular the dyads ZH/WB (resp. BW/HZ) and the dyad WF/DH (resp. HM/SW) that gain most significance as *bā-mayika*. *Bā-mayika,* the Jēnu Kuṛumba say, can demand each other support in everyday interaction and they should also share and distribute among each other. They should support each other if any one of them runs into difficulties in everyday life like having no cloth, no money, no cigarettes, food provisions, *et al.* And they should help each other in processes of work, e.g. in the dangerous work of honey-gathering. It should be pointed out, however, that only marriage legitimises this kind of demands. Thus, among genealogical affines of the same generation (MBS/FZS, MBD/

16. Since the present paper is concerned with the more general patterns of sociality, we do not need to describe the dyads and their respective attitudes in detail here. Such a description is provided, however, in Demmer, 1996.
17. Cf. L. Dumont, 1983: 75.

FZD), demands of mutual support are not regarded as proper behavior. Moreover, *bā-mayika* should not only support one another with regard to issues of everyday life. In rituals too this category is of central significance. Thus, all those who are tied to each other through marriage should contribute, as we will see below, in rituals, particularly in death rituals (*pole*). There the husbands of Ego's sisters, resp. daughters, are obliged to contribute, i.e. the ZH has to contribute in Ego's father's *pole* and/or DH has to contribute in Ego's death ritual. In other words, all these relatives, the *bā-mayika*, are situated or "bound"[18] in a complex network of everyday sharing and cooperation.

This principle of mutual support among *bā-mayika* is supplemented by another social evaluation of this affinal relationship. For *bā-mayika*, the Jēnu Kuṛumba hold, are those who are "one" and those who are "equal" — *bā-mayika* are *ondeve* and *sāmave*, they are the people in whose company one really likes to go into the forest for gathering, they are those who are seen likewise with pleasure in ones own company, they are those, who are "close relatives" (*daṇḍe sontagāru*) who, moreover, should also marry among each other. Among the Jēnu Kuṛumba this category is conceptualised even to encompass relations of conjugality. The women one is married to is called the "woman of ones hut" and as my interlocutors pointed out to me, these two people are *bā-mayika* too — husband and wife, the conjugal pair (*okkal*), are *bā-mayika* and, furthermore, husband and wife are thus regarded as being equal (*sāmave*) too.

As an ideal type the category of "*bā-mayika*" encompasses a set of relatives as shown in the figure below:

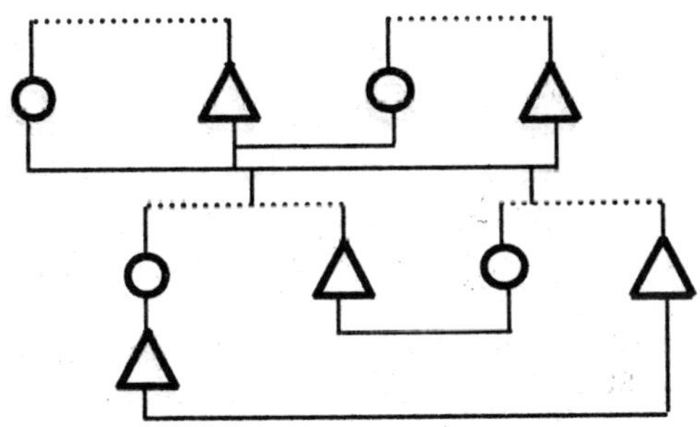

— — — — — — — = Classificatory Kinship

Figure 4 : The Category of Bā-mayika as an Ikeal Type

18. As in many other Dravidian languages to marry someone is called in Jēnu Kuṛumba, "to bind (*kaṭṭale*) someone".

In sum, and with regard to the narrative representations of these concepts provided below, we can state that the category *bā-mayika* is conceptualised as a specific domain of sociality with associated moral values. In it equality, sharing and support is stressed and expectations of positive relatedness dominate.

In contrast to this positive social evaluation of the affinal domain, the sphere of kin/consanguinity is marked by rather negative evaluations fore-grounding hierarchy and asymmetrical expectations. In fact, the conceptualisation of *bā-mayika* as equals stands in opposition to expectations of behaviour in the "kin" sphere, particular to those between brothers, i.e. elder and younger brothers. Even though it is commonly held that those being in this dyadic relationship should support each other as well, no Jēnu Kuṟumba I spoke to thought it appropriate to speak of brothers as equals. Thus it is that this dyad is not only the locus of hierarchy proper, but that this feature dominates this dyad to an extent that it excludes sharing and mutual support in everyday life. While in the domain of affines people should show confidence in the sharing of things and in mutual support, transactions among brothers are rather exceptional and treated with suspicion. This relationship dyad is asymmetrical then because the younger brother has in common understanding no right to approach an elder brother in a demanding manner. An elder brother, in contrast, is right to do so. In the sphere of everyday life this results in the common state of affairs that brothers regularly avoid each other and only seldom do they cooperate.

Moral Concepts in Narrative Genres

Certainly it is not enough to simply claim the existence of the above mentioned moral schemes without referring to indigenous contexts of their articulation. In other words we also need to ask where and how these moral schemes are articulated and transmitted by the people themselves.

Recent research in social and moral knowledge has increasingly shown that narrative forms and practices play a decisive role in the transmission of social concepts. Thus Taylor (1989) has argued that the members of a moral community acquire their understandings of values through narrative processes. In fact, narrativity is shown by him to be a precondition for the maintenance of the virtues a moral community is based upon. But narrativity is also of central significance with respect to the cognitive and experiential dimensions of social life. As Bruner (1991) has explored it is through processes of narration that experience and knowledge of the domain of social interaction is directed.[19]

Both of these observations are relevant for the Jēnu Kuṟumba. In this culture narrative genres are important means for the acquaintance and maintenance of concepts of sociality. At the same time, however, social concepts mediated through narratives also direct the experiences of people as well as their social evaluations and expectations. Indeed, as we will see, both of the above mentioned moral schemes — those related with the affinal domain of relationships as well as those associated with the sphere of kin/consanguinity — are made explicit in narrative forms. The range of narrative forms is, at least among the Jēnu Kuṟumba, broad. Social meaning is, for example, explicated in the rather short songs that are sung during rituals. Thus a song performed during the puberty ceremony for girls articulates the value of the relationship among affines of unequal generations, namely among ego and wife's father (*māvan*), resp. husband's mother (*atte*).

Give the pot, *atte* and *māvan,*
give the pot, the necklace, the necklace
we need rice.....
(*sembu kōḍu, atte māva, sembu*
kōḍu, kanne māle, kanne māle, arisi bēku,..)

Performed by unmarried girls this song is about the social expectation of support among affines and the giving of gifts, as example a cooking pot, a necklace or even rice for consumption, among relatives in this social domain. More elaborately articulated, however, is social knowledge in narratives proper and in the so-called "honey song" of the Jēnu Kuṟumba. Moreover, these narrative forms not only depict the moral schemes associated with specific social domains but these genres develop their meaning also in a contrastive, structural manner. Indeed, the so called honey narrative (*jēnu-parasanga*) constructs the value of affinal relationships — here the meaning of conjugal relatedness — in *explicit contrast* to relatedness in the kin-domain, exemplified with the dyad of "elder and younger brother".

---

19. For a related argument in anthropology, cf. Carrithers (1992).

The Honey Narrative[20] (*Jēnu-parasanga*)

In the story six younger brothers and one elder brother go out for honey into the forest. The elder brother, however, is making his younger brothers to do all the work that is necessary to gather the honey in the huge tree that they finally found. They had to make the rope, they were ordered to make the ladder, to make the baskets, and so forth. Finally he also asked them to prepare his food and then to get the honey. This last demand, however, the younger brothers refused. They argued that he, the elder brother, should climb up the tree because he has the superior knowledge of honey gathering. Accordingly the elder brother climbed into the tree. Then the elder brother pierced comb after comb and let the honey down to his younger brothers who catch it and fill it in tins.

Yet, as soon as the elder brother has pierced all the honey and attempts to climb down, the younger brothers cut of the bamboo ladder being the only way down. Laden with honey they return to their huts leaving the elder brother helpless to the bees, who return in the evening and sting him terribly. After the younger brothers return to their huts the wife of their elder brother asks them about their elder brother. The younger brothers lie, pretending that he must have come back already. She however does not believe them, takes her small child on her hips and goes into the forest to search for her husband, even though it is getting dark already.

Ultimately, having faced many perils courageously on her way[21] she discovers her husband, sitting helpless and weeping in the huge tree. He asks her to return to their hut and to bring him his ceremonial utensils. This she does, but after she brings them, he asks her to leave him alone. He himself wants to turn into an eagle and to fly away into the deepest jungle. But that request she refuses with the argument that without him she is nothing and that her place is at his side. Finally her husband gives in and when all three of them were transformed into eagles by and by, they fly into the deepest jungle.

But in the end, after the parents have brought their child up in the jungle, all three return to the settlement of the younger

20. For the transcriptions and translations of all narratives referred to in this article, cf. Gossel n.d.

21. For example a strange hunter who invites her but whom she ignores; tigers and elephants that cross the tree where she takes rest in with her child, *et al.*

> brothers. There, the old-aged parents of the brothers see the three eagles sitting on a huge tree outside their settlement. To them the elder brother discloses his identity and the whole story of his brothers' misdeeds. In the end however he forgives them, even promises to protect the whole family, and then flies away with his wife and child.

As we can see, this narrative places the relationship between brothers in a clear-cut opposition to the affinal relationship *par excellence*, namely the conjugal pair. What is construed with the means of narrativity then is the meaning of the affinal domain which, in turn, is explicitly put in contrast to the kin domain of sociality. Thus this narrative demonstrates clearly what husband (*gaṇḍan*) and wife (*ëṇḍru*) should mean to each other and what value the conjugal relationship has for the Jēnu Kuṛumba: it is imagined as the real locus of solidarity, cooperation and support. In contrast, the agnatic relationship between elder brother and younger brother is represented as being unreliable, marked by self-interests and — in fact — treachery. With its implications of sharing, unity and support, the conjugal bond carries the implications of reciprocal support and accordingly the positive expectations that prevail in the affinal domain. The affinal relationship, *okkal*, is therefore set in clear opposition to the kin domain of elder and younger brother, where sociality is not marked by mutual support. In that way, the agnatic domain is negatively evaluated as being the locus of hierarchy and inequality.

The moral principle of mutual and reciprocal support as the distinguished feature of the affinal realm is also the theme of another narrative form, namely the honey song (*jēn-paduna*). This song is sung during the process of gathering rock-honey in steep and dangerous rocks. In it the gatherers construct a common identity with the bees, addressing the queen of the bees as mother-in-law whose potential sons-in-law, i.e. the gatherers, have come to take their wives from her. However, the song goes, this should not make the mothers angry. To the contrary, the honey gatherers claim the support of their affinal relatives *in spe* and ask them not to sting but to give the honey to their son in laws. How could a mother of one's wife refuse to support her son-in-law in his work, how could she do anything bad to her sons in law, her *bā-mayika*, is the argument here. In this song, then, the meaning of the affinal domain is constructed with explicit reference to marriage mother. While the honey narrative concentrates on the conjugal pair (*okkal*), the honey song explicates the social meaning of the affinal realm in focusing on the more encompassing category of *bā-mayika*.

Honey Song[22] (*Jēn-paduna*)

Gatherer:

They climb down the rock and pierce. The honey bees they make rise. I am the son-in-law.

In the storming of the wind he pierces the honey. Your blossoms, the girls, they scare them. The girls arise and dance. They pierce the girls, in the storming of the wind, they pierce the honey, in the wind, they pierce the girls. Don't bite children. Rise in the wind and dance, my dear ones.

Baregų eragi kuttidar-alla. Jēn uḷune ē:lsidan-alla. nānu aḷen-alla. gāḷi Īṭalu jēnune kuttidanu. ninna ūne eṇṇu makkane jaḍedaru. eṇṇu-makka eddu āḍidaru. eṇṇu-makkane kuttidaru, gāḷi Īṭalu jēnune kuttidaru, eṇṇu-makkane gāḷilu kuttidaru. kaccāde-ka makkale. gāḷilu eddu āḍuna-ka.

Others:

Kihihi, kihihi

Gatherer:

In the leaves they climb up, standing steady in the storming of the wind. In this wind they climb. Having come across seven mountains, seven ravines, they climb. Having cut the bōka-blossoms which they were asked to bring, they climb. The rock he climbs down, they say. In the rope, in the fibreladder he climbs down in the wind. It lifts up the cloth. I am the son in law. The honey bees, they plaster the rock.

soppulu attidaru, gāḷi ōtalu nindu deyira Ī gāḷilu attidaru. ēḷu beṭṭa, ēḷu aḷḷa, sutti bandu attidaru. bōka-ūne kuydu, tarsida ū kuydu attidaru. baregamba eragidanu. agga, mālulu eragidanu

---

22. Usually the honey gatherer who is engaged in the rocks is singing this song. The other people present, all together or only some of them, reply to his verses with cries of joy. The atmosphere during this work in the often very steep rocks is a mixed one where moments of danger and excitement alternate. The Ālu Kuṟumba of the eastern Nilgiris sing also honey-songs. As Kapps ma-terial (1983) suggests these songs carry social meanings similar to those presented here.

gāḷilu. baṭṭene ella tūkidadu. nānu aḷen nān. jēnu-kunni kallugu metidde.

Others:

Kihi, kihihi, kihi

Gatherer:

Having cut the *bōka*-blossoms, seven mountains, seven ravines. Don't make a fight. Until I take, you remain peaceful. Having entered the cave they take the girls. The girls they restrain. Seven mountains, seven ravines. An empty fortress for the girls who cut and came.

bōka-ūne kuydu, ēḷu beṭṭa, ēḷu aḷḷa jagala māḍāde-ka. nān eṭṭa gaṇṭa summag iru. eṇṇu-makkane ettidar-alla aḷe oḷage ukku. eṇṇu-makkane taḍedaru. ēḷu beṭṭa, ēḷu aḷḷa. kuydu banda eṇṇu-makkagu āku koṭṭe.

Others:

Kihi, kihihi, kihi

Gatherer:

Remain peaceful for awhile. Still awhile they climb down and pierce. Seven mountains, seven ravines. In the empty fortress. They take the girls. Seven fortesses, seven places. All having cut jasmine-blossoms, they climb down in the wind. Having cut the jasmine-blossoms, they pierce the honey. I am the son-in-law.

selpa ottu summag-irnu. selpa ottu eragi kuttidar-alla. ēḷu beṭṭa, ēḷu aḷḷa. āku koṭṭelu. eṇṇu-makkane ettidaru. ēḷu koṭṭe, ēḷu jāgalu. mallige-ūne kuydu ellaru, gāḷilu eragidaru. mallige-ūne kuydu jēnune kuttidaru. nānu aḷenu.

Others:

Kihi, kihihi, kihi

Gatherer:

Children, I am the son-in-law. They pierce the girls. I am the son-in-law. Seven rivers, seven blossoms, seven mountains, seven ravines.

makkaḷē, nānu aḷenu. eṇṇu-makkane kuttidaru. nān aḷen-alla. ēḷu nāru, ēḷu ū, ēḷu beṭṭa, ēḷu aḷḷa.

Others:

Kihi, kihihi, kihi

Gatherer:

I am the son-in-law, having climbed down in the wind. They bite. They pierce the girls. Don't bite, dear mother. The honey bees who cut the jasmine blossoms and came. On the rope itself I am the son-in-law. In the storming of the wind he climbs down and pierces the girls in the wind. I am the son-in-law.
eṇṇu-makkane kuttidaru. nān aḷenu gāḷilu eragi. kaccidaru. kaccāde-kavva. mallige-ūne kuydu banda jēnu-kunni. aggaleve nān aḷenu nān. gāḷi Ītalu eragi kuttidanu eṇṇu-makkane gāḷilu. nān aḷen-alla.

Others:

Kihihi, kihi, kihihi

Gatherer:

Having climbed down and having cut *bōka*-blossoms. Seven rivers, seven ravines, seven mountains. I am the son-in-law, yours. Having climbed down in the wind they pierce. For the girls that cut the jasmine-blossoms and come, for them there is an empty fortress. Girls rise up and dance. Don't bite. Rise up (as) from (old) times in the wind. It is again you girls. In the wind rise up and dance. I am the son-in-law. Mother, after you gave to us, we, having made your hands empty, we leave you (alone), yes? I am the son in law.
eragi bōka-ūne kuydu. ēḷu nāru, ēḷu aḷḷa, ēlu beṭṭa. nān aḷenu, ninna. gāḷilu eragi kuttidaru. mallige-ūne kuydu banda ennu-makkagu āku koṭṭe. eṇṇu-makka eddu āḍnu. kaccādenu. eddu kālainda gāḷilu. tirigi idder-alla eṇṇu-makka. eddu āḍidar-alla gāḷilu. nān aḷenu. avva, nangagu koṭṭoṭṭu, ningagu beru kayi māḍi, buṭṭeo(n)alla? nān aḷenu.

Others:

Kihi, kihihi, ki

Gatherer:

Seven rivers, seven mountains they surround. Girls, don't bite. Don't bite children. I. Just a little while more. I am the son-in-law.

Those who have trembled your fortress, they did wrong. I am the son-in-law. You made (that we) came together peacefully. I am the son-in-law.

ēḷu nīru, ēḷu beṭṭa suttidaru. eṇṇu-makka kaccādenu. makkale kaccādenu. nān. innu selpa ottu ganṭa. nān aḷen-alla. ninga āḷa asidavaru mōsa mādi buṭṭaru. nān aḷen nān. ninga summane sērsi idderu. nān aḷenu alla.

Others:

Ki, kihi, ki

As a close reading of this song shows, it is the morality among *bā-mayika* that is made the central theme in it. The gatherers address the bees as potential marriage partners and the mothers of the bees as mother of their affinal partners, who should not harm their sons-in-law but protect and support them. Through narrative means the honey gatherers thus construct a shared social identity as affinal relatives and they also explicate the moral meaning of this domain of sociality: *Bā-mayika,* the song makes clear, should care for each other — they should not withhold the "gift" of honey but they should support and protect one another.

Social Structures in Everyday Life and in Ritual

If we follow the theories of "praxis" as outlined above the social structure of a society can be seen as an active accomplishment of actors who use specific cultural and social concepts to bring forth the structure of their social configuration. In what follows we will therefore analyse how the Jēnu Kuṛumba employ their moral concepts in fields of social practices and how they structure their social world accordingly. We will explore two fields of practice. First we will investigate the structure of camps as they are formed in the foraging process. Then we will interrogate into the process of cooperation and gift giving in the death ritual. Let us first focus on the structure of everyday life as it appears during the extended periods of gathering in the forest.

As a detailed structural analysis of actual participants with regard to their mutual kinship relationships shows it is the moral concepts outlined above that give the gathering camps a specific social structure.[23]

23. Cf. Demmer 1997 for the details of that analysis.

If we consider the process of foraging itself it is an outstanding feature of that process that all minor forest products, except rock-honey, can be gathered by the cooperation of husband and wife. Only the gathering of rock-honey requires the cooperation of at least three people. And indeed, in the process of economic production it is the conjugal pairs (*okkal*) that constitute the basic structure of camps. As a structural analysis of camp formations show, it happens quite often that okkal either go out gathering alone or they move in groups where they are only accompanied by some unmarried youths (puṇḍagāru). In those cases the conjugal pairs go with their own unmarried elder children and/or with elder unmarried youths, being related to the couple otherwise, for example as terminological children[24] or bilaterally.[25]

In most cases, however, camps are formed by more than one conjugal pair and several of them will move together in search for minor forest products.[26] This is so because even though the members of these camps don't cooperate in the actual process of gathering, nevertheless they are, due to their kinship position, expected to support and help each other in cases this becomes necessary: one may detect honey, somebody has an accident, *et al.* Of course, as it could be expected of a foraging society, the personal composition of gathering camps is very flexible in the sense that their actual membership is configured anew each time people go out into the forest. However, the respective camps show a clear-cut pattern in terms of social relationships. First, the structure of all camps is based predominantly on affinal relations. Second, within this overall pattern, two types of camp structures can be seen to exist. One type has an "extended" affinal structure, the other type is more or less restricted to the conjugal, affinal pair.

The structure of the first type consists of people who are related immediately through marriage. In particular these are the dyads ZH/WB and WF/DH, a category that corresponds to Dumont's subcategory of "immediate affines" (1983: 75). On the other hand, there are in this type of camps genealogical affines as well, even though less frequently, i.e. MB/ZS or MBS/FZS. Camps showing such an "extended" affinal pattern

24. BS, BD (from male Ego's point of view), ZS, ZD (from female Ego's point of view).
25. As ZS, ZD (from male Ego's point of view) or as BS, BD (from female Ego's point of view).
26. The camps are called jōḍi by the Jēnu Kuṛumba, a term denoting a "pair," a "couple," but also more generally 'those who are one, united and equal' (Cf. Kittel, 1893).

can be observed in particular at times preceding rituals because at those times kinship duties are instantiated. As we will see below, this is the case when a death ritual (*pole*) is to be carried out and when the gifts of ZH resp. DH play a significant role. But this is also the case when one really needs reliable partners to work with, e.g. for the difficult and dangerous task of collecting rock honey (*bare jēnu*). Apart from this type we can also find a second type of gathering camps. This type is based essentially on conjugal pairs with more distant classificatory relationships.

Finally, and in contrast to the above structures, it is only in very rare cases that "real" brothers, i.e. those who are not terminological kin, move together in the same gathering camp.[27] Agnatic relations, therefore, are rather exceptional. This result of structural analysis can be supplemented with the fact that many of my Jēnu Kuṛumba friends also told me that they usually avoid going for gathering with their brothers. Moreover, some of them made it quite explicit that they do so because they don't trust their brothers. Accordingly, here in the field of gathering, brothers typically avoid each other, they do not cooperate and do not support each other. In sum, then, affinal structures emerge as the significant feature of everyday life. This structure, in turn, is based on the application of the moral schemes of kinship and their positive evaluation of the domain of affinal relationships.

The moral significance of affinal ties that dominates everyday life is also stressed in another context of social practice, namely the death ritual (*pole*) of the Jēnu Kuṛumba.[28] Death rituals proceed, as in many other cultures, in two phases.[29] In the first phase, performed immediately after the death of a person, the corpse of the dead person is buried. In a second phase, performed later on, the "spirit" (*gāḷi*) of the dead person is brought into the underworld. In both phases of the ritual, however, the reinforcement and representation of social structures and their associated moral values is a central concern for the people engaged. In particular people enact the value of affinity and the unity of affines in the course of the performance.

The first part of the ritual is, in comparison to the second part, of relatively short duration and is accomplished within a day's time. It is

27. There were only two cases in a sample of twenty-five camps.
28. For a more detailed description of Jēnu Kuṛumba death rituals, see Demmer, 1999.
29. Cf. Hertz, 1960; Huntington & Metcalf, 1979; Bloch & Parry, 1982; Pfeffer, 1991.

performed as soon as possible after a person has died and consists mainly in the burial of the dead body and in public wailing. This is accomplished in several sequences of acts. First, relatives prepare the corpse for burial, construct and decorate a barrow and subsequently carry the corpse, that lies on the barrow, to the burial place. There they dig the grave, put the dead body in it and finally fill it with earth.

All sequences involve as many as affinal relatives of the dead person as possible and here, as in all parts of the whole ritual, not only the brothers, sisters and children of the deceased play important roles but also the affinal kinpeople. In fact, all those who regard each other as *bā-mayika* are expected to cooperate. Thus, in this first part the close male relatives [B, S, DH, ZH, WB, F *et al.*] of the personal kindred of the dead, constituting a circle of affinal relatives, help each other to carry the barrow, they dig the grave together and all, male and female participants, are expected to throw a handful of earth into the grave. In addition to these performed acts, intended to support and help the dead and one another, these first sequences of actions are interspersed with discursive articulations that underline the unity of affines. Here it is in particular the female circle of affines who stress the morality of kinship (W, Z, D, M, FZ, WM, SW, *et al.*) but also the above mentioned male relatives of the deceased take part. Addressing the spirit of the dead person, all these relatives express in one way or another their positive relatedness and their solidarity with the dead person. But they also articulate the unity among themselves, i.e. among the living. They bemoan that the dead relative is now alone and that it has no support any more. They bemoan that they, the living, miss the dead person's contributions to communal life and they memorise the good sociality of the dead person when it was alive and contributed to the well being of the relatives.

In the second phase of the ritual the expression of the morality of kinship is even more elaborate. After the burial of the body it may take weeks or months until this part can be carried out but finally, after all relatives have come together, they present themselves in a sequence of symbolic actions as supportive and unanimous relatives gathered together to help their dead relative to reach the underworld. In this process they ultimately present themselves as "children of one hut" (*onde mane makka*).

The ritual as a whole proceeds in sequences, each sequence being devoted to the performance of certain supportive contributions of specific

30. This music is called the "tune of the footpath": dāri-koḷal. Whenever people move, this music is played.

relatives. The first sequence is called the "the cutting and bringing of leaves." In it all the male relatives of the deceased walk, accompanied by a certain type of music, in a line to a nearby river.[30] At the river they cut branches with green leaves from a specific tree and take these branches in a kind of procession to a prepared ritual ground. These branches are later used to build a small leave hut. This hut is meant as a protective hut (*udi-mane*)[31] where later on in the course of the ritual the spirit will take rest and where it is feeded and entertained with music and dance, all essentially performed by his circle of affines.

After that the second sequence takes place, the so-called "bringing of water and the circumambulation of the protecting-hut". In this sequence all assembled relatives of the dead, not only the male members, again walk, as usual led by the "tune of the footpath," to the river. The women also carry water vessels with them. After reaching the river bank, and after the *yajman*, the ritual priest, has performed *pūje*, close relatives of the dead, kin and affines, assemble in order to call the dead person, to bemoan that they miss it, they also memorise the good times which they had with the dead and thus express verbally their good relationships with the dead. But they also point to the good relationships among themselves and underline the good sociality among the living relatives.

At one point or another the dead person, persuaded by these appeals, is usually willing to join his living relatives and embodies itself in a medium. Embodied that way it takes water from the river and distributes it to the women. These take it up then and the whole group, including the dead person, walks back to the ritual ground. Two small children also walk in the group, they carry a small clay pot each. In one pot the ancestors are said to have taken their place. The other pot is intended to be the seat for the spirit of the dead, after it has left its medium. When the group has reached the ritual space, a small leave hut is constructed. Finally, affinal male members of the dead person join this group carrying a range of foodstuff with them. This foodstuff (oil, rice, vegetables, etc.) is provided by the *bā-maiyka*, i.e. the sons of the dead person and their affinal relatives and it is also meant as a sign of support and solidarity. This whole group ultimately circumambulates the leaf hut three times, screaming loudly and joyfully. After that, the spirit of the dead will leave

31. "*uḍi-mane*" literally means "hut of dust". "Dust," however, means also dryness and thus symbolizes the protection from rain which the hut provides. Taken the meaning further it also symbolizes a *social* meaning, namely the support and care of the relatives who build it.

its medium and takes its seat in one of the small clay pots being placed in the leaf hut in the meantime. The other small clay pot too is seated in the hut so that both, spirit and ancestor, can sit together in this protected space. The water, however, that has been carried by the women is used to cook food for all assembled relatives. This will be served and communally consumed later in the night, when the people make a brake and pause from their dances and songs. The spirit and the ancestors too, of course, are served a portion from the food.

In the course of the ritual, however, close relatives of the dead not only demonstrate their support and their good sociality with symbolic actions. They are also engaged in a series of dialogues with their dead relatives. In these discourses too they express the good relatedness with the dead and thus the sociality of the assembled relatives.[32] Moreover, as these elaborate dialogues show, all the above-mentioned contributions to the ritual, enacted in public by the relatives, are meant to help and support the spirit. They are meant to reconcile it and make it happy (*santosha*), as people they, so that it is willing to reach the underworld the following day.

Here is not the space to explicate the moral concepts articulated in these discourses in detail. What is important in the context of the present article, however, are the overall social meanings presented in the ritual. These meanings essentially focus on the relationships of the kindred and thus basically on the relatedness of affines. As we could already see affines present themselves as a group of supportive relatives. And in crucial passages of the discourse in this ritual too, they view themselves as the "children of one hut" (*onde mane makka*) and as people who should help each other and who offer one another support. Indeed it is this meaning, this idea of affinally related people being a household, that is step by step enacted in the process of the ritual. The following figure, based on the actual performance of one ritual, may suffice to illustrate the various "gifts" and contributions of the relatives according to their kinship position.

If we consider the various contributions of the relatives involved in the ritual the basic social meaning of the performance as "people of one hut" becomes evident. The relatives present themselves as people who contribute through their doings to the good maintenance of the web of

32. The figure below provides one example for the particular living relatives engaged in such dialogues with the dead. For the ritual process and the dialogues in detail, cf. Demmer, 1999.

kinship, in turn understood as a common household: All male relatives of the dead present contribute the leafy branches, the women bring the water and the sons, daughters and their affines carry the food. Other unmarried members of the kindred contribute the firewood, affines cook the food, male members play the music, female members carry the water pots and, finally, the children carry the deity. They all together contribute to the construction of the "*uḍi-mane*" for the spirit to sit in and present themselves in that way as members of a peaceful and unanimous "hut".

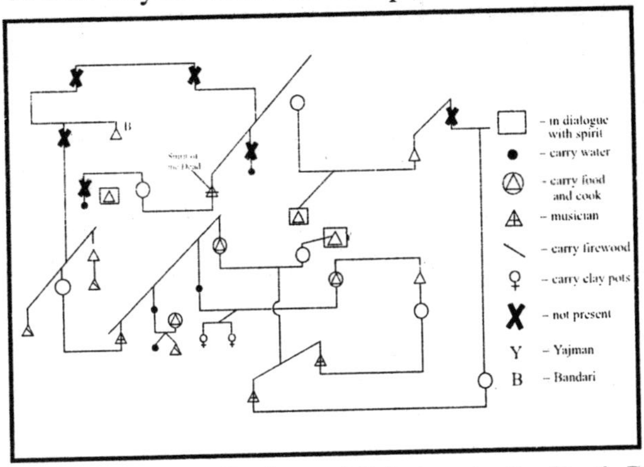

Figure 9.5 : The Contributions of Relatives in the Death Ritual[33]

The Structure of the Regional Tribal System

The preceding sections of this article outlined the main internal structures of relationships and the moral concepts that the Jēnu Kuṛumba employ to realise these structures in fields of social practices. However, the Jēnu Kuṛumba do by no means represent an isolated community confined to its own social world. Rather they are an "encapsulated society" (Woodburn, 1988) and part of a surrounding social landscape to which they relate themselves as much as they are given a position in it by others. Today this social landscape is the "Indian" society at large with its government agencies and with its immigrated but since many decades settled, local village people, comprising Hindu castes, Muslims and several sections of Christians. But this social landscape also includes a range of tribal cultures too. In between the two levels, the Jēnu Kuṛumba

33. *Yajman* and *bandari* are the ritual offices. The *yajman* is concerned with the communication between the living and the dead. He performs all the *puje*. The *bandari*, in contrast, organises the communication among the human participants. Cf. Demmer, 1999 for a more detailed description. In the ritual context all actions, i.e. verbal and non-verbal acts, are regarded as contributions (cf. Demmer, 1999).

culture on the one hand and the "Indian" society on the other hand, do we have a third level, a level that one might call the "regional tribal society". It is mainly with regard to this "regional tribal society" that the Jēnu Kuṟumba articulate a model of social structure. The remainder of the present article will show the structure of this regional society: how the Jēnu Kuṟumba are positioned in it and how they themselves articulate it.

The region of the northern Nilgiris is the home of several tribal cultures. Apart from the Jēnu Kuṟumba we find Baḍaga, Irula (Kasaba), Shōlega and the Betta Kuṟumba. All of these groups are also located in a social order that, conceptually, encompasses all of these tribes. Furthermore, this order is a hierarchical order. That means, each of these tribes is given either a lower or a higher status in relation to the other tribes in the social order. Finally, the members of this order are classified according to a simple scheme, namely that of elder brother and younger brother. Tribal relations in the "regional society," then, are ordered by a principle of relative seniority.

From the perspective of the Irula, for example, the Jēnu Kuṟumba are classified as "younger brother" in relation to themselves, the Irula, who are classified as "elder brother". However, in relation to the Shōlega, who are regarded as "elder brother," the Irula attain a lower status — they are regarded as the "younger brother" of the Shōlega. In the same way all tribal cultures in the area are given a status as younger brother or as elder brother.[34]

Elder Brother		*Younger Brother*
Badaga	related to	Shōlega
Iruḻa (Kasaba)	related to	Betta Kuṟumba
Shōlega	related to	Iruḻa (Kasaba)
Betta Kuṟumba	related to	Jēnu Kuṟumba

Figure 9.6 : The System of Inter-tribal Relationships

As to the present there is, unfortunately, no material that gives us a comprehensive overview as to the social practices associated with this scheme of classification. Nevertheless it is evident, at least from my

34. Cf. Ẓvelebil, 1973 for ethnographic material on the Iruḷa. The Badaga, in turn, regard the Iruḷa as younger brothers (F. Heidemann, personal communication).

own observations in the region, that this scheme does have implications for several domains of social practices, regulating social distances and restrictions as well as possible fields of cooperation. The Shōlega, for example, are consulted by some Jēnu Kuṟumba with regard to the conduct of ritual affairs. Marriage relations too are restricted between the two tribes according to this scheme of classification. And in the economic domain there are a range of implications that make the hierarchy between the two tribes a relevant factor. The Shōlega nowadays are, for example, at least on the Karnataka side of the region, land-owners and the Jēnu Kuṟumba are employed by them as caretakers of their fields or as field laborers. Finally, in everyday interaction the hierarchical relationship is also relevant and most visible.

The same is true for the relationship between the Iruḷa and the Jēnu Kuṟumba. While the Iruḷa are less dominant in their ritual and economic relationship with the Jēnu Kuṟumba and both seem to share equally in the worship of local deities, nevertheless marriages between the two groups are restricted. The Jēnu Kuṟumba themselves, however, do not restrict those hypergamous marriages with Iruḷa and in praxis it happens, according to my data not even seldom, that Jēnu Kuṟumba women are married to Iruḷa men. Yet, in those cases the Iruḷa men have to face the consequences of being excluded from vital domains of their own community. They are not allowed to reside in the settlements of Iruḷa any more, they are not entitled to participate in Irula rituals, e.g. in death rituals, and they are even not allowed to share their food with Iruḷa in public as it is practiced, for example, in Iruḷa festivals.

The system of regional tribal hierarchy, then, constrains the interrelationships of the local tribes and their interaction to a considerable amount. Yet it should be noted that the system is not based on a concept of purity. Rather is hierarchy legitimised with reference to the inferior status of "younger brothers" in relation to "elder brothers". This, in turn, is associated with a relative lack of religious knowledge, a lack of economic wealth and property and, in fact, a kind of cultural backwardness. Thus, as I have shown elsewhere in more detail,[35] the Iruḷa criticise the Jēnu Kuṟumba for the latter's intimate relationship with the forest and regard them as a "forest caste" (*kādu jāti*).

This label does not only serve to signify the closeness of the Jk to the forest but it is also a marker of their inferiority. Being a "forest caste"

35. Demmer, 1996, chapter III.

means being without a proper knowledge of the Iruḷa deities, it means being fearful and with no power and, finally, it means having no knowledge of agriculture or even property of land or cattle. Those depictions are also maintained in local narratives and they are most explicit in the story of "Billayan and Kārayan". In the several versions of this story Billayan is presented as the elder brother, with superior knowledge, related to powerful deities and accustomed to the world of the village people and to agriculture. The Jēnu Kuṛumba, in contrast, are represented in the narrative figure of the younger brother, Kārayan, being in all the above aspects inferior to his elder brother, the Iruḷa.

In the region we are concerned with here, this type of narrative serves not only the Iruḷa to represent a system of tribal order. In fact, it is the blue print for the social order of all tribes in the area. Thus the Shōlega and the Kasaba have developed versions of the narrative and articulate the local system of tribal relatedness in the same manner as the Iruḷa. And the Jēnu Kuṛumba too narrate versions of the Billayan/ Kārayan story. It should be no surprise, though, that the Jēnu Kuṛumba do not place themselves at the bottom of this system of tribal hierarchy. Their view of the regional tribal system is indeed an attempt to redefine the tribal hierarchy.

In the context of the present article it seems appropriate to close this section on the regional system of the tribal social order with a reference to the voices of the Jēnu Kuṛumba as they can be heard in that narrative.

The Story of Billayan and Kārayan

> Elder brother and younger brother, Billayan and Kārayan, they lived in the dense forest. They had only little knowledge. They did not know how to make fire, they did not know their parents and they had no wives. One day the elder brother decided to get fire from the Gauḍa[36] and he left the forest. To this his younger brother agreed but he also begged the elder brother to return soon — he was small and needed the support of his elder brother. The elder brother assured him that he will be back soon and left. When he reached the settlement of the Gauḍa and asked for fire, they gave him fire, plus food and a wife but — he had to do work for that. And not any work but only dirty and low work he had to do. He had to carry the garbage out of the Gauḍa settlement, he had to

36. Gauḍa are a peasant caste in the region.

clean it. Yet — the elder brother did not mind — He agreed to these conditions and did not return into the forest. When the elder brother did not return, the younger brother also left the forest to search for his elder brother. But when he found him in the Gauda settlement and saw that he was carrying the garbage the younger brother was roused to anger and sad. "Hey" he called him without respect. "You are a Kasaba (Iruḷa), one who carries garbage. Don't come close to me. I am a Jēnu Kuṛumba. Oh, your company I don't need, and my company you don't need. Go!"

That way the elder brother became a Kasaba (Iruḷa) and he stayed in the village. The younger brother, however, returned into the forest, without fire and without a wife. But when he reached there he approached his deity, Billuru Māri, and she showed him how to make fire by rubbing wooden sticks together. That way he lived alone in the forest, only in company with the animals.[37] Later on the elder brother came into the forest to hunt boar. At that time the deity, Billuru Māri, helped the younger brother also to get a wife. She wiped out the footprints of the boar and the elder brother lost its track. The younger brother, who was gathering honey in a tree that time, realised that as the work of his deity and he approached the elder brother. The elder brother asked the younger brother: "You track the boar and bring it to me". The younger brother said: "I will bring the boar. You give me your smallest daugther". The elder brother also agreed. The younger brother tracked the boar, found it and "*grrrr, grrrr*" killed it with his spear. Then he dropped it at the foot of the elder brother, took the smallest daughter from the elder brother and disappeared into the forest. That is all; that is the end of the story.

If we analyse this Billayan/Kārayan story, and the one presented above is only one of many similar versions, we can see that these narratives turn evaluations upside down which, in the stories of their neighbors, serve to signify the low status of the Jēnu Kuṛumba in relation to the other tribes in the region. Interestingly enough, the Jēnu Kuṛumba do not refuse being the younger brother — but the younger brother from their point of view has no inferior status. Thus, while from the point of view of the other tribes a close relationship with the forest

37. There is no word for animals in Jēnu Kuṛumba except the term "kādu jāti," lit. this means "forest tribe," or "forest caste".

is regarded as a marker of inferiority, stigmatizing the Jēnu Kuṛumba as the lowest of all tribes in the region, the younger brothers relationship to the forest in this narrative secures him independence. Hunting, for example, makes him free from laboring for others, as sections of the Iruḷain fact need to do. And also the deities of the forest are not seen as powerless or inferior but rather as the ultimate source of power for the younger brother, the Jēnu Kuṛumba. Those elements then reevaluate the position of the younger brother in the system of regional hierarchy. Here the Jēnu Kuṛumba place themselves in the position of superiors, looking down upon their elder brothers as powerless and, in fact, a dirty and dependent *jāti* without, though, putting into doubt the general formal system based, as it where, on the principle of seniority in the domain of agnatic relationships.

Conclusion

The recent anthropology of South Indian foraging cultures argued that the social structures of these societies are less to be found on the level of a group model of society but rather on the level of personal relatedness. As we have seen in the present article this is most relevant for a study of the social structure of the Jēnu Kuṛumba. In this society structures do not demarcate the tribe as a whole, e.g. in terms of a society made up of clans, moieties, lineages and so forth. Likewise, pantribal institutions or structures of encompassing political leadership or of judicial authority are absent. Social life among the Jēnu Kuṛumba is rather confined to a web of interpersonal relations — a web of kinship, moreover, where relatedness is constituted with reference to specific concepts of morality. In fact, the Jēnu Kuṛumba understand themselves explicitly as a moral community or, in other words, the maintenance and structure of this community is based on a morality of kinship.

In terms of structures kinship constitutes this community as a classificatory kindred of approximately three hundred adult persons. It's structure is based primarily on affinal structures, in particular on classificatory cross-cousin marriage. In moral terms affinal structures are evaluated as a domain of positive sociality. Ultimately, then, it is the "good" sociality among affines that leads people towards a closure of their marriage relations. In that way kinship serves as an integrating force: in accordance with a Dravidian system of classification affinal circles of relatives are maintained that constitute the community.

But kinship is not only important for the direction and closure of marriage relations. Rather, the morality of kinship attains significance among the Jēnu Kuṛumba as an encompassing system of classification through which moral obligations of reciprocity, of various transactions in everyday life and of contributions in ritual life are articulated and directed.

On the most abstract level we could see that this morality is embedded in the terminological system of classification. This classificatory system differentiates, roughly conceived, two broad domains of sociality: a domain of affinity and a domain of agnatic-consanguine (kin) relationships. Each domain is marked by specific social expectations and attitudes. The kin-domain is dominated by hierarchical and asymmetrical attitudes. The affinal domain, in contrast, is dominated by egalitarian and symmetrical attitudes. Thus, one should respect the elder brother, but one does not expect sharing with or equal reciprocity from an elder brother. Among affines, in contrast, the expectation of reciprocal support and help is appropriate. Here, in the domain of affines, two categories of relatives, namely the category of affinal relatives, the *bā-mayika*, and the category of the conjugal pair (*okkal*), in itself understood as a affinal domain of relatedness, appeared as most important. Within those circles of affines a morality of sharing, of contribution and of distribution of things prevails.

Moreover, these concepts are not only embedded in the system of classification. The present article could rather show that they are also explicitly articulated in narrative genres like the honey song or the honey narrative. And, finally, these concepts are not only represented in narratives but they are also enacted by the actors. The JK use them to structure the various fields of social practices. Thus gathering camps are structured on the base of the morality of kinship. Their structure is accordingly marked by affinal ties. Agnatic relationships, in contrast, are avoided resp. excluded, because in this domain negative expectations with regard to sharing and reciprocal help are dominant.

Likewise is ritual life, at least in the death ritual considered here, structured in accordance with the significance of affinal ties and their positive morality. In the rituals the relatives of the dead person present themselves as a circle of relatives and through their various contributions to the ritual they stress the morality of kinship. These symbolic actions are understood as evidence for the care and support that these people are providing to one another. In this ritual, at least, all participants contribute something to keep the moral community alive. Accordingly it is this circle of relatives that is enacted and presented in the ritual as the good community.

Finally, the social and moral concepts associated with kinship are not only relevant with regard to intracultural structures but they are also employed to structure interethnic relations in the region. Thus, the structure of the regional tribal system is construed in analogy to the same model of hierarchy that the Jēnu Kuṛumba employ to structure their internal relations in the kin domain, namely the model of elder and younger brother and their antagonistic relationship. And it carries the same moral evaluation in the sense that this hierarchy is regarded as an undesired form of domination. Accordingly they are, just as the agnatic forms of hierarchy within the community, considered in negative terms.

The several tribes in the region are ordered hierarchically according to their relative status in terms of seniority. All tribes regard one another as elder brother resp. younger brother. And this goes hand in hand with an evaluation of the respective positions. Seen from the positions "on top" of the model, the Jēnu Kuṛumba are attributed the lowest position in this hierarchy. Their inferiority is derived from their closeness to the forest, from their relationship to forest deities and from their lack of property, in particular a lack of land and cattle.

The Jēnu Kuṛumba themselves, however, do not share this view. They challenge this system in several ways and at least in their own narratives that deal with the intertribal social order this system is turned upside down. For them, their closeness to the forest means independence and sovereignty rather than inferiority, and we heard the voices in the narrative who consider other tribes as low because these work for other castes or for tribal groups, e.g. in cattle herding or agriculture. To be sure, the Jēnu Kuṛumba agree that they are the younger brothers. But yet, as their own narratives make clear, they are not low and inferior. Rather the Jēnu Kuṛumba claim, due to their closeness to the forest, to their independent work in it and, last but not least, due to their relationship to the forest deities a highly valued position in the social order of the regional tribes.

REFERENCES

Barnett, S. 1975. "Coconuts and Gold," *Contributions to Indian Sociology*, 133-156.

Bird-David, N. 1987. "Single Persons and Social Cohesion in a Hunter-Gatherer Society," in P. Hockings (ed.), *Dimensions of Social Life: Essays in Honor of David Mandelbaum*. Berlin and New York: Mouton de Gruyter.

____. 1988. "Hunters and Gatherers and Other People — A Re-examination," in T. Ingold, D. Riches and J. Woodburn (ed.), *Hunters and Gatherers. Vol.1. History, Evolution and Social Change*. Oxford: Berg.

____. 1990. "The Giving Environment: Another Perspective on the Economic System of Gatherer-Hunters," *Current Anthropology*, 31 (2): 189-96.

____. 1994. "Sociality and Immediacy: Or, Past and Present Conversations on Bands," *Man*, (NS): 583-603.

____. 1995. "Hunter-Gatherers' Kinship Organisation: Implicit Roles and Rules," in E. Goody (ed.), *Social Intelligence and Interaction: Expressions and Implications of the Social Bias in Human Intelligence*. Cambridge: University Press.

____. 1999. " 'Animism' Revisited. Personhood, Environment, and Relational Epistemology," *Current Anthropology*, 40 (Supplement).

____. Forthcoming. "Puja, or Sharing with the Gods?: On Ritualised Possession among Nayaka of South India," *Eastern Anthropologist*.

Bourdieu, P. 1979. *Entwurf einer Theorie der Praxis* (auf der ethnologischen Grundlage der kabylischen Gesellschaft). Frankfurt/M.: Suhrkamp.

____. 1987. Sozialer Sinn. Kritik der theoretischen Vernunft. Frankfurt/M.: Suhrkamp.

Bruner, J. 1991. "The Narrative Construction of Social Reality," *Critical Inquiry*, 18 (Autumn): 1-21.

Burkhart, G. 1978. "Marriage Alliance and the Local Circle among some Udayars of South India," (pp. 171-211) in S. Vatuk (ed.), *American Studies in the Anthropology of India*. New Delhi: Manohar.

Carrithers, M. 1992. *Why Humans have Cultures: Explaining Anthropology and Social Diversity*. Oxford, New York. University Press.

David, K. 1973. "Until Marriage Do Us Part. A Cultural Account of Jaffna Tamil Categories for Kinsman," *Man*, 8 (4): 521-535.

Demmer, U. 1996. *Verwandtschaft und Sozialität bei den Jenu Kurumba. Vom Arbeiten, vom Teilen, und von (Un)gleichheit in einer südindischen Sammler- und Jägergesellschaft*. Stuttgart: Franz Steiner Verlag.

____. 1997. "The Structure and Structuration of Gathering Camps among the Jenu Kurumba Gatherer/Hunters of South India," *Journal of Indian Anthropology*, 28: 249-259.

____. 1999. "How to Make the Spirit of the Dead Happy. The Rhetoric of Words and Deeds in a Jenu Kurumba Death Ritual," in E. Schoembucher and C. P. Zoller (eds.), *Ways of Dying. Death and its Meaning in South Asia*. New Delhi: Manohar.

Dumont, L. 1983. *Affinity as a Value*. Chicago: University of Chicago Press.

Gardner, P. 1966. "Symmetric Respect and Memorate Knowledge: The Structure and Ecology of Individualistic Culture," *Southwestern Journal of Anthropology*, 22: 389-415.

____. 1969. "Paliyan Social Structure," in D. Damas (ed.), *Contributions to*

Anthropology: Band Societies. Ottawa: National Museums of Canada. National Museum of Canada Bulletin No. 229.

____. 1972 "The Paliyans," in M. G. Bicchieri (ed.), *Hunters and Gatherers Today*. New York: Rineholt and Winston.

____. 1988. "Pressures for Tamil Propriety in Paliyan Social Organisation," in T. Ingold, D. Riches and J. Woodburn (eds.), *Hunters and Gatherers. Vol. 2. Property, Power, and Ideology*. Oxford: Berg.

____. 1991. "Pragmatic Meanings of Possessions in Paliyan Shamanism," Anthropos, 86: 367-384.

Giddens, A. 1979. *Central Problems in Social Theory — Action, Structure, and Contradiction in Social Analysis*. Berkeley: University of California Press.

Gossel, M. n. d. *Untersuchungen zur Sprache und oralen Tradition der Jēnu Kuṟumba in Südindien*. Heidelberg: Unveröffentlichtes Manuskript.

Harre, R. 1990. "Commentary by Rom Harr," in R. Bhaskar (ed.), *Harr, and his Critics: Essays in Honour of Rom Harr with his Commentary on them*. Oxford: Blackwell.

Kapp, D. B. 1982. *Ālu Kuṟumba Nāyan. Die Sprache der Ālu Kuṟumba. Grammatik, Texte, Wörterbuch. Neuindische Studien*. Herausgegeben von H. Berger, L. Lutze und G. Sontheimer. Band 7. Wiesbaden: Otto Harrassowitz.

____. 1983. "Honigsammeln und Jagen bei den Ālu-Kuṟumbas," *In Anthropos*, 78: 715-738.

Morris, B. 1978. "The Family, Group Structuring and Trade among South Indian Hunter-Gatherers," in E. Leacock and R. Lee (eds.), *Politics and History in Band Societies*. Cambridge: Cambridge Univ. Press.

____. 1982. *Forest Traders, a Socio-Economic Study of the Hill Pandaram*. London School of Economics: Monographs on Social Anthropology. New Jersey: The Athlone Press.

____. 1981. "Hill Gods and Ecstatic Cults: Notes on the Religion of a Hunting and Gathering People," *Man in India*, 61: 203-236.

Ortner, S. 1984. "Theory in Anthropology since the Sixties," *Journal of Comparative Studies of Society and History*, 26 (1): 126-166.

Pfeffer, G. 1982. *Status and Affinity in Middle India*. Wiesbaden: Franz Steiner.

____. 1991. "Der intra-agnatische 'Seelentausch' der Gabada beim grossen Lineageritual," in M. S. Laubscher (ed.), *Beitraege zur Ethnologie Mittel- und Sued-Indiens*. Muenchen.

Taylor, CH. 1992. *Sources of the Self. The Making of the Modern Identity*. Cambridge: University Press.

Woodburn, J. 1988. "African Hunter-Gatherer Social Organisation: Is it Best Understood as a Product of Encapsulation?," in T. Ingold, D. Riches and J. Woodburn (ed.), *Hunters and Gatherers*. Vols.1. and 2. Oxford: Berg.

Yalman, N. 1962. "The Structure of the Sinhalese Kindred: A Re-examination of the Dravidian Terminology," *American Anthropologist*, 64: 548-573.

Zvelebil, K. V. 1973. *The Iruḷa Language*. Wiesbaden: Otto Harrassowitz.

____. 1979. *The Iruḷa Language*. Part II. Wiesbaden: Otto Harrassowitz.

SECTION II

TRIBAL SOCIETIES ABROAD

TEN

THE PASHTUN TRIBAL SYSTEM

BERNT GLATZER

Introduction

We have inherited a somewhat fuzzy usage of the term "*tribe*" and "*tribal*" from early British anthropology. "*Tribe*" was often used in a rather derogatory manner for relatively small ethnic groups who lived as "underdeveloped" (formerly called "*primitive*" or even "*savage*") minorities, far from the majorities' cultural and social mainstream. No wonder that the term "*tribe*" became obsolete in many continents, and former objects of anthropological investigation are nowadays less ready to accept labels for their respective ethnic groups which seem derogatory to them.

However, in the usage of English in the north-western parts of Subcontinent and in West Asia the term "*tribe*" or in its equivalents in the local languages ("*qawm,*" "*qabila,*" "*il,*" "*tayfah,*" etc.) has no derogatory connotation. To the contrary, it is used with pride as a marker of nobility. Belonging to a tribe means to be of distinguished and old ancestry, to belonging to genuine people, to be dependable. As a *tribal* one is bound by a network of primordial obligations on the solid basis of well-structured genealogical ties. Such notions are linked to pride and honour, not to inferiority. Arab rulers would be deeply offended if their tribal background was questioned, Afghan dignitaries and intellectuals increasingly use their tribal names as a second name, a similar tendency is noticeable in Pakistan, e.g. Ghulam Ishaq Khan, a former President of Pakistan preferred to appear in tribal costume on official occasions.

This encourages me to come to the rescue of the useful anthropological term "*tribe*" under the condition that it is well defined and free of all connotations of simplicity, primitiveness, exoticism, or periphery. "*Tribal*" may also be applied to certain aspects of highly complex and technically developed societies, e.g. in Central Europe or in the Indian or Pakistani Punjab. I consider "*tribe*" as just one of the many interwoven structural components of a given society, no matter how complex and "developed".

I suggest the following definition:

By "*tribe*" I understand a social segment based on a genealogical concept of social structure. According to such concept the society is segmented by a principle of descent from a common ancestor or from common ancestors. Tribes (i.e. segments in a tribal system) are constituted by the people's notion of being distinct from others through sharing closer common ancestry. Like an ethnic group, a tribe is always constituted *vis-à-vis* one or more equivalents. On a higher genealogical level different tribes may join into one segment in relation to another segment which is made up of tribes who are genealogically closer to one another than to the tribes of the first segment. Since tribes are social segments *per definitionem*, there have to be at least two tribes on each level.

Often the terms *clan* or *lineage* are used instead, but the latter two have unilineal descent and — usually — exogamy as a defining criterium which is not obligatory with *tribe*. In addition, most of us associate with *clan* and *lineage* small and more or less localised social units, so it would sound odd to be used for categories like the Pashtun Durrani which count several million members.

Many authors define, or at least characterise *tribe* as a *political* unit. I would prefer to omit this as a defining criterion because at this point of the discussion, I use *tribe* merely as a structural concept, as a principle of social order, rather than to define "real" social groups or acting political units. When it comes to tribes "out there" the interesting question whether or not "*tribes*" are political units, should not be blocked *a priori* by a definition, but should be the subject of research and analysis.

At this point I want to stress that the tribal system is usually not the only structural principle of a tribal society. The example of the Punjab (both Indian and Pakistani) makes it clear that tribe or tribal structure is only one guideline of social orientation in a complex network of different principles and patterns of the social landscape. The society or societies in which Pashtuns live are not much simpler. In Afghanistan which recently has sunk into chaos and turmoil and where tribes have gained considerably in importance, the tribal system is only one component within a much more complex social and political web. This is true as well for areas populated homogeneously by Pashtuns. The tribal system does or did not only reside in remote and backward areas but permeated and still permeates all levels of the society from the nomad camp up to the royal palace, from the remote mountain village up to the university and to the head quarters of the armed forces.

The "Largest Tribal Society"

Pashtuns are said to having developed the world's largest tribal society,[1] and in local thinking the tribal system even encompasses all humanity, as Barakhan, one of my informants, an Atsakzay nomad of Badghis, Northwest Afghanistan, has put it:

> "When God created the animals and humans he first created one ant and his spouse, then one buck and his goat, one ram and his sheep ... finally one man and his wife, and from these ancestors sprang the tribes (*qawm*) of the ants, of the goats, of the sheep and finally the tribe of Adam. The offspring of the first ant became the grandfathers (*nikagan*) of the various tribes (*qawm*) and subtribes (*qawm* and *khel*) of ants ..., as Adam's sons became the *nikagan* of the peoples of the world (*qawm*), and their sons the *nikagan* of the tribes (*qawm*) within these peoples. One of Adam's sons or grandsons was Ibrahim, the *nika* of all nomads."[2]

An equation of animal and human society is what one might expect from a pastoral nomad, but the main structural elements in this statement are shared by pastoral, agricultural and other Pashtuns: the notion that the divine tribal order unifies and divides all human beings or even all creatures. The unifying cognitive ordering concept of tribe is clearly laid down in the Qur'an:

> Men, we have created you from a male and a female, and made you into nations and tribes, that you might get to know one

1. To my knowledge this often repeated stereotype was first formulated by J. Spain in his *The Pathan Borderland*. The Hague: Mouton, 1963, p. 17.
2. From an interview in 1970.

another. The noblest of you in God's sight is he who is most righteous. God is all-knowing and wise" (XLIX, 13).[3]

Local folklore has it that all Pashtuns are (mainly) patrilineal descendants of one founding father, even if there is no agreement about the apical ancestor's name. Some call him Qays Abdurrashid, others say his name was Daru Nika, or Baba Khaled (Khalid bin Walid — the legendary General of the Army of Prophet Muhammad). The name of the common ancestor is less important than the Pashtuns' belief of belonging to one huge kinship group or family. The common ancestor had many sons, grandsons, great-grandsons and so forth, each being the ancestor of one of the innumerable branches and sub-branches or tribes and sub-tribes, clans and sub-clans down to the local lineages and families. The ordering principle of each tribal subgroup is similar to that of the larger group, yet the segments do not have a fixed or repetitive number of sub-divisions such as many Turkish tribes who have a binary system of segmentation. The common Pashtun ancestor is said to have had four sons: Sarban, Bitan (*alias* Batni or Sheykh Beyt), Ghurghusht and Karran, the latter was adopted. Sarban had two sons: Sharjnun and Kharshbun; Bitan three sons: Isma'il, Ashbun, Kajin, and one famous daughter: Bibi Matu; Ghurghusht had three sons: Danay, Babay and Mando; Karran was blessed with two sons: Koday and Kakay. From all these sons and grandsons of Qays Abdurrashid or his aliases sprang the thousands of tribes, subtribes and local lineages of the Pashtuns.

There have been many attempts to codify the Pashtun tribal system, the most famous being the *Makhzan-e Afghani* compiled in India by Ni'matullah in the early 17th century. This genealogies lists thousands of tribes and relates anecdotes and legends about the tribes' origins and how they joined or split.[5] The tribal charter is based on patrilineality, but in some conspicuous cases this principle is set aside for notable

3. *The Koran.* Translated with notes by N. J. Dawood. London: Penguin Books, 1995, p. 516.
4. Khwaja Ni'mat Ullah b. Khwâja Habîb Ullah al-Harawî: *Tarîkh-e Khân Jahânî wa makhzan-e Afghânî.* ed. by S. M. Imâmuddîn (Dacca: Asiatic Society of Pakistan, Publ. No. 4, 2 vols.) 1960-1992.
5. Khwaja Ni'mat Ullah's grand national genealogy (see footnote no. 4) written in the 17th Century AD. is considered among literate Pashtuns as the classical one. B. Dorn issued a translated version in 1829 under the title *History of the Afghans* (repr. by Susil Gupta, London and Santiago de Compostela 1965). Another, more handy genealogy is the *Hayat-i Afghan* by Hayat Khan, translated to English by H. Priestley, Lahore, 1874 (reprinted by Sang-e-Meel Publ., Lahore 1981).

exceptions. In principle, one has to be born into a tribe, but Afghan pragmatism allows exceptions. Through consensus of the tribe, outsiders may be allowed to take residence in their area. If such outsiders and their offspring honour the tribal code of behaviour and succeed to intermarry with the tribe they may be accepted as members after a generation or two.

Cherchez la Femme: The Ghilzay Case

Some of the more famous and powerful tribes such as the Afridi or Ghilzay are connected to the rest of the Pashtuns by adoption and/or by female links. In the genealogical books adventurous or romantic stories usually adorn these deviations from the patrilineal rule. Adaptations to social and political realities were always possible as the tribal system was managed in a flexible manner.

An example is Bibi Matu the Mother of all Ghilzay who embodies the genealogical link of that grand and famous tribe to the rest of the Pashtuns:

The story begins with an account of the non-Pashtun Kings of Ghor (western Central Afghanistan) and why one Shah Hossain, a Prince of that dynasty had to flee to the pasture lands of Sheykh Bayt, a son of Qays Abdurrashid, the apical ancestor of the Pashtuns. The text is taken from Bernhard Dorn's classical translation of the Makhzan done in St. Petersburg in the early 19th Century:

> "...Shah Hossain, leaving his father, came alone, and in a miserable condition, to the village of Sheikh Batni [a synonym of Sheikh Beyt], and presented himself to him. the marks of felicity being engrossed on Hossain's forehead, Sheikh Batni allowed him to reside among his tribes, made him his friend, and evinced paternal affection towards him. He would not occupy himself with worldly affairs, but gave himself up entirely to devotion, austerity, reading the Koran, and devout meditation; and by this integrity and prudence everything was well administered. Destiny bringing on an eventual display of affairs, Shah Hossain, conformably to human nature and youth, paid his addresses to the daughter of Sheikh Batni, Matu by name; and matters gradually went so far, that they, by mutual consent, but without the sanction of either father or mother, proceeded into intimacy, that, a short time after, the symptoms of pregnancy appeared, and the case no longer

> admitted of concealment. The damsel's mother becoming aware of it, assailed her daughter with reproaches: she, perceiving that there was no remedy, but by the adoption of a speedy resolution, informed Sheikh Beyt of it, and said to him: "Before the secret come to light, and reach the ears of our relations, we must give our daughter in marriage to that young man". The Sheikh, however, objected: "That youth is no match for us, as I am entirely unacquainted with his former condition and origin: how could I then consent to it?" To this the mother replied, "Truly, his dignified appearance bears sufficient evidence of his nobility". The Sheikh still refusing his consent, his consort closely examined Shah Hossain about his origin and family: in reply to which he declared: "My ancestors were princes and rulers in the province of Ghor: if you do not believe it, despatch a confidential person to ascertain the truth of this statement". The lady, overjoyed at this declaration, reported it to the Sheikh, who despatched one Kaghdoor, with a letter of Shah Hossain to Ghor, in order to obtain a faithful account of his origin. The messenger, on his arrival, duly ascertained the truth of his statement, as to his noble descent, and returned with written documents… the messenger made his report of Hossein's noble origin to the Sheikh, whose mind, previously clouded with distress, brightened up. In a propitious hour they married Bibi Matu to Shah Hossain who soon after married also Kaghdoor's daughter. After a certain time, Matu was delivered of a charming and auspicious boy, who, being the fruit of a clandestine amour, was called Ghilzye: *-Ghil*, in the Afghan language, signifying a "thief"; and *zye*, "born, a son".[6]

This legend of the Ghilzay is one of many examples when the written genealogies try to cope with the fact that Pashtuns are obviously of heterogeneous origin, and that the tribal structure is not left to a strict patrilineal principle alone, but is open to convenient arrangements.

The notion of a non-Pashtun origin of the Ghilzay has not only stimulated the fantasy of local genealogists but also that of western historians who consider it likely that the Ghilzay tribe represents the survivors of the medieval Turkish tribe of Khalaj, who joined a Pashtun

6. Bernhard Dorn: *History of the Afghans. Translated from the Persian of Neamat Ullah.* London, Santiago de Compostela: Susil Gupta, 2nd Ed. 1965 (1st Ed. 1829-1836). "Book the Third", p. 47f.

tribal confederation or formed one of their own.[7] Even the *Makhzan* hints at a Turkish ancestry of the children of Bibi Matu by counting among Shah Hossain's forefathers Turkish princes.[8] Ni'matullah's *Makhzan* reports more than 63 instances when the rule of patrilineal descent is broken either by statements that a tribal ancestor was of unknown origin but adopted by a Pashtun, or by female links, sometimes by a combination of both.

qawm, khel and -zay

A few more words about terminology: People, ethnic group and tribe are called *qawm* in Pashtu and in most other languages in Afghanistan. This reflects the traditional view that ethnic groups and tribes are structured in a similar way, i.e. by genealogical links. Subtribe or clan is *khel* in Pashtu, but it may also be called *qawm*, as any tribal unit may be seen as a tribe or sub-tribe at the same time, depending on the level of ramification it is viewed from. Thus a subtribe or sub-clan of a *khel* is also a *khel* down to the village level.

A frequent suffix of names of larger tribal units is *-zay*, e.g. Mandozay, meaning "Son of Mando," plural form Mandozi, "Sons of Mando," and *-khel* for the sub-units. Some *khels* have grown to such an extent that they became recognised as tribes of their own, such as the Sulaimankhel, a branch of the Ghilzay. The suffix *-zay* indicates in most of the cases a southern or western origin (e.g. the Yusufzay of Swat originate from Kandahar), whereas most of the eastern tribes lack this typical tribal suffix, such as the Afridi, Mohmand, Zadran, Dzadzi (Jaji), Mangal, Shinwari, as well as many smaller tribes in Khost such as the Tani, Saberi, Lakan, Ghorboz, etc.

Tribes as Social and Political Groups and Factions

Most of the tribes in Afghanistan are neither corporate nor political entities, yet the tribal system has more often than not served as a blue print for political alliances. Political entrepreneurs found kinship and tribal links most convenient as a basis for alliances or confederations in order to challenge even imperial powers and to secure areas for their clients.

7. Bosworth, C. E. "Khaladj," in *The Encyclopedia of Islam*. New Ed. IV. Leiden: Brill 1990 (1978).
8. Dorn, op. cit. III, p. 46p.

There is a dilemma in tribal societies: the very tool, which enables tribal leaders to establish powerful political entities, the charter of segmentary solidarity, is also instrumental for segmentary division. Once a charismatic leader who masters the instrument of segmentary alliance looses influence or dies the divisive character of the segmentary tribal system will gain the upper hand. Tribal systems do not usually develop institutionalised political power, which could tolerate fluctuations in the abilities of individual rulers.

The Pashtun ideal of equality is based on the tribal system. The idea is that all Pashtuns are born equal, and are children of one common ancestor; social and economic inequality, which of course exists, is not given by nature or birth but is achieved individually, and is threatened and open to change at any time.

Whereas the tribal order discourages social hierarchy, it defines social nearness and distance. Pashtuns use their tribal order to mark lines of conflict and solidarity. If I see two men fighting I am supposed to side with the one who is "closer" to me, i.e. the one with whom I share the nearest common patrilineal ancestor.

In the Pashtun tribal areas in East Afghanistan and Northwest Pakistan we find a socio-political division into two opposite sections: Tor Gund ("white faction") and Spin Gund ("black faction"). The following example is from Khost in East Afghanistan: The Saberi, Dzadran (Jadran), Tsamkani (Chamkani), Tani, Mandozay, etc. are named Spin Gund in opposition with the Tor Gund, the Mangal, Ismailkhel and others. Today this dichotomy has become practically obsolete, but people clearly remember which tribe belongs to which *gund*. The recent violent land dispute between members of the Tsamkani and the Mangal, however, is between two opposing *gund* and the sympathies of the Saberi who are not part of the conflict lie with their *gund* fellows, the Tsamkani.

Tribes are localised to various degrees. The Ghilzay, for example, are scattered all over Afghanistan; thus there is no proper Ghilzay land. Yet, there are areas where Ghilzay and certain of their subtribes predominate. Other tribes, such as the Afridi, have a clearly defined homeland. The latter is true for most of the eastern tribes along the Afghan-Pakistani border. Tribal land is sub-divided along tribal sub-divisions. Belonging to a tribe therefore means having access to the land of that tribe. There are also landless tribals, e.g. those who have sold their inherited land to another member of their tribe. If a member of a tribe loses ownership of his land, he retains at least his right to re-acquire land if he regains the necessary means. Localised tribes also own common and undivided property: pastures and forests which every member has an equal right to use. When a member of a tribe defends the land of his tribe he defends his own security and future of his family.[9]

Those tribes who inhabit a coherent area are able to define and enact a common policy. Even where influential persons (*khan*) or commanders have emerged, decisions of importance for the whole community are reached at community councils (*jirga*). According to tribal ideal of equality, every free and experienced male person of the tribe has the right to attend, to speak and to decide. Only *jirgas* on very high levels (provincial or all-tribe, which is very rare) need a system of representation. When the tribes of Mandozay and Ismailkhel sent a joint *jirga* to Peshawar in order to attract international aid, they nominated two representatives from each sub-tribe to participate.[10] *jirgas* traditionally have neither leaders nor chairmen. The participants prefer to sit in circles in order to avoid any dominant position. Decisions are reached only through consensus. Therefore discussions last until everyone is convinced or until it becomes clear that there will be no consensus at that time. Once a decision is reached at a *jirga*, it is binding for every participant.

During the anti-Soviet war a new political term came into use in Afghanistan: *shora*. This is the Arabic term referring to the first meetings of the Muslim *ummah*. The word *jirga* is derived from Mongolian and lacks religious connotation. Other differences between *jirga* and *shora* are the more representative character of a *shora*, a relatively permanent membership, and more regular intervals of the meetings. *jirgas* in contrast meet *ad hoc* when a problem arises.[11]

In southeastern Afghanistan tribal and/or local communities maintain militias, *arbaki* or *lashgar* called. *Jirgas* can also summon ad hoc militias, even if their constituencies are tribally mixed. Such militias are made up of young unmarried men not yet experienced enough to

9. For a comprehensive account of the legal aspects of the tribal system in Khost see W. Steul, *Paschtunwali: Ein Ehrenkodex und seine rechtliche Relevanz* (Wiesbaden: Steiner) 1981.

10. At that time (1991) I worked with the NGO (Danish Committee for Aid to Afghan Refugee) which was approached successfully by this *jirga*.

11. For a good analysis of the Afghan *shoras* see: Lynn Carter & Kerry Connor, *A Preliminary Investigation of contemporary Afghan Councils*. (Peshawar: Paper prepared for ACBAR, 52pp) 1989.

participate in *jirgas* or *shoras*, but strong and loyal enough to sanction the decisions. The classical sanction for not adhering to a *jirga's/shora's* decision is the house of the offender to be burned down by the *arbaki*, and the worst sanction is expulsion from the tribe and tribal land.

I have already mentioned leaders, a closer look at them reveals that their power is rather limited. Whereas tribes and their divisions are structurally stable and dependable, tribal leadership is not. Political leaders can hardly build their power on the tribal structure alone because that is egalitarian. They need continuously to convince their followers and adversaries of their superior personal qualities and have to procure and redistribute resources from outside the tribal realm, for the followers expect from them material or symbolic advantages and in times of political chaos people demand from their leaders to provide security. Clients may quickly be disappointed by a *khan* or commander and may switch overnight to another one, there is no institutional safety net for tribal leaders.

In a tribal setting one can gain power by

I. controlling tenants;
II. attracting many regular guests through lavish hospitality;
III. channelling resources from the outside world to one's followers,
IV. superior rhetoric qualities and regular sound judgements in the *shoras* and *jirgas*; and
V. gallantry in war and conflict.

All these qualities are transitory and have constantly to be re-enacted against ever-present competitors.

In spite of the proverbial unpredictability of tribal leadership, the tribal system provides an element of stability and resilience in times of turmoil and when state authority has disappeared. To the Pashtuns it means relative safety, legal security and social orientation in an otherwise chaotic and anarchic world. Where the tribal system is well functioning the new radical Islamist rulers of Afghanistan, the Taliban, have not dared to touch it, instead they continue the practice of earlier Afghan Governments to let peripheral areas (i.e. the largest part of the country) be organised by local authorities and institutions only loosely connected with the state rulers.

In the post-war time (after 1992) I have experienced that in areas where the tribal system was dominant and intact (e.g. in Khost) civil order and security were faster restored and rehabilitation of local economy and the return of refugees went more smoothly than in areas where the tribal system was not functioning anymore.[12]

Although tribal structures can be found all over Afghanistan, they do not have everywhere the same ordering and organising quality as they do in the East of the country, and even there the tribal system is only one of various ordering principles within the society. In the predominantly Pashtun South and Southwest of Afghanistan the tribes are less localised and most communities and political units are multi-tribal. Here tribal structure is an organising factor too, it allows people to form solidarity groups when the need arises, creates bonds of social cohesion over long distance, and it structures the attachment of locally dispersed people and groups to the rest of the Pashtuns. It helps for example nomads to claim obligations of mutual help from sedentary farmers in different areas of Afghanistan.

Tribes, Politics and History

In the anthropological literature "*tribe*" is often seen and analysed as a politically organised or politically acting unit.[13] No doubt, the Pashtun tribal system does have an eminent political relevance, although only in exceptional cases do Pashtun tribes form actual social groups or organisations which are able to act collectively as political units. Whether Pashtun tribes today are in a state of decay under the onslaught of modernism,[14] whether the tribal *khans* fail to "*tie the knot of the tribe*,"[15] or whether the underlying segmentary lineage structure was never more than just an "*ideology of social relations*"[16] is another question, but as a matter of fact in most cases tribes do not have observable organisations which could enable them to perform collective actions *as a tribe*. Where

---

12. Bernt Glatzer, "From Refugee to Resident: Effects of Aid on Repatriation," in E. Eide & T. Skaufjord (eds.), *From Aid During Times of War to Aid for Reconstruction and Development*. Seminar Report (Peshawar: Norwegian Afghanistan Committee) 1992, pp.161-168.
13. cf. Richard Tapper: "Introduction," In: R. Tapper (ed.), *The Conflict of Tribe and State in Iran and Afghanistan*. London etc. Croom Helm and St. Martin's Press, 1983: 1-82.
14. Louis Dupree: Tribal Warfare in Afghanistan and Pakistan: A Reflection of The Segmentary Lineage System. In: Ahmed & Hart (eds.): *Islam in Tribal Societies: From the Atlas to the Indus*. London: Routledge, 1984: 266-286.
15. Jon Anderson: There are no khans anymore: Economic Development and Social Change in Tribal Afghanistan. *The Middle East Journal*. 32, 1978: 167-183.
16. Dale F. Eickelman: *The Middle East: An Anthropological Appraisal*. Englewood Cliffs; NJ: Prentice-Hall, 1981: 104

they are able to act collectively they are only small groups, e.g. populations of a single valley or of a cluster of villages as the above-mentioned Mandozai and Ismailkhel. In some cases the organisational weakness of Pashtun tribes may be due to recent detribalisation which Evans observed among the Safi.[17] Two centuries ago, the pioneer of Afghan anthropology, Mountstuart Elphinstone, had observed the phenomenon of political inconsistency of Pashtun tribes when he struggled with describing and analysing the Ghilzay confederacy:

> "The system of government which I have described is so often deranged ... that it is seldom found in full force; and must, therefore, be considered rather as the model on which all the governments of tribes are formed than a correct description of any one of them. There is probably no case where some link is not wanting in the chain of authorities, which ought to descend from the Khaun to the heads of families...The whole constitution is also sometimes overturned...frequently the chiefs are neglected, and every subdivision, every quarter, and even every family, throws off its dependence ... and acts according to its own interest and inclination".[18]

In the same chapter Elphinstone stressed also the interesting fact that when tribes formed viable constituencies it was instigated by the royal court's policy which tried to extend its influence by organising local populations along tribal lines and by pampering local big men as tribal chiefs:

> "On the whole, it is generally observable that the tribes most under the King's influence are most obedient to their Khaun, though there are some striking exceptions to the rule". (ibid.: 217)

"*Striking*" here is to be understood literally: Elphinstone had in mind cases when tribes succeeded in organising themselves in such an efficient way that they managed to invade well established empires. This was the case in 1722 when a Ghilzai army under their chieftain Mahmud succeeded in conquering and usurping the throne of Safawid Persia. Yet the Ghilzai rule of Persia lasted only till 1729, it was so

---

17. Jeffrey H. P. Evans: *The Social Structure and Organization of a Pakhtu Speaking Community in Afghanistan.* (Ph.D. thesis; Durham), 1977: 3.
18. *Mountstuart Elphinstone*: *An Account of the Kingdom of Caubul.* 2 vols. London: Longman 1839 (1st ed. 1815), vol.2, p. 215f.

short-lived mainly because the Ghilzay lacked any organisational basis to sustain an imperial rule. In 1749 the rivals of the Ghilzai, the Abdali — another Pashtun tribal confederacy — where more successful: On their home ground they forged together the larger part of Pashtuns and neighbouring ethnic groups to an intertribal confederacy which became known as Afghanistan. As the Ghilzay experienced before, the Abdali (later "Durrani") rulers could not relly on their own tribal organisation, but from the beginning (1749) had to base their rule on state institutions which they found in the former Safawid and Moghul provincial centres of Herat, Kandahar, Kabul and Peshawar. The higher the tribal chief Ahmad Shah Abdali (later Durrani) rose to royal power and the more successful he was in conquering neighbouring territories the more he got estranged from his tribal basis. Eventually he had to resort to purchasing loyalty from tribal chiefs who owed him their position. These tribal chiefs in turn became soon alienated from their own tribal basis because they were more loyal to the king and more oriented toward the royal court than to their local followers. In this way an urban élite emerged which up to this day is culturally, politically and economically remarkably distant from the mainly rural Afghan population. When the ever widening gap between the ruler and the ruled became deep enough the bond of social and cultural cohesion, *asabiyah*, the tribal solidarity, as Ibn Khaldun named it, broke and the kingdom sank in anarchy leaving the rulers to be overthrown by their rivals who could muster a stronger tribal following (*lashgar*) — the classical Ibn Khaldunian scenario.

Yet, in one important respect the Pashtun example does not corroborate Ibn Khaldun's model:

It were not the Pashtun tribes who set out to overthrow a dynasty, but it were the political leaders (such as Mahmud or Ahmad Shah, later Dost Muhammad, Abdurrahman and Nadir Shah, the father of Zaher Shah) who made skilful use of tribal networks, of tribal identities and solidarities (*asabiyah*) to gain a devoted following, to raise to supreme power in a state. Once such leaders ascended to supreme power the tribal structure had little to offer for sustaining power and for running the state, and the rulers had to find or to create alternative institutions outside the tribal network, the more successful they were in this respect the more they became severed from their tribal basis.

This does not make tribal structure politically obsolete. Outside the sphere of the state, in the central, western and southern hinterland of

Afghanistan where even under the Taliban state power hardly ever reaches, the tribal system is still the main structuring and ordering principle of the local society. The tribal system consists not only of a the patrilineal model of an ever ramifying society, but also of rules of solidarity and conflict resolution, of social forms how to gain and loose political power, and of a very elaborate code of honour and shame: the pashtunwali which is linked with historical memories of the tribes and lineages.[19]

Tribes in the Recent Afghan War

Tribalism, and ethnicity are often lumped together, and both are blamed as main factors of turmoil, war and of the break-down of state order, but there are reasons to assume that the tribal structure of Afghanistan is rather a factor of stability, even if it does not support durable political leadership.

As mentioned before a high degree of ethnic and tribal dynamics is observable in Afghanistan. Ethnic and tribal boundaries and identities are not fixed since ages, but are often a matter of negotiation. Whether social action is based on tribal and ethnic criteria depends on opportunities and tactics and may change quickly. For example, the Pashtun party leader and warlord Gulbudin Hekmatyar initially laid a stress in his public speeches on panislamism and the Muslim *ummah*. Boundaries between Muslim states should become obsolete. Later, during his campaigns for recruitment in Pashtun areas he appealed to the ethnic and tribal solidarity of the Pashtuns who should defend their identity and honour against the rest of the world.

During the guerilla war against Soviet troops in Afghanistan and against the pro-Communist regime in Kabul the front lines cut through almost all ethnic groups and the larger tribes. In all those groups there were (a) sympathisers and collaborators of the socialist regimes, (b) fierce enemies of these regimes, and (c) people who decided to wait and see who would be the winner. I know many families whose strategy was to place one member among the communists, another one or two among the mujahedin of various parties, and to sent yet another one as a refugee to Europe or USA, while the rest of the family set up their household

19. More on *pashtunwali* in B. Glatzer: Zum Pashtunwali als Ethnischem Selbstportrait. In: R. Kößler und G. Best (Hg): *Festschrift für Christian Sigrist.* (in press).

in a Pakistani refugee camp. Of course the family continued communicating among all its members.

During the early years of the war foreigners and Afghan intellectuals on both sides of the front expected a soon end of tribalism and ethnicity. Some hoped for the "achievements of socialism" and for the "brotherly help of the USSR" to transform the society into a supra-ethnic class society and eventually into a harmonious socialist state, the others expected the grand *jihad* against the formidable common enemy to do the job of creating one Afghan nation.

During the long war it became obvious that the regimes in Kabul and the *mujahedin* were divided into numerous hostile factions. It became also obvious that ethnicity and tribalism were additional factors but not the most important ones. In early 1980 the Sunni *mujahedin* had formed about 100 different parties who ran 60 offices in Peshawar. During the following year the Pakistan Government forced the *mujahedin* to unite and acknowledged only 7 parties who were given administrative tasks for millions of Afghan refugees in Pakistan. The rest of the parties had to close their offices in Pakistan. The 7 parties issued identity and ration cards thus forcing the refugees to make a choice between one or another of the parties. Even more relevant was the Pakistani policy to distribute military equipment and money for the *mujahedin* exclusively through the 7 parties.

The Shia *mujahedin* formed another eight parties, who found support in Iran. Over the years Iran succeeded in uniting most of them, today the significant Shia parties are the two wings of the Hizb-e Wahdad which organise the great majority of the Hazarah, and the Harakat-e Islami (Mohseni) which appeals more to the urban Shia and is relatively independent of Iran.[20]

Between 1978 and 1992 the Soviet-installed governments, the army and the civil service of Kabul where divided into hostile factions as well. Two presidents, innumerable ministers, generals and other dignitaries were killed in factional fights.

Ethnicity and tribalism are often held responsible for the Afghan disunity. Indeed practically each of the conflicting parties and groups, including the Taliban, show a certain emphasis towards one or another ethnic group. This, however, is no proof that ethnic and tribal divisions are the cause of political cleavages and violent conflicts. Every Afghan

---

20. Jonathan Lee, pers. comm.

belongs to one of the ethnic groups and every Pashtun belongs to one of the tribes, thus a quarrel between two Afghans who incidentally do not belong to the same ethnic group or tribe may easily be misinterpreted as ethnically or tribally motivated.

A closer look at the history of the present conflicting parties reveals that ethnicity and tribalism are an epiphenomenon in the Afghan war.[21] Or as Canfield puts it: "Contrary to what might be supposed, the actual operating units of socio-political coalition...are rarely genuinely 'ethnic' in composition".[22] The undeniable fact that the parties do have a recognisable ethnic stamp has mainly to do with the local background of their founders and leaders rather than with their ethnical identity. If in that local background exists a demographical majority of one ethic group or one tribe it is most likely that the closest companions of the founders and leaders will belong to the same group. They will usually recruit from their home area and use the local language for internal communication thus creating a barrier to those unfamiliar with that language. Olivier Roy points at the example of the Persian speaking Nurzay Pashtuns of Southwest Afghanistan who initially joined the Jamiyat-i Islami which is mainly Tajik because Persian is the Language spoken in that party, whereas the Pashtu speaking Nurzay went to Harakat-e Enqelab.[23]

Outlook

Due to its inherent primordial connotations ethnic and tribal identity is connected with strong emotions and therefore easily leads to particular aggressiveness when conflicts arise. Organisers and leaders of conflicts use ethnic and tribal emotions and instrumentalise the feelings of honour and shame connected with it as a most effective tool or weapon. Although Afghanistan's national unity is on the agenda of all conflicting groups ethnic arguments are increasingly used in the political agitation. There is an obvious tendency towards ethnisation of the conflict. In October and November 1996 I carried out a survey on popular concepts of locality, ethnicity and tribe among peasants, artisans, traders, and students who recently came from different parts of Afghanistan to Peshawar and intended to return soon. To my surprise all of them without an exception

21. see O. Roy, *op. cit.*; Canfield, *op. cit.*
22. Canfield, *op. cit.*, p. 76.
23. Roy, *op. cit,* p. 178.

stressed the importance of Afghan national unity incorporating all ethnic minorities. A partition of Afghanistan, be it on ethnic or other lines, was seen as a terrifying perspective to be avoided by all means. In autumn 1998 I continued the survey with the same questions and noticed an even increased longing for national unity and a deep fear of ethnic disunity. The Taliban were praised on the one side for their success in pacifying the larger part of the country, but were criticised at the same time for their ethnically imbalanced attitude and for their administrative shortcomings. On the other hand, tribal identity was considered by most of the respondents not as a fissive but rather as a stabilising factor in present day Afghanistan, as an ordering social principle of rural Pashtuns which provides them with a stable social orientation in a chaotic world.

ACKNOWLEDGEMENT

Research underlying this article was funded by the Deutsche Forschungsgemeinschaft, Bonn, I wish to thank Ursel Siebert-Glatzer for her substantial collaboration.

REFERENCES

Anderson, Jon. 1978. "There are No Khans Anymore: Economic Development and Social Change in Tribal Afghanistan," *The Middle East Journal*, 32: 167-183.

Bosworth, C. E. 1990 (1978). "Khaladj," in *The Encyclopedia of Islam.* (New edition, IV) Leiden: Brill.

Carter, Lynn & Kerry Connor. 1989. "A Preliminary Investigation of Contemporary Afghan Councils," paper prepared for ACBAR, Peshawar.

Dawood, N.J. 1995. *The Koran* (translated with notes). London: Penguin Books.

Dorn, Bernhard. 1965 (1829). *History of the Afghans.* Translated from the Persian of Neamat Ullah. London, Santiago de Compostela: Susil Gupta.

Dupree, Louis. 1984. "Tribal Warfare in Afghanistan and Pakistan: A Reflection of the Segmentary Lineage System," (pp.266-286) in Ahmed & Hart (eds.), *Islam in Tribal Societies: From the Atlas to the Indus.* London: Routledge.

Eickelman, Dale F. 1981. *The Middle East: An Anthropological Appraisal.* Englewood Cliffs; NJ: Prentice-Hall.

Elphinstone, Mountstuart. 1839. *An Account of the Kingdom of Caubul.* (2 vols.) London: Longman.

Evans, Jeffrey H. P. 1977. *The Social Structure and Organization of a Pakhtu Speaking Community in Afghanistan.* Unpublished Ph.D. thesis, Durham.

Glatzer, B. (in press). "Zum Pashtunwali als ethnischem Selbstportrait," in R. Kößler undG. Best (ed.), *Festschrift für Christian Sigrist.*

Glatzer, Bernt. 1992. "From Refugee to Resident: Effects of Aid on Repatriation," (pp. 161-168) in E. Eide & T. Skaufjord (eds.), *From Aid During Times of War to Aid for Reconstruction and Development*. Seminar Report. Peshawar: Norwegian Afghanistan Committee.

Imâmuddîn, S. M. 1960 (1992) *Tarîkh-e Khân Jahânî wa makhzan-e Afghânî*. Dacca: Asiatic Society of Pakistan, publication no. 4, 2 vols.

Khan, Hayat. 1981. *Hayat-i Afghan* (translated to English by H. Priestley) reprinted by Lahore: Sang-e-Meel Publication.

Spain, J. 1963. *The Pathan Borderland.* The Hague: Mouton.

Steul, W. 1981. *Paschtunwali: Ein Ehrenkodex und seine rechtliche Relevanz.* Wiesbaden: Steiner.

Tapper, Richard. 1983. "Introduction," (pp. 1-82) in R. Tapper (ed.), *The Conflict of Tribe and State in Iran and Afghanistan*. London, etc.: Croom Helm and St. Martin's Press.

ELEVEN

BEDOUIN

ULRICH BRAUKÄMPER

Classification

The English term Bedouin is derived from the Arabic "bada," meaning "to live in a plain desert". The noun *Badw* (*Badu, Bedu*) traditionally refers to those Arabic-speaking people who live according to the Bedouin way of life as nomadic livestock-herders. They are strictly differentiated by themselves and by outiders from Arabs gaining their livelihood as sedentary peasants (Arabic: *fallahin*) or town-dwellers. However, in parts of northern Africa the term ᶜArab is sometimes employed for mobile pastoralists in general, e.g. for the non-Arabic Beja. It thus becomes synonymous with Bedouin. Here, Bedouin is restricted as a label for nomads of Arabian speech and culture inhabiting parts of western Asia and northern Africa. The term refers to a considerable number of tribes (Arabic: *qabail*, sg. *qabila*), often genealogically interrelated. Because of the vast distances separating them, they have usually developed a tribal/ethnic consciousness of their own.

A first general classification can be made according to the livestock, their dominant economic resource. The "classical" and presumably original type of Bedouin is a herder of sheep, goats and one-humped camels of the *Camelus dromedarius* subspecies well adapted to an arid habitat. In some parts of the southern Arabian peninsula, particularly in the Zufar region of Oman, where sufficient rainfall is provided by the summer monsoon, humped cattle (*Bos indicus*) constitute a major resource of Bedouin livelihood. Cattle of this breed became the primary economic base for (semi-)nomadic Arabs in fringes of the African savannas adjacent to the Sahara desert. In the eastern Sudanic zone between the White Nile and Lake Chad these people are collectively labelled *Baggara*, meaning "cattle people" (derived from the Arabic word *baqar* = "cattle"). They are thus differentiated from their Bedouin neighbours in the north, the *Abbala* or "camel people". In the marshlands of southern Iraq, Arabic herdsmen raise water-buffaloes, mostly pasturing them in reaped and fallow fields within a very limited geographical range. This specialisation is usually not considered a typical form of Bedouin culture.

The Bedouin tribes speak various dialects of Arabic, a language belonging to the southern cluster of the Semitic language group. Although the huge extension of their habitat between the Atlantic coast of Mauretania and the Iranian highlands made them adopt various linguistic and cultural features of their neighbours, i.e. Berbers, sub-Saharan Africans, Turks, or Iranians, essential aspects of their way of life and values remained relatively homogeneous. Nomadic fractions of the latter ethnic groups, on the other hand, share many similarities with the Arabic-speaking Bedouin.

Geographical Location

Bedouin tribes or tribal fragments are to be found in 12 states of western Asia and 15 states of northern Africa. Major areal clusters are northern and southern Arabia, the Mediterranean regions of Africa, the Sahara and the African Sahel. In most countries, however, the Bedouin constitute only small and steadily dwindling minorities. The total number of "real" representatives of Bedouin culture may not amount to more than five million people.

In order to avoid conflict with sedentary peasants their herds have to be kept away from the areas of permanent cultivation. Since rain-based agriculture has consistently expanded in many regions over the last decades, pastures became scarcer or had to be shifted to niches of more arid habitats. Whereas on the one hand the life of many Bedouin has thus become more difficult, they have, on the other hand, benefited in the oil-producing states from the general increase of national income. This is one of the numerous factors of culture change, converting former nomads into sedentary dwellers of towns and villages.

Bedouin tribes are mainly found in areas where rainfall is too low and unpredictable for the permanent cultivation of crops. In most areas of the *Dry Belt* of western Asia and northern Africa rainfed agriculture becomes too risky when average precipitation is less than 300 mm *per annum.* In such regions — apart from irrigated cultivation in oases — nomadic pastoralism usually provides the only strategy of livelihood. Camels are best adapted to arid climatic conditions and can even be pastured in waterless deserts where rainfall sometimes leads to a thin cover of vegetation for short periods. For example, the Kababish and other nomads of the northern Sudan regularly utilise the so-called *djizu* pastures consisting of succulent plants which grow after occasional precipitation in areas of the Libyan desert where no wells exist. During such a grazing phase of a few weeks they mainly live on camel milk. Regarding fodder and watering, sheep and goats are more demanding than camels, even though the former can be kept in relatively arid zones with annual rainfall of less than 200 mm. Cattle need a cover of grass and have to be watered daily (at a minimum every second day) during the dry season, which means that their radius of pasture cannot be extended more than 20 km from a permanent source of water. The Bedouin are thus to a large extent dependent ecological preconditions of the animals the are primarily herding.

The Arabic Bedouin, raising camels, sheep and goats, are scattered over the vast arid zones from Syria and Irak to the southern shores of the Arabian peninsula and over the northern part of Africa from the Mediterranean Sea to the *Sahel Belt* between the Atlantic Ocean and the Red Sea. The cattle-keeping Bedouin — apart from small pockets, e.g. Oman and the Libyan Cyrenaica — are concentrated in the sub-Saharan regions of dry savanna between the thirteenth and the tenth parallel. For most of the Baggara the cultivation of crops, particularly millet, serves as a second pillar of their economy, whereas for the Bedouin of the arid zones, agriculture usually plays a far less important role.

The Evolution of Bedouin Culture

Since the keeping of livestock is the core element of Bedouin culture, the question of its origin leads back to the beginning of domestication of the respective animals in western Asia. The earliest focus of the breeding of sheep from the wild species *Ovis ammon* most probably occurred in mountainous parts of this area from the end of the ninth millennium B.C. onwards. The goat derived from *Capra aegagrus* appeared as a domesticated animal in the region between Iran and Palestine during the eighth millennium. Sheep and goats became highly important for agropastoralist economies and the surplus production of the early civilisations and empire states of the region. The period of domestication of the dromedary from an ancestor that has since become extinct is still contested, but most experts seem to believe that this process occurred between the third and the second millennium B.C. in the Arabian peninsula. From there the domestication of the dromedary spread to northern Africa since the sixth century B.C. The horse, also an integral part of Bedouin culture, originally seems to have been domesticated in central Asia from where, during the first half of the second millennium B.C, its use as an object of prestige and a mode of transport during warfare was spread via Iran and Mesopotamia as far as Egypt. The African donkey (*Equus asinus*) and the Southwest Asiatic onager (*Equus hemionus*) had already been in use as transport animals during earlier periods.

Parts of the present habitat of the Bedouin belong to the earliest centres of mankind, where the so-called *Neolithic Revolution* was initiated, i.e. a productive economy with plant domestication and sedentary settlement. In Jericho, Palestine, the beginning of this process can be traced back archaeologically to about 10,000 B.P. The evolution of animal and plant domestication, however, seems to have lead to mixed forms of economy, favouring the rise of complex civilisations rather than a nomadic way of life of the Bedouin type. The latter must be assumed to be a cultural specialisation of a later period, when the camel, as an essential innovation by the pastoral-oriented societies of western Asia, was increasingly adopted. By its unique adaptation to arid conditions, this animal enabled its keepers to use pastures in areas inaccessible before. They could also utilise ecological niches outside the fertile land controled by the agricultural-oriented empire states. Such favourable conditions for the evolution of Bedouin culture seem to have existed in Mesopotamia at the end of the second millennium B.C. when the expansion of the Assyrian empire exerted a growing pressure upon the semi-sedentary agropastoralists around the fringes of intensively cultivated land.

The rise of empire states around the fertile regions of western Asia — from Mesopotamia, Syria, Palestine as far as Yemen and Hadramawt — presumably accelerated the evolution of a highly specialised mobile pastoralism, finally developing into the type of the present Bedouin.

Also, the empire states' access to camels not only enabled them to establish long-distance trading connections across arid regions, but also to induced military expeditions to pillage or pursual of nomads far into the waterless deserts. This fact gradually forced the agropastoralists to change their way of life into the Bedouin style, thus improving their general mobility and swiftness. Simultaneously, the Arabic-speaking nomads learnt to employ this new flexibility for suprise attacks upon caravans, peasants and town dwellers.

In general, the evolution of Bedouin culture is to be seen as a reaction to the increasing power of empires in the fertile areas surrounding the arid zones of the Semitic-speaking populations. This growing pressure, initiated around 1,300 B.C., resulted in the evolution of a more and more specialised and increasingly mobile society which then developed a peculiar type of cultural pattern, henceforth to be labelled as Bedouin.

To some extent such a vision of Bedouin society as unavoidable consequence of external pressures would be contradicting the view of the famous Tunisian historiographer Ibn Khaldoun (A.D. 1332-1406). The latter was propagating a "theory of (cyclical) conquest" basically blaming the aggressive and martial Bedouin for the destruction of urban civilisations. After such a destructive campaign, the conquerors, would adapt to the features of urban life, maintaining their tradition while, at the same time, losing their military qualities. As a result of this process, they themselves would be prone to be conquered by other groups of Bedouin who had retained their martial character in the desert, and the whole cycle starts again.

This theory of conquest, famous in the Muslim world and of considerable importance in European anthropology and sociology during the first half of the 20th century, was developed by Ibn Khaldoun under the impression of the invasions of the Banu Hilal Bedouin. The latter's exodus from the Arabian peninsula prompted them to cause enormous destructions in the urban civilisations of northern Africa during the 11th century. Ibn Khaldoun's theory, however, has only a limited explanatory value with regard to the evolution of Bedouin society. The theories on these processes have to be revised consistently in the light of new archaeological, historical, linguistic and anthropological research.

The Role of the Bedouin in Documented History

A growing interest in the history and culture of the Arabic-speaking nomads arose in the 19th century and was further stimulated by pioneer studies such as those of Max von Oppenheim (1939, 1942). Ancient literary and visual sources frequently offer reports of populations representing the early Bedouin cultural type. From the second half of the second millennium B.C. onwards mounted warriors of mobile pastoralist groups entered the scene in the vicinity of the western Asiatic empires. We know about subsequent waves of Semitic-speaking nomads such as Hebrews, Aramaeans, and Nabataeans invading the settled civilisations of Palestine, Syria and Irak. As indicated above, camel-riding had been developed in Arabia, whereas horse-riding was adopted from the mountain people of Transcaucasia and Iran. The first cuneiform documents recording the existence of camel-riding nomads dates back to 880 B.C. Its content has been interpreted as the story of "Aramaean Bedouin" fighting a vassal of Assur Nasirpal somewhere in the vicinity of Mesopotamia. During the subsequent centuries the Assyrian kings were continuously involved in military encounters with mobile pastoralists of Aribi, identified as the northernmost region of Arabia between Syria and Mesopotamia. The first explicit mention of the name cArab in the Bible, referring to people of the desert, occurs in the book of Isaiah in the late 8th century B.C. Evidently this term, in the sense of "true Arạbs," particularly referred to the desert nomads, sometimes including oasis-dwellers without further distinction. Even Prophet Muhammad used the term A^{c}rab denoting the Bedouin in particular.

In the southern parts of the Arabian peninsula, i.e. south of the Rub^{c} al-Khali, the development of Bedouin culture seems to have started several centuries later than in the north. According to inscriptions of South Arabia, Bedouin became involved in local conflicts towards the second century A.D. Between the third and the sixth centuries, when a general sense of insecurity grew all over the region, they seem to have been involved in the disputes between the Sabaean state and the Aksumite empire in Ethiopia as well as in the constant wars between Rome and Persia. The Byzantines were mainly confronted with the tribes of the Ghassanids between Sinai and Syria, the Persians with the Lakhmids in Irak.

In the areas of Yemen and Oman the concentration of power in the hands of the rulers of highland peasants, fortified in castle-like residences, furthermore induced parts of the population to join the Bedouin way of life. A growing tendency of internal feuds and rivalries over pastoral resources as well as natural catastrophies destroying parts of the irrigation systems obviously gave rise to far-reaching migrations towards the north and to the African shores of the Red Sea. This migratory inclination has characterised the Bedouin of southern Arabia ever since. The Blemmyes, who can most probably be identified as ancestors of the present Bedja tribes of northeastern Sudan, adopted the Bedouin type of nomadism, including the camel, from Arabic immigrants and were mentioned as fierce enemies of the Ptolemaean rulers of Egypt and their Roman successors.

Information on the Bedouin of pre-Muslim Arabia has been preserved in pre-Islamic poetry as well as in the writings of poets and scholars during the first centuries after Islamisation. The town-dwellers, including the Kuraysh, the clan of Prophet Muhammad in Mecca, had always maintained intensive relations with their Bedouin neighbours who were able to secure or to threaten the trade routes, or the base of their economic existence. The nomads were also interested in commercial links and social alliances with urban people who secured their supply with vegetarian food, handicraft articles and luxury goods.

During the wars in the beginning of the seventh century A.D., fought by Prophet Muhammad for the establishment of Islam, he was supported by some of the Bedouin, but fiercefully opposed by others. At the time of his death (A.D. 632), however, most of the nomadic tribes of the Arabian peninsula were united under his religious and political command. In the Muslim armies conquering large parts of western Asia and northern Africa over the subsequent eighty years Bedouin forces occupied a leading part. Khalif ᶜUmar (634-44) for example, i.e. Muhammad's second successor in the theocratic rule of the Muslim empire and the most effective Arabic conqueror, is said to have preferred the modest and arduous Bedouin way of life.

For many Bedouin the wars of Islamic conquest can be equated with migration movements, because they were not only carried out by male warriors, but considerable parts of the latter's domestic groups joined or followed the military expeditions. Thus in some of the most important migrations of the early Middle Ages Arabic nomads spread as far as Iran and Morocco. In most regions outside the Arabian peninsula the Bedouin obviously preferred to preserve their traditional culture. They abstained from intermarrying with the local populations to a notable extent. Occasionally, however, the Bedouin tended to enlarge their ethnic body by processes of assimilation, particularly when they met nomadic groups of similar cultural orientation in ecological conditions comparable to those of Arabia. In the case of the Berber pastoralists of southern Morocco, the western Sahara, and Mauretania ethnically mixed tribes of Arabic-Berber origin came into existence from the eighth century onwards. In the Nile valley and in other areas of northern Africa dominated by peasant cultures the Bedouin tended to pursue their life as mobile pastoralists along the arid fringes of the cultivated land.

As mentioned above, the second important wave of Bedouin from the Arabian peninsula into northern Africa occurred during the eleventh century A.D. This occupation of Libya and Tunis by the Banu Hilal proved to be disastrous for these regions causing a further series of turbulent migrations in regions as far away as the central and southern Sahara.

One of the most important Bedouin groups in northern Africa originates from the genealogical cluster of the Djuhayna, to be traced back to places in today's Yemen and Saudi Arabia. They invaded Egypt in 641 and parts of them pursued their way with the conquering Islamic army towards the Maghrib. The bulk of the Djuhayna, however, seem to have moved upstream along the Nile until their further advance was blocked by the Christian kingdoms of Nubia. According to the historical traditions of the former, the Arabs were camel-breeding Bedouin facing an increasing lack of pastures in the narrow Nile valley. Furthermore they had to face the hostile policy of the Egyptian rulers, after the Bahriya Mamluks had taken power by the middle of the 13th century. Only after the collapse of the Christian stronghold of Dongola in 1315/16 the Arabic nomads were able to infiltrate the Sahel region of the Sudan and make use of its vast grazing areas stretching out as far as Lake Chad.

In the middle of the 17th century, some of these Bedouin groups of these regions became involved in internal struggles for power resulting in some divisions being forced to move southward into the savanna regions. The latter struck an ecological borderline demarcating areas in which the keeping of camels proved to be increasingly difficult or impossible. For them the adoption of agriculture or cattle-breeding or a combination of the two became a question of survival. This enforced change led them to develop a special agropastoral system characterised by cattle-rearing and the cultivation of millet. They adopted cattle from the non-Arab Fulbe (Fulani) who had been migrating from the west to the savanna zones east of Lake Chad from the sixteenth century onwards. The result was a new type of Bedouin culture based on mobile cattle-breeding. This process of becoming Baggara, "cattle men", in savannas between the White Nile and Lake Chad receiving rainfall of 500 to1000 mm was more or less completed by 1800.

The Baggara Arabs became the most active partisans of the theocratic Mahdist rule in the Sudan between 1882 and 1898. This political orientation obviously resulted from pragmatic considerations such as economic advantages, rather than from motives of religious conviction and passion.

Between the 16th and the 19th centuries most of the Bedouin tribes were subjected to the Turkish Ottoman empire, although at times their state of dependency was not very strict. Subsequent foreign rulers until the second half of the 20th century came from Great Britain, France, Italy and Spain. The decidedly liberty-loving Bedouin frequently revolted against their alien overlords and sometimes retreated to territories outside of the latters' control. For example, two waves of the Awlad Sulayman tribe fled from Fezzan in southern Libya to Kanem northeast of Lake Chad: the first group migrated out of the range of Turkish rule in 1842 and the second tried to escape Italian oppression from 1928 to 1930. Only the Bedouin of the interior parts of present Saudi Arabia, united by the ideology of the Wahhabiya brotherhood since the 18th century, successfully resisted in place any attempt at establishing colonial rule.

In the 20th century the Bedouin of all categories became politically and economically more and more marginalised. Because of the increasing density of population in their countries they are today confronted with the steady expansion of cultivated land at the expense of the grazing reserves. The colonial powers as well as the independent states have been interested in transforming them into sedentary peasants and town-dwellers thus depriving them of the core element of their culture, mobile pastoralism.

The Bedouin, like nomads everywhere in the world, were often accused of causing environmental destruction and constituting backward and troublesome relics in the modern societies. On the other hand, a growing attitude of romanticism with respect to the Bedouin traditions can be observed. For example, in Saudi-Arabia, Jordan, Israel or Libya they are valued as an important part of the cultural heritage of these countries and also exploited for folkloristic purposes and tourism.

Economic Patterns

As already pointed out, the core element of Bedouin subsistence is the keeping of mobile herds of camels or, in the case of the Baggara, cattle, usually combined with sheep and goats. Horses of the famous Arabian as well as of Berber and Nubian (Dongola) breeds used to be important objects of prestige and warfare. They had to be fed on grain. Furthermore donkeys facilitated transport and dogs guarded camps and herds. Today some of the Bedouin groups are exclusively nomads relying on the products of their animals only, but most of them practise some farming or horticulture. For the Baggara the cultivation of millet in fact became the second pillar of their economy.

Agricultural work, however, has a low reputation in general. The Bedouin therefore try to employ labourers for cultivation. Until the colonial period slaves were kept for irrigated and rainfed agriculture. The traditional ideal of a Bedouin, as far as the economic activities are concerned, is to take care of the animals he possesses. The work of herding and rearing tends to be extremely arduous, but it is considered far preferable to the monotony of farming or crafts. Hired labour is sometimes employed during the dry season for the watering of animals from wells, since some herd owners can afford the wages for impoverished nomads. The latter work for the acquisition of a herd of their own. Towards their animals the Bedouin display a commercial attitude, so they usually do not hesitate to sell parts of their surplus production every year. Particular emotional links are restricted to the camels and horses mounted by the men.

The considerable range in the sources of income, at the disposal of the Bedouin in former times, has mostly disappeared in the 20th century. Hunting in the deserts and savannas for example was either forbidden by law or became unproductive because the most relevant animal species had become extinct. Formerly the Baggara had been renowned hunters, killing elephants from horseback with lances. In the 19th century, they traded in large amounts of ivory and ostrich feathers. Collecting vegetarian items, however, i.e. undomesticated rice or Arabic gum, continues to be important in savanna regions. Before the establishment of colonial rule razzias (Arabic: *ghawza*), military expeditions against other nomads, settlements of peasants and caravans of traders, was a common practice of many Bedouin tribes. The Baggara and the Arabs of the western Sahara regularly raided slaves among Black African peasants and sold some of them abroad. The Bedouin could also gain subsidies by protecting caravans or offering them safe-conduct while passing through the tribal territories. Enforced pacification and the replacement of camel caravans by railways and lorries terminated these means of income during the first decades of the 20th century.

The keeping of livestock continues to be the most typical and most important economic sector for the Bedouin. Animal husbandry is usually not a restricted economic strategy of mere subsistence, but rather surplus production, utilised for the purchase of vegetable food as well as handicraft articles and industrial objects. To a certain extent the Bedouin live on the products of their animals, i.e. milk, clarified butter, cheese and meat, but their most important staple food consists of grain, usually not provided by their own subsidiary agriculture in sufficient quantities. They are therefore dependent upon the exchange of milk poducts, hides and live animals for vegetarian foodstuff and other items of the peasant and urban population. In the areas of the Arabic-speaking nomads varieties of millet, followed by wheat and barley, are the cereals mostly used for daily consumption. Dates and vegetables, such as onions, okra as well as different leguminous plants cultivated in the oases, also constitute an important part of the Bedouin diet.

In arid zones the herds always have to follow a pattern of migration determined by a combination of seasonal and areal variability in the supply of pasture and water. If vegetation becomes scarce in a particular area, survival implies movement to locations of sufficient pasture. The grazing resources are usually assigned in a regular fashion according to the geographical particularities and seasonal climatic conditions known by the experience of many generations. The nomadic movements are therefore not performed at random but follow more or less standardised cycles of transhumance, to be changed only under extraordinary circumstances such as drought or political insecurity. The most common pattern of transhumance is the annual migration between dry and wet season pastures. The more arid an area, the more far-reaching the cycles of transhumance tend to be. Camel-keepers in a desert or Sahel habitat will sometimes cover distances of more than 1,000 km per annum, whereas cattle-keepers of the savanna rarely surpass 400 km.

Camels mainly feed on thinly scattered shrubs and bushes over vast grazing-grounds. The herders, mostly young men mounted on specially trained riding-camels, have to control mobility of the herds and to keep them away from the cultivated plots. In the dry season the dromedaries on their own would regularly return to the wells to be watered. For sheep and goats the demands of pasture differ when compared to those of camels. The former have to be watered more frequently. They are therefore kept at closer distances to the camps and usually herded by women and children. Because of their high rate of reproduction, sheep and goats provide the major source of meat and the most important commodity of trade for the Bedouin. As mentioned above, cattle need a cover of grass vegetation and daily watering in the hot season rendering them unsuitable for arid zones and thus restricting their existence to savanna regions. Along the fringes of the wet savanna in Africa, cattle are furthermore threatened by *trypanosomiasis* caused by tsetse flies (*Glossina morsitans*). These perils limit the southern extension of Baggara transhumance.

Among the Bedouin the three-generation extended family is the most common domestic unit. If such a group cannot muster enough manpower to cover all of the daily chores in the rearing of livestock either relatives or hired labourers must be engaged. The latter will usually be poor tribesmen trying to raise a herd of their own.

A basic requisition of all mobile pastoralists is the formation of herding units manageable by a single herder or by teams in accordance with the household and camping units. These herding systems depend upon pastures and species of animals concerned. Any numeric description would therefore be an inapproriate generalisation. In the Sudan, for example, the average size of a camel herd manageable by two herdsmen amounts to 80-100 individual animals. One adult herder can take care of about 70 cattle or 200 sheep. If the numbers of animals surpass these quantities, the herding units have to be reorganised. The manageable size of herds does not necessarily correlate with the actual ownership of animals according to the households. Frequently, nomadic relatives, peasants, or town people entrust livestock as a kind of live capital to Bedouin herders. The latter are then allowed to use the milk of the animals in addition to the compensation for their work in the form of agricultural products and a certain quantity of the foals, calves or kids. Throughout Bedouin history this exchange of goods and services has been essential for the establishment of socio-economic alliances between mobile pastoralists and sedentary villagers and townsmen.

Although the living conditions for the Bedouin have become more and more precarious in some respects since the second half of the 20th century, the nomads experienced enormous advantages with regard to herding practices. The extermination of predatory animals such as lions, leopards and hyenas in most regions has facilitated their work considerably minimising the risk of night grazing for example. Pacification has furthermore reduced the necessity of their permanent alert against enemies and thiefs. Since the 1960s, however, civil wars in several states of northern Africa have again created a growing state of public insecurity. Increasingly nomads in Chad and Sudan, for example, have reacted to this serious interference by acquiring modern rifles.

Settlements and Material Culture

The Bedouin type of economy requires a material culture fitting their mobile life-style. All of their belongings, including the shelters, regularly have to be removed and reinstalled in different localities for the limited grazing periods. The items are transported by camels, donkeys and, among the Baggara, pack-oxen. Traffic conditions permitting, lorries and pick-up trucks may also be employed since the last decades. Over long distances these loads would not usually exeed 200 kg per camel and 100 kg per oxen.

The tents (*buyut*, sg. *bayt* = house) of camel-keeping Bedouin living in regions of low precipitation consist of woollen tarpaulins of black goat hair fixed upon a rectangular system of poles and ropes. The space within the tent is divided into a larger part for the women and children, including the kitchen and the storing facilities, and a smaller part for the men where visitors are also received and hospitality is extended to guests. The nomad's tent in savanna regions with higher rainfall is usually smaller than the "black tent" used by the camel-keeping Bedouin. It consists of a circular cupola-shaped skeleton of bent wooden branches covered with water-proof mats made of fibre of the dum palm. In the interior a platform for sleeping and storing provisions is installed. Among all Bedouin groups the erection and dismantling of the tent is women's work.

Provided the grazing capacity is sufficient, each camping unit would usually consist of about half a dozen tents of related people. During the dry season bigger concentrations can be observed around places where water is available in natural pools, barrages or wells. Bedouin groups, in the habit of spending the cold season regularly in the same places, would sometimes construct stone houses (*buyut hajar*) at these sites.

Most objects of Bedouin inventory, i.e. household utensils as well as equipment for nomadic activities, are made of unbreakable materials such as wood, leather, wool, grass, calabash and fibres. For cookers and tea-kettles metal is preferred, while ceramics are hardly used. In many regions between Syria and the Sudan, roving tinkers of Gypsy origin

(Halab) provide their services and handicraft objects to the Bedouin. A remarkable creation of Bedouin material culture is the camel-litter (Arabic: *cutfa* or *shibriya*) consisting of a wooden frame, cloth and leather mats decorated with cowries. It is still used in some areas, for example in Syria and the Sudan, to shelter women and babies on nomadic migrations and the bridal procession to the place of the bridegroom. The Baggara vainly tried to transfer the *cutfa* to pack-oxen, since it proved to be disfunctional for the backs of these animals and in the relatively dense vegetation of their savanna habitat. The litter was therefore restricted to ceremonial occasions and has meanwhile been abandoned completely.

The traditional clothes of the Bedouin vary in many details because of the local influences in the vast area between Morocco, the African savannas, Irak and Yemen. The basic dress for men is flowing garments, baggy trousers and turbans made of cotton, woollen caftans and leather slippers or boots. The clothes of girls and married women are usually differentiated. Unlike the uni-coloured, white or brownish, clothes of men the blouses and gowns of females are often composed in a variety of colours. Bedouin women usually go unveiled, wearing heavy jewelry made by the silversmiths of urban centres. The dress of small children was in former times restricted to breechclouts made of wool, cotton or leather.

The most common musical instrument among the Bedouin is the lute-like rababa. Various types of guitars and tambours are also widespread. In some regions, particularly in the Sudan, big copper drums (Arabic: *nahas* or *nuggara*) played an outstanding role as symbols of tribal identity.

The most frequent Bedouin weaponry consisted of curved or straight swords, lances and daggers the handles of which were decorated with silver, ivory and other materials. Muzzle-loader rifles and coats of mail were occasionally used until the first decades of the 20th century. In regions beyond full state control the Bedouin presently possess a considerable amount of modern fire-arms, particularly Kalashnikovs.

Life Cycle, Kinship and Social Structure

Within the vast Bedouin habitat, their social structure and political organisation differ according to their tribal affiliation and their cultural, ecological and economic variations. Certain patterns of interactions and institutions appear to be characteristic, however. First of all, in the typical small-scale communities, face-to-face relations are essential for the patterns of social control. The details of these encounters is elaborated below at some more length in the context of the value system. Similarities of the life cycle ceremonies and the rites of passage are obvious among all Bedouin tribes. The customs associated with birth, name-giving, circumcision, wedding and death are more or less standardised according to the Islamic rituals. Pre-Islamic survivals in all of these fields do exist, but such variations are scarce and difficult to prove.

Among most of the Bedouin groups newborn children are made household members by rites of seclusion and purification conducted between seven and forty days after birth. Circumcision (*khitan*) is performed on boys at the age of two to eight years, and this event is accompanied by a feast. Girls of the Baggara and of a number of southern Arabian tribes are subjected to clitoridectomy at approximately the same age. This is not demanded by religious law, so it may be assumed that it was adopted from a pre-Muslim substratum of female genital mutilation that has traditionally been common among peoples of northeastern Africa, such as Nubians, Ethiopians and Somali.

Bedouin children of both sexes, having reached the age of six years, are employed in household tasks and in herding sheep and goats. If their parents decide to send them to schools they usually have to leave their families and stay in urban hostels. Attempts by governments to provide facilities of modern education in the nomadic camps have rarely proved to be successful.

With regard to marriage, it can be assumed that in former times certain obligations of exogamy at the lineage or clan level played an important role among the Bedouin, as it is still the case in many nomadic societies of the world. However, the Muslim preferences of marrying the closest relatives permitted by the Quran (4, 23), particularly the daughters of the father's brother (*bint camm*) and of the mother's brother (*bint khal*), have gained ground to a considerable extent. This fact has also strengthened the trend towards a reduction of interethnic marriages and thus reinforced ties of endogamy among the Bedouin tribes. Such a change of concepts and practices is clearly seen in the traditions of the Baggara Arabs. Before parallel and cross cousin marriages became preferential in the 20th century, the Baggara contracted numerous interethnic marriage relations with neighbouring African groups, leading to their dark physical complexion.

Cousin marriages are valued as strengthening the cohesion and the authority of the lineage. Brideprice and dowry are usually reduced in the case of such alliances and the property remains within a limited circle of relatives. According to Quranic law (*shariʿa*) daughters inherit half of the property which is attributed to sons. Since among the Bedouin heritage mainly consists of livestock, and females are not considered capable of looking after camels or cattle, their animal holdings are usually entrusted to male relatives only and incorporated into their herds.

Polygyny seems to be comparatively rare among Bedouin. Only a few chiefs and rich livestock owners can afford to marry up to four wives as permitted by Islamic law. Such men are often interested in having at least one of their wives live in a permanent settlement of agriculturalists or in a town in order to diversify the means of income and to minimise economic constraints. Segregation of women, common in urban or village societies, is not practised in the nomadic conditions, and Bedouin women can carry out their economic activities in public. Political decisions, however, are almost exclusively restricted to male responsibility. Divorce, initiated by either husband or wife, seems to be frequent in most Bedouin groups. Until her remarriage the divorced woman will return to her family of orientation.

The Bedouin fully observe the general Muslim practices associated with death including the simple funeral rites. The body of a deceased person must be buried within twenty-four hours after death. Graves are usually unmarked, even though at times conspicuous mausoleums are erected for persons considered particularly holy during their lifetime or after death. Such sites can then become locally or even regionally important places of pilgrimage. As elsewhere in the Muslim world, such a cult of ancestors or saints may be opposed by rigid puritanical Muslim brotherhoods such as the Wahhabites in Arabia.

Socio-political Organisation

Throughout their history the Bedouin were exposed to natural conditions of great harshness. The struggle for survival was merciless and induced a constant tendency for the strong to capture the property of the weak, i.e. the livestock or the grazing rights. As a result Bedouin group solidarity at the level of lineages, clans and tribes has been developed to an extraordinay degree. Such a necessity of forming large and strong groups was, however, adverse to the requirements of the nomadic economy demanding a thin spread over huge areas in search of pasturage. Thus for groups beyond a certain size it was difficult to coordinate their activities as a unit in a coherent and efficient manner. The constant opposition of centrifugal and centripetal forces therefore exposed Bedouin society to the incessant dynamics of fusion and fission.

Like all Arabs, the Bedouin are strictly patrilineal, even though some indicators suggest numerous traces of matriliny at the time of Prophet Muhammad superseded by patriliny after Islamisation. The smallest residential unit, the *bayt* (house) is usually named after its senior male resident. The kinship terminology is characterised by distinctive terms for kin on the side of both parents in Ego's generation and for the first ascending generation. This descriptive system indicates the specific kin position and sex of the person designated. Adult Bedouin men are usually able to name more than five generations of agnatic ancestors and tend to conceptualise relations among descent groups in terms of a segmentary model with its typical aspects of a complementary opposition. This is characterised by a saying, recorded by Edward Evans-Pritchard (1949) among the Bedouin of the Lybian Cyrenaica, that Ego acts against his brother, Ego and his brother against their cousin, and Ego, his brother and his cousin against the rest of the world.

Most of the nomads are members of larger patrilineal descent groups, lineages (*khashm al-buyut* = "mouth/entrance of the houses") linked by agnation. In some areas, particularly in western Asia, these lineages are sub-divisions of units called *fakhadh* ("thigh") which might be labelled maximal lineages or clans. In some regions such as Cyrenaica the clans divide into sub-units called *aila*. Among many Baggara, the level of a minor lineage, *surra* ("navel"), is situated below the *khashm al-bayt*. The highest socio-political unit is the *qabila*, the tribe. The concept of "tribe," which has received a pejorative meaning in parts of Africa and Asia during colonial time, does not carry any negative implication in the emic understanding of the Bedouin. Despite of the fact that "tribalism" is opposed by the modern nation states, they openly talk about *qabila* and regard it as an honourable criterion of socio-cultural identification. Most of the tribes and even clans possess individual brands for the identification of their animals.

Qabail such as the Shammar in northern Arabia or the Salamat in southern Chad sometimes constitute tribal federations, connected by special relations called *ʿurf*. The Arabic word *ʿurf* means beneficence, kindness, tradition, customary tribal law. It implies a wide-spread network of regulations and alliances of mutual support in socio-economic and political activities. These include the right of mutual use of the respective territories, called *dar* or *watan* (homeland) in Arabic. The *ᶜurf* groups in northern Africa are usually permitted to pass through their partners' dar with their herds and they can exploit their grazing reserves in times of need. The system thus acts as a factor minimising the risks of ecological crises and economic contraints. *ᶜUrf* also includes the obligation of mutual assistance in searching for stray animals and in fighting and pursuing robbers of livestock. In former times they also implied military alliances for defending the common territory.

Institutions of settling disputes and mechanisms for the regulation of conflicts are highly elaborated all over the Bedouin territories, because interethnic warfare as well as intra-tribal feuds appear to have been frequent events. In the olden days a life had to be avenged by a life. After the rise of Islam this destructive obligation has increasingly been replaced by the payment of blood-wealth (Arabic: *diya*), although conservative Bedouin kept on propagating the unmanlyness of the "substitution of milk for blood". Among the camel nomads (including the Somali of northeastern Africa who are culturally related to the Arabic Bedouin) the *diya* usually amounts to 100 camels for a slain man and 50 for a woman. The Baggara of the Sudan pay 40 cows for a man and 20 for a woman. Among several Bedouin tribes of northern Africa representatives of the curf alliances are mostly involved in decisions regarding bloodwealth. According to their oral traditions this system had always functioned so well even in the pre-colonial times that blood revenge was rarely practised. Among most Bedouin groups, a particular social body called *ᶜakila* has survived until the present day, acting as a diya-paying unit.

Another type of traditional organisation, to be found in many Bedouin regions above the qabila level, is called *khuwa*, meaning "friendship". This refers to a more or less formalised category of alliances not normally involving neighbouring groups. With a contract of *khuwa* the partners agree on the mutual granting of *muhanna*, goodness or confidence, implying solidarity in socio-political actions and the permission to graze livestock on the partner's land whenever needed. Among the Sudanese Bedouin, *khuwa* is settled by a kind of ceremonial treaty of the chiefs, dignitaries and elders of the groups intending to be linked under such conditions. Pastoralists performing cycles of transhumance which temporarily lead through the territories of other people are usually allied with these groups by *khuwa* contracts. Such contracts are not limited to Arabic-speaking people, but have to be extended by necessity to non-Arabic ethnic units in many cases.

Bedouin society has always been characterised by egalitarian standards. It consisted primarily of *ᶜArab hurr*, free-born people with (theoretically) equal rights. The position of an individual was mainly dependent on his physical and intellectual capacities and on his wealth of livestock and other property which permitted him to be generous and to attract supporters and clients. Ascribed status could be important, for example, in the case of a "noble" *sharific* origin, i.e. the alleged descent from the family of Prophet Muhammad, or of "sacred" tribal segments particularly in the Maghrib. Social strata based on professional or other cultural differentiations hardly exist among the Bedouin. Specialised craftsmen are mostly associated with sedentary societies. In the pre-colonial times, the Bedouin owned a limited amount of slaves, mainly of Black African origin, who were employed in activities such as herding and watering livestock or in household services. Moreover, some Bedouin tribes possessed groups of vassals or serf-like clients in oases or zones of rainfed agriculture, and the latter had to pay a part of their production as tribute to their masters. Such conditions were mostly terminated during the colonial and post-colonial periods.

If a paramount chief was accepted by a tribe, his position was hardly more than the one of a *primus inter pares*, and his power was efficiently controled by a council of elders (*madjlis*). Elected leaders, mostly carrying the title *shaykh*, presided over the various levels of tribal segments. Since colonial times they have also acted as intermediaries between the taxpayers and the government.

Religion and Concepts of Value

The Bedouin of Arabia were among the first people in the world who were converted to the newly established world religion of Islam in the 7th century A.D. Apart from minorities having adopted Christianity or Judaism, they had been partisans of various indigenous folk religions before. Only few relics of information on the pre-Islamic beliefs and practices were transmitted by Arabic literature and poetry. The original faith of the Bedouin had obviously been centred around the belief in the quasi-religious dynamism of tribal human energies. A widespread belief in fate suggested that the world was constructed in a way that human efforts to avert disaster would be thwarted by circumstances. Various cults were performed by the Bedouin at particular shrines. During the sacred times blood feuds were strictly interdicted at these places so that trading activities and the establishment of alliances could flourish. The *Ka^cba* in Mecca was apparently one of the most venerable places of the pre-Islamic Arabs including the Bedouin. Festivals which had traditionally been held at the tombs of tribal ancestors were, at a later stage, often superimposed with the celebration of Muslim feasts such as *^cId al-kabir* in memory of Prophet Ibrahim's sacrifice.

Islam is by no means a Bedouin "religion of the desert," since it was created in an urban milieu. Its requirements can therefore best be fulfilled by town-dwellers, whereas rural people and particularly nomads face more difficulties in properly following its rules and obligations. For these reasons the Bedouin have never been strict in the observance of religious duties when compared to sedentary Muslims. Their active role in the early spread of Islam is usually recognised, but nowadays they are often blamed by the orthodox Muslim authorities as being people who do not fulfil their religious duties seriously enough. However, the Bedouin partisans of certain brotherhoods, such as the Wahhabites in Saudi Arabia, the Saidites in Yemen and the Sanussi in northern Africa, are fervently devoted to their religion.

The majority of the Bedouin are Sunnites and followers of the orthodox school of law which happens to be dominant in their region, i.e. they are either Hanafites, Shafi'ites, Malikites or Hanbalites.The majority of the Bedouin perform their daily prayers regularly and also observe the fasting period of *Ramadan*, although this is extremely difficult under conditions of the harsh climate in their habitat. The Bedouin also vividly believe that spirits (e.g. *djinn*, mentioned in the holy book, the Quran), some of them benevolent and others malevolent, interfere in the life of humans. Orthodox Islam, however, opposes cults of possession spirits (*zar*) mainly found in northeastern Africa and employed by specialised human media, frequently women, to cure deseases and to ward off evil.

Bedouin groups rarely have formal religious specialists, but they usually depend on Quranic teachers trained in sedentary communities. Such persons are either invited to the nomadic camps in order to give courses in religious knowledge, or Bedouin children are sent to Quranic schools established in adjacent villages and towns. A very important means of income for these literary religious specialists is the fabrication of leather amulets containing bits of paper with verses of the Quran. Bedouin people strongly believe in the power of such objects to protect them against malevolent spirits, the "evil eye" and the multiple dangers of everyday life.

The Bedouin are partly influenced by Islamic mysticism which found its most prominent expression in the so-called Sufi brotherhoods or dervish orders. Their founders often developed their theological ideas around the fringes of the desert. The method of following the Sufi path (*tariqa*) tends to be moderate among Bedouin people. It is usually confined to individual contemplation and to group services where the *dhikr*, the tireless repetition of an ejaculatory litany, is performed as a kind of prayer. Bedouin membership in Sufi brotherhoods such as the Qadiriyya and the Tidjaniyya is relatively frequent. However, mystical exercises culminating in orgiastic dances, a widespread phenomenon in many societies of sedentary Muslims, seem to contradict their sober mind.

As pointed out above, the Bedouin have rarely been outstanding in their religious devotion. When they were mobilised for the spread or defence of Islam, their support was motivated by personal advantages and a pragmatic solidarity for a basic value of pan-Arabic culture rather than zealous fanaticism. Islam as a religious system undoubtedly introduced a considerable set of basic moral innovations into Bedouin society, and these are likely to increase in importance the more intensively the Muslim patterns become rooted. This process, together with that of global modernisation in the socio-economic and technological spheres, inevitable leads to far-reaching changes in the traditional values of the Bedouin.

As far as historical records can trace — sporadically they inform us about the situation in pre-Islamic times — a more or less standardised ideal of Bedouin cultural values had existed. Regard of prestige or reputation (Arabic: *hasab*) is said to have been a driving force in much of their activity. Highly admired qualities were those required for a successful life in the harsh conditions of their habitat. These consisted of a special amount of fortitude or manliness (Arabic: *hamasa*) demanding bravery in battle, patience in misfortune, persistence in revenge, protection of the weak and defiance of the strong. In this respect, the *ʿArab hurr*, the free-born man of Arabic tongue, referred primarily to the Bedouin. Certain values and practices, which are nowadays observed by the elites of Arab countries, such as the passion for thoroughbred horses and riding-camels and for hawking, have to a large extent been adopted from a Bedouin cultural background. In fact, many of the present rulers and elites lay claim to a Bedouin origin, but their separation from the actual living-conditions of the nomads mostly occurred several generations ago.

Another central criterion of Bedouin culture is their esteem for hospitality, expressed by their saying: "I am the servant of my guest as long as he stays with me; but otherwise there is nothing of a servant within me". Guests are treated with special care and are usually offered the best type of food affordable by their hosts. Frequently an animal is slaughtered for them in the manner of a ritual sacrifice as prescribed by Islam. In case of armed conflicts, guests from other groups have to be protected by their hosts as if they were members of the latters' families.

The concept of a highly ritualised hospitality is part of a sophisticated code of honour and shame serving to control all kinds of social behaviour within Bedouin society. This honour called sharaf in Arabic has to be constantly defended and asserted. It is an integrated part of the cultural legacy inherited in Bedouin families from generation to generation. Sharaf can be changed in quality and reputation according to the conduct of individuals and their respective kin groups. People regarded as being in a state of dishonour (*ᶜar*) or shame (*ᶜaybca*) are exposed to a very comprehensive set of social sanctions. Individuals committing grave misbehaviour are threatened by the punishment of expulsion (*dlalaᶜ*) from the community. It is one of the most important duties of the elders to deal with affronts to dignity.

Another prominent concept associated with honour among the Bedouin is expressed by the notion of *ᶜird*, implying a quasi-sacred connotation since pre-Islamic times. In the history of the ancient Arabs *ᶜird* was mainly associated with fighting. Any sign of failure in warfare or loss of independence humiliated and dishonoured the Bedouin. Weakness was conceived as the reason for dishonour, power the foundation for honour or *ᶜird*. At present, the meaning of *ᶜird* has evidently become more restricted and is particularly related to women. In Transjordan country, for example, it is clearly associated with the virtue of a woman and even with her beauty. In Egypt the *ᶜird* of a man largely depends on the reputation of his wife and of all his female relatives. In Syria the honourable position of every member of the tribe reflects on a man's *ᶜird*.

In contrast to *ʿird*, sharaf can be acquired and augmented through men's correct behaviour, whereas *ʿird* of a person or a group can only be lost by the normative "misconduct" of their female members. In case of loss it is extremely difficult for honour to be regained. Unlike *ʿird* the honour involved in deviating from "ordinary" dignity is not reflexive. Every individual is free to decide how to react in a particular case.

Honour and dignity have found their expression as central themes in Bedouin literature and the poetry. Poets seem to have played an even more important role in their pre-Islamic than in their present society. The Bedouin obviously felt there was something supernatural or magical about them. The range of literary genres is considerable. There is prose with a particular emphasis on folktales, proverbs, fairy tales and fables, and there are different categories of poems. The ode, for example, contains boastings, i.e. praise of one's own tribe for its fortitude and other virtues, and/or revilings, satiric verses dispraising one's adversaries. It is held that the possession or the lack of human excellence is mainly inherited. Many of the poetic texts deal with the esteem of men outstanding for their bravery, wisdom and generosity and with warrior-heroes who carried out successful raids and fought dangerous animals or even monsters. Other categories of poems praise the beauty and virtue of women and talk about love. In Bedouin society the tales are often told and the poems recited when people sit together in their camps or when travelling. A considerable proportion of the literature even created at present continues to be oral. Arabic is one of the richest languages in terms of its vocabulary and it offers an extraordinary range of artistic expressiveness which the Bedouin poets and novellists can dispose of.

Modern Changes and Prospects

During the the 20th century Bedouin societies have undergone far-reaching changes all over their homeland. Particularly the steadily increasing production of petroleum in numerous countries of western Asia and northern Africa since the 1950s has exerted a considerable impact on their socio-economic patterns. The Bedouin citizens of the oil-producing countries, just as the other parts of the population, benefited from the enormously augmented national income and frequently decided to quit the arduousness of their traditional way of life. A large amount of jobs in the public sector, in services and trade became available to them. When their pastures were covered with oil-producing facilities or polluted they had no alternative to abandoning mobile pastoralism. For those who stayed Bedouin certain technical facilities for herding and livestock trade such as mechanical water pumps and automobiles as well as an improved network of veterinary services tended to render the conditions of life less difficult and risky. The growing purchasing power of the populations of all the countries with Bedouin minorities increased the demand for livestock products.

These conditions, however, partly acted to the damage of the traditional nomadic patterns, and structures of rural capitalism started developing threatening Bedouin existence as well as the precarious equilibrium of the arid and semi-arid environment. In the savannas, the Baggara nomads are facing serious challenges from the growing density of population. Arable land is more and more occupied by peasants so that the grazing resources dwindle. Most governments advocate a policy which considers non-sedentary livestock-breeding an inappropriate and undesirable economic activity.

The Bedouin way of life is generally regarded as an anachronism in the modern world, but it is at the same time often idealised in nostalgic romanticism. As already indicated, the rulers and elites of several states in western Asia and northern Africa like to recall their Bedouin roots, and for the sake of their political credibility they consistently appeal to the values and virtues of the Arab nomads. Leaders of states symbolically demonstrate their esteem for Bedouin culture by temporarily residing in tents which are usually equipped with all sorts modern facilities and luxury. However, people still continuing the traditional Bedouin way of life are still confronted with exceptionally harsh conditions of existence.

REFERENCES

Asad, Talal. 1970. *The Kababish Arabs: Power, Authority and Consent in a Nomadic Tribe*. London: C. Hurst & Co.

Beck, Kurt. 1988. *Die Kawahla von Kordofan. Ökologische und ökonomische Strategien arabischer Nomaden im Sudan*. Stuttgart: Franz Steiner.

Behnke, Roy. 1980. *The Herders of Cyrenaica: Ecology, Economy, and Kinship among the Bedouin of Eastern Libya*. Urbana: University of Illinois Press.

Braukämper, Ulrich. 1993. "Notes on the Origin of Baggara Arab Culture with Special Reference to the Shuwa," *Sprache und Geschichte in Afrika*, 14: 13-46.

Caratini, Sophie. 1989. *Les Rgaybat (1610-1934).* Paris: L'Harmattan.

Chatty, Dawn. 1986. *From Camel to Truck: The Bedouin in the Modern World.* New York: Vantage Press.

Chatty, Dawn and William Young. 1995. "Bedouin," in Middleton, John and Amal Rassam (eds.), *Encyclopedia of World Cultures.* Vol. IX. Pp. 42-45. New York: G.K. Hall & Company.

Cole, Donald. 1975. *Nomads of the Nomads: The Al Murrah of the Empty Quarter.* Chicago: Aldine Publishing Co.

Coon, Carlton S., Hermann von Wissmann, Friedrich Kussmaul, W. Montgomery Watt. 1960. "Badw," (pp. 872- 92) in *The Encyclopaedia of Islam.* New Edition. Vol. I: Leiden, London: E.J. Brill.

Cunnison, Ian. 1966. *Baggara Arabs. Power and Lineage in a Sudanese Nomad Tribe.* Oxford: Clarendon.

Dostal, Walter. 1959. "The Evolution of Bedouin Life," (pp. 11-34) in Gabrieli, Francesco (ed.), *L'antica società beduina.* Roma: Centro di Studi Semitici.

____. 1967. *Die Beduinen in Südarabien. Ethnologische Studien zur Entwicklung der Kamelhirtenkultur in Arabien.* Wien: Berger.

Evans-Pritchrad, Edward E. 1949. *The Sanusi of Cyrenaica.* Oxford: Clarendon Press.

Goody, Jack and Emanuel Marx (eds.). 1991. *The Bedouin of Cyrenaica. Studies in Personal and Corporate Power.* Cambridge: Cambridge University Press.

Herzog, Rolf. 1983. "Beduinen," (pp. 255-73) in Müller, Klaus E. (ed.), *Menschenbilder früher Gesellschaften. Ethnologische Studien zum Verhältnis von Mensch und Kultur.* Frankfurt a.M.: Campus-Verlag.

Lancaster, William. 1981. *The Rwala Bedouin Today.* Cambridge: Cambridge University Press.

McMichael, Harold A. 1967(1922). *A History of the Arabs in the Sudan.* 2 vols. London: Cass.

Marx, Emanuel.1967. *Bedouin of the Negev.* Manchester: Manchester University Press.

Oppenheim, Max von. 1939/1942. *Die Beduinen.* 2 vols. Leipzig: Harrassowitz.

Scholz, Fred (ed.). 1981. *Beduinen im Zeichen des Erdöls. Studien zur Entwicklung der beduinischen Lebenswelt Südost-Arabiens.* Wiesbaden: Dr. Ludwig Reichert.

Stein, Lothar. 1975. *Wandervolk der Wüste.* Leipzig: VEB Brockhaus.

Stewart, Frank H. 1988-90. *Texts in Sinai Bedouin Law.* 2 vols. Wiesbaden: Harrassowitz.

TWELVE

THE TRIBAL SCHOOLS OF IRAN: Sedentarisation through Education

SOHEILA SHAHSHAHANI

Introduction

Almost all anthropologists working on Iran, and all Iranian students doing field-work for an anthropology degree have been directed towards research among pastoral nomads. The original system of education of these populations has never been studied anthropologically, but we see the system of education which has been installed to change their society, applauded in various articles. This is not surprising, since all attempts to study and then "modernise" pastoral nomadic areas ever since Reza Shah's period has been through forced sedentarisation. The government never had a reasonable economic project to replace this nomadic mode of life with a sedentarised one. If under Reza Shah forced sedentarisation was exercised, under Mohammad Reza a more delicate measure had to be adopted. It was a more manipulative measure as will be seen in the following article.

> *"Par quoi se transmet encore l'heritage d'un people? Par l'education qu'il donne à ses enfants..."* Albert Memmi (1973).

An ex-peace corps officer calls the tribal schools, "the most exciting successful educational experiment in modern Iranian history" (Barker 1981: 141). Clarence Hendershot (1965) in "A Report on the Tribal Schools of Fars Province" published by AID says, "The development of this system of moving schools is one of the miracles of modern Persia". This school system, about whose foundation some words will be said shortly, was established in the early 1950s and in the school year

1977-78 (the Iranian year 1356-57), it boasted of 111,819 students (32,406 girls and 79,413 boys, according to Census of Department of Education, Iranian year 1356-57). It was apparently an educational system adapted to a pastoral nomadic mode of existence, but as clearly noted by P. Barker (1981) it also had very distinct political ambitions. Similarly C. Hendershot (1975: xiii) stated, "The Technical Assistance Programme was born in politics and was weighed with politics throughout its two decades of existence." The chief executive of the programme in 1976 claimed that the project impinged upon the economic life of the people (Bahmanbegi, 1355: 16). I am very far from knowing the economic and political magnitudes of this educational system, but what I would like to do in this article is to unravel the mystifications which lent glamour to this system, and see it as it was intended, i.e. as an oppressive pedagogy. Inspired by Paulo Freire's *Pedagogy of the Oppressed* (1970), I define oppressive pedagogy as (1) one which decides people's mode of existence for them, but lies about it to them; (2) One which serves the dominating class in the society at large; (3) One which prevents authentic thinking and orders what is to be learned. The project of the tribal schools succeeded phenomenally in pursuing this scheme. Interviews with young men and women who attended the schools will substitute this paper and provide revealing insights.

History and Extension

In 1948 the construction of three boarding schools for children of pastoral nomads started in the city of Fasa. In 1950 this project was stopped because of budgetary cuts. In 1949 a project called "*Seven-year Development Plan for the Plan Organisation of the Imperial Government of Iran*," the overseas consultants suggested the formation of "moving schools, designed to accompany the tribe while in its annual migration" (Hendershot, 1965: 7). By 1951 when "historians" of the tribal school project (Barker and Hendershot) spoke of a man called Mohammad Bahmanbegi becoming interested in an educational project, the Point Four consultants and advisers were already in Iran. Glen Gagon, a graduate of Bragham Young University, was the Point Four Education Adviser for Fars. A meeting between the two men, Gagon and Bahmanbegi, started years of cooperation. Practically, what Bahmanbegi (1355: 9) needed at this time for the realisation of his project were tents, teachers and class-room supplies. G. Gagon promised the first and the last which would cost a total of US$ 200. Bahmanbegi was to search for teachers and their salaries. After the collapse of the school project at Fasa, the ministry of education was not likely to respond positively. Another possible source of help would be the Qashqa'I khans. It was through their initial help that Bahmanbegi provided the teachers with their first salaries. Hendershot (1975: 23-24) says that for the "1953 fiscal year programme" tribal education was one of the five fields of concentration. "On August 1st, 1953, 109 teachers met for six weeks of training" (Hendershot, 1965: 3), teaching began in autumn 1953 with government approval of the project. Different dates are given for the foundation of the tribal school, Hendershot (1975: 14) gives 1955 in one publication, but October 1956 in another publication (Hendershot, 1975: 90), Bahmanbegi himself, writing in 1976 (1355: 3), gives the date of foundation as 1957. In any case, this school started by training 60 teachers, and the first school was set up in the Qashqai'I area in 1953. by 1956 there were six tribal schools in five ostans (provinces) with an enrolment of 172" (Hendershot, 1975: 90). In 1957 the Boyer Ahmadi Tribe received the white tent school, these white canvas tents themselves stood out as something new in an area where tents are otherwise of black goathair. Statistics for the school year of 1973-74 indicate their presence, additionally in the provinces of Fars, in Azerbayejan, Kurdestan, Chahar Mahai-e Bakhtiari, Khuzestan, Sistan and Baluchestan, Kerman, Kermanshah, Ilam and Lorestan. At this time the total number of students was 53,814. From this number 37,033 were from Fars and the rest from other provinces. For the school years 1974-75 to 1977-78, their respective numbers are 61,948 / 80,485 / 96,645 and 111,819. Here again the total of students from Fars was 63,072 (C.D.E. 1356-57). It should be noted that more than half of the "tribal schools" had permanent locations. The number for the school year 1977-78, for example, was 1253 tribal moving schools to 1587 tribal permanent schools. As often noted by scholars who work with statistics from Iran, figures should not be taken very seriously. Cross references help to show the errors which exist, although one cannot be sure of either reference! For example, for the school year 1976-77 the number of students from Boyer Ahmadi and Kogiluyeh areas is given to be 4954. For the same period 2757 is given as the total at the Plan Organisation Seminar (Taheri, 1355: 28). For Kerman, for the same date, again the ministry of education gives a higher number, 3306, than a report from the area, which gives 2500 as the total of students having been taught at these schools (RPN, 1355

Vol. I: 15). Finally for the province of Lorestan, the total number of 6940 is given for the students of five grades, while 9100 is given as the possible number of students' to be taught by the end of the year in three grades (ibid.: Vol. II: 17).

Aims

> *"All domination involves invasion at times physical and overt, at times camouflaged, with the invader assuming the role of a helping friend"* (Freire, 1970: 150).

It is significant to note what Barker discusses as the four elements important for the early 1950s as the "climax of the Qashqai'I struggle for autonomy": "(1) Nationalist movement built around the figure of Mohammad Mossaddeq; (2) American fears that the world's largest proven oil reserves fall into communist hands; (3) The farsighted dreams of an idealistic young tribesman; (4) the ambitions of a young Shah to consolidate his control over a divided and rebellious country" (Barker, 1981: 144). It is difficult to understand what Barker means by "struggle for autonomy" in the above four points. There is no consideration given to the powerful Qasha'i people. What is definitely to be avoided, however, is a threat to the oil reserves by the Qasha'i being attracted towards communism. In a few paragraphs the above author refers to the "abundance of communists in the ranks of the teachers" as one of the major problems "plaguing the Iranian educational establishment" (Barker, 1981: 145). Thus the author very clearly portrays U.S. economic and political interests in the programme. A few words on the other three points quoted above are necessary. During this period the U.S. had decided to help the young Shah to consolidate his control over a divided and rebellious country". The idealist young tribesman, Bahmanbegi, will be the local means to this end; finally, the "nationalism" of Mossaddeq will be otherwise incorporated into the programme (will be discussed later).

"Nomadic tribes throughout the Middle East have frustrated the efforts of numerous central governments to modernise their societies, centralise their powers, and develop national consciousness among all segments of their populations" (Barker, 1981: 140). The efforts of Reza Shah to brutally sedentarise the pastoral nomads not having attained the desired aim, this time education is to be used as the means toward sedentarisation. This is why Bahmanbegi is so useful for the Point Four education project:

> "It was the strong belief of Mr. Bahmanbegi that the only way for the Government to make useful loyal citizens of the tribal people was to educate them. It was also the surest way of promoting the Government's objective of getting the tribes to settle" (Hendershot, 1965: 8).

The first characteristic of oppressive pedagogy now becomes evident. Planners decide people's mode of existence for them, and they lie about it to them. In the case under study, the planners actually want to sedentarise the pastoral nomads, but they say they want to give them education. They want to keep communism out of the region and they want to have access to the oil reserves, but they say they want to give education to the people. More than twenty years after the foundation of this project when Bahmanbegi and the peace corps officer speak about their successful enterprise (in different articles) some very significant observations are made Barker (1981, 1567) writes:

> "...there is no doubt but that the overall impact of the schools has been to encourage settlement. The schools do not give the students tools with which to become better managers of a livestock-based economy, but rather a those which they will need in order to successfully make the transition to a settled life and urban employment".

Although Barker writing from the U.S. in 1981 speaks very enthusiastically about the job possibilities that these schools have opened up to the children of pastoral nomads, Bahmanbegi writing from Iran in 1976 says:

> "Tribal people's attraction toward settlement, and the development of villages have increased the people's need for specialised workers in construction working, electricity, carpentry, etc." (Bahmanbegi, 1976: 12).

This is a second way in which the people are given wrong information. While the students grow up expecting to become doctors, teachers, government employees and so on, what awaits them is a different future. This adds to the first characteristic of oppressive pedagogy. It has been necessary to indulge in giving long quotes from the organisers of the tribal school project because it has always been praised as a purely educational project. No serious academic consideration has been given to it as a political project and one which has had aims other than its name obviously indicates. My use of data from the organisers themselves must prove to the reader the objectivity of my point, while a rapid reading of such writings padded with a mass of propaganda hinders the comprehension of facts.

The project largely attained its aim through "manipulation".

> "By means of manipulation, the dominant elites try to confirm the masses to the objectives. Through manipulation the dominant elites can lead the people into an inauthentic type of 'organisation' and can thus avoid threatening alternatives: the true organization of the emerged and the emerging people" (Freire, 1970: 144-45).

Having mentioned the aims of the tribal school project and its achievements, it is now necessary to consider the means through which these aims were attained. The first means is the person who helped its realization; the second is the method this school used to convince the people of its utility.

Means A: Mohammad Bahmanbegi

It has been US policy to intervene in the affairs of other countries under the rubric of aid. The following, which is written from American perspectives, and must be read with a critical eye, shows the initial steps for the Technical Assistance Programme.

> "Barely two months after President Harry S. Truman signed the Act of International Development in June 5, 1950, Dr. Franklin S. Harris was dispatched to negotiate an agreement to provide technical assistance to Government of Iran. Conditions in Iran were critical economically, socially, and politically, as a result of growing crisis with the British over their oil concession, and becoming steadily worse. Haste was important. Consequently when the President's signature was affixed to the Act, Iran was the first country to receive attention. Dr. Harris arrived in Tehran in Mid-August. Early in September a draft agreement was sent to Washington, and on October 19, Ambassador Henry Grady and Prime Minister Ali Razmara signed a Memorandum of understanding providing for American technical cooperation for a rural improvement programme, the first Point-four international agreement" (Hendershot, 1975: 1).

I do not know exactly how the project started, whether it was first Bahmanbegi who "used" U.S. economic aid and ideas (1949 Overseas

Consultant suggestion), or whether the idea and interests were already there, and the advisors in Fars were only waiting for the ambitious man to arrive on the scene. At any event, Bahmanbegi was identified as the local person to cooperate with, and, "to facilitate American assistance, Mr. Bahmanbegi was placed on the Point Four pay-roll" (Hendershot, 1965: 11), Mohammad Bahmanbegi, born in 1920, son of one of the Qasha'I khan's cooks, finished his law degree in 1945. During this same year he published his book Orf o Adat dar Ashayer-e Fars (Moeurs et Coutumes des Tribus du Fars). Already in this book signs of a feeling of "superiority"of the educated tribesman *vis-à-vis* his fellows are evident. His description of the Boyer Ahmadi below shows the complex psychology of the "colonised" who in hope of a prosperous future uses the logic of the "coloniser" and thus misrepresents and depises his countrymen (and of course part of himself too):

> "Le courage et le denuement d'un Boyer Ahmadi, par exemple, sont inégalables: il va nu-pieds ... déuenillé ... et nourri de glands.... Comme il ne fait rien, tout attise le feu de la misère et de la violence — ce qui accroît la proportion de querelles, de meurites et de banditisme, tandis que la franchise, la simplicité et le courage desnomades reduisent de beaucoup le nombre des tricheurs et des felons" (translation by Montel, 1966: 119).

The theme of the "lazy native" is nothing, new to anthropologists (and fortunately good critical analyses of the subject have already appeared (e.g. Leclerc, 1972: 17-18), and the idea has repeatedly been used by colonisers to justify towards their own countrymen their activities abroad. But, of course at the same time some of the colonised accept this concept.

> "For cultural invasion to succeed, it is essential that those invaded become convinced of their intrinsic inferiority. Since everything has its opposite, if those who are invaded consider themselves inferior, they must necessarily recognise the superiority of the invaders. The values of the latter thereby become the pattern for the former" (Freire 1970: 151).

At any event, Bahmanbegi with such a mentality returned to the Qasha'I area, stayed there for five years and then in 1951 he went to the U.S. for the first time. Hendershot (1965: 7) comments on this visit, saying:

> "In 1951 Mr. Bahmanbegi visited the U.S. where he took a keen interest in social process. He was particularly impressed by the public schools. The following year he returned with a mission".

Two phrases are ambiguous. It is not clear what the author means by "social process"; the "mission" with which Bahmanbegi returned is not evident. The author does not specify. After beginning his work with the Point Four (perhaps in 1953, Bahmanbegi revisited the U.S. "to observe with special attention the schools for American Indians" (Hendershot, 1965: 7). I cannot exaggerate the importance of this man for the tribal education project, as there are statements that the Point Four officers and the peace corps officers considered him as a charismatic leader who was one of the few critical elements measures for the success of the "miracle," which was "the result of the dreams and plans of one man" (Hendershot, 1965: 32; Barker, 1981: 153, 155). Bahmanbegi was the missing link to domination:

> "In their passion to dominate, to mold others to their patterns and their way of life, the invaders desire to know how those they have invaded apprehend reality — but only so they can dominate the latter more effectively"(Freire, 1970: 150-1).

In affirmation of the above:

> "His tribal origins and intimate knowledge of tribal customs and problems made him uniquely able to communicate with tribes people... Bahmanbegi's thorough understanding of tribal 'psychology' enabled him to appeal to tribal values in order to sell his program to the tribes..." (Barker, 1981: 153).

This point about knowing the psychology of one people in order "to sell" them something is furthered by the statistics given above. These indicate better success of the program in the province of Fars. Of course other reasons might have added to greater interest in sedentarisation in this area, but "in 1975 he attempted to repeat the high school experiment in Sanandaj for Kurdish students, but when he examined the stuents at the end of the first year, he was dissatisfied and closed the school" (Barker, 1981: 154).

Means B: The School System

Although Iran never became a colony, yet certain programs had definitely the character of colonial institutions. In the case of the tribal school programme, the pastoral nomads were treated as the "primitive" who is dangerous, whose land has resources, which the coloniser cannot neglect. This educational institution was the means toward colonisation of a king. In this same line of thought Geard Leclerc (1972: 39) writes: "Le colonialisme n'est pas seulement expansion et domination economique, mais aussi ethnocentrisme culturel. Le colonialisme suppose la croyance en une seule culture...." This supposition is best exemplified by the benevolent coloniser who was formerly often the missionary; today this benevolence comes in the form of technical assistance programs which are based on the belief that the "primitive" is at a much lower technical, cultural and spiritual level, and in order to have him progress to a higher level, he must be educated. In keeping with this line of thought Bahmanbegi (1355: 12) wrote,

> "Before twenty four years ago these people (pastoral nomads) did not have any kind of culture and educational institutions, and for long years they existed in ignorance. Twenty-four years ago following his imperial Majesty's benevolent intentions, I who am of pastoral nomadic origins, established the tribal school".

Note that in the above quotation, lack of institutions of formal education is equated with the absence of culture and the presence of ignorance. How did this school system operate in order to attain its aims? The first characteristic to be considered is bilingualism. The pastoral nomadic populations of Iran have ethnic names, which are also the names of their languages: Baluch, Kurd, Turk, Lor, Talesh, etc. The Qasha'I, who are Turkic, speak Qashqai'I Turki. Other important tribes in Fars are Lor and Arab. Therefore, the studies of bilingualism done in colonial contexts can very well apply to these tribal schools.

> "Le colonise n'est sauve de l'analphabetisme que pour tomber dans le dualisme linguistique... La possession de deux langues n'est passeulement celle de deux outils, e'est la participation a deux royaumes psychiques et culturels. Or ici les deux univers symbolises, portes par les deux langues, sont en conflit: ce sont ceux du colonisateur et du colonise" (Memmi, 1973: 135-6).

During my own field work in the Mamassani (a Lor population) are, I was confronted with the same phenomenon. The children who had gone to school would make fun of their elders and mostly those less exposed to Persian, i.e. women (Shahshahani, 1366, 1981: Ch. 5). In my interviews with university students who had gone to tribal schools

I found their language still a source of discomfort. They felt inferior because they did not possess fluency in Persian. In the tribal school project great emphasis was laid on Persian, and in high school, on English. The second major element of education and a very important one which does not favour autonomous thinking, is the method used for learning, i.e. memorisation. The aim of the programme was not to make sure that the students had understood their lessons, but rather to have them respond word by word and very rapidly. "Two times two, *befarma*". (If the *befarma* "please answer") was left out, the student would not know the answer. If the student hesitated in the middle of a poem he was reciting, or a geographical description he was giving, then he could not continue, and had to start from the very beginning. "At the end of elementary school," one student told me, "all knew was how to multiply and divide like a fast moving tape, and recite the story of *zaq o kabk* as swift as thunder, and become the thief, the beast or the king in plays we were ordered to stage for the monitors who came to examine us".

The curriculum of these schools was entirely the same as that of other Iranian schools, but the teaching methods were very different. Perhaps at the time it would have been possible to measure the difference, but to try and do so today would only be speculative. This is why I cite the students themselves, and try and recall their red cheeks while trying to recite in as high a voice as possible all their courses, from geography to poetry. This technique was not practiced in urban or rural schools, and was in my opinion part of a process of trying to divert the tribal temperament. The reasoning went like this: the tribal people are mountain people, used to self-expression in a rough and courageous manner and in loud voices. These qualities must be rechanelled in such a manner that the energy is spent, but the tribal spirit is not strengthened. Both in school and at annual celebrations the students had the opportunity, within a very well defined structure of school programmes to spend their young "tribal" energy, without strengthening tribal cohesion.

The school year was arranged according to the mode of existence of the population, that is to say according to the cycle of transhumance. Those who transhumed did not have classes during their migration period. Otherwise school started in fall and ended in late spring. The tribal school system tried to keep the students for as many hours as possible at school. Depending upon its location and the season, children went to school from approximately 7 to 11.30 and from 13 to 18 hrs, that is for as many as 8½ hours daily (with recess), while schools run by the ministry of education held classes for no more than 6 hours per day. The project adapted itself to the basic model of existence of the community it was inserted into, but it tried to occupy the children for as many hours as it could. The hours were not marked by the bell; so the school allowed for certain flexibility, but when the student was at school, his greatest concentration was demanded. A teacher should be absent for a day, but then he had to make up for his absence another day. These adaptive measures to the pastoral nomadic way of life demanded the students' cooperation in another domain too:

> "The concentration of mind, the alertness to every development, the complete absorption of their minds in the learning situation make for a speed of accomplishment not found in many schools" (Hendershot, 1965: 17).

Anyone who has visited a tribal school is amazed by the enthusiasm in the classroom. As soon as a question is asked, everyone raises his hand to respond. When there is recitation to be done, the student raises his/her voice as loudly as he can; his face becomes red. When I questioned a tribal schoolteacher about the reason for this behaviour, I was told that "tribal people are courageous and independent people. In keeping with this spirit, the children have to express themselves in loud voices, not timidly like urban children." In my opinion, this is giving the children (and their family and their society) the false myth of continuing their traditional way of life. This is preserving a characteristic, emptying it of its original meaning, and filling it with another cont. Another example, perhaps more clear, of this use of traditional cultural traits for accomplishing other ends is the following:

> "Another tradition of tribal warfare upon which Bahmanbegi drew was the war camp or ordu. In previous generations the ordu had been a large gathering of khans and warriors to make war preparations. In the Qashqa'i collective memory these were times of great excitement and tribal pride. Under Tribal Education, ordus underwent a metamorphosis and became a sort of education inspection festival. School children from a large radius were bused to the white tent camp so that the students might be tested by Tribal Education officials, participate in dancing, and share in the large meals and general excitement" (Barker, 1981: 154).

Another basic point must be considered in this discussion about method of accomplishment and that is the functioning of the school through the teacher-student relationship and the monitor-teacher and monitor-student relationship, "the whole school structure was like military camp," I was told by a teacher. To an outsider the teacher gave the impression of working with the students, and he did not have a special place apart and above them. C. Hendershot (1975: 91) remarks, "A high degree of cordiality was shared by the children, their teachers and the supervisors". But "a peculiar fear existed between the teacher and the students," an ex-student told me. "Between the teacher and the students no friendly relationship existed, there was a great distance between them ..." another said. "The teacher did not care if the student really understood the lesson, he only wanted us to respond very quickly". The teacher had great power over the student because he could greatly humiliate the child who did not study well, and praise one who did well. News of both was easily carried outside the white tent into the heart of the community. The place of the school within the community was marked by the promise of the future of the children. "My sister wove carpets to pay for my school accessories,"remembered one Qashqa'i student. The children received cakes and cookies (something also appreciated by the parents), and some other aids such as free books and pens. Also, as university students who had attended tribal schools explained,

> "People had realised that their production of sheep and goat and all their hard work was not bringing a good life for them. Therefore, they did not want their children to do the same. They wanted them to sit in offices like government employees and do nothing and gain their lives".

This is why they insisted that their children study well. The traditional economic system had been undermined, and hence the community turned to the school as the possibility of securing a future for their children. The school became the link with the future: As one ex-student put it, "Before the children were in the service of their elders, now all the community was in the service of the children's education". Naturally, a child was keen on getting the approval of his parents, his teachers and his community. Besides, the teacher who examined and had power over children, there were monitors who often visited the schools. They examined both the teacher and the students. Monitors had cars at their service and they traveled to different tribal schools. Besides guiding the teachers, their performance was noted and reports were sent to the administration, at the pinnacle of which was Bahmanbegi. "His spirit was always four meters above everybody's head". Another ex-student said, "We were under strict control. In high school we knew that because of the turmoil in the tribes, we were under strict surveillance. I dare say all the important figures of our school were working for the intelligence service." Thus a spirit of terror and suspicion reigned and this is why, "everything was done by force and obligation; studying was obligatory, eating was obligatory, dancing for the feast was obligatory ... perhaps our fear too was obligatory". The teachers also felt terribly observed.

> "The teacher knew that Bahmanbegi was as apt to humiliate a poor teacher in front of his students at an ordu as he was to praise a good one. They believed him when he said that he would beat any teacher who beat his students" (Barker, 1981: 154).

This ordering about in the process of learning is what at the beginning of this paper I called the third quality of oppressive pedagogy, one which prevents authentic thinking and orders what is to be learned.

Before concluding this article, there is one more point I must raise and this is in relation to "nationalism," also referred to earlier. While among the four points quoted from Barker's article, the "nationalism"of Dr. Mossaddeq was mentioned, in another quotation, the Shah's regime is projected as a nationalist one. Hendershot states the American position more directly when he portrays Mossaddeq as a prime minister who wanted"dictatorial powers," the Shah as a benevolent monarch who "could no longer see his people being killed in the streets," and the Americans as innocent victims who were passing "a trying period... For several days United States personnel were confined to quarters ... Walls were plastered with 'Yankee go home' signs and the safety of American personnel was imperiled" (Hendershot, 1975: 10-11). Such use of term "nationalism" once again constitutes its appropriation by political organisers according to what they wanted it to mean. This is a false use of the term, just as the tribal school project was in fact a colonial enterprise. Its aim was to make future urban dwellers and its first method was to humiliate those leading a tribal way of life. It praised urban ways of life, the climax of which was the American lifestyle. One of the first measures of humiliation used for the teachers themselves concerned cleanliness.

> "Mr. Bahmanbegi has his own ideas of education for the tribes ... the first lesson the prospective teacher needed to learn was personal

hygiene ... Household and camp sanitation followed ..." (Hendershot, 1965: 9-10).

When I was doing fieldwork I was amazed by the constant remarks on cleanliness made by local physicians and urban visitors to children and even more so to women. This was a subtle but effective means of humiliation. Finally, if the government had a nationalistic character its education programme would emphasise knowledge of the countiy and national heroes. Speaking of the French colonial school Albert Memmi wrote:

> "L'histoire qu'on lui apprend n'est pas la sienne. Il sait qui fût Colbert ou Crom wel mais non qui fût Khuznader; qui fut Jeanne d' Arc mais non la Kahena. Tout semble s'être passé ailleurs que chez·lui, son pays et luimême sonten l'air..."(Memmi, 1973: 133-134).

An eight-year old girl who had doubled the first grade was still trying to memorise the words for "iron," "fan", "oven" and so on. She had never seen any of them. "Students know about the Western world, but they do not know their own heroes or the mountain peaks or the rivers one kilometre away from them," a teacher told me Barker (1981: 139) corroborates this. "The school has peddled the Shah's version of Iranian nationalism and contributed to the undermining of some of the bases of tribal society".

Thus, very clearly, this system of education was at the service of the pro-American regime, and was meant to serve the interests of the dominating class of society. Thus completes the definition of oppressive pedagogy as defined at the beginning of this article. As a postscript I would add the following information, which I obtained from Mr. Shahbazi, a Ph.D. student as personal communication, in 1994: after the Islamic revolution this school program was briefly interrupted, but was resumed thereafter. The change in curriculum in these as in other schools consists of greater attention being paid to courses in religion. The number of teachers is the same, but only a minority (100 out of 1200) is still transhuming; the rest are teaching in tribal schools in rural or urban areas.

REFERENCES

Bahmanbegi, Mohammad 1355 (2535). "Tarikche-ye mokhtasari az fa'aliyathaye edare-ye koll-e amusesh-e ashayeri" Sazman-e barname va budje, seminare barresi-ye mas'ale-ye jame' eye ashayeriye iran" ("A short history of the activities of the "Institute for Tribal Teaching," Organisation for programming and budgeting, seminar on research on tribal problems in Iran").

Bahmanbegi, Mohammad. 1945. *Orf of Adat dar Ashayer-e Furs (Moeurs et Coutumes des Tribus du Fars*).

Barker, Paul. 1981. "Tent Schools of the Qashqa'i: A Paradox of Local Initiative and State Control," (139-157) in M.E. Bonine and N. Keddie (eds.), *Modern Iran, The Dialectics of Continuity and Change*. Albany: State University of York Press:

C.D.E. 1356-57. *Census of Department of Education for Different Years*. Teheran: Government of Iran.

Freire, Paulo. 1970. *Pedagogy of the Oppressed*. New York: Seabury Press.

Hendershot, Clarence. 1965. *White Tents in the Mountains. A Report on the Tribal Schools of Fars Province*. Teheran: Communications Resources Branch, U.S. Aid/Iran.

Hendershot, Clarence. 1975. *Politics, Polemics and Pedagoges*. New York: Vantage Press.

Leclerc, Gerard. 1972. *Anthropologie et Colonialisme. Essaie sur l'histoire d'africanisme*. Paris: Fayard.

Memmi, Albert. 1973. *Portrait du Colonisé*. Paris: Payot.

Monteil, Vincent. 1966. *Les tribus du Fârs et la sédentarisation des nomads*. Paris: Mouton.

RPN 1355, *Report Regarding the Situation of Pastoral Nomads in Iran. (Gozaresh-e-vaz'e mojud-e jame'eye ashayeri-e iran)*Teheran. 2 Vols.

Shahshahani, Soheila 1981, (1366). *The Four Seasons of the Sun. An Ethnography of Women of Oyun, A Sedentarised Village of the Mamasani Pastoral Nomads of Iran*. Ph.D. Thesis, New School for Social Research, New York (published in Persian, Tehran: Tus.).

Taheri, Ata. 1355 (2535), *"Ashayer-e Kohgiluye va Boyer Ahmadi" sazman-e barname va budje, seminare barresi-e masa'ele jame'eye ashayeri-e iran. ("Tribes of Kohgiliye and the Boyer Ahmad Report on the Contemporary Situation of the Tribal Community in Iran. Evaluation of Rural Activities. Vol.I, Organisation for Programming and Budgeting, Seminar on Research on Tribal Problems in Iran").* Teheran: Government of Iran.

THIRTEEN

INTRA-FAITH AND INTER-RELIGIOUS TENSIONS IN EAST AFRICAN TRIBAL ENVIRONMENTS

R.E.S. TANNER

Introduction

The definitions of "religion" are probably as variable as the numbers of those who attempt to provide them, but most implicitly ally their responses to the four great international religions: Buddhism, Christianity, Hinduism and Islam for which there is substantial theological and social background data. Such definitions leave out perhaps the majority of activities involving metaphysics and thus makes much of these into "magic". We propose to have no such distinction and use the category religion for all activities related to or directed at metaphysical realities. "Tribe" is another difficulty as historically a tribe may well have been a loose category, which varied with the circumstances and had no clearly defined boundaries. The colonial governments with administrative needs, defined tribes as living in specific areas and indeed during the colonial period in Tanzania, the number of tribes recognised for census purposes doubled. The tribal connections of any individual may then as now depend on whatever matrilineal, patrilineal or affinal connections were advantageous at a particular time.

Since there are no Buddhist or Hindu East Africans, it is proposed to treat the practices of the three faiths operating there, the quasi-traditional, Christian and Moslem, without distinguishing or dividing their practices into magical and non-magical or religious categories.

This has the advantage of eliminating any definition of religious practices, which would automatically relegate most quasi-traditional ones to a position of ideological and social inferiority, which their contemporary popularity cannot justify.

"Tribe" has a rural flavour to it whereas in practice individuals have always been on the move particularly now between the expanding towns and the rural areas, whenever they deem it necessary. Few are so permanently committed to the towns that their tribal ways of thinking and perhaps behaving no longer apply. Certainly some like the pastoral Maasai, Pokot and Karamajong are more committed to a rural way of life but they certainly visit the towns and are aware of what urban life offers. Others such as the Ganda, Kikuyu and Sukuma often commute to towns for work and business living most of their lives beyond the urban fringe. Children may spend their time equally between rural and urban relatives so that their patterns of thought and behaviour will be that of their natal tribes as modified by circumstances beyond their control and where the best opportunities are located.

The legal definition of urban areas may well exclude the septic fringe of peri-urban slums, which are clearly not rural or in any way connected to subsistence agriculture. In these circumstances there can be no defined dividing line between town and country in either social and religious practices. It is highly porous situation in which language, histories and identities are constantly subject to mutation (Chambers, 1994: 5).

The East African Religious Paradigm

The history of religion in this region antedates the arrival of Christianity in the late 1800s and Islam by at least the 12th century by many millennea. Its development in the mists of antiquity will have correlated with the social and ecological environments, which have lasted to a very similar extent to the present-day. Geographically dispersed social systems, which only in the colonial period came to have static administrative rather than social characteristics.

Overwhelmingly this must be a picture, which has rarely involved anything approaching semi-centralised states except perhaps in the inter-lacustrian "kingdoms" of Uganda. Without a social structure, which would at least in part be maintained by literate administrators, the social structure was and is segmentary with constant adaptations to social, political, economic and ecological circumstances.

The absence of towns except for some clustering round the houses of chiefs, the fortified villages of the Ssonjo near to their irrigated fields, and the villages of the Yao, shows that the social practices of these people, their pattern of living was centrifugal rather than centripetal. These people lived as they do now in family groups away from rather than near to their neighbours.

Since these people lived dispersed, they did not develop centralised religious institutions. Their religious practices just as much as their social ones will have been developed under these conditions of virtually permanent dispersal. This was not a social environment in which there could be any permanent centralising cults imposing a pattern of religious behaviour on their followers. The Buchwezi cult exists both north and south of Lake Victoria with virtually nothing in common beyond the similarities of the officiants' headresses. The initiation ceremonies of a Sukuma Buchwezi group observed over a ten year gap had almost nothing in common; there could be no question of the cult having a specific ritual, only some possible shared ideas of their spirit origin.

Thus it would seem that religious practices must have had in antiquity characteristics, which now form a paradigm of contemporary importance predisposing these people to accept certain religious ideas and practices.

Firstly, religious ideas and practices focus on individuals and their families. The protective activities of individuals shown in the amulets they wear on arms or loins (Tanner, 1969), the domestic cults of family, lineage and clan with identifying taboos and the cults related to various levels of chiefs. Low key regular practices, which were not sustained under any burden of social or religious sanctions.

Secondly, cyclical and linear rites of passage involving a wider range of people, neighbours as much as relatives but usually of sufficient importance to overcome the centrifugal pattern of their social lives. The main factor will have been a balance between the benefits and costs of such ceremonies in terms of time and cost.

Finally, there are reactive religious activities, overwhelmingly the most common, in which the numbers involved are related to the importance of the problem experienced. At its minimum the problems of particular individuals or families over illness, infertility and accident involving a few people to the problems of drought in an area for which thousands would attend a rainmaking ceremony. Again these would be evaluated on a cost-benefit basis; infertile women may go to many quasi-traditional healers in search of a cure. It is cults reacting to public anxieties, which come to public attention with their potentiality for violence typified by the mass killings in which the Movement for the Restoration of the Ten Commandments in western Uganda was involved in March 2000.

The contemporary East African has inherited a highly dispersed pattern of religious behaviour overwhelmingly client and problem oriented (Whyte, 1997). The form that it takes now as it has always done depends on particular personal skills rather than on office holding. It thus has the capacity to expand and contract with the circumstances such as the Holy Spirit Movement in northern Uganda which grew in disruptive strength with widespread popular anxieties among the Acholi tribe, discharged and unemployed soldiers and the easy availability of arms (Behrend, 1991).

This inherited religious and social paradigm into which they have been socialised, would not give them any background for the development of centralising and centralised religions. There is rarely an "either/or" religious commitment to either an inter-national or quasi-traditional faith. Personal religious systems of parallel practices in which individuals keep several options open according to their circumstantial interpretation of their needs based on economics and personal factors, anticipated returns on the performance of a prescribed ritual, the advice of friends, relatives, the propinquity of the suggested quasi-traditional healer and public opinion.

The Pattern of Segmented Religious Practice

The paradigm of a religious system in which there are great variations in dealing with the spirit world, shows that it can only be described as a single system in very general terms. Ancestors influencing the living, malevolence passing between the dead and the living and between the living as well as the influence on the living of spirits with which they have no lineal connections. Only in this last category is there any corporate activity of individuals not previously connected by blood or marriage.

The fact that anthropological studies have perhaps shown a greater interest in religious than economic matters, does not make it an activity in any way comparable to the observable religious preoccupations of Hindus and the regular devotions of devout Christians and Moslems.

East African religion has been a response to demand one, a practical rather than a practising system in which those involved, except for a few popular quasi-traditional healers, are part-time, depending more on their subsistence farming and livestock tending (Platvoet, 1993).

The basis of social segmentation is competition and quasi-traditional healers as much as the Christian leaders of the major and Independent Churches are in covert competition with each other within their ostensible commitment to and involvement in the more general spirit world and spirituality. Thus in what these quasi-traditional healers practise and prescribe for those who consult them, there are idiosyncratic themes, eccentricity and inspiration (Tanner, 1997). In effect it is always competition to draw clients to them and away from their rivals. Numbers mean status as well as economic and social security.

Anthropologists see few ceremonies and may thus tend to assume a pattern of stability in form and practice, which is far from being the case. How could it be otherwise when there are no written requirements for rituals, no centralised training schemes and subsequent supervision. It seems certain that almost all-religious activity, which is not related to infrequent rites of passage, is based entirely on particular situations involving different people, which invites if not requires disparate responses. The six million Sukuma have a traditional system of involvement with their ancestors whom they propitiate in times of difficulty when such causes are diagnosed by diviners. A list of these propitiations show virtually different rituals for what are different situations according to the ideas of the officients and the materials and participants as to what is available and what can be afforded.

East Africans as they experience the processes of continual and rapid social change, start with the assumption of disparate rather than monolinear responses to their problems involving the spirit world. This traditional segmentary religious system and the religious paradigm that sustains it, transfers easily to the growing towns and cities.

What centripetal socio-religious activities existed in rural areas relating to rites of passage involving larger numbers of people than single families, have disappeared in the urban areas with their mixture of tribal cultures and the development of a class structure coming from a combination of literacy, regular employment, corruption and nepotism (Iliffe, 1975).

In the urban areas there is not only a proliferation of quasi-traditional healers relating to the opportunities there and to the larger population.

In the early 60s it was estimated that on any one day in Dar Es Salaam, the then capital of Tanzania, there were more people consulting quasi-traditional practitioners than were using all the government's welfare and medical institutions (Swantz, 1974). There are far fewer in rural areas where the social sanctions on deviant behaviour are operative and the opportunities fewer. These men and women have developed a working relationship with non-ancestral spirits rather than ancestors who are less active influences on the members of dispersed families, combined with a growing concern over witchcraft.

Since witchcraft is not defined or perhaps definable, it is an explanation for almost any real or imagined unpleasantness. In societies which have undergone many radical changes due in part to factors over which people have little or no control, it is not surprising that this has become a matter of growing popular fear and national concern. Amongst the Sukuma and Nyamwwezi particularly there has been widespread killings of suspected witches. In 1970-84 there have been 3693 killings amongst the Sukuma alone of whom 62 per cent were of women over 41 years. This epitomises the cultural clash between the idealised modernisation goals of the state and the cosmology of the Sukuma people (Mesaki, 1992). Whatever rapid political and social changes that may occur, the pattern of thinking within their quasi-traditional paradigm is likely to continue relatively unchanged despite the fact that the social institutions with which they were originally correlated have ceased to exist.

Most areas have Christian churches of various denominations with their conspicuous buildings and permanent staffs as well as those of the so-called Independent Churches and similar Moslem institutions and groupings particularly along the coast and in townships.

In economic terms this is a consumer society for religion in which all can choose from goods displayed in the religious market place. In this respect there are factors which have accounted for increased tensions reflected in part in more religious involvements and their accompanying stresses.

The colonial period with its "us and them" dichotomy came to an end in Eastern Africa in a wave of universal optimism rather than of violent political tensions. Over the years since then this has been replaced by the severe depression of what almost all the people expected. In addition the end of apartheid in South Africa meant the loss of an emotional political focus of which everyone was aware.

All three countries on gaining political independence ceased to balance their budgets and indulged in wide-ranging policies designed to make up for the years of what the new politicians saw as the minimal and lethargic development programmes of the previous colonial regimes. This resulted in an expanded civil service, which became increasingly underpaid as inflation took hold of the economy. These civil servants had to find alternative ways of maintaining their livelihoods and were less and less able to fulfil the functions for which their posts were designed. No doubt this was caused in part by a widespread feeling that administration was relatively easy led to many ambitious schemes for which there were not enough competent long-service African civil servants to replace the expatriates whose contracts had terminated with the transfer of sovereignty.

A series of long droughts was bad enough for subsistence farmers but in Tanzania this was aggravated by the Villagisation policy which uprooted a high proportion of cultivators without providing them with the facilities there which the government had hoped to provide and which these people considered to have been promised them. The resentment engendered by this mass internal migration carried out with little planning and some force will not only be long lasting, but reduced the capacity of the country to feed itself.

Uganda suffered the inefficiency and brutality of the Idi Amin regime which was overthrown by an invasion from Tanzania which further impoverished the economies of both countries and resulted in a long lasting civil war there, aggravated by the Holy Spirit Movement. The fact that Amin was a Moslem led to Moslem aggression against their Christian neighbours (Whyte, 1997: 53). Both Tanzania and Uganda abolished their chiefs and chiefdoms which had both emotional and political functions and these were not replaced in the peoples' hearts by politicians and political parties. Kenya suffered droughts and inter-tribal tensions as well as a lack of economic growth. All three states had serious problems from corruption which led to the increased wariness of donors supporting inefficient regimes.

Further all three countries suffered border problems and floods of refugees from Zaire, Ruanda, Urundi, Ethiopia, Somalia and the Sudan for which international aid was needed. The control of mass diseases with the exception of AIDS engendering widespread fear, and some reduction in infant mortality led to an increase in the youthfulness and size of the population rather than any marked lengthening of life.

Overall the people who had expected a marked and early improvement in their standard of living, have in fact suffered a decline and a growth of cynicism over the political process and their politicians in particular; "a revolution of rising disappointments" (Geertz, 2000: 32). In addition the growth of the tourist industry has meant that more and more poor East Africans have been faced with wealthy foreigners. Possibly a far more invasive "us and them" emotional rather than ideological situation than prior to independence.

People now have a largely recreated traditional religion running parallel to or as an alternative to Christianity or Islam rather than a having a religion coinciding with their tribal identity. In this situation practitioners who are able to show that they have some links with what the people see as their traditional beliefs, have great advantages since there are few institutional or ideological barriers to discourage consumer utilisation and personal initiatives.

The Latency of Inter-Religious Tensions

If East African religions are considered in terms of their three foci, the modernised traditional, Christianity and Islam, there are structural difficulties in comparing them in terms of beliefs and practices. Attendance at Christian ceremonies and Friday prayers in the mosques can be assessed, but beyond that there can be no accurate details of private prayers and none at all on the frequencies of using traditional rituals.

The East African modernised or quasi-traditional religion has no intellectualised core which can be grasped as the model to which there are conformities and deviations. The simplicity of belief in active spirits and the transmittable malevolence of innumerable and unknown ancestors, relatives and outsiders and the innumerable ways in which this can be interpreted by individuals, gives it an immediate adaptability which is institutionally absent from the major Christian Churches and to a lesser extent from Islam.

Whether this widening faith indicates, correlates to or follows after secular, economic, political and social problems is difficult to evaluate. There are widespread examples of this religion being involved in the expression of social and political unrest in the last century. The Nyabingi cult in south-west Uganda (Hopkins, 1970), the 1905 Maji rebellion in German East Africa (Iliffe, 1979), the Mau Kikuyu revolt in Kenya

(Nottingham and Rosberg, 1966), millenneal cults in Gusii, Kenya (Whipper, 1970), as well as repeated rebellions in Southern Rhodesia (Ranger, 1967). All involved divination and the use of protective religious preparations.

We can perhaps see these modernised traditional religious activities, which do develop into cults and sects, as having the potential to embody and exemplify difficulties in any society where there are no other ways beyond violence of expressing their misery. It will not take the form of open tension between cults until other factors come into play such as the prolonged civil war in Uganda, where the cultic origins of those acting more or less in the name of the Holy Spirit Movement became obscure.

However there seems little doubt that the increase in personal and collective difficulties has been accompanied by an increased use of what the people themselves consider to be their traditional religions and not just in its violent corporate manifestations. Such tensions as do occur are related to the gossip associated with competition rather than ideological rivalry for hearts and minds. People speaking in tongues while possessed can be believed or not but the predisposition is to believe as it is a basic feature of their religious paradigm. Ideological rivalry would be hard to initiate without the prior formulation of beliefs and practices in writing; they cannot rush to the Bible and Koran for support for or against schismatic activities.

Any secular evaluation of missionary Christianity in Eastern Africa has to consider rivalry between Churches as important. Colonial administrators were always wary of missionaries who couched their expansionist and rival aims in ideological terms. The enunciation of the aim of doing God's work invited secular and defensive responses from civil servants trying to prevent possible tensions while promoting the social services which these Churches could provide and for which the government did not have sufficient funds.

Whether they said as much or not, they were all aiming at area exclusivities in the siting of their churches, schools and medical centres for which overseas personnel and funds were available. This was known in colonial Tanganyika as "ecclesiastical chess". In the 1960s a Roman Catholic bishop in Usukuma thought that the building of a church anywhere would produce 2000 converts, but the Sukuma have never taken to Christianity with any marked enthusiasm as the parish of Bukumbi where there have been resident priests for over a century, does not have a majority of Roman Catholics in its neighbourhood; the majority remain in effect traditional believers.

As these mainstream Churches came under national leadership, the staff to run their institutions has shrunk considerably, so that despite overseas capital to initiate projects, accredited personnel has become the main problem. It has become more a question of servicing their existing followers than in embarking on any obvious rivalry, which the new governments would not have tolerated as in some ways as instigated from abroad and thus a relic of colonialism. Rome is hardly a centre of economic influence but Churches with Scotland and England in their titles raise eyebrows in an ostensibly anti-tribal political set-up.

It is hard to consider that there is any real possibility of tensions between the main Christian denominations at the institutional level. Their leaders are well aware that ecumenism is now not only a part of overall Christian ideology but a political necessity as well.

In Islam the African Sunni majority have had tensions over the Ahmaddiya translation of the Koran into kiSwahili which circulates but is not widely known. Many Indians are Shia, but their internal differences have never spread into the surrounding African Sunni communities from whom they have never sort converts. Sufi prayer groups have in some ways the characteristics of quasi-traditional spirit cults and depend on the personalities of their leaders.

Religious Inspiration and the Formulation of New Cults

Independent Churches have been infrequently conspicuous in the East African religious scene, although they have existed in some distinctive forms (Welbourn, 1961). They do not have sufficient economic support to maintain any large institutional and separate presence, although under the cloak of universality they are in fact tribally based. There are not as numerically distinctive as they have been in their thousands in South Africa (Barrett, 1968).

However there is no reason to suppose that Independent Churches do not have the potential to respond collectively to the need for locally based Christian institutions in which people can feel "at home" in the impersonal wilderness of an increasingly mass society (Welbourn and Ogot, 1966: 144-5).

While many are inclined to see these Independent Churches in derogatory terms as the semi-pathological creations of individuals disrupting the lives of simple peasantry, some have developed impressive support for those in misery. The Legio Maria, a breakaway Church from the Roman Catholics, with its Latin liturgy, ecclesiastical hierarchy, and intense ritualism, provides for the laying on of hands for the cure of illness and misfortune which the main denominations are reluctant to perform. The African Israeli Church Ninevah with its distinctive dress and jogging to services has many social attractions. Overall the major ones in Zambia and Zimbabwe and their quasi-traditional counterparts, have the function of knitting together tribal areas divided by the ecclesiastical boundaries of the main-line Churches (Werbner, 1977). These Churches are very much the creation of their originators' inspirations and accordingly have difficulty in maintaining an identity independent of these charismatic figures. As with the leaders of quasi-traditional cults, it is the combination of charisma and ritual exclusivities couched in mainly natal languages, which attract and retain supporters.

A recent example was the Lumpa Church of Alice Lenshina in Northern Rhodesia in the 1950-60s (Lehmann,1961; Roberts,1970). This was a popular movement originating in her breakaway from the Church of Scotland which drew members from other Churches as well. The emotional intensity shown by its members who were prepared to die in defence of their wish to live in separate communities and its popularist approach to salvation and the elimination of witchcraft, is not the framework of thinking in which mutual tolerance develops.

That this was likely to be the form of any future religious protest movements was shown in the Holy Spirit Movement in northern Uganda (Behrend, 1991). Alice Lakwena and those who carried on the movement after she went to Kenya, through prophetic and spirit communication were able to create an armed movement, which nearly captured Kampala.

The Rise in Inter-Faith Tensions

It has perhaps been one of the axioms of western thinkers that religion would recede as one of the major confrontational issues in public life and that it would remain as a personal or at the most a small community issue. This has not happened and inter-religious violence has been a major part of political and social in the Sudan, Ethiopia and Uganda.

While there have been many violent confrontations within and between faiths in the past since 1820 a third of all fighting has had a religious element in which over two thirds have had a Christian component and a half Moslem (Wilkinson, 1980). Of these fighting between Roman Catholics and Orthodox Christians in what was once Yugoslavia was the worst, while there has been sectarian violence in Northern Ireland for nearly a century. In addition there has been substantial religion backed Moslem-cum-tribal violence in the Sudan and northern Nigeria against Christians, of which the former has flooded Uganda with refugees. The Libyans supported the Amin regime with both arms, men and money and Amin himself is now a refugee in Saudi Arabia.

East African Moslems have not been isolated from these events and there has been a general rise in Moslem sense of corporate identity aided by oil money in attempting to overcome its muted political voice and its reputation for backwardness. The Zanzibar region of secular Tanzania recently attempted to affiliate itself independently with pan-Islamic Middle-Eastern organisations.

The fundamentalist frame of Moslem thinking as a background for Islamic actions is clear, combined as it is with some religious rigidity as to how to cope with rapid social change. There seem to be parallels here to the much earlier Christian approach to missionary work, which was both culturally and theologically aggressive. During this period Islam was not specifically expansionist (Tanner, 1992) except though marriage and trade.

Now Islam in Eastern Africa is becoming much more visible with the building of mosques with oil money and audibly as well with amplified calls to prayer. This is apart from the Yao, Zigua Digo and the coastal Swahili who are almost all nominal Moslems, while continuing to practise quasi-traditional rituals. There is also the national Bakwata missionary organisation. There have been some commercialised conversions, the modern equivalent of earlier "rice" Christians.

Nevertheless Islam still remains handicapped by having its one holy book written in Arabic, although this always has been used for divination, its historical association with the coastal people's sense of cultural superiority and its economic backwardness there. However it does affiliate easily into the social lives of those who consider their tribal affiliations to be important A Sukuma chief had children in all three religions with perhaps a fine sense of opportunism, and Uganda chiefs who converted to the new faiths on almost a pro rata basis, do not seem to have brought into their new faiths many others.

Islam has the advantages of tenets which are easy to learn and to follow in comparison to Christianity, no catechuminate and a more institutionally relaxed view of what is religiously permissible, combined with the absence of a supervisory priesthood interested in morals rather than ritual practices (Tanner and Wijsen,1995). Even senior Moslems are concerned at the activities of their coreligionists as in the development of "zar" cults among Moslem women in many communities including Eastern Africa (Boddy, 1989; Kenyon, 1999; and Messing, 1958).

Entering the Religious Ambivalence of the Modern World

If the East African could be typified, then it is as a subsistence farmer with a vague tribal paradigm dictating thoughts rather than specific behaviour but with a very clear and calculated idea of how to make the best out of a possibly increasingly difficult life. While not denying those who have religious vocations as such, almost all their religious behaviour has a cost-benefit dimension; an outlay of time and materials against a calculation of the expected returns. In this religious rituals are seen in much the same terms as social activities and their agricultural practices.

While it is obvious that almost all those involved in religious activities see themselves as acting for religious rather than secular reasons, it is these secular reasons in a tribal framework of thinking that may dictate membership of a particular Christian denomination and now to a certain extent Islam.

Some of course convert and maintain their commitment for almost exclusively religious reasons, but others convert or maintain membership for more material reasons, some of which involve considerable foresight (Tanner, 1969a).

The main-line Churches have material resources, schools, hospitals, training colleges, educational bursaries and access to funds for charity. In the absence of anything more than minimal welfare provisions by governments, this is bound to be an important factor. Others convert in order to marry or to join new social groupings such as the Legion of Mary (not the Legio Maria) or because membership provides physical and ritual protections (Tanner, 1970).

Islam and the major Christian denominations could have become closely connected to particular tribes by couching their rituals in their languages. Protestantism particularly produced the Bible in a number of tribal languages. Their missionaries as well as the Roman Catholics preached and did their parochial work in them. Both Roman Catholics and Moslems were stuck with canonical languages, Latin and classical Arabic, which were of little pastoral but considerable ritual value.

The Moslems were not in a position to change, as the Koran in Arabic was the literal Word of God. The Roman Catholics can and did change after Vatican II to local languages but here there were difficulties. In Tanzania the change was to kiSwahili, the national lingua franca from the end of the 19th century, thus tacitly allying itself with national political rather than tribal ambitions. While this may have been justifiable with small tribes for which the expense of translation and publishing would have been out of the question. Its effect on the six million Sukuma and Nyamwezi who have already been reluctant to become Christians, would have become more marked.

However in Uganda and Kenya there are no such widely acceptable and commonsense use of a lingua franca. Thus the main-line denominations and of course the Independent Churches have no alternative but to be involved with tribal languages; Roman Catholic dioceses among the Luo and Kikuyu whatever their views, are in practise tribal dioceses and this of course aids the paralleling of religious practices. Their sense of nominal religious identity will be denominational and readily relatable to their tribal paradigms of thought sustained by their languages.

Even with the use of tribal languages there are the persistent problems of translation. The semantic battle between languages which have no common background is complicated by theological abstractions. Whatever words are used for God, including the use of the upper case, spirit, sin and the list is virtually endless, they carry with them a seemingly dominant Western paraphernalia of meaning; ostensibly equivalent words may not mean equivalent popular understandings (Tanner, 1993). The kiSwahili use of the word "mungu" for the Christian all-loving God to a Sukuma congregation, will not mean that the word is accepted in this framework of religious thinking however admirable. The tribal linguistic paradigm will always be present in the subconscious if not in the forefront of their minds that their God is a backup figure whom they hope would leave them alone (Tanner, 1956). Tribal languages are more used by women than any lingua franca and thus these traditional pattern of thinking is likely to be stronger with them than men.

There may indeed be cross-conversions between denominations but this will not be towards any greater experience of Christian unity, but towards varying levels of conformity to denominational practices, a periodic lapsing much the same as with Western Christians (Tanner, 1969b), and as always a paralleling of religious practices between the ostensibly non-tribal Christianity and the quasi-traditional tribal practicalities of dealing with immediate problems.

But it is in quasi-traditional religious practices that there is constant adaptation to the needs of those sharing loose traditional paradigms. They are up to date because the changes that individual practitioners make are not related to past texts and resolutions, nor are the changes that occur the result of long and laborious institutional processes. Perhaps they have a feel for what is useful in the beliefs as much as the practices of the main-line Christian denominations. Modern quasi-traditional religions are now making use of non-African spirits as an important part of their help for people adjusting to modern life (Krings, 1999; and Masquelier, 1999). The Holy Spirit Movement in Uganda had an Italian spirit guiding their mobile force and a Korean one their weapons and transport (Behrend, 1999).

Conclusions

The picture of a traditional religious system which at one time coincided with the tribe one was probably always an illusion except where uninhabited areas isolated communities. Even then there would have been areas of unconformity and change enabled by non-literacy.

It is possible to identify tribal rural areas as specifically different to urban ones in which a single tribe may be in the majority and urban areas in which there are tribal enclaves. The population is constantly on the move between rural and urban locations for both short and long term reasons. Only the old in the rural areas and a small minority of committed urbanites are excluded from this peripatetic cross-cultural life-style.

It has always been possible for non-literate people to claim a traditional basis for their religious practices which overall enabled them to feel comfortable with what they were doing. Any memory of the past is always subject to considerable social adjustment as time goes by. So it seems that the religious and social paradigm in which East Africans think is a tribal one adjusted to modern circumstances.

Political and economic circumstances may change in the short-term but the semantic usages of their tribally based languages are as well at the back of Christian and Moslem practices and are likely to remain so for many decades to come. Translations of meaning for ambiguous terms allows plenty of areas for private reinterpretations and adjustments.

When it is recognised that there are more Sukuma than Scots and Welsh put together, it should be accepted that thinking within a tribal paradigm in East Africa is not only acceptable but to be expected. It is in the private as much as public areas of personal need that the tribal paradigm there fulfils important functions that can only be met by a broad largely non-literate interpretation of religion, the quasi-traditional.

It seems likely that tensions will remain between Christians and Moslems at the local level and may well increase for which the rising political and religious expectations of the latter may be responsible.

All quasi-traditional religious practitioners and their cults are in covert competition with each other as they have always been, but it seems unlikely that this would create tension which would diminish the opportunities for personal service; their most popular feature.

Covert competition between the mainline Christian denominations is no longer so obvious issue because the governments are much less tolerant of such manoeuvrings. Independent Christian sects are likely to be part of any popular movement encouraged and enabled by civil unrest and particularly when they act in support of the widespread fear of witchcraft.

REFERENCES

Barrett, D.B. 1968. *Schism and Renewal in Africa*. Nairobi: Oxford University Press.

Behrend, H. 1991. "Is Alice Lakwena a Witch? The Holy Spirit Movement in its Fight against Evil in the North," in H.B. Hansen and M. Twaddle (eds.), *Changing Uganda*. Currey: Oxford.

____. 1997. "Power to Heal, Power to Kill. Spirit Possession and War in Northern Uganda (1986-94)," in H. Behrend and U. Luig (eds.), *Spirit Possession Modernity and Power in Africa*. Currey: Oxford.

Boddy, J. 1989. *Women and Alien Spirits. Women, Men and the Zar Cult in Northern Sudan*. Madison: Wisconsin University Press.

Brett, A. 1996. "Testimonies of War Trauma in Uganda," in T. Allen (ed.), *In Search of Cool Ground*. Geneva: United Nations Institute for Social Development. Chambers, I. 1994. Migrancy, Culture, Identity. London: Routledge.

Dewey, J. 1981. "Experience and Nature," in J.A. Boyd (ed.), *J. Dewey. Later Works.1925-53*. Vol. 1. Carbondale: University of Illinois.

Gable, E. 1995. "The Colonisation of Consciousness; the Local Sceptic and the Will to be Modern in a West African Village," *American Ethnologist*, 22 (2): 242-57.

Geertz, C. 2000. *Available Light. Anthropological Reflections on Philosophical Topics*. New Jersey: Princeton University.

Heald, S. 1991. "Divinatory Failure; the Religious and Social Role of Gusii Diviners," *Africa.* 61 (3): 299-317.

Hopkins, E.1970. "The Nyabingi Cult in South-western Uganda," (pp. 258-336) in R.I. Rotberg and A.A. Mazrui (eds.), *Protest and Power in Black Africa*. New York: Oxford University Press.

Iliffe, J. 1975. "The Creation of Group Consciousness among the Dock Workers of Dar Es Salaam.1929-56," in R. Sandbrook and R. Cohen (eds.), *The Development of the African Working Class; Studies in Class Formation and Action*. Toronto: University of Toronto Press.

____. 1979. *A Modern History of Tanganyika*. Cambridge: Cambridge University Press.

Kenyon, S.M. 1999. "The Care of the Butcher's Wife. Illness, Possession and Power in Central Sudan," in H. Behrend and U. Luig (eds.), *op.cit.*

Krings, M. 1999. "On History and Language of the European 'Bori' Spirits," in H. Behrend and U. Luig (eds.), *op.cit.*

Lehmann, D. 1961. "Alice Lenshina Mulenga and the Lumpa Church," (pp. 248-268) in J.V. Taylor and D. Lehmann (eds.), *Christians of the Copper-belt.* London.

Lubeck, P.M. 1985. "Islamic Protest under Semi-industrial Capitalism," *Africa*, 55: 369-89.

Marquelier, A. 1999. "The Invention of Anti-tradition. Dodo Spirits in Southern Niger," in H. Behrend and U. Luig (eds.), *op.cit.*

Maton, K.I. and K.I. Pargament. 1992. "Religion as a Resource for Preventive Action," in K.I. Pargament *et al.* (eds.), *Religion and Prevention in Health, Rsearch, Vision and Action*. New York: Narworth Press.

Mesaki, S. 1992. "The Preponderance of Women as Victims in Sukuma Witch Killings," in P.G. Foster and S. Maghimbi (eds.), *The Tanzanian Peasantry: Economy in Crisis*. Aldershot: Avebury.

Messing, S.D. 1958. "Group Therapy and Social Status in the Zar Cult of Ethiopia," *American Anthropologist*, 60: 1120-5.

Nottingham, J. and C.C. Rosberg. 1966. *The Myth of Mau Nationalist in Kenya*. New York: Praeger.

Platvoet, A.G. 1993. "African Traditional Religions in the Religious History of Mankind," *Journal for the Study of Religions*, 6 (2): 29-48.

Ranger, T.O. 1967. *Revolt in Southern Rhodesia*. London: Heinemann.

Roberts, A.D. 1970. "The Lumpa Church of Alice Lenshina," (pp. 513-568) in R.I. Rotberg and A.A. Mazrui (eds.), op.cit.

Schimmel, A.1994. *Deciphering the Signs of God. A Phenomenological Approach to Islam*. Edinburgh: Edinburgh University Press.

Swartz, L.1974. *The Role of the Medical Man among the Zaramo of Dar Es Salaam.* Ph.D. Dissertation. University of Dar Es Salaam, Tanzania.

Tanner, R.E.S. 1956. "An Introduction to the Northern Sukuma's Idea of the Supreme Being," *Anthropological Quarterly,* 29 (2): 45-56.

____. 1967. *Transition in African Belief.* New York: Maryknoll.

____. 1968. "Reasons for Rejecting Christianity in Usukuma," *African Ecclesiastical Revue*, October.

____. 1969(a). "Reasons for Entering the Christian Community," *African Ecclesiastical Revue*, April.

____. 1969(b). "The Christian who does not Practice in Usukuma," *African Ecclesiastical Revue*, July.
____. 1970. *The Witch Murders in Usukuma: A Sociological Commentary*. Uppsala: Scandinavian Institute of African Studies.
____. 1973. "Economic Factors in East African Ecumenism," *Journal Ecumenical Studies*. January.
____.1974. "Conversion to Christianity and Islam from African Religions," *Heythrop Journal*. April.
____. 1992. "The Impact of Christianity and Islam on two East African Societies," *Studia Missionalia,* 20 (3): 201-215.
____. 1993a. "African Traditional Religions and their Reactions to other Faiths," *Studia Missionalia,* 42: 371-394.
____. 1993b. "East African Ethical Ideas and Translation. Some Possible Consequences of a Bilateral Process," *Anthropos*, 88: 29-37.
____. 1997. "Cognitive Development. Socialisation and Cognitive Mutation. A Critique and Elaboration of Boyer's Naturalness of Religion. A Case Study of the Sukuma of Tanzania," *Journal of Social Sciences,* 1 (2): 91-8.
Tanner, R.E.S. and F.S. Wijsen. 1993. "Christianity in Usukuma: A Working Misunderstanding," *Nouvelle Revbue de Science Missionnaire,* 49 (3): 177-194.
Trimingham, J.S.1964. *Islam in East Africa.* Oxford: Oxford University Press.
Welbourn, F.B. 1961. *East African Rebels: A Study of Some Independent Churches.* London: SCM Press.
Welbourn, F.B. and B.A. Ogot. 1966. *A Place to Feel at Home*. London.
Werbner, R.P. 1977. "Introduction," in R.P. Werbner (ed.), *Regional Cults.* London: Academic Press.
Whyte, S.R. 1997. *Questioning Misfortune. The Pragmatics of Uncertainty in Eastern Uganda.* Cambridge: Cambridge University Press.
Wijsen, J.S. and R.E.S. Tanner. 2000. *The Recreation of Cultural Identity among the Sukuma of Tanzania* (In press).
Wilkinson, D. 1980. *Deadly Quarrels. Lewis F. Richardson and the Statistical Study of War.* Berkeley: University of California Press.
Wipper, A. 1970. "The Gusii Rebels," in R.I. Rotberg and A.A. Mazrui (eds.), op.cit.

FOURTEEN

THE GROUP ETHIC VERSUS INDIVIDUALISM AMONG NORTH AMERICAN MICMACS

LAWRENCE F. VAN HORN

Introduction

A member of the Algonkian language family, Micmac Indians speak an eastern Algonkian language of northeastern North America. In Canada, Micmac-speaking groups reside in parts of Quebec, New Brunswick, Prince Edward Island, and Nova Scotia. At one time they occupied a portion of Newfoundland. In the United States, Micmacs live in Maine. From both countries, they work for extended stretches of time in such cities as Boston and Worcester, Massachusetts. They also serve as harvesters in the potato fields of Maine and the blueberry patches of Nova Scotia. Often while away they will maintain ties and send money back to home bases in the state of Maine or in one of the Canadian Maritime provinces above (Guillemin, 1975: 83).

Already we have coupled the old with the new. Speaking the Micmac language is old, but working in the economies of the United States or Canada is relatively new. This is so given the long tradition of the Micmacs as hunters, gatherers, and fisher folk in a northern climate of limited horticulture due to the short growing season.

The Micmacs have the "dubious distinction of being among the first North American Indians to have been contacted by Europeans — with the discovery of Cape Breton (Nova Scotia) by the French Bretons in 1504" (Hoffman, 1955: 7). For New Brunswick Micmacs, with whom

I am directly familiar, the first contact with Europeans is traced to 1534, when Jacques Cartier entered Miramichi Bay and the Bay of Chaleur and traded with Micmacs from ships and later on shore (Guillemin, 1975: 25-27).

The Micmacs were not pushed westward as happened to many indigenous peoples as a result of European settlement in North America. Although they lost vast amounts of land to Europeans, Micmacs still stayed on portions of their own land, now called reserves in Canada (Patterson, 1972: 4). In the United States, such reserves are called reservations. Maine Micmacs lack a reservation. They are federally recognised by the United States Government as the Aroostook Band of Micmac Indians but without a formal land base (Bureau of Indian Affairs, 1997: 21).

During the Seven Years' War (1756-1763), the Micmacs sided with the French against the British in the struggle of these European powers for control of North America. Micmacs were able to help hide some of the Acadians, who were French speaking, and save them from the deportation out of Nova Scotia that began in 1755 by the British (Anderson, 2000: 75, 100-114). Acadia included what is now western Nova Scotia and eastern New Brunswick. New Brunswick was part of Nova Scotia until 1784 when it became a separate British colony. It became a founding province in the Dominion of Canada. Confederation was a result of the British North America Act of 1867. That same year, the Indian Act was passed that established the initial Micmac reserves in the Maritime Provinces.

Starting in 1765, many Acadians eventually settled in Louisiana, having gone to France upon their 1755 expulsion by British from Nova Scotia. They continued to speak a certain dialect of French, and became known as Cajuns. They are so known today.

The Micmac community of Burnt Church in present-day New Brunswick derives its name from the Seven Years' War. The incident is one of Acadian fugitives building a stone church in the Miramichi area in 1755 as a tribute in thanks to their Micmac benefactors and for mutual French and Micmac use. Through missionaries many Micmacs had become Catholic, at least nominally. But on September 17, 1758, a British patrol from a man-of-war in Miramichi Bay set fire to the church (Ganong, 1914: 304). The name "Burnt Church" stuck. Burnt Church today is situated between the primarily English-speaking community of New Jersey, New Brunswick on one side and on the other, the primarily French-speaking community of Neguac, of Acadian ancestry.

Members of Burnt Church, like those of other Indian communities reasonably near the international border, enjoy the freedom to cross at will between Canada and the United States. This freedom extends to working, often being employed as wage labourers in agriculture or industry, in the other country. The privilege stems from the American Revolution and the Jay Treaty of 1794 between the United States of America and what was then the United Kingdom of Great Britain, following the 1707 Act of Union of the kingdoms of England and Scotland. Like the Micmacs whose aboriginal range was divided by the 1794 boundary line, "border tribes were free to travel back and forth ...for hunting, fishing, and trading purposes" (Prins, 1996: 48).

According to their aboriginal social structure (Nietfeld, 1981), the Micmacs traditionally regarded the patrilocal extended family as a very important unit in which different types of political, economic, and social cooperation occurred. Kinship was traditionally bilateral. It still is. One's relatives are determined equally through both the mother and father. The desired rule of residence at marriage was traditionally, and still is, patrilocal. Practice calls for the couple to live near the groom's father's household. A Micmac reserve typically can be mapped by identifying each household's kinship affiliations. A pattern soon emerges. Different patrilocal extended families can be seen to have clustered in different parts of the reserve. Each patrilocal extended family pretty much will reside in its own section.

Extended families heads would band together to govern a region, such as the Miramichi Peninsula in eastern New Brunswick, with the Bay of Chaleur on the north and Miramichi Bay on the south. Band leadership was in the hands of a headman who held the office partly by way of inheriting it from his father, and partly through consensus of the family heads that he was worthy to lead. For analysis below, we refer to this headman of a band as a Micmac chief. He and his family heads, who later served as the prototype for the contemporary elected band council along with the now-elected chief, would meet annually as the leaders of a regional band to assess the re-allocation of hunting territories among extended families. Variables were used such as rough population estimates of the fluctuations in the species preyed upon, plus changes in Micmac family size to adjust the boundaries of the family hunting territories. Today, beyond identifying with one's home community in Canada or the United States, Micmacs say they see themselves, not just as regional groups as before, but rather as one people united into an Indian nation, the Micmac Nation (Prins, 1996: 65).

This paper focuses upon two aspects of Micmac character and culture — cooperation and individualism. These traits are described and analysed. And the circumstances are explored under which one value might prevail over the other in work and education groups and in Micmac businesses.

Egalitarian Values and Leadership

Cultural values are those concepts utilised by a society or group as criteria for desirable behavior (Williams, 1967: 23). Micmacs "find it virtually impossible to accept authority of any kind" (Bock, 1966: 55). Micmacs are well known for their egalitarian values and down-to-earth, teasing sense of humour. Micmac humour encourages people to make puns. It is self-depreciating, and pokes fun at the ironies of life. On the more serious side, Micmacs are known, too, for their "kindness, loyalty, strength, and quiet dignity" (Bock, 1974b: 385).

It has been said that the Micmacs have survived over 450 years of acculturation, to maintain a Micmac identity by clinging to their egalitarian values, aided by the Micmac language as a conduit of Micmac culture (Bock, 1974a: 225-226; Upton, 1980: 171). Egalitarian values are expressed through cooperation, reciprocity, and the use of the Micmac language *versus* English among fellow bilingual Micmacs (Van Horn, 1975 and 1977).

Egalitarianism means that a Micmac person will normally take great pains to avoid any implication that he or she might somehow be setting himself or herself "above others" economically, socially, or politically. The importance of not being perceived as "too proud" is a concomitant and corollary of Micmac egalitarianism. An example may be found in the role of a modern Micmac chief.

The now-elected chief of the Burnt Church Micmac Indian Band at Burnt Church, New Brunswick, Canada, leads by persuasion rather than by coercion. Power is exerted by way of example and convincing rather than by applying hierarchical authority (Miller, 1955: 287). The workday in the Burnt Church community begins at eight in the morning when the men who are engaged in work projects report to the chief at the community hall. The women assemble across the road in the handicraft center in this Micmac reserve along the southern shore of Miramichi Bay. They make beadwork products, wooden baskets of a traditional style, and items of leather and fur for the tourist trade. One of their most popular artifacts is a substantial beadwork necklace called an Indian tie that both men and women wear. Outlets are local and national, the latter through the Canadian Bureau of Indian Affairs via a certification process. This federal agency attaches an informative tag to each item indicating that it is an authentic product, handmade by a Canadian Indian. After talking with the men, the chief crosses the road to the handicraft centre to meet with the women.

Separate consultation with the men and then the women workers has to do with the chief sequentially presiding over daily morning meetings to discuss work assignments. Under the chief's leadership, the group decides upon that day's assignments. Assignments relate to fishing, building new homes on the reserve, re-modelling homes to up-grade them as major construction projects, and clearing brush to attract tourists to picnic spots along Miramichi Bay and to the handicraft center. Tasks are generally carried out in teams of two or more men. With handicrafts and the women's work group, individual artisans are seemingly an exception to teamwork. Yet more than one craftsperson may help design and make particular products and items. And the group keeps a group production schedule.

The chief is the leader of an egalitarian community who holds his elected position because of demonstrated ability to be fair with his people and to fight for community benefits that generally come in from outside the community. To do so, the chief must see to it that his workers deliver products "on-time" in European Canadian terms. He accomplishes this by marshalling support from his kinsmen, friends, and followers who are indeed to be found among the workers. A Micmac chief is expected to distribute benefits and goods in such a way that the material needs of the people are met before those of the leader. It is a classic case of the first shall be last.

The seventeenth century missionary Chretien Le Clercq, says of a Micmac chief that he "made it a point of honor to be always the worst dressed of his people and to take care they were all better clothed than he" (Le Clercq, 1691: 235 in Ganong, 1910:10). Historian William F. Ganong refers to this practice as a traditional value of "noblesse oblige among Micmac chiefs" (Ganong, 1910: 10). The same is true today at Burnt Church. The chief is quite unostentatious in everyday life in presenting himself and referring to his possessions. Recently he insisted that homes in most need were repaired first and then that everyone else's renovations were made, before fixing up his own house.

Burnt Church, like other Micmac reserves, originally had a subsistence economy based upon hunting, fishing, and gathering. Today in modern times, the economy depends upon a little gardening, some commercial fishing, and occasional hunting for sport and table. Plant gathering still occurs, too. There is no plow agriculture and no animal husbandry, except for the raising of a hog or two by a few families. Income derives from fishing, cutting evergreens for pulpwood and "Christmas" trees, constructing new houses and other buildings as they are needed on the reserve, and manufacturing and selling handicrafts. Portions of these activities are funded directly by the Government of Canada as work projects, or as potentially self-sustaining programmes after initial capital investment. Once set up, the projects and programmes are administered by the chief with the advice and consent of the band council.

In addition to work projects and programmes, a few people in Burnt Church have salaried jobs paid through the elementary school, the health clinic, or the band council. These jobs include those of school teacher; nurse; social assistance or welfare officer; community janitor for the school, clinic, and community hall; and police constable attached to the Royal Canadian Mounted Police (RCMP). A Micmac small business exists — a grocery store run by one family. The handicraft center, fishing cooperative, and the operation of removing brush, cutting trees, and collecting pulpwood are run by the chief through the band council. Potential exists for more businesses, but Burnt Church is not as developed as the Micmac reserve of Eskasoni in Nova Scotia, as referred to in the article mentioned below by Daniel Strouthes (1998).

The Group Ethic

For sharing money and for performing household and other tasks, the patrilocal extended family is a basic economic unit as well as a traditional political unit. This is what I have observed at Burnt Church and learned there through ethnographic interviewing and collecting family histories. Jeanne Guillemin refers to a Micmac reserve or reservation as a conglomeration of extended families with "the extended family…[including] three or even four different generations" (Guillemin,

1975: 83).

Ideally within the patrilocal extended family, cooperation is the norm. In family groups especially, but also in other types of groups such as classroom and work groups, Micmac Indians value people over things and freely share their knowledge and material possessions (Guillemin, 1975: 149). Within these groups, people freely share environmental data consistent with continuing aspects of the traditional hunting, gathering, and fishing subsistence economy. Related to the community's participation in the larger society, they also share economic data such as information about jobs available both on and off of the reserve.

The Micmac emphasis on sharing freely within a reference group is brought out in the classroom. Micmac students readily share their knowledge. This happens even during tests, much to the chagrin of their mostly European Canadian teachers. As part of my fieldwork, I was permitted to teach the sixth grade class at Burnt Church on a substitute basis. On one occasion, having given a presentation on famous Indian leaders in history, I gave a quiz to see what the class had learned. When talking occurred, my prior European American teaching experience led me to tell the students to be quiet and do their own work individually. But I quickly realised that ethnocentrism had prompted me to say this. I changed my instructions to permit talking during the test, and thus, the sharing of information. I was delighted to learn afterwards that the entire class got an "A". Not only did my students listen to explanations from each other, but also they voluntarily took the information home and elsewhere in the community. The fact that they freely shared the information with others came back to me in several different community settings. Many adults, including parents, shared with me what I had taught in the classroom the previous day. The father of one boy telling me about the lesson in the grocery store is but one example. The information I presented was seemingly much appreciated. Presumably, it was well learned, too, judging by the number of times it was accurately told and re-told.

European Canadian and European American teachers tend to motivate students through individual competition, that is, by encouraging competitive performances among individuals. I have found this approach not to be effective among Micmacs. As related above, I observed in a Burnt Church classroom a group response that produced a very meaningful result for the group and the community.

The school principal at Burnt Church, who also teaches sixth grade as part of his duties, confirmed my analysis. The most effective teaching device that this principal has found for working with Micmac children is the group project. He has come to use this method for virtually every subject covered in the sixth grade. Students work together in small groups to gather data analyzing and answering a series of questions in a joint report written by the group.

A Micmac atmosphere prevails in the third grade. This is the only class at Burnt Church that is taught by a Micmac teacher (Van Horn, 1983: 101). This woman is a fully qualified elementary school teacher with a bachelor's degree and the required certificate from the province to teach. Interestingly enough, learning takes place in her classroom through group activities. She fosters group projects and a great deal of class discussion to accompany each project. In fact, the principal borrowed the methodology of the group approach from her. From personal observation and talking with the students, I believe that that this method of teaching maintains a level of interest and participation in the classroom that might otherwise be lost by the methods of the European Canadian teachers. They, by contrast, stress individual recitation and other forms of performing individually in the context of personal competition.

Pride in-group achievement takes precedence over individual accomplishments among the Micmacs. As part of group dynamics and leadership, this value is coupled with at least two other values as follows. As explained above about the expectations of a Micmac chief, egalitarian persuasion takes precedence over hierarchical coercion. And generally in the context of expected reciprocity and cooperation, the needs of others take precedence over one's immediate personal interests and use of material personal possessions.

As I have inferred above and emphasise here, pride in-group achievement may be seen in the classroom at Burnt Church. An instance in the third grade is a case in point. Visiting one day, I ended up sitting next to a delightfully alert third grader who, with no prompting from her Micmac teacher, took out the arithmetic project book her group was working on and proceeded to give me an arithmetic lesson. She volunteered what was going on — what problems were being solved. She certainly demonstrated enthusiasm, and I felt she demonstrated pride as well, in showing me the work of her group.

Other activities in which pride in-group achievement is apparent include work groups and on baseball and ice hockey teams. Whether cutting brush, doing bead work, or playing sports, the idiom is not what "I did," but rather what "we did".

Motivation

The way to motivate Micmacs is to recognise one's role in a group, and to appeal for the best performance of each one as relevant to group tasks. As noted earlier, men's work groups at Burnt Church include construction workers, skilled carpenters, fishermen, and wood-cutters. Women comprise the work group of handicraft manufacturers. There are three permanent committees of men and women: the Church Committee, the Health Committee, and the School Committee. Members are appointed by the chief. The committees report to the Burnt Church Indian Band Council, of which the chief is the presiding officer. Members are elected biennially. There is also an occasional ad hoc committee to advise the band council.

Three informal political groups exist, which are comparable to local political parties and which are generally congruent with the three patrilocal extended families of Burnt Church. The patrilocal extended families vie for office, and in essence, take turns holding office over the years. Men's sports groups include an adult baseball team, a Little League baseball team, and an adult ice hockey team. There are no women's groups for sports, although women enjoy being fans of the men's teams. When asked what the most important type of group might be in the community, people invariably name the family of which they are a member. That is, the answer is the patrilocal extended family. This is true socially, economically, and politically.

A health-care problem has been noted among Micmacs involving inactivity, obesity, and overuse of prescription drugs as "3.3 times the average Canadian rate" (Barkow, 1981). The social prescription was "to train local [Micmac] people into teams of counsellors...under the control of local [Micmac] band councils ...equipped to advise on activities and diet, provide counselling ...and in other ways to function as a ...social worker" (Barkow, 1981). As an applied anthropologist recommending a means of social change, Jerome Barkow recognised and has subsequently followed through with something very Micmac — teamwork!

As a matter of culture and personality, a Micmac person will tend to find personal satisfaction and social identity as a member of a group.

Work is done and effort expended for the group. Identity is found in competing along with group members in the name of the group, rather than individually. This situation is consistent with Micmac egalitarian values.

Micmac Businesses and Individualism

Daniel Strouthes (1998: 42) brings out the point that medium-sized businesses invariably fail on Micmac reserves. The practice of federal, economic development monies coming to Micmac reserves from the Government of Canada for this purpose is several decades old. It continues without financial success necessarily following. Strouthes speaks from direct experience at Eskasoni, Nova Scotia's largest Micmac reserve, which is on Cape Breton Island. He documents the lack of business acumen among Micmacs about operating to make a profit (1998: 42-43). The tendency is to hire as many people as possible, rather than grow gradually and allow a steady profit to justify new jobs. Delegation of authority is a problem. People have trouble accepting authority over them and supervising workers under them. However, "Micmac businesses with single operators usually do quite well" (Strouthes, 1998: 43).

Analysis

> [At Eskasoni, Micmac] businesses are small and never grow to a medium size. This is because of cultural values limiting authority to single individuals....but more importantly, an absolute inability to share authority.... The sharing of authority between [business] partners does not last long. The significance of this pattern is that is does not allow the kind of shared responsibility and shared/delegated authority which medium-sized and larger businesses require (Strouthes, 1998: 43-45).

Sharing occurs at Eskasoni much as I have described it above for Burnt Church. Although personally owned, material possessions are freely shared and all sorts of information as well. Strouthes establishes the relationship between sharing and leadership as follows:

> [Micmac] people strive to share with others at least partly to increase personal prestige, and seek to avoid being the recipient of shared wealth so as to avoid being seen as needing charity. Those who work hard and productively and who share the fruits of their labor enjoy prestige and, if their other qualities warrant,

> positions of leadership....This certainly makes sense in light of the realities of surviving in a harsh environment (during the hunting and gathering era)....People ...[would and do] stay close to productive hunters/fishers in order to benefit from their greater hunting and fishing expertise (Strouthes, 1998: 44).

Strouthes, thus, sees cultural continuity in "the traditional value on individualism in authority" (1998: 44). This according to Strouthes interferes with modern economic development among the Micmacs, leading to the failure of medium-sized businesses, "because the Micmac culture places such a strong high value on individualism" (1998: 43).

Discussion

George Stankey (1977: 154) comments that the social sciences — including psychology, cultural anthropology, economics, and sociology — have a common thread in that, combined, they focus on three basic elements of human behavior. These are the individual in society, groups in society, and the human use of resources. The question of the impediment of Micmac individualism that Strouthes (1998) applies to the problematic viability of medium-sized Micmac businesses raises a question in turn. At what point does a group form or come into play? Could a medium-sized Micmac company be formed and be led effectively by the positive role model of a Micmac chief?

Jerome Barkow (1981), as noted, sees forming a Micmac group of counsellors as a solution to certain health problems. Daniel Strouthes suggests forming a group of businessmen to manage the needed medium-sized businesses. He says that these businesses must be created and managed "by competent business people whose only interest is the success of the project....[and the] experience [that] would allow Micmac managers to learn how to share and delegate authority in business" (Strouthes, 1998: 45).

Implied by Strouthes is the fact that the positive role model of a Micmac chief works in Micmac-led small businesses, as mentioned above. But when authority must be shared and delegated in medium-sized businesses, a problem arises. Individualism takes over and competition becomes rampant. Strouthes (1998: 43-45) documents several instances where this has happened, so that only one person ends up running the business. Where does this individual competition come from? Acculturation? Cultural survival of a traditional custom?

As previously stated, patrilocal extended families do compete for the elected positions of members of the band council and chief. The family in power controls much of the distribution of resources with a Micmac reserve community. Before European contact in the traditional subsistence economy, patrilocal extended families competed to some extent for resources, but that was countered by the annual adjustment of family hunting territories as an economic and political matter. This was a significant aspect of traditional Micmac egalitarianism.

Could the patrilocal extended family serve as a model for a medium-sized Micmac business? It probably is the model for the small-sized successful Micmac businesses. A better model, however, might be the traditional banding together of families in the annual, regional adjustment of family hunting territories. Here authority was shared. The group reference was the band associated with a geographic region.

Daniel Strouthes feels that Micmac "economic self-sufficiency would...tend to preserve rather than erode traditional culture" (1998: 45). One way to offer encouragement might be to point out the similarity above between traditional Micmac band structure and that applicable to a medium-sized business. Although Strouthes is an academic anthropologist with a Ph.D. from Yale University, now teaching at the University of Wisconsin at Eau Claire, perhaps he could play the role of an applied anthropologist. Perhaps he could advise and educate both Micmac officials and those from the Government of Canada on this possibility, especially at Eskasoni, which as a friend and colleague I know he knows so well.

Conclusion

Given the goal of economic self-sufficiency for Micmac communities, the way to motivate people in work projects and programmes and businesses on the reserves is to invoke the group ethic. In both work and education, group assignments, group tasks, and group activities lead to consensus to work together and, if competition is called for, to compete as a group. Group consensus is the key to success to sustain and increase Micmac productivity and, financially speaking, to make a profit.

REFERENCES

Anderson, F. 2000. *Crucible of War: The Seven Years' War and The Fate of Empire in British North American, 1754-1766*. New York: Alfred A. Knopf.

Barkow, J. H. 1981. "Curing the Medicalisation of Micmac Social Problems," paper presented at the Forty-first Annual Meeting, Society for Applied Anthropology, University of Edinburgh, Edinburgh, Scotland, United Kingdom, April 15, 1981. Available from the author, Department of Anthropology, Dalhousie University, Halifax, Nova Scotia, Canada B3H 1T2.

Bock, P. K. 1966. "The Micmac Indians of Restigouche [Quebec, Canada]: History and Contemporary Description," *National Museum of Canada Bulletin*, 213.

____. 1974a. *Modern Cultural Anthropology*. Second edition. New York: Alfred A. Knopf.

____. 1974b. Review. *Urban Renegades: The Cultural Strategy of American Indians [Micmacs Who Work Away from Home at a Distance in Boston, Massachusetts, USA]*. By Jeanne Guillemin (New York: Columbia University Press). Ethnohistory, 21 (4): 384-386.

Bureau of Indian Affairs. 1997. *A Development Resource Guide for American Indian Tribes*. Washington, District of Columbia: Bureau of Indian Affairs, United States Department of the Interior.

Ganong, W. F. 1914. "The Official Account of the Destruction of Burnt Church [New Brunswick, Canada]," *Collections of the New Brunswick Historical Society*, 3 (9): 301-315.

Guillemin, J. 1975. *Urban Renegades: The Cultural Strategy of American Indians [Micmacs Who Work Away from Home at a Distance in Boston, Massachusetts, USA]*. New York: Columbia University Press.

Hoffman, B.G. 1955. *The Historical Ethnography of the Micmac of the Sixteenth and Seventeenth Centuries*. Ph.D. Dissertation, Department of Anthropology, University of California at Berkeley.

Miller, W. B. 1955."Two Concepts of Authority," *American Anthropologist*, 57 (2): 271-289.

Nietfeld, P. K. L. 1981. *Determinants of Aboriginal Micmac Political Structure*. Ph.D. Dissertation, Department of Anthropology, University of New Mexico, Albuquerque, New Mexico.

Patterson, E. P., II. 1972. *The Canadian Indian: A History since 1500*. New York: Macmillan.

Prins, H. E. L. 1996."Tribal Network and Migrant Labor: Mi'kmaq Indians as Seasonal Workers in Aroostook's Potato Fields, 1870-1980 [Aroostook County, Maine, USA]," (pp. 45-65) in A. Littlefield and M. C. Knack (eds.), *Native Americans and Wage Labor: Ethnohistorical Perspectives*. Norman: University of Oklahoma Press.

Stankey, G.H. 1977. "A Sociologist among the Economists: Some Social Concepts for Outdoor Recreation Planning,"/(11. 154-161) in *Proceedings of a National Symposium on Outdoor Advances in the Application of Economics*. Washington, District of Columbia: Forest Service, United States Department of Agriculture, General Technical Report Number WO-2.

Strouthes, D. P. 1998. "Impediments to the Economic Development of Nova Scotia's Largest Micmac Reserve [Eskasoni. Cape Breton Island]," (pp. 42-46) in L. F. Van Horn (ed.), *Grounds for Indigenous Knowledge: A Symposium — The Importance of Being Emic in an Etic World, High Plains Applied Anthropologist 18* (1, Spring 1998): 2-46.

Upton, L. F. S. 1980. *Micmacs and Colonists: Indian-White Relations in the Maritimes, 1713-1867*. Vancouver, British Columbia: University of British Columbia Press.

Van Horn, L. F. 1975. "Switching to Micmac [from English] as an Egalitarian Symbol: The Police Example in a Bilingual Micmac Indian Community [Burnt Church, New Brunswick, Canada]," *Anthropological Journal of Canada*, 13 (1): 23-24.

____. 1977. *Differential Language Use at Burnt Church [New Brunswick], A Bilingual Micmac Indian Community of Eastern Canada*. Ph.D. Dissertation, Ph.D. Program in Anthropology, Graduate School, City University of New York.

____. 1983. "The Group Ethic among Micmac Indians [of Eastern Canada]: Implications for Education and Work," (pp. 99-107) in K. T. Molohon (ed.), *Challenge for Change: Education and Modern Society, Laurentian University Review*, 15 (2, February 1983): 1-137.

Williams, R. 1967. "Individual and Group Values," *Annals of the American Academy of Political and Social Science*, 371: 20-37.

FIFTEEN

LAW AND DISORDER ON THE WINNEBAGO AND OMAHA RESERVATIONS OF NEBRASKA

PETER T. SUZUKI

This chapter will examine a recent court case regarding crimes that took place on the Winnebago Reservation in Nebraska perpetrated by a nineteen year old man. For these crimes he was tried in the Winnebago Tribal Court, found guilty and then was tried by the Federal Court for the same crime. After some background information on the Winnebago Tribe of Nebraska, the attention will shift to the case itself. The concluding portion analyses the case and points to its significance.

The Winnebago Reservation is situated on the Missouri River in the State of Nebraska. Its neighbours are the Omaha Indians, whose reservation centre, Macy, is only eight miles away. The City of Omaha, the largest city in Nebraska, is, respectively, 80 and 75 miles from these reservations.

The Winnebagos ("People of the Salt Water") or *Hochungra* ("People of the Parent Speech"), branched off from the main tribe in the State of Wisconsin in 1840. According to the 1990 census, those on the Nebraska reservation numbered 1,156, while those in Wisconsin totalled some 5,000. However, it is estimated that the 2000 census will have around 3,500 as the final count for residents of the Nebraska reservation. This steep increase is due to two significant facts. One is the growing prosperity on the reservation and its concomitant sense of tribalhood among those who consider the Nebraska reservation as their home. Both have contributed to the return of tribal members to the Nebraska reservation (Anon., 1997b; Suzuki, 1999).

The number given for the Winnebagos living on the reservation does not include other living there. The figure of 1,156 does refer to those who are *enrolled members.* Enrolled means that a person of Indian heritage is officially noted to be a member of a specific tribe by proving through genealogical records his/her affiliation with the given tribe. Most tribes have an enrollment office headed by a person whose task is to enroll members, provide enrollment cards, and check enrollment claims. Typically, a plastic identification card has the person's picture, vital statistics, official signature(s), name of tribe, and an assigned identification number on it. It is a card that resembles a driver's licence, and can gain entry to any Indian Health Service Hospital (there is one on the Winnebago Reservation) in the United States, where services and medicines are provided without charge. It is also used whenever a person has to prove his/her official status as a tribal member of a particular tribe.

Since 1986 the Winnebago Nation has had its own tribal court, and whenever new judges are appointed, the tribal authorities point with pride to the event (Anon., 1996). (Likewise, as a means to keep crime under control through the sanction of shame, the tribal newspaper, *Winnebago Indian News* publishes its "Weekly Conviction List" (e.g. Winnebago Tribal Court, 2000). More details will be provided regarding the development of the Tribal Court below as it plays a critical point in the analysis of the case to be examined. Like all reservations, the system of law and order on this reservation is also shored up by a police force, which happens to be under the aegis of the Bureau of Indian Affairs (BIA) so that the police officers are BIA employees. In turn, the BIA is a branch of the U.S. Department of the Interior that was founded in 1824 (originally the BIA was a part of the Department of the Army) (Taylor, 1984).

The following are the facts concerning the crimes, about which there is no dispute. Robert Lee Weaselhead, Jr., was an enrolled member of the Blackfeet Tribe living on the Winnebago Reservation. In February and March 1997, when he was 19 years of age, he had a girl friend fourteen years of age, a Winnebago tribal member. His involvement with her included sex. As this broke the Winnebago law, he was prosecuted in the Winnebago Tribal Court and confronted with the evidence of First Degree Sexual Assault, Child Abuse, and Contributing to the Delinquency of a Minor (Winnebago Tribal Court, 1997), he pleaded *nolo contendre* ("no contest"). During the discovery process before getting to this point, the prosecution found other acts that Weaselhead had engaged in that were prosecutorial. It was only because he was threatened by the prosecution that these latter charges were also to be added against the initial First Degree Sexual Assault, etc. charge, did he offer the no-contest plea. Thus, he entered into a plea agreement with the Winnebago Tribal Court that dismissed charges hanging over his head relating to "other acts" (Winnebago Tribal Court, 1997).

The Winnebago Tribal Court then sentenced him to 280 days in jail, of which 100 were suspended (*U.S.* v. *Weaselhead,* 1998: 818). On the very day that he entered into a plea agreement in the Winnebago Tribal Court, a federal grand jury indicted him and charged with Counts I, II, and III. His plea was "not guilty".

His defence team, Federal Public Defender, District of Nebraska, and Jennifer L. Gilg, Assistant Federal Public Defender, State of Nebraska (she did research and authored the briefs), made a motion for dismissal on the grounds of *double jeopardy*. Double jeopardy is a constitutionally expressed feature, that a person cannot be tried for the same offense twice. As succinctly stated by Burns (1978: 396):

> ...a defendant need not be charged with identical offenses before separate courts for double jeopardy to exist. Jeopardy [is also] ... where every element of one charge necessarily constitutes an element of the other.

This part is clear-cut. However, a murkier aspect emerges when the discussion of sovereigns appears. Thus, one of the fifty states of the U.S. might prosecute someone of a crime; if the crime in question violates the laws of the U.S., then the person can be charged with the same crime by federal authorities because the crime is "deemed as two separate offenses" (Burns, 1978: 396). In the case of Indian tribal courts, however, whether they are or are not a unique extension of the federal government becomes critical.

The appeal to dismiss was heard by the Magistrate Judge, who agreed with the defendant, concluding that [the] dual prosecution of the defendant by both the tribal court and now the federal government does not implicate separate prosecutions by separate sovereigns. Rather, the tribal court was exercising jurisdiction over the defendant, which flowed from a delegation of power from Congress and a subsequent prosecution by the federal government for the same offense is barred by the Fifth Amendment [the double jeopardy amendment to the Constitution of the United States] (*U.S.* v. *Weaselhead*, 1998: 820).

His thesis was that the tribal court was a creation of the U.S. Congress (technically speaking, the U.S. Congress, the legislative branch of government, is the only entity that can make laws affecting Indian tribes, and, by the same token, Congress is part and parcel of the federal government).

The federal prosecutors, whose headquarters are in Omaha (as are the offices of the federal public defenders) then appealed to the U.S. District Court (in the city of Omaha) presided over by Judge Thomas M. Shanahan. Shanahan overruled the Magistrate Judge's ruling (Shanahan, 1998), which was then appealed to the Eighth Circuit Court of Appeals in St. Louis to reverse it.

In both Judge Shanahan's ruling and in Gilg's appeal, references are made to previous cases in support of their respective positions.

One is *U.S.* v. *Wheeler*, a case that involved a Navaho, Robert Anthony Wheeler, who, on October 16, 1974, was arrested by Navaho police for disorderly conduct, based on his involvement with a juvenile female. He pleaded guilty two days later to both counts and was fined and jailed for each of the counts (disorderly conduct and contributing to the delinquency of a minor). A year later, he was indicted by federal prosecutors for the same crimes, and so asked the U.S. District Court of Arizona to dismiss the charges on grounds of double jeopardy. The latter concurred, thus, the prosecutors appealed to the Ninth Circuit Court of Appeals (San Francisco). This appeals court affirmed the District Court's decision. In 1977, the case ended up in the U.S. Supreme Court (Washington, D.C.) whose decision was unanimous: that the Ninth Circuit Court ruling was wrong because tribal courts and federal district courts were indeed separate entities (thus, Indian tribes were "sovereign") (Burns, 1978: 397-398, 400).

Quite understandably, both the prosecutors, in their appeal, and Judge Shanahan, in his ruling, cited *U.S.* v. *Wheeler* en *extenso* as it supported their respective positions (Monaghan & Norris 1997: 2, 12, 24, 25, 28, 29; Shanahan, 1998: 4a, 7a; passim). However, as Gilg has pointed out, the Weaselhead case differed substantially from Wheeler's because Weaselhead, being of the Blackfeet Tribe, was not a member of the Winnebago tribe, whereas Wheeler and his victim were both Navahos.

She relied upon the *Duro* v. *Reina* case, which was decided by the U.S. Supreme Court. At its heart the Court affirmed that "in criminal matters, a tribe's inherent sovereign powers extend only to tribe (sic) members" (*U.S.* v. *Weaselhead*, 1998: 822), irrespective of whether the non-member is an Indian, and that a tribe is dependent upon the U.S. government delegated by Congress (Gilg, 1998: 7; italics added). When this Supreme Court ruling came down, Congress became alarmed and amended the Indian Civil Rights Act of 1968 with language that would cover the gap; viz., that non-member Indians would also fall under a tribal court's jurisdiction.

These amendations, too, were cited by the prosecutors and the District Court judge to reinforce their stands. To counter this, Gilg made the following powerful point, after recognizing that Congress indeed tacked something onto to the Indian Civil Rights Act. That Congress through its amendments to the Indian Civil Rights Act delegated a new, federally created right to prosecute nonmember Indians. Accordingly, both the Winnebago tribal court's jurisdiction over Weaselhead and the federal court's power to prosecute him *emanate from the federal government*...therefore violates Double Jeopardy (Gilg, 1998: 7; italics added).

She then argued that Congress could not reinstate an inherent power that the U.S. Supreme Court — and here she cites the Court's decision in *the Duro* case, "necessarily surrendered by the tribes in their submission to the overriding sovereignty of the United States" (Gilg, 1998: 15).

There were other issues that were also argued, such as *implicit divestiture*, meaning the extent to which Indian tribes had acceded their powers to the federal government when they became dependent upon the United States through treaties — so too the concept of *federal common* law and its connection to congressional intent *vs.* constitutional principles (Gilg, 1998: 16; Monaghan & Norris, 1997; Shanahan, 1998). Although fascinating and cogently argued by Gilg to support her client, these issues need not detain us here inasmuch as the Court of Appeals ruled against Weasel, emphasizing that two sovereign entities were indeed involved and that there was no basis for a reversal based on double jeopardy. The defence team then put the case before the U.S. Supreme Court, but it refused to hear the case.

It is of some interest to note that soon after the *Weaselhead* case was decided, a somewhat similar case arose. With reference to *U.S.* v. *Enas*, the double jeopardy defence was also used. Michael J. Enas, an enrolled member of the San Carlos Apache Tribe on August 18, 1994, stabbed Joseph Kessay on land governed by the White Mountain Apache Tribe. He pleaded guilty to two violations of the White Mountain Apache Tribe's criminal code and was sentenced to 180 days in prison plus a fine of $1,180. Almost a year after the attack, on June 21, 1995, the federal grand jury indicted him for the same crimes (assault with a dangerous weapon and assault resulting in serious bodily injury). The District Court in Phoenix, Arizona, dismissed the indictment on the basis that he was being tried twice for the same crimes. The District Court's reasoning was that the power of the tribe to prosecute criminal deeds flowed from the U.S. Government rather than from "inherent tribal authority" (*U.S.* v. *Enas*, 2000: 917). Its position, then, was diametrically opposed to the District Court's position as occupied by Judge Shanahan in Omaha, Nebraska. The federal government appealed to the decision, and at the U.S. Ninth Circuit Court of Appeals in San Francisco, won. The appeals court's rationale was that the 1990 amendments to the Indian Civil Rights Law recognised "the sovereign power of Indian tribes to prosecute non-member Indians who commit crimes on tribal land, [accordingly,] the dual sovereignty doctrine applies in this case" (*U.S.* v. *Enas*, 2000: 920). Interestingly, it was also diametrically opposed to this same court's ruling in 1976 in the *Wheeler* case, which, it will be recalled, did find double jeopardy, even though the year 2000 court's ruling made reference to *U.S.* v. *Wheeler* in deciding the *Enas* case. Obviously its institutional memory was rather short.

It is also significant that in deciding the *Enas* case, the Ninth Circuit Court cited the Eighth Circuit Court's ruling in *U.S.* v. *Weaselhead* on several occasions to support its position (*U.S.* v. *Enas*, 2000: 918).

It is to be lamented that Weaselhead's defence team did not delineate the history of the Winnebago Tribal Court to buttress its position, that the court was indeed an arm of the federal government through Congress.

Prior to 1953, there was a hodge-podge of statuses that existed between the states and the tribes. In an attempt to bring about greater order, Congress passed Public Law (PL) 280. This statute transferred to five states — plus the Territory of Alaska — that were willing (one included Nebraska) to assume civil and criminal jurisdiction over Indian reservations. Quite understandably, tribes in these states (California, Minnesota, Oregon, and Washington), including Nebraska's, were leery because it was well known that states were less tolerant of Indians in their midst than was even the federal government.

Considering the absence of any significant investigation of the Indians' state of social development prior to the broad delegation of jurisdiction to every state by PL-280, it seems unlikely that Congress knew or cared about the Indians' readiness for state jurisdiction. Furthermore, it is difficult to reconcile this theme of advanced acculturation with the prevailing notion that state criminal jurisdiction was necessary because the Indians were disorderly and incapable of self-government. Most likely, civil jurisdiction was an afterthought in a measure aimed primarily at bringing law and order to the reservations, added because it comported with the pro-assimilationist drift of federal policy, and because it was convenient and cheap (Goldberg, 1974-75: 543-44).

By 1968, the chaotic conditions that PL-280 engendered moved Congress to incorporate in the Indian Civil Rights Act the retrocession feature so that the states that first willingly accepted control over criminal and civil cases could return back (i.e. retrocede) to the federal government their roles with the concomitant proviso that the tribes would take over criminal and civil matters on their reservations.[1]

The Omahas did not hesitate to retrocede so that the federal government gave to the Omaha Tribe of Nebraska jurisdiction over criminal and civil matters, with the result that it developed its own police force and tribal court. Primarily because of economic reasons, the Winnebagos did not retrocede until 1986 (Suzuki, 1991: 1-2). Consider the complexity of the situation regarding the application of Winnebago tribal law after retrocession by examining the table below (Samuelson, 1987).

NON-AUTO CASES

Offenders	*Victims*	*Jurisdiction*
1. Non-Indian	Non-Indian	State
2. Non-Indian	Indian	Federal for felonies: state and federal for misdemeanors
3. Non-Indian	Victimless	State
4. Indian	Indian	Federal and/or tribe
5. Indian	Non-Indian	Federal and/or tribe
6. Indian	Victimless	Federal and/or tribe

1. When Nebraska took over the judicial functions of its reservations, "..the reservations were left without any law enforcement at all.... The situation was so desperate that in 1957 [four years after the state had taken over], the governor of Nebraska flew to Washington to demand that the B.I.A. take back jurisdiction, something the Bureau was not authorised to do under PL-280" (Goldberg, 1974-75: 553; 553 fn91)

AUTO CASES

Offenders	*Victims*	*Jurisdiction*
1. Non-Indian	Indian	Federal for felony state and federal for misdemeanors
2. Non-Indian	Victimless	State
3. Non-Indian	Non-Indian	State
4. Indian	Non-Indian	Federal or tribe
5. Indian	Victimless	Tribe
6. Indian	Indian	Federal or tribe

Obviously this is predicated on the existence of a tribal court, and for the Winnebagos, this came into being in 1986 with retrocession. The major difference with the Omaha Tribe is that the latter have their own police force, unlike the BIA force on the Winnebago Reservation. From the above it is not clear that even the type of road can form another variable in the calculus; namely, whether accidents/incidents take place on a state, reservation, or BIA road (Suzuki, 1991: 4-8).

This brief digression into Winnebago tribal law is by way of pointing out that since 1986 the reservation has had a system that has been primarily in Indian hands, and the years since retrocession have not proved to be detrimental to the White population as it once feared when retrocession was being considered (Stern, 1986: 9-B). More importantly, in connection with the Weasel case, the history of PL-280 and retrocession — and the establishment of the Winnebago Tribal Court — shows the clear fingerprints of Congress. The defence's position that the Winnebago Tribal Court was a progeny of Congress, thus prosecution by it and by the federal authorities had emanated from one sovereign source (the U.S. Government), would have shown more convincingly the basis for double jeopardy. This is not to say that the federal prosecutors, Thomas J. Monagahn, U.S. Attorney for the District of Nebraska and his assistant Michel P. Norris, or Judge Shanahan would have been moved by this revelation to come to conclusions other than those they drew.

In support of the position just stated, consider the following. The plea-bargain agreement that the Winnebago Tribal Court and Weaselhead entered into was undertaken while "the United States Bureau of Indian Affairs was in contact with both the Winnebago tribal prosecutor and the United States Attorney's Office [i.e. Thomas Monaghan] throughout the investigation of the matter" (Gilg, 1998: 20). This meant little to

Monaghan to the degree that the plea agreement is made light of in his brief for appeal (Monaghan and Norris, 1997: 7).

As the plea bargain is one of the major and fundamental strategic tools to lubricate the legal and criminal justice system, it is not a small matter when, once entered into, one of the parties reneges or ignores it. When such a turnabout action takes place, it diminishes and tarnishes the officials and office they occupy. In the Weaselhead case, where there already is skepticism and mistrust about "White man's justice" among all Indians, the status of the Winnebago Tribal Court and the BIA could be severely damaged. There already is a sense of lassitude and cynicism concerning the BIA so the damage to its image among Winnebagos may not prove to be severe and desolating. However, for the relatively young and tender Winnebago Tribal Court and its occupants, to this observer, and probably to many Winnebagos, it is an entirely different matter. The Tribal Court can ill afford to have its status and image tarnished in any way, especially in light of the attempt to create a "true democracy" on the Winnebago Reservation resting on an established set of rules and laws.

An observation by David Stickman, the defense attorney, is apposite because it is highly revealing. The tribal court sentence should have been the end of the case, Stickman said, but the U.S. Attorney's Office *began a two-year battle to try Weaselhead in federal court* (Alexander, 2000: 15; italics added). Monaghan, a Clinton appointee via Janet Reno (head of the U.S. Department of Justice), is the same person who, in 1997, had the Nebraska State Patrol seize 53 slot machines just 5 miles from the Santee Sioux Reservation, Nebraska, as they made their way on a truck to the reservation casino, slot machines which had been shipped from New Mexico where they had been purchased. In 1996, he seized $87,194 from the same tribe's casino bank on the argument that the Santee Sioux were illegally operating a casino on their reservation. This latter seizure was undertaken in the face of the fact that there were numerous illegal gambling operations in Nebraska's bars and taverns (Dorr, 1997: 19). The seizure by the Nebraska State Patrol, on the other hand, was directly at variance with the tribe's sovereignty as a nation. Had there been any seizure at all, it should have been the federal authorities (e.g. the FBI) to undertake it.

As for the issue of sovereignty — surely the most critical one facing nearly all tribes across the United States — the Santee Sioux had requested the then-governor of Nebraska, Ben Nelson, a Democrat, to enter into a compact with the state in accordance with a critical feature of the 1989 Indian Gaming Regulatory Act passed by Congress. His steadfast refusal to meet with the Santee Sioux on this issue as a first step toward drawing up a compact to enable the reservation to have a casino because, among other reasons given by the governor, the Santee Sioux was not really a nation, was at the basis for the tribe's opening up the casino anyway (his successor, a Republican, has continued the same policy).

The governor's rationale was also one that was readily accepted by Monaghan in his seizures of Santee Sioux property and money. Parenthetically, as of this writing, through many court battles, the tribe was vindicated to the extent of the court allowing the casino to stay open but not expand its operation and the seized bank account being returned to the tribe, although the seized slot machines have yet to be released.

Monaghan's actions focused on the issue of sovereignty as raised by the Santee Sioux and their Indian supporters (but also the gaming lobby) across the nation. As concerns the Weaselhead case again, the supreme irony, quite obviously, was Monaghan's (and Shanahan's) forceful position that the Winnebago Tribe unarguably constituted a sovereign entity so that double jeopardy was out of the question.

In discussing *U.S.* v. *Wheeler*, Burns has brought out a searing observation made by the Ninth Circuit Court of Appeals in deciding another case with respect to Indians and their tribal courts:

> In spite of the theory that *for some purposes,* an Indian tribe is an independent sovereignty, we think that in light of their history, it is *pure fiction* to say that the Indian courts...are not in part, at least, arms of the federal government (Burns, 1978: 398; italics added).

Although this statement was expressed in 1970, the situation has not altered since then. The Weaselhead and Santee Sioux cases convincingly show that Monaghan's office *for some purposes* an Indian tribe in Nebraska is truly an independent sovereignty and for others, it is not. However, lest the reader assume that how public officials interpret sovereignty in Nebraska is unique, the history of Indian treatment by the courts and officials of other states shows how thoroughly embedded is the notion of sovereignty as an arbitrarily interpreted one, a concept subject to suit whatever situation arises for the benefit of the non-Indian officials.

Now it is a canon of anthropology that the researcher place actions in their proper context in order to arrive at a more meaningful interpretation. In examining Monaghan's actions, in particular his use of the Nebraska State Patrol instead of the FBI because according to his office, the Santee Sioux had violated the federal 1989 Indian Gaming Regulatory Act, light is shed on an aspect of a law enforcement agency that should be of concern to all Americans. As an integral part of the U.S. Department of Justice, Monaghan's actions make sense in so far as they were consistent with the disturbing slide toward arbitrary and intrusive actions by the Department of Justice ever since Clinton assumed office. The most dramatic and violent actions, of course, were the killings of a mother and baby at Ruby Ridge, Idaho, and the mass killing of some eighty individuals at Waco, Texas (in the latter, Reno justified the attack because there was "child abuse," which, it is important to point out, is not a federal crime. She later admitted that this had been just a rumour). Add to these some of the following: the illegal transfer of FBI files on over one hundred individuals to the White House; the illegal release of Internal Revenue Service tax records on certain Americans to the White House; the refusal of Reno to appoint a special prosecutor to investigate the president and vice-president's questionable roles in fund raising (as was strongly recommended by the head of the FBI to Janet Reno); the illegal release of confidential background information on Linda Tripp when she was a teenager in order to damage her reputation because she had taped evidence implicating Monica Lewinsky and Clinton; the illegal release of private letters written by Kathleen Willey in order to embarrass her because she had charged Clinton with sexual harassment, etc. Compounding these are the lies that Clinton has told to the American people (the most infamous one being the one on television, that he did not have sex "with that woman") including the bombing of a Sudanese pharmaceutical factory that purportedly was making poison chemicals but, in fact, was an attempt to divert attention away from the Lewinsky case when it was reaching its apex. The result has been the creation of a culture of government deception and deceit. A palpable fallout of what the Clinton administration has wrought has been mistrust and distrust of the government, and especially of the one department that was established to foster justice and equity before the law.

Sadly, what Monaghan's office has done, the seizures and the wanton disregard of the plea agreement, is in harmony with what has been outlined with regard to the what the Justice Department and the other departments of the Clinton administration have brazenly undertaken, to the detriment of all Americans.

Beyond the fact that Robert Lee Weaselhead lost in the courts, more troubling issues raised in the case have not been resolved by the courts and linger even through the *Enas* case. One is surely the elusive nature of sovereignty, a concept that has been applied by public officials not of the Indian nations to use as they see fit when it suits their purposes. Another, as aptly pointed out by Gilg is the failure of the courts to examine whether Congress' amendments permitting tribal criminal jurisdiction over nonmember Indians constitute a delegation of a new power rather than a reaffirmation of an inherent power, and transform the prosecuting tribal court into an arm of the federal government. The language and history of Duro indicate that the answer to this question is "yes" (Gilg, 1998: 21).

As in a standard anthropological approach, by drawing a cultural framework around the Weaselhead case, with Monaghan and the present decadent Department of Justice under a tainted U.S. president in the centre, the questionable practices of Monaghan can be better apprehended, but certainly not better appreciated.

In the fall of 1997 with much fanfare, the Department of Justice made public a final report by the Executive Committee for Indian Country Law Enforcement Improvements that dwelt on the alarming rise in crime on Indian reservations (Executive Committee, 1997; Anon, 1997a, 1997c). Statistical data were supplemented to prove this point, one that could not be argued away (Greenfield, 1999). While the situation on reservations is starkly true, this paper takes the position that decisions such as evinced in the *Weaselhead* and *Enas* cases are the basis for engendering disorder on the reservations (in the title of this paper, the Omaha Reservation, because it is a neighbouring reservation to the Winnebagos' is used as a symbol for all the other reservations in the U.S. Also, it is on the Omaha Reservation that Weaselhead would have been jailed because the Winnebago Reservation has no jail, had the tribal court prevailed). Because of such rulings, Indians do truly face double jeopardy. Given its criminal code, the tribal courts will have to prosecute Indians, members or non-members, for crimes; it then follows that the federal authorities will simultaneously or later indict and prosecute Indians for the identical crimes. In this kind of scenario, it might be that tribal courts would have to stop adjudicating criminal cases in order to obviate Indians from suffering from two courts for the same crimes. In the *Weaselhead* case, the prestige and status of a theretofore solid institution, the tribal court, has been severely damaged and will be further weakened. In this fashion, the very federal government agency that is supposed to guarantee law and order on the reservations will generate law and disorder. In this era, this situation is but a true reflection of the tragic state of the Department of Justice and the present administration in Washington, D.C. which views with contempt laws and rules they dislike, and whose values have seeped down into the U.S. Attorney's office in Omaha, Nebraska.

Finally, some years ago, an astute analyst of the legal system in Indian Country described the system as a "maze," an appropriate metaphor that was picked up some years later by another scholar on the same subject (Clinton, 1976; Vetter, 1992). Given events that have come to pass since 1992, perhaps a more apposite term would be "mess".

ACKNOWLEDGMENTS

I thank Jennifer Gilg for giving me copies of relevant documents used in this paper. I also thank the following persons on the Winnebago and Omaha Reservations who, over the years, enlightened me about tribal law and the court system (all were either former tribal court judges, prosecutors, or public defenders): J. Balille, R. Bossman, K. Cleary, D. Leblanc (nee Blackbird), T. Mathis, R. Smith, and E. Zendehas.

REFERENCES

Alexander, D. 2000. "Winnebago Man Gets Second Term," *Omaha World-Herald*, Feb. 26, p. 15.

Anon. 1996. "Winnebago Supreme Court Sworn In," *Winnebago Indian News*, December 7, p. 4.

Anon. 1997a. "[President] Clinton: Policing Poor on Indian Reservations," *Omaha World-Herald*, August 29, p.3 (evening ed.).

Anon. 1997b. "American Indian Population Growing in Thurston County," *Omaha World-Herald*, November 10, p. 14 (morning ed.).

Anon. 1997c. "Police on Reservations Fight Losing Battle Against Crime," *Omaha World-Herald*, November 30, p. 20-A.

Burns, L.A. 1978. "Criminal Jurisdiction: Double Jeopardy in Indian Country," *American Indian Law Review*, 6: 395-402.

Clinton, R.N. 1976. "Criminal Jurisdiction Over Indian Land: A Journey Down a Jurisdictional Maze," *Arizona Law Review*, 18: 503-583.

Dorr, R. 1997. "Santee Say Police Seized Slot Machines on Way to Casino," *Omaha World-Herald*, November 25, p. 19 (evening ed.).

Executive Committee. 1997. "Final Report on Indian Country Law Enforcement Improvement," U.S. Department of Justice. Typescript.

Gilg, J.L. 1999. "U.S. Appellee vs. Robert Weaselhead, Appellant," Omaha, Nebraska. Typescript.

Goldberg, C.E. 1974-75. "Public Law 280: The Limits of State Jurisdiction Over Reservation Indians," *UCLA Law Review*, 22: 535-594.

Greenfield, L.A. 1999. "American Indians and Crime," U.S. Department of Justice. Typescript.

Monaghan, T.J. & M.P. Norris. 1997. "U.S. v. Weaselhead: Brief of Appellee," Omaha, Nebraska. Typescript.

Samuelson, M. 1987. "The Winnebagos after Retrocession: A Chart." Pender, Nebraska. Typescript.

Shanahan, T.M. 1998. U.S. Plaintiff vs. Robert L. Weaselhead," Omaha, Nebraska. Typescript.

Stern, G. 1986. "Argument Heard for and Against Separate Indian Law Enforcement," *Omaha World-Herald*, January 5, p. 5-B.

Suzuki, P., 1991. "Retrocession and Jurisdictional Issues Facing the Omaha Tribe of Nebraska," *Man and Life*, 18 (1 & 2): 1-10.

____. 1999. "The Rebirth of a Nation: The Winnebago Tribe of Nebraska and Managed Ethnicity," (pp. 71-82) in D.K.Behera and Georg Pfeffer (eds.), *Contemporary Society: Tribal Studies*. New Delhi: Concept Publishing Company

Taylor, T.W. 1984. *The Bureau of Indian Affairs*. Boulder: Westview Press.

U.S. v. Weaselhead. 1998. *Federal Reporter*, 3rd Session, 156: 818-825.

U.S. v. Enas. 2000. *Federal Reporter*, 3rd Session, 204: 915-920.

Vetter, W.V. 1992. "A New Corridor for the Maze: Tribal Criminal Jurisdiction and Nonmember Indians," *American Indian Law Review*, 17: 349-457.

Winnebago Tribal Court. 1997. "Winnebago Tribe of Nebraska v. Robert Weaselhead, Jr., Case CR 97-193," Winnebago, Nebraska. Typescript.

____. 2000. "Weekly Conviction List," *Winnebago Indian News*, May 13, p. 14.

SIXTEEN

TRIBAL PEOPLE OF MEXICO

ULRICH KÖHLER

Indigenous Groups and Tribes within the National Context

Mexico was conquered by Spanish troops in 1521 and remained a colony until 1821. Within these three hundred years, many Europeans emigrated to the big middle American country also known as "New Spain" during that time. Today the indigenous population amounts to about 10 per cent of the total number of inhabitants.

These groups differ from the Spanish-speaking majority. Nevertheless they cannot, as whole, be considered tribal. The difference between them and ordinary Mexicans is not due to their physical appearance,[1] but primarily due to their linguistic and cultural affiliation. By law, all Mexicans are supposed to be equal. No particular legal regulations discriminate the indigenous population. Members of the latter may pass over to the demographic mainstream in case they learn to converse in Spanish and adopt the cultural ways of the majority. With regard to their outward appearance, the Spanish-speaking majority is rather heterogenic. About 65 per cent are Mestizos, descendents of Indios and Europeans, about 25 per cent have the appearance of Indios[2] and only about 10 per

1. The indigenous people of Mexico are of medium height, have brown skin, black straight hair and black eyes frequently characterised by the mongol lid. Most of their distant forefathers migrated to America from Asia about twelve thousand years ago, passing through the area of the Bering Strait which now separates Siberia from Alaska. At that time, however, a land bridge existed between the two continents.

cent look like Europeans. The first category, defined culturally and linguistically, is called "Ladino" in Guatemala and southern Mexico. For the sake of convenience, the term is used in the following article for Mexico as a whole.[3] Before entering into details of the ethnic and social composure of Mexico, a few geographical characteristics should be clarified.

Very similar to India, most of Mexico is situated between the 30th and 15th degree of latitude. Like India, Mexico is also a sea-bound country, i.e. sea shores are the borders of the country in the east, the west and the south. As a result rainfall in the form of monsoon and other regular winds, crossing the country from the sea, are quite comparable. As for the morphology of the country, however, one important difference can be registered. While India — in spite of the Eastern and Western Ghats and the Deccan plateau — is characterised by a moderate altitude, plateaus of great altitude and enormous mountain ranges dominate the topography of Mexico. The high plateaus around Mexico City and of Puebla have an altitude of more than 2,000 m and the chains of peaks of the long mountain ranges of the eastern and western Sierra Madre average between 2,500 and 3,000 m. The proximity of highland areas, lowland valleys and coastal plains is ideal for commercial interchange and has shaped much of the cultural history of Mexico, because the different soils and climates allow typical crops for each eco-type.

According to census data of the year of 2000, Mexico has 97 million inhabitants (*La Jornada*, 21-6-2000). The 10 per cent of indigenous population hence amount to about 10 million people. In spite of the continuous absorption of Indios into the group of Ladinos this ratio has not changed over the last five decades. The level remains constant mainly due to the fact that the increase in population is higher than the national average among the Indios.

Within the territory of Mexico the settlements of the indigenous population are not equally distributed. About 85 per cent of the Indios live in the central and southern Mexican states, of Veracruz, Puebla,

2. This term is employed here for the sake of convenience only. The English translation being "Indian", it might cause confusion, especially in an article addressed primarily to readers in India. In Mexico the term "Indio" has at times a derogative connotation and should be used with caution. On the other hand some indigenous leaders of Mexico use it with pride and I may thus be pardoned for employing it here.
3. Renowned Mexican social scientists have already employed it this manner.

Hidalgo, México, Guerrero, Oaxaca, Chiapas, Tabasco, Campeche, Quintana Roo and Yucatán. The percentage of the Indios within the total population of any of these provinces varies considerably. While it is close to 50 per cent in Yucatán and Oaxaca, it amounts to about 25 per cent in Chiapas and Hidalgo and is less than 10 per cent in Tabasco. Thus the demographic distribution within the country shows the Indios of today principally living in the regions where the pre-Columbian civilisations[4] had flourished. The largely arid north of Mexico had at that time only been sparsely settled. Only few remnants of the indigenous population are therefore encountered in the northern regions. Within the main settlement area of the Indios in central and southern Mexico, one important change since the advent of the Spaniards has occurred: Having been the masters of the whole country in pre-colonial times, the Indios lost most of the land in the fertile plains to the invaders. Today they are mostly met on land in the less advantageous mountain region. The former inhabitants of the valleys and high plateaus were either expelled and or assimilated to the Spanish-speaking society of Ladinos.

Within the Indio population of Mexico the linguistic diversity is considerable. Depending upon the particular definition, some 40 to 60 indigenous languages are spoken belonging to several different linguistic families. Nahuatl, the language of the ancient Aztec and spoken by about two million individuals, is the tongue most widely spread. The second position is taken by the Maya of Yucatan, the language of about 800,000 inhabitants of the peninsula of Yucatan. With regard to their demographic basis Zapoteco, Mixteco, Otomí, Totonaco, Tzeltal and Tzotzil are also of considerable importance. Some 350,000 and 600,000 speakers of these languages can be counted. These rather impressive numbers indicate that at least some of the indigenous languages of Mexico are not yet threatened by extinction.

An outside observer could imagine the fairly large linguistic units to stand for groups of common interests exercising some political influence. This, however, is not the case. The speakers of these languages, for the most part, are nowhere near a common political organisation. Furthermore, several of these languages are not spoken within a specific territory but spread over a large area, resembling smaller or larger islands within a sea of Spanish-speaking Mexicans. Such a situation is

4. Before Christopher Columbus arrived in America in 1492, the middle American states had maintained a very high administrative and scientific standard.

typical for Nahuatl in particular. Joint action for political purposes is further impeded by the fact that, within a common linguistic area, popular identity and political representation is associated with the particular locality, usually the municipio,[5] and not to the totality of the speakers of the particular language.

Regarding the type of environment and settlement, most Indios favour a particular kind. Mexico, like India, is a country of modern industrialised cities, provincial towns, agrarian villages, and dispersed hamlets. While Indios can also be found in the national Capital or in provincial towns, their typical type of settlement is the village or the hamlet. Distinguishing between town and countryside — or the corresponding gradual shift of cultural affiliation — Robert Redfield has differentiated urban and folkways of life, connecting the latter to the concept of the peasant. Apart from this dichotomy, Redfield (1941) added a third category, called "tribal," in his classic book on the peninsula of Yucatan. By this definition, people classified as "tribal" may also entertain economic relations with towns, but in contrast to peasants, they do not share a feeling of belonging with the urban people. They consider themselves as a separate ethnic group. This tribal-peasant-urban model of Redfield has proved to be a useful classification beyond Mexico and it has also been adopted by anthropologists of India. The distinction between, on the one hand, Spanish-speaking peasants, conceiving themselves as Mexicans, and, on the other hand, indigenous cultivators without a habitual reference to the larger whole, is indeed of major significance in this middle American country.[6] Tribal Indios typically associate the term Mexico only with the Capital, to a lesser extent with the territory of the republic, and least of all with the nation.

Not all speakers of indigenous languages can be termed tribal in Mexico. Those living in cities or towns have largely cut off the ties to their original villages. Their children are usually assimilated into the group of Ladinos. Indios living as a minority in small towns or villages of Ladinos are not under the same pressure of assimilation, but they do not have a strong identity of their own or an organisational set-up providing them with a tribal definition of the own group. They are simply a culturally and linguistically different minority within the world of the Ladinos. Typically an indigenous tribe of Mexico consists of a

5. This is the smallest official territorial unit in Mexico, comparable to a tehsil in India.
6. Legally the tribal people have the same rights as all Mexicans.

cluster of villages inhabited only or mostly by Indios. The common political and religious organisation of these inhabitants is designed for the worship of a local patron deity. Furthermore, a particular dress and a specific dialect of the respective language serve as distinctive traits. The language group of the Tzotzil in Chiapas, for example, is subdivided into about 20 of such tribes. The fact that almost all of them locate the navel of the world within their respective territory underlines the feeling of cohesion within the own tribe and distinction with regard to the others.

Within those societies of Indios which may be called tribal a further distinction seems to be useful. In the north of Mexico, or the region without pre-Columbian civilisations, tribal Indios of today also have a tribal social background. A typical example is the Tarahumara in Chihuahua. They and other ethnic groups like the Yaqui, Mayo, and Seri are not considered to be part of the cultural area of Mesoamerica (see below), but to belong to that of the Greater Southwest, which includes several ethnic groups of the USA like the Pueblo, Navaho, and Apache. On the other hand, most of the forefathers of present-day tribal Indios in central and southern Mexico had not been tribesmen at the advent of the European colonial power. These ancestors had rather been peasants, oriented towards the urban centres of the pre-Columbian civilisations. Their descendants were tribalised in the course of the colonial regime.

The transformation of the peasants of central and southern Mexico into tribal groups was due to the destruction of the former indigenous urban centres by the Spaniards. Since that time a foreign culture, introduced from Spain, has been dominating such centres for almost 500 years. Nowadays Spanish-speaking peasants of the countryside are linked to the towns by language and culture. The former indigenous peasants have been marginalised and relegated to a tribal status.

Historical and Cultural Background

To understand the cultural background of the Indios, it will be necessary to give a brief outline of the cultural history of Mesoamerica (cf. Wolf, 1959), the cultural area where the pre-Columbian civilisations of Middle America flourished. Geographically it comprises central and southern Mexico, all of the countries Belize and Guatemala, and the western parts of Honduras and El Salvador. In pre-classic times, the first complex civilisation emerging was that of the Olmec. It flourished between 1000 and 500 BC. The classic period (200-900) was dominated by three different cultures: Teotihuacan in central Mexico, Monte Alban in Oaxaca, and the Maya in the southeast. During the post-classic period there have been a number of different nations with special cultural centres of which the Aztec are the most famous, because they were politically predominant at the time of the European conquest in 1521.

As distinctive traits of these pre-Spanish civilisations a monumental architecture can be mentioned, such as pyramids, palaces, temples, and courts for ball games. Moreover calendars and a script, an advanced educational system, and a stratified society with a proper public administration mark the development of these empires. The Maya of the classic period (300-900 AD) deserve special mention, because, judged at a worldwide level, they had reached the highest standard in the fields of mathematics and astronomy (cf. Sharer 1994), ahead of the counterparts in China, India, and Europe. Some outstanding achievements are the invention of the zero and a meticulous calculation of the duration of the year, improved only by modern technical devices of the twentieth century.

Traditions derived from the pre-Columbian civilisations are conspicuous in the fields of arithmetic and the native calendar. They possess a rich mythology and an extensive oral literature in general. The old Mesoamerican vigesimal system of counting[7] has been preserved among most indigenous people. Some illiterate Indios have no problems in handling multiples of four hundred and eight thousand.

The old calendar — dividing the year into 18 periods of 20 days and 5 additional days — is still widely used. As an indicator of the planting season and the regulation of the annual cycle of festivals, it remains indispensable. In recent years, under the influence of formal education in schools, this calendar is gradually substituted by the European calendar, however, normally used at the national level. Of the ancient divinatory calendar of 260 days few traces are left in Mexico, but it is still widely employed by Maya-Indios in the highlands of neighbouring Guatemala.

Apart from the mythology and the narration of stories and historical events, the oral literature is conspicuously present in prayers and orations of the Indios, when communicating with the deities.[8] In a transcribed

7. The number twenty is the basic unit of the system.
8. These principally aim at securing good crops and ensuring the health of the members of the community.

written form[9] such texts often amount to 50 pages or more. They are admirable for their wealth of metaphors, stylistic nuances, and aesthetical diversity.

Such cultural traits are usually absent in Ladino peasant communities of similar economic status. We have to conclude accordingly that traditional tribal Indios generally have a richer and more sophisticated intellectual life than their Spanish-speaking counterparts. The high cultural level does not, however, exist among all communities of Indios in Mexico. It is encountered mostly in those villages, which have been able to preserve at least some kind of autonomy as well as their own social institutions throughout history since the 16th century.

The opposite picture is offered from the 17th century onward by the enslaved communities. The Spaniards had established haciendas, or large plantations, on which Indios had to work as landless labourers under the conditions amounting to serfdom. Their personal rights were extremely restricted. In the wake of the Mexican Revolution of 1910-17, most of these haciendas have been broken up by the government from the 1930s onward. The landholdings were divided and granted to the former labourers who have now formed villages of their own on the lands of their former masters. In some areas of Mexico, the inhabitants of these new agricultural settlements speak only Spanish, in others they have preserved their native language. But the conditions, suffered by their forefathers on the plantations for centuries, have resulted in a process of deculturation, a loss of cultural knowledge. Thus communities of this type, in spite of the fact that their members still speak a native language, can hardly be qualified as "tribal". Within the whole social context of Mexico, they rather represent some kind of marginalised peasants. Their living conditions resemble those of poor rural Ladinos, but their relations to the urban centres and the national social network are weaker because of the language barrier.

Life-style among Indigenous Mexican Tribes

A typical tribal unit in Mexico consists of a municipio, a kind of tehsil inhabited by Indios sharing the same language and culture. Such a municipio consists of a head village, distinguished by the location of the civil and religious organisations, and the surrounding minor villages

9. Effected by anthropologists.

and hamlets. The demographic size of a municipio varies from 2,500 to 50,000 individuals. Almost no feeling of commonality or identity is extended to the inhabitants of adjacent municipios of Indios, sharing the same language and culture. The unit of identification is clearly the own municipio with such characteristic features as an own patron deity, a particular dress, and independent civil and religious institutions. In areas of Mexico, predominantly inhabited by Indios, it can therefore be concluded that the tehsil or municipio typically defines the individual tribe.[10]

In the economic field most tribes of Mexican Indios dedicate themselves to subsistence agriculture, supplemented by certain cash crops. Most prominent staple foods are maize (*Zea mays*), beans (*Phaseolus vulgaris*), squash (kinds of pumpkin), cultivated and wild vegetables, and different kinds of chilli-peppers (*Capsicum annuum*). All these plants originated in the New World and were domesticated by the forefathers of the Indios in pre-Columbian times.[11] In addition to cultivation, usually a few hens, turkeys and pigs are held.[12] In most areas of Mexico cattle is rare in villages of Indios, but some families may raise one or more young bulls, bought from Ladinos, and later again to be sold to the same group. In arid areas with soils poorly suited for agriculture, goats are frequent, and in some cold highland zones sheep are bred, with the principal aim of "harvesting" their wool.

The types of cash crops vary according to the respective altitude. Most of them are raised for regional and national markets but some are even sold abroad. On the regional scene, an exchange between towns and villages (utensils against foodstuff) as well as between different altitudes is typical. Thus bananas and other tropical fruit are sent to the highlands and from there wheat, potatoes, and fruit of European origin (apples, pears) returned to the lowlands. The most important cash crop to be sold overseas is coffee. While rendering high profits at times of high prices, the cultivation is a risky affair, because of the fluctuation of the international coffee price at the principal market in New York.

---

10. There are a few examples of large municipios containing several tribes. These, however, are granted a degree of autonomy on their own.
11. It may seem hard to imagine, that chili-peppers, so prominent in South Asia food for centuries, were non-existent in India before the European discovery of the American continent.
12. Although Mexican Indios are fond of meat, these animals are mostly sold, because they offer an easy cash income, required for the purchase of tools, flashlights, radio-recorders and batteries to keep them working.

The direct effect is noticeable even in remote mountain villages of Mexico (Early 1982) or any other coffee growing country.

Where the production of subsistence goods and cash crops does not meet the necessities of a household, members of tribal villages (mostly men) look for an outside income like other rural people of Mexico. Some of them find temporary jobs on plantations, others in construction work of nearby towns, and still others venture to work as vagrant labourers in the USA. Although the illegal crossing of the frontier is a risky affair, the much higher wages to the north of the border make it an attractive alternative. Among tribal Indios of Mexico those of the centre of the county have been involved in this kind of far-distance migration for decades, but those from the further away in the south-east seem to be catching up.[13]

Regarding the social organisation of the Indios the nuclear family is most frequent. Descent is reckoned bilaterally, although a certain preference is given to the male line, i.e. land is usually passed on to sons only. Marriage is contacted formally after several petitions, the groom having to pay a bridewealth which varies in content and amount from area to area. The residence of a new couple is mostly viri-patrilocal or neolocal. Among many tribal Indios of Mexico, the young husband customarily spends about a year after the wedding with his wife in the house of her parents, working for his father-in-law.[14]

In the field of religion, varying forms of syncretism between Roman Catholicism and traditional Mesoamerican religions are typical. It is important to point out that the present religions of tribal Indios of Mexico are not just a blend of the two sources mentioned, but many new ideas and rites have been created by these Indios in the course of almost five centuries. Strongly reminiscent of the pre-Columbian pantheon are the powerful female earth goddess although in some places the Christian devil has also entered her realm. The mountain gods are responsible for rain and thus the life-givers for agriculture. The mountain gods often have a female counterpart, the goddesses of springs and rivers.[15]

---

13. From there it takes about three days by bus to reach the border of the US.
14. This custom of temporary residence of the husband in the house of the parents of his young wife seems to have proven advantageous in several ways. The young man has a possibility to learn the special knowledge of his father-in-law or of the family of his wife, and her parents have a chance to watch his manners - not the least towards his wife - and to give him further education, if necessary.
15. This is very similar to the Aztec concepts of Tlaloc and Chalchiuhtlicue.

On the other hand, a strong Christian influence is evident in the case of the santo, wooden statues in the church or on domestic altars. The church in the capital village of a municipio usually houses at least one dozen of these santos. Their names are invariably derived from those of Catholic saints, but in contrast to that Christian theological concept, they are mostly considered deities of their own right by the Indios who worship them.[16]

While the earth goddess and mountain gods on one side and the santo on the other have undergone changes, but have not fused with aspects of the other religion involved, this has happened in some other cases. Most prominent are the sun god, now associated with Jesus Christ, and the moon goddess linked to his mother Mary. The fusion of the latter two was facilitated by the fact that Mary is frequently associated with the moon in Spain and other parts of southern Europe.

The fiesta cycle, the round of religious festivals, is almost exclusively directed to the santo in the church. Its foundations were laid in the 16th century by the Spanish clergy, but in the course of time alterations have been introduced varying from one community to the next. The only other widespread kind of rite among Indios of Mexico are offerings to mountain gods and other deities considered responsible for the sending of rain.

With regard to the concept of souls, two principal forms can be distinguished among tribal Indios of Mexico: an internal soul living in the body and leaving it at death, and an external soul, or an intimate relationship with one or more animals or natural phenomena. This relationship has the quality of an Alter Ego, meaning that both have a parallel life. Most dramatically this becomes evident at the moment of death, because if one of the two Egos dies, the other perishes as well. The animals serving as Alter Ego mostly belong to the predatory species of the wilderness (jaguar, puma, fox, weasel, eagle, hawk, owl, snake), but in the process of acculturation some domesticated animals (cat, dog, goat) have entered their realm as well. While the relationship between person and Alter Ego is normally limited to a parallel evolution of their respective lives, some individuals can act at their will in the guise of their Alter Ego(s). In these cases the latter are termed "Nagual". They

16. The degree to which the official Catholic point of view is accepted largely depends on the continuous presence of a priest in the village (which is rarely the case) and his capability to convince his audience.

may be used by curers to heal a patient, but also by witches to do harm to other people. The attitude towards the power derived from Naguals is therefore ambivalent.

The soul which normally is located within the body may leave it under certain circumstances, e.g. during a dream. At such a time of travelling the soul will be in danger.

In the worst case, the soul, on being frightened, may be lost, or it may be robbed by malignant forces. As a matter of fact, the finding of souls and their restitution into the body of the respective patient is the primordial office of indigenous curers in Mexico. This is effected in a curing ceremony, during which as many deities as possible are asked to co-operate. Although they deal with the finding and liberation of souls, these curers are no shamans, because they do not send out their own soul in order to find that of the patient. They, on the contrary, contract gods to perform that task for them.

No uniform picture can be presented regarding the ideas on life after death. Although Christian ideas of heaven and hell have had some impact, the widespread expectation of a limited duration in either place is more common. This is especially the case among those Indios who believe in a reincarnation of the soul after the same number of years the person has lived on earth. Such a reincarnation is, however, not confined to a particular individual. What survives is only a kind of force of life. In fact the soul of a man will be reincarnated in the body of woman or that of an Indio in the body of a Ladino according to a widespread belief.

For quite some time Protestant missionaries hailing from the USA have tried to convert members of indigenous tribes of Mexico. Over many decades their success was insignificant, but since the mid-seventies they could get a foothold in a number of communities. The result has been frequent intra-communal strife in addition to considerable cultural loss. These incursions from northern America are all the more problematic, since several rivalling Protestant sects make it a policy to enter a single community at a time, dividing its members along several lines by creating dissent. The success of these more recent missionaries was partly due to their efficient use of modern means of communication. Knowing that most houses contain a radio-recorder, they have made their songs and their indoctrination available on tapes at a low price. Compared to the delegation of more missionaries and their families in the past, the production of such materials has undoubtedly been much cheaper for the particular North American sects of activists.

Local government within a tehsil or municipio is officially headed by a "presidente municipal," a kind of mayor, and several other hierarchically ordered civil offices. In communities of Mexican tribal Indios an additional hierarchy of offices is dedicated to the cult of the santo in the church. In a great number of cases these two administrations have fused and form a common hierarchy of offices. Typically a man enters this system by taking a low office on one of the two sides, and then moves up in his career alternating between civil and religious offices. Until recently, the service has always been without remuneration,[17] and the holders of higher offices must bear considerable costs in addition, especially those, who have to finance major religious feasts. As a compensation for this economic loss, however, they gain social prestige. The process involved is thus similar to that of "feasts of merit".[18]

Interpreting this hierarchy of ascending prestige has been a matter of anthropological controversy. For a long time it was held that the system ensured economic equality, i.e. that no member of the community could ascend economically much higher than the rest, because any surplus was consumed by the expenses of the feasts. This point of view was challenged by Cancian (1965) who, in the community he had studied, had found out that members of well-to-do families mostly took over the offices of the highest expenses. This was an important observation, but it did not completely invalidate the other interpretation. One could argue on solid grounds that the better economic position of some families would have grown out of dimension,[19] if some of the accumulated wealth were not periodically consumed by organising and financing the religious feasts.

With their well-organised community organisation, prevailing endogamy and seemingly strong group-solidarity such communities have been characterised by Eric Wolf (1957) as "closed corporate communities". This picture would seem to be quite appealing and may be correct in some cases. But in many others the contacts with the outside world and their influences on village affairs are greater than

17. In some Mexican states office-holders now receive a moderate remuneration.
18. In India those of the Naga are especially famous and well documented, but similar 'feasts of merit' are known everywhere in the peasant and tribal population.
19. In these communities envy is a widespread phenomenon. It is fostered by a basic mental concept termed the Image of Limited Good by George Foster (1965). Since things desired in life are conceived to exist only in finite quantity, logically the advantage of one person must be to the disadvantage of others. Consequently, such "unsocial" behaviour leads to envy, criticism and even social sanctions.

assumed in this ideal type of concept.

Contacts to the Outside World and Interethnic Relations

Relations to the outside world are principally confined to the economic sphere, be they to market towns in the surroundings, to regular markets in nearby villages of other Indios or of rural Ladinos, or to the coming of itinerant merchants who buy products at the house of the producer.

The most important impact from the outside has been the establishment of government schools which have gradually been reaching even remote mountain villages during the last decades. Although the teachers are not well prepared for their job, and although they usually work only few days a week, the schools are a major impact tending to undermine the existing tribal structures and to weaken local identities. Although there have been several attempts to teach in the indigenous languages — at least during the first classes of primary school — most of the teaching is actually done in Spanish. This corresponds with the tacit intention of the Mexican government to establish Spanish on the long run as the only language of the country.

Medical centres of the government, usually without a resident doctor, are now also present in many tribal villages of Indios. Although mostly of poor quality, these medical centres have after all contributed to the enormous demographic increase of the last decades.

Official connections with state agencies are principally in the field of the administration of justice, because cases of homicide and grave personal injury have to be transferred to the Mexican authorities. The various elections on state and national level, in which the Indios are entitled to participate, have only been a weak tie between them and the national scene. Only since a few years, this voting is done in some places in a conspicuous and deliberate way, so that a voter could choose a particular candidate or party. Until recently, however, this task was frequently executed by the scribes of the municipal administration with the aim to please higher government officers.

Regarding interethnic relations between Indios and Ladinos, the former are usually in an inferior position. Broadly speaking, at the time of independence from Spain in 1821, the Ladinos inherited the dominant role from the Spaniards. This type of interethnic relations has been recognised in the middle of the twentieth century by Mexican social scientists, who have keyed the term "internal colonialism" to characterise the attitude of the dominant Spanish-speaking society towards the indigenous population living in the same country. Invariably, Ladinos feel themselves superior to Indios and they try to draw economic advantages from all forms of interaction with them (Köhler, 1980). Indios do indeed mostly appear timid or even submissive when appearing in towns of Ladinos, but this does not necessarily mean that their self-esteem has been broken. In their own villages they appear more confident, and in a few cases they have begun to dictate conditions of behaviour to itinerant Ladino traders of the local market. With regard to self-esteem among Indios and their opinion about Ladinos no general picture can be drawn. While some groups of Indios seem to have internalised the low social status ascribed to them for centuries, others have not lost their pride. For example the Tzotzil and Tzeltal in the state of Chiapas consider only themselves as batz'i(l) vinik, "real people," only their respective languages are regarded as real languages, and their superior position in relation to that of Ladinos is underlined in creation myths. According to one version, the forefathers of the Indios were made of honest clay while those of the Ladinos of horse excrements. Another myth defines today's Ladinos as the offspring of Ladino-women and dogs. Their "brutish and uncultured" manners are regarded as a proof for this type of ancestry.

Recent Developments

One of the aims of the Mexican Revolution of 1910-17 was to improve the economic and social situation of the Indios. It took decades, however, until the first serious steps into that direction were undertaken. During the twenties cultural missions were sent into villages to promote at least superficial literacy and other kinds of skills. A real start was achieved in the late thirties by the implementation of a land reform resulting in the donation of agricultural plots to landless Indios and Ladinos. In 1948 the Instituto Nacional Indigenista (INI), the National Institute of Indigenous Affairs, was founded. Initiating a regional development project, work began in the highlands of Chiapas (Köhler, 1968). Since then it has created about one hundred similar institutions. Originally this kind of intervention was conceived as an integrated development programme covering the fields of schooling, economic welfare, health programmes and judicial assistance. In the course of time the educational programmes have, however, come to dominate the scheme with the effect that today government schools have been erected in almost every village inhabited by Indios. As a result of this policy, their social position has considerably improved during the last decades. While still looked down upon by Ladinos, extreme forms of abuse — like robberies on the way to the market — no longer occur. Growing bilingualism among the Indios of today is enabling them to operate more efficiently when having to settle affairs in town.

Amazingly national and even regional associations for the defence of common interests of Mexican Indios have come to be created relatively late (Köhler, 1995). Initial attempts in that direction were not sponsored by Indios themselves, but came from outside institutions. In 1974 the Catholic Church organised the first indigenous congress, and a year later, the national government instituted tribal councils for the different indigenous groups. These councils and their spokesmen are expected to serve as a centre of communication between government and the various indigenous ethnic groups.

In 1979 a national federation of indigenous associations was founded, the Coordinadora Nacional Plan Ayala (CNPA), and now dozens of regional associations have come into life. In 1994 the uprising of the Ejercito Zapatista de Liberación Nacional (EZLN), named after the famous revolutionary leader Emiliano Zapata, has received much public attention all over the world.[20] After eleven days of war, the rebels retreated into the jungle of eastern Chiapas and have, since then, kept a kind of armistice with government troops. The rebels postulated several changes in national policy and demanded the improvement of social and economic conditions of the indigenous people of Mexico, especially the donation of land. The uprising in effect caused many changes in the political scene at the national level. Further democratisation and clean elections were implemented, but on the other hand, it has aggravated the situation of the Indios in Chiapas. For ideological reasons, further distribution of land for the benefit of Indios was postulated, ignoring the fact, that in the Indio inhabited area of Chiapas, all land formerly held by Ladinos had already been passed over to these Indios. Following the slogan of the EZLN, its sympathisers now turn against their own tribesmen, trying to expel those who own a little more than the average. In some municipios this has already lead to a situation of

20. This movement is usually described as an uprising of Indios. They do indeed constitute the majority of the followers, but Marcos, the principal leader and spokesman, is an academically trained white man.

civil war with gloomy prospects for the future. As a result of the policy of the EZLN, the main line of social division in Chiapas is now no longer the ethnic division between Indios and Ladinos, but between factions of Indios of the same municipio, divided according to their political position in favour or against the EZLN.

As a result of this development tribal institutions, like the civil-religious hierarchy, are relegated to a peripheral role and tribal solidarity is weakened, if not lost. Unintentionally, the revolt of 1994 has had rather more negative than positive results for the Indios — at least with regard to the state of Chiapas.

Outlook

Regarding Mexico as a whole, some tribal people indeed consider themselves as distinct from the Spanish-speaking society of Ladinos. Over the last decades, however, multiple additional ties have been established between the national society and the indigenous tribes. Of these efforts the government schools have had the greatest impact in the sense of gradually ladinoizing the Indios. On this path, radio-programmes, in some regions even television, gain considerable influence. Although there are examples of tribes vigorously defending their identity by warding off the entry of unwanted ideas and customs and restricting the activities of North American Protestant sects, the general trend operates towards a levelling of cultural differences and towards the diffusion of national customs. As a consequence, quite a few of the tribal ethnic groups of Mexico will probably pass to a status of bilingual peasants within the coming generations, still somehow apart from Ladinos but with a way of life quite similar to that of the general rural folk.

Regarding ethnic identities, the present division of linguistic groups into various individual tribes may possibly be overcome in the future. New entities of identification may evolve, based on a common language.[21] Such new groupings could achieve political power, especially within the particular region or federal state. To be successful they would have to create modern organisational structures, similar to nations[22] rather than tribes.

21. This does not necessarily mean the inclusion of all speakers of the particular language. Especially in the case of Nahuatl, dispersed over a wide area, the creation of groupings with an additional regional basis could be imagined, like the Nahua of the Huaxteca, of Guerrero or the Sierra de Zongolica.
22. This term is already used for self-identification by organised indigenous linguistic groups of North- und South America.

REFERENCES

Cancian, Frank. 1965. *Economics and Prestige in a Maya Community: The Religious Cargo System of Zinacantan*. Stanford: Stanford Univ. Press.

Early, Daniel K.1982. *Café: Dependencia y Efectos. Comunidades Nahuas de Zongolica, Ver., en el Mercado de Nueva York*. México: Instituto Nacional Indigenista.

Foster, George M. 1965. "Peasant Society and the Image of Limited Good," *American Anthropologist*, 67: 293-314.

Handbook of Middle American Indians. 1967. Vol. 6: *Social Anthropology*. Austin: University of Texas Press.

____.1969. Vols. 7-8: *Ethnology*. Austin: University of Texas Press.

Köhler, Ulrich. 1968. "Neuere Methoden zur Integration der Indianer in Mexiko: Die Regionalprogramme des Instituto Nacional Indigenist (INI)," (pp. 59-83) in *Zur Integration der indianischen Bevölkerung Mexikos in die moderne Gesellschaft Lateinamerikas*. Arnold-Bergstraesser-Institut, (ed.). Freiburg.

____. 1980. "Patterns of Interethnic Economic Exchange in Southeastern Mexico," *Journal of Anthropological Research*, 36: 316-337.

____. 1995. "Voces del México Profundo: Iniciativas y luchas Indígenas," *Antropológicas, Nueva Época*, 13: 22-28.

La Jornada 2000 Daily Newspaper. México.

Redfield, Robert. 1941. *The Folk Culture of Yucatan*. Chicago: University of Chicago Press.

Sharer, Robert J. 1994. *The Ancient Maya*. 5th edition [original by Sylvanus G. Morley]. Stanford: Stanford Univ. Press.

Supplement to the Handbook of Middle American Indians 2000. Vol. 6: *Ethnology*. Austin: University of Texas Press.

Warman, Arturo and Arturo Argueta. (eds.). 1993. *Movimientos Indígenas Contemporáneos en México*. México: UNAM — Miguel Ángel Porrúa.

Wolf, Eric R. 1957. "Closed Corporate Peasant Communities in Mesoamerica and Central Java," *Southwestern Journal of Anthropology*, 13: 1-18.

____. 1959. *Sons of the Shaking Earth: The People of Mexico and Guatemala. Their Land, History and Culture*. Chicago: University of Chicago Press.

SEVENTEEN

TRIBAL WHEN OTHER OPTIONS ARE UNAVAILABLE: Reflections on Appalachia as Precursor

ROBERT J. GREGORY

Introduction

In growing up in the Southern Tier of New York State, I never heard from my parents, relatives and friends that we were an integral part of Appalachia. I was never told that we were at the Northern end of that culture spreading up the big mountain chain on the East Coast of the United States. No one ever spoke about tribal membership, the "various systems of social organisation comprising several local villages, bands, districts, lineages, or other groups and sharing a common ancestry, language, culture and name" (Morris, 1980: 1369) either. The orientation of parents, teachers, and local leaders was all toward the industrial Northeast, or to New York City. In fact, we lived in the periphery of Appalachia, and experienced daily much of the same culture as these people. Yet because we were on the periphery, and because we were in economically good times, some of us had aspirations, access to power and careers, and self-identities that enabled us to escape. But we could not help but be influenced, even though we did not at the time recognise the strength of the connection.

In later life, after experiencing a variety of other, alternative cultures, the slow realisation grows that, yes, yes indeed, Appalachia was part of my own upbringing, a goodly chunk of my identity ties me for ever to the mountain culture. The perhaps not so surprising thing is that the recognition brings a satisfaction and further realisation that just may be, possibly, my experiencc in growing up that way is that we served as a precursor for the population of the larger world. Who would have thought back then, that Appalachian culture served as a signal to or gateway for the future? Or, that Appalachian people could be designated as a tribal group, because of their strong kinship links and religious beliefs, their distinctive language and history, and their very limited economic situation?

Now, as the Millennium begins, the evidence is increasing. Specifically, we were at the mercy of systems of power that controlled us, and we had relatively little say in creating or managing our own destinies. Tribal communities are typically found in the backwash of modern societies, without power or control over their own destiny. Appalachia is like that.

Area studies, like tribal studies, have played a significant role in anthropology, political science and geography for decades. The following sketches characterise experiences and encounters in Appalachia, encapsulate the rich specifics, and permit the drawing of important themes to our attention. By so doing, the author points out that Appalachia represents a precursor for the population of the world as we advance into the future.

Sketch 1 — Living in the Hollers

As a beginning university lecturer, I was challenged by my new role and by cultural differences with my students, particularly the mature students returning to university after long absences. My Northeast United States background seemed out of "place" in the deep heart of Appalachia.

One such student sat just in front of me, but revealed she was a bit perplexed about one of my lectures. "You do need to understand what it is to grow up in the hollers," she proclaimed, "and it will take some thinking, some serious thinking or learning, for you to catch on."

"Well, I am willing to try," I said. "Can you give me a for instance, then, something I can think about to try to comprehend what it is to grow up in a holler in Appalachia?" I asked.

"Let me tell you a story about the next ridge over from where I grew up," she decided. "This would have been back about twenty or twenty-five years".

"Okay, I am listening," I said.

"This family lived in their holler just over the ridge from my family for several generations. The government folks came in during the 30s to build a road through their valley. The government didn't have a lot of success, but they did make a little windy road down through that ran right along the stream, and why today, it is nothing but a lonely half forgotten trail. Not much ever goes along it, cause there are better roads and lots better places to go. Once in a while, someone drives through, sure enough, but not many. Now, the family lived up on the side hill, for they knew that the valley sometimes flooded where the stream went through. Sides, they didn't want to have anything to do with the road anyway." She had captured my attention by this time, and I wondered where this shaggy dog story might lead.

"The family had a couple of sons, let's call them Ron and Jim. They never went to school. The parents never even registered them with the health department. As far as the rest of the world knew, they did not exist. They were less than 10 years old, when their Pop let them use the .22 to catch rabbits or coons or whatever. From about the time they were 12 or 13, they used to sit up on the side hill, hidden in the trees and big rocks there, and watch the valley from their spot. About once a week, some vehicle would drive through on the road, and Ron and Jim would aim their .22, and shoot at the vehicle. It would be over a thousand yards, pretty much the limit a .22 bullet could go. Usually they missed.

Every once in a while, they would make a hit and then the driver would stop, get out and inspect the car, find a bullet hole, then drive off in a hurry. Ron and Jim might sit in their spot and watch, or sometimes, they would run and hide in a secret cave for the rest of the day, then go on home. They never had anything to say about their version of hunting to the rest of the family".

"That is pretty bad behavior," I said, offering a moral judgement, along with encouragement for her to continue.

"Well, that is what they did, now you need to think about all this to begin to understand our ways," she stated firmly, coming to the end of her story.

Over the years, I have thought about Ron and Jim and my student from the neighbouring holler. I have thought about that situation and culture, but I confess, I still have not figured out what it is really like to live in the hollers.

Sketch 2 — Family

"Family comes first," she said, "and no matter how black the sheep, each person is part of the family. We stand together, no matter." These words, spoken to me with pride, answered my question, about why Appalachian people were different from others elsewhere. I was talking about the unemployment rates, then well over 20 per cent in the county, and 80 per cent in much of the state, with a well educated young woman in West Virginia. Coal country meant economic booms and busts, mostly busts, especially when nuclear power plants replaced coal almost altogether. The 80 per cent unemployment rate was only a vague number, the lives of those involved spoke another reality altogether.

She was a person who could have made a good life elsewhere, but chose to remain close to her own extended family and her own culture. By so doing, she knew that she would suffer unemployment, temporary at best jobs, low wages, eternal poverty, and poor quality working conditions for the rest of her life. But, like her contemporaries, she could not trust the outside world enough, based on her personal experiences, to go exploring elsewhere for jobs, marriage partners, or futures. She was content to stay with what she knew, kinfolk she could trust, and belief in a way of life that still satisfied.

Sketch 3 — Departmental Dinner

"My gosh, Bob, that was fun," my colleague admitted. "I was surprised that you and your wife were able to get all of us to have dinner at your place," he added. "You know, in my nearly two decades of teaching at the university, the members of our department never got together outside of committee meetings. After work, we have all gone our separate ways, and I will be willing to bet that none of us even went to each other's homes for a visit".

Coming in from the North to a university setting in Appalachia adds new ideas, new activities. For us from the Northeast, such activities seem perfectly normal and natural. For those living in Appalachia however, social innovations are rare, and the expectation is that things will not work out, no matter how much planning or preparation or enthusiasm goes into them. Making a departmental dinner a success was, it turned out, a very rare event. After this successful dinner and gathering, the members of the department never again attended a dinner or other non-university event together. This failure to extend kin or work groupings to a social community, even in a department that included only six persons, was not atypical in the region.

Sketch 4 — Christian Values

Among gifts I received near the end of the summer for my birthday was a lovely, bright, carmine red bath towel. I liked the brightness and the colour, and this one was my favourite. The thickness and absorbency were just right.

We had learned sometime before about a nearby swimming hole, and decided that, since it was a blazing hot summer day, we would go early in the evening to try it out. This swimming place had been traditionally open to all but was now called the Christian Camp. Church people held a summer camp each year, to preach along with assuring that their "Christian children" learned proper Christian values and had a good chance to enjoy some Christian recreation with other like-minded Christian children and Christian families. The local Christian leaders had raised a building through their fundraising efforts, and a young minister was put in charge, to supervise and guide the children present and to serve as a role model example to all.

Well, our carload arrived hot and dry, and we were eager to cool off in the stream. We parked near twenty or thirty other vehicles, then walked over to the stream and put our towels and shoes in proper little piles near each other. I still remember parting with my new towel reluctantly for that towel was a special gift. Then we waded in to cool off in the delightful clear water.

A large number of Christians were distributed in the water, on the banks of the stream, and near the sole building. Soon, we hurled a Frisbee around, both in and then out of the water. We frolicked, played and enjoyed ourselves, and even met a couple of interesting people to talk with. Everyone seemed to be having a good time. The smell of barbecues cooking food wafted about in the air, and the heat of the day dissipated gradually.

We returned from the stream to find that my towel was missing. My shoes and everything else were in their proper place, but my towel was clearly gone. With a feeling of distress, I cast my eyes about the entire scene, noting several red towels, but none with the distinctive carmine color. The sinking feeling in my heart was dramatic. I felt grief.

Then, my quickly emerging anger mixed and focused on the strong principles of the Christian religion so evident in the Appalachian region. I asked myself, "how can this be? What are these Christians about?" Then I asked members of my family, "how can this be?" They too helped me look, and walk about the camp to see if they could spot the lost towel.

Eventually, I approached the young minister. He calmly looked at me, and said, "just look about and take another red towel — really, they are all the same. We are Christian here. We share." He then pointed out a couple of old ragged red towels laying in among shoes and other gear, obviously left while people were in swimming.

I could believe neither his words nor his casualness. Christian beliefs in the Appalachian region are fundamental, extreme, and strange to anyone from outside the region. Obviously, I had not acclimatised and adjusted to the prevailing standards. Although I say standards, I mean a lack of standards, as measured by the larger world.

Sketch 5 — Story Telling

"All you have to do is to watch for the distinctive colour," the Appalachian native told me, "and you will be able to find 'sang most everywhere round here." I learned much later that yes, 'sang can be located by the colour, but only at a certain time of the year, and further, only in certain and very selected locations. Sang or Ginseng is a popular topic, for if you can find quantities in the autumn, you can sell this popular and very profitable herb and make quick and easy money. Ginseng roots sometimes grow into carrot or parsnip like tubers that are valued by those of Chinese origin. Even small bits of ground up roots are treasured for their reputed positive effects. Possibly too, if you can find the right market, you won't even have to pay taxes, for the 'sang market is frequently gray in terms of the "revenooers". Much of the lore about finding 'sang is hidden away, available only to kinfolk who have earned a role within the extended families living way back in the mountains.

At one point in my life, that hope and promise, and the lure of easy cash, led me to send away for 100 ginseng seeds, plus instructions. I planted the seeds in rich soil in shady second growth forest. The dream of easy money, of participating in something out of the ordinary, and maintaining the secrecy of the Appalachian mountain people all brought me, and countless others, to try to raise ginseng. Raising your own however, is not as valued as finding wild ginseng, but it is a good start.

Unfortunately, my ginseng patch failed to grow.

Still, ginseng provided many rich stories, with rich common to the Appalachian area: government agents and especially the revenooers, secret knowledge and places that had to be protected from foreigners, the good guys *versus* the bad guys who were not always exactly who you thought, and the many culturally important issues of destiny and fate. In particular the inability to control one's own life, to stay on the side of law and order and avoid its opposite, and to maintain ever present kinship networks and alliances rather than engage in feuds, seemed tied up with and bound to these themes. In truth, ginseng takes up only about one or two per cent of the talk for other important topics are discussed more frequently and all year round.

Popular story telling topics range from bear traps hidden in the nearby hills to gold mining in the local stream to alcohol made in stills back in the hollers, or to marijuana and Blue Grass music festivals. If one had to pick a specific topic that occupied minds and hearts more than any other, this would have to be making "home-made likker" with a still, then running the freshly brewed alcohol to distribution points, followed by all sorts of stories about consumption of such products. Good story telling always demands an attentive audience, so anyone intent on visiting, playing the role of tourist, or from another part of Appalachia could be subjected to some fine oral history art forms, free for the taking. The story-teller of course, could build a reputation and gain status, and sometimes, even sell something that might represent a symbol of the region.

Sketch 6 — Power

The word came through official channels that we were invited to attend the speech to dedicate the new hall. This meeting would allow us to listen to a candidate for high political office. Various other select groups in town and in neighbouring towns were similarly issued a formal invitation. The honour of being invited did not extend to everyone, and in fact, only certain numbers of people from each organisation were scheduled to attend. Lists of names were circulated, so that there could be no mistakes. No special news appeared in the papers about the event, and no general public invitation or notification was made. "Security," they said.

The day came and we, dressed in our finest outfits, trooped along to the hall an hour before the event. The State Police were in full evidence, with dozens of vehicles displayed prominently in each and every direction. I dawdled behind my group, to see more of the goings-on, but a State Police Officer asked me what I was doing. Noting that I did not appear to be a troublemaker, but an honest and concerned citizen, he took me aside for a little chat. "No, you can't watch the arrival of the candidate. He may come by helicopter or limousine, even I don't know things like that. Security, you know," he concluded. "Now, you go on in so you are not in the way," he stated flatly, with implications that if I did not do as he demanded, then there would be big trouble.

I entered and found my assigned group and seat waiting. Collectively we sat for a long time, with nothing much to do but observe. I did note a group of local police officers, stationed around the inside of the hall. A couple of men in the audience seemed out of place, as if they too were police officers but in suits for the occasion. In the distance we heard the sounds of a helicopter, but we never knew or found out if the candidate was aboard. Security, you know.

A little variety show to take up time and give us something to do eventually occupied the stage. We watched, a bit bored with these preliminaries.

Suddenly, the stage burst into life, with the entrance of five or six burly big men, dressed in deathly black suits. An older thin man, equally dressed, accompanied them. These men did not just stroll in, but took charge, leaving no doubt in anyone's mind that they controlled the scene. The Police Officers present stiffened to attention, and the thin man strode to the microphone and protective bullet-proof lectern to the opposite side of the stage. Tapping the microphone, he listened to hear if everything worked properly, then announced that he had the deep pleasure of introducing the candidate. He appreciated that we had waited, that it was a hot and stuffy day, and then he assured us all that we would be very pleased to have the wonderful opportunity to listen to this famous man. The burly men were casting their eyes over the audience carefully, looking for movement, watching for too much or too little eye contact, identifying the locations of police and audience members and exits, and staging their presence and utter control over everything and everyone. No one in the audience dared move, or blink, or whisper questions to others seated nearby. Security, you know.

First, we had a prayer, conducted by a local minister of a prominent church. The pastor strode over, gowned in white finery akin to a peacock, and asked the audience to stand. He led a prayer dedicated to the health and well-being of the leaders of the community and state, and then asked everyone to join him in a Pledge of Allegiance to the Flag. Everyone present put their hands on their hearts, and recited the familiar words carefully and correctly. The Pastor joined the thin man in a seat near the centre of the stage and we waited a minute or two.

Finally, entering from the side of the stage nearest the lectern, a very tall, personable looking man, again in a deathly black "power" suit, strode up to the microphone and began speaking. His voice boomed forth over the loudspeakers, proclaiming "how wonderful it is to again be in Appalachia," while he stood smiling broadly and confidently at us. His eyes cast about too, seeking eye contact with those near him (mostly police officers) while he went on to talk about the strengths of those living in Appalachia, such as "strong families and honesty and integrity". The dedication of the local people was the backbone of the community. He was personally honoured to come to town to dedicate the hall. The little cloth cover over the plaque near the lectern came down when he pulled a drawstring, and the audience clapped as if on cue. The man continued to talk about the lack of jobs but he assured everyone that "with economic development, things would get better". The man praised the hard work and difficult role for the police officers, the strenuous and valuable efforts of the men and women working for the political party he represented, and begged everyone to be sure to exercise their patriotic American duty by voting in the coming election. He thanked everyone again for coming and then walked decisively off the stage, to mild applause by the people and rapt clapping and even modest cheers by the police officers. His departure was carefully arranged, obviously, for security, you know.

We were then entertained by the thin man for a couple of minutes while the burly men departed after their boss, then the local police stood and watched carefully as we too stood up ready to depart the now dedicated hall. In the distance we heard a helicopter again, but that may have been a disguise for the limousine. We departed, noting that half the State Police were already gone, and the others were packing up, leaving the local police to disperse the audience and carry on. Security, you know.

Afterwards, upon reading the warm and positive accounts of the dedication and speech in the local and state newspapers, I thought about the power of money, glib tongues and a commanding presence to hypnotise people into performing exactly as the rulers desired. It looked so easy that almost anyone could do the same act, if they had enough money, speech-writers, helicopters, limousines, body-guards, and such.

Sketch 7 — Financial Power

One of the strangest experiences I had in the Appalachian region occurred when a young acquaintance of mine stopped by and asked for some advice. He stated that his grandfather passed away, and he was expecting to inherit several millions of dollars. His father was setting up trust funds for each member of the family as well, and collectively they were very well off. This young man wanted my thoughts and suggestions on what he might do to live quietly and peacefully, but help the people of the community. Since I was an outsider, having only lived there for a couple of years, I might be unbiased. And further, since I had an extensive education, I might have some notions as to how people in other areas handled their wealth constructively. "Fair enough ideas," I said, "and I suspect that things will crop up from time to time that will interest you as opportunities to help people along." I promised to share with him any great ideas I came up with.

In a few weeks, a local politician happened by my office to tell me about a charitable programme being designed for the community. "This programme will benefit everyone, but especially the poor, the homeless, the people with disabilities, and those hardest hit by the economic downturns," said the politician. The only thing we need is either government grants or local wealth to get it off the ground. Can you help us write a grant request?

"I know the very best way you can raise some local funds to do good work," I suggested, and gave him the name of the young man.

Sure enough a few days later, the young man came by and asked, "Did you suggest to the politician that we might be able to help with a local charity?"

"Yes," I said proudly, "for in terms of what you were saying the other day, and in terms of the plans for a new and positive programme, why the connection just made sense".

"Well, I talked it over with my Dad, and he said that we should never disclose any wealth we happen to have to anyone outside our family. Please, please, do not ever let anyone know that we are well to do".

"Okay, I can understand that, but what about the programme that the politician is trying to get going to benefit your community?" I put an emphasis on "your" to assure him of his past interests.

"Well, my Dad says that any philanthropic giving should be initiated by us, and not by someone else. That way, we can choose what we do, when we do it, and to what extent we help out. We can choose to be anonymous or to have our name put on a programme or building. He also suggested that it is more important to let the trust funds grow for the next few years, even several decades, and that way, we can help more, when it comes time".

He had concluded his speech, and I understood how locally raised wealth accrues from the members of the community to lodge in one family, or even one person, and there remain, for ever. Actually, the money did not remain even with the local individual or trust fund but went to the big cities to investment funds. The likelihood that any money would ever contribute to the well-being of local communities in Appalachia was zero.

Sketch 8 — The Library

Teaching in an Appalachian institution of higher learning is not like teaching elsewhere in the United States or around the world. An example concerned the conditions in the university library.

From the exterior, the library appeared to be an imposing building, with stairs leading up to a formal double door entrance. The building seemed to be a solid, two-story fortress, like most elsewhere. On the inside, the stacks of books seemed relatively open for easy access, and the few librarians or more likely librarian helpers visible were busy with paperwork or answering queries. The books were relatively few, for the basketball team always took any extra funds from the university coffers, and the library rated well down on the food chain.

It was in the journal collection that the clearest difference lay. If you assigned journal articles to your students, by giving them a list of the best articles for your subject, or even by mentioning a specific article in class, the students would pay special attention. If you then went on the next day to the new journals rack, or back into the stacks to find older volumes, you could be sure to locate the specific issue or bound volume. However, and this is where the difference came in, if you sought out the specific article, you would find that the pages had been carefully cut out, presumably with a razor. This was not just a rare occurrence, but something that happened frequently, each and everyday, for virtually all the journals in the entire library. If you took a count, probably one-fourth of all the articles had disappeared.

Seems the students had the idea that if they had the article, and no one else could get a copy, then their grades would be just fine, but no one else could complete the required work and study. When you asked the students about this situation, they simply passed it off as, "first comers win big, that is just the way it has always been". When you asked the staff about this situation, they shook their heads, and said "nothing can be done about it, ain't it awful?" When you asked the librarians, they shook their heads sadly and ignored you for the rest of the day.

Sketch 9 — Making Music

Sunday morning brought red-eye gravy on home made biscuits, black coffee, and home grown bacon and eggs. As if to make up for a too vigorous Saturday evening, Sundays were days of rest and relaxation. What better way to celebrate than church for the believers, and making music for the fiddlers.

Whether dulcimer, guitar, cello, violin, or fiddle, several men would gather at someone's home, play for a couple of hours, drink some beer or better, white light'ning; then head for another home, there to continue. The pattern would last all day, and far into the night, depending upon crowds, availability of alcohol, and energy and co-ordination to make music.

Sometimes, the gathering would begin on Friday night or Saturday afternoon, then continue on through to Sunday night. From time to time, these naturally occurring local music performances would bring these men together and they would drive to a nearby music festival, or sundry other gatherings. Country music, bluegrass, rock and roll, and local variants of mountain music enthralled visitors, tourists, and the musicians themselves.

Occasionally under the influence, social tensions and rifts would be revealed, at other times, the harmonious music would blend together these mountain music men, their families, and a few fortunate guests.

Sketch 10 — Personal Awareness

When I was but a child, the older people would claim, "Yessir, Elmira and the Southern Tier is a great place to work. Why, we have the typewriter plant, Remington Rand, the grey iron foundry, General Electric, and the fire-truck plant, Ward LaFrance, and at least three other large industries. No unemployment here". The speaker would then claim, "they all pay good wages and have plenty of benefits. We are blessed!" They might then add, with an optimistic voice, "we worked hard for it".

Our second-generation immigrant parents worked hard indeed in those big industrial plants, enabling some of us young folk to "get an education," or "find a trade". Most of us were not so lucky, but some were and that enabled many of us to move up and onwards. Those that did not seize the opportunity to move out however, were soon watching six major industrial plants shut down, not temporarily but for ever, throwing thousands of loyal workers out into the local streets. High unemployment, powerlessness to act, and poverty are part and parcel of Appalachia, just like in our times the "downsizing" of the multi-national corporations has become an everyday event. We fail to appreciate the impact, the blighted lives of those individuals and their family members who are thrown asunder. The Southern Tier was on the edge, and according to the Appalachian Regional Development Act of 1965 (PL 89-4) my home region of Chemung County was definitely part of Appalachia (Rothblatt, 1971: 3). During World War II, the boom times gave us power, self-control, wealth, and hope. Not long after, power, self-control, wealth, and hope disappeared as economic hard times hit and have remained so for many decades. Many young people grew up without work experience or hope for the future. Worse, they had little awareness that other places in the United States or the world might be different. The impact of economic decline seemed far greater for those who had seen but narrowly missed the alternatives, the almosts, the possibilities, the others were not even aware. The major growth industry in that particular region since has been a prison complex. Nothing more needs be added.

A Brief Look at Some Literature

Early history in Appalachia is covered albeit sparsely in many volumes (Langman, 1971; Rothblatt, 1971). Whether the region's culture, as portrayed, is due to politics, religion (Humphrey, 1984), geography, socialisation and media indoctrination (Gaventa, 1984), history (Rothblatt, 1971), or even the mountainous environment (Beaver and Purrington, 1984), depends to a large extent upon the vision of the authors. The multi-hued disciplinary viewpoints reveal a complex culture area. The homespun philosophy emerging from the region (Berry, 1991; Porter, no date) too, is far more complex than any one point of view can represent.

The most important factor in Appalachia, however, concerns power, decision-making and control. Power, and especially the failure of bottoms-up revolutionary or reformation forces to alter inequities, served as the key subject for Gaventa (1980). He noted that power is concentrated at the top, and though power may appear to be diverse (pp. 259-261) the appearance of diverse sources and types of power is limited to those at the top, which means, exterior to the Appalachian region. From the perspective available from the bottom, power is held by an elite, exterior to the region. This power is further bolstered, covertly and only rarely, overtly, by those in the local region. Gaventa (1984) also notes that this elite used "the most sophisticated media ideology and socialisation machinery that any society has ever seen" (p. 154) to block any resistance. Now, rivalry with and mistrust of "outsiders" is characteristic, for even "back to the land" immigrants into Appalachia do not fit in easily or readily (Staley, 1999).

Another facet of the powerlessness and failure to band together may be due to the fundamental religion prevalent in the region (McCauley and Farmer, 1996). Humphrey (1984), for example, states, "The evangelical faith offers believers an escape from the terrors and insecurities of modern life. The emphasis is not on community or place but upon the individual" (p. 132). The churches then, have not enabled these forlorn individuals to band together to bring about social, political or economic change but instead, has operated to divide, separate, and weaken groups so they have few ties with each other, other than the final bond of kinship and extended families. Appalachian people have been vanquished and reside, one could say in a state of "plight" akin to that of the Native Americans (DeLoria, 1969).

Even vast government schemes cannot resurrect the society or rehabilitate the people to a state similar to that of the Northeast, the South, the Mid-west, or the West Coast. The regional planning approach set up by the Appalachian Regional Commission demonstrated "that an institutional setting can adjust and reconcile conflicting preferences of those involved in decision making . . . ." and that with incentives, states "can reach a consensus about a complex programme." (p. 197). Still, many would observe that the Commission, like development projects anywhere in Appalachia, has not been a full-fledged success.

Conclusions

Well, what can we conclude from this brief adventure into Appalachia? Several themes run through the sketches, including extreme power differentials, value differences, alternative motivational patterns, distrust of outsiders and even of each other, and a great deal of difficulty in achieving meaningful communication. Kinship and strong religious beliefs mark the area as tribal, whether formal definitions agree or not (Quentin-Baxter, 1998) and whether "weak insiders" or "powerful outsiders" provide the definition (Gregory, 1997), the reality is that Appalachian people live in tribal units. The power differentials are most important and are clear, for Appalachia has absentee landlords, absentee government officials, and absentee commercial powers-that-be with almost infinite wealth, technology, and savoir faire. And yet, these people with power are not regarded as, and are not in fact, local, accessible, or in an ultimate sense, meaningful. The powers-that-be are ignored, not with disdain or hatred, but simply denied any role in or relationship with the daily lives of the people of Appalachia, except for their perennial and constant looting of any financial or environmental or human resources. Like floods, chemical spills, coal mining disasters, or other natural phenomenon, the decisions these powerful people make are a mystery, and only fate holds any clues.

No one in Appalachia cares, really, what the people with power do or say or claim anymore. They know they are being looted, and they know that there is nothing they can do about the situation. Unlike the connections between the rich and the poor in the Northeast, or in other locations around the major countries in the world, there are virtually no such connections in Appalachia. There is no middle class. Those living in the region have no aspirations to engage with these powerful outsiders, nor bother to fight against their power. The battle took place many years ago, and today, there is no contest, no struggle for power, and accordingly, no hope of redress.

Value differences are many. Since there is no point in aspiring to power, there is also no sense worrying about such things, for worry will not make any difference. Appalachian people simply accept their own selves, and the most distant they can extend their trust is to their families. They appear guarded to their neighbours, friends and work place associates. They have learned through bitter experience not to care about life, people, or activities beyond their local kinship based niche in their own part of their own mountains. Foreigners are easy to reject, or to be made fun of, or to be ignored. In fact they can even be shot at, typically without repercussions because no one else cares. If repercussions do occur, then such events were destined to happen by arbitrary fate, not by anything that the people themselves could have influenced.

Why do something? Motives are complex and multiple, for all of us. Why do Appalachian people do something? Because this was and is the way such things have always been done. The classic saying, "what was good enough for Pappy is good enough for me," confirms that traditions are valued, and behaviour that is in accord with tradition is correct. Innovation is foreign, and therefore to be avoided. Sayings such as "America first," or "love it or leave it," are common. If avoidance of new technology is impossible, then such technology is incorporated in ways so that tradition is not altered.

Communications span the world today, and go even beyond into the far reaches of space. Communications in Appalachia are limited, the focus is still on the family, the local, and the necessary, not the frivolous, not the global, and certainly are not extended beyond the small number of people involved in local kinship networks. If you are resident in Appalachia, you cannot trust or work effectively with local or external leaders, so you end up trusting family, kin, and not a local hierarchy and not an exterior power. Those in the hierarchy, anywhere above the bottom, only seek to control, exploit, and rip-off. This includes the few locals who have been co-opted as well as the outsiders. They are the enemy.

Appalachia then, is a region of local tribes, united by kinship, guided by tradition and fundamental religion, and separated from the rest of America by a different history, economy and culture. The residents are people "whose social, cultural and economic conditions distinguish them from other sections of the national community, and whose status is regulated wholly or partially by their own customs or traditions..." (http://panda.org/resources/publications/sustainability/indigenous2/annex1.html). Therefore, they fit the definition by the International Labour Convention 169 of the United Nations, as tribal people.

Appalachia as Precursor

In terms of the future of societies around the world, differentials in power, wealth, and scope are now enormous, and appear to be increasing rapidly. A few individuals and some corporations with enormous power control most if not all of the world's wealth (Korten, 1995; Mander, 1997). Their ambitions and demands are virtually unlimited in scope and scale. The rest of the world's population is due to be left financially bereft, if not already so. As this flow of wealth to a few occurs, less and less interest in the global scene is likely for "local" people, for there will be no reason for them to take any interest in what life is like elsewhere. After all, the MacDonalds and KFC restaurants, the crowded super highways, and the tourist attractions are all the same anywhere. Identity will be gained from local tradition. Each local group may retain a few symbolic memories, a few tokens, of what about life was meaningful to re-enact and to recreate meaningful activities, suitable for tourists and entertainment. While communications will continue to span the world, the surveillance sector will see to it that meaningful communication will become local, family or small group oriented. E-mail messages flow everywhere, but given the acronym agencies spying on us, the collected outpourings of feelings and information will be used, sooner or later, to target trouble-makers, dissidents, radicals, and more. When trust breaks down on the regional, national and global level, then for the masses, communication patterns will be restricted. The elite will soon enough have total control, military, financial, and thought patterns. The weather, sports, psycho-babble, advertisements and product information stemming from the mass media, are all that remains available as common denominator forms of communication.

The lifestyles, culture and patterns of Appalachia are precursors for the future for all of us, around the world. The few elite will and in fact, do now, have unprecedented power, and there will be no point in trying to influence, change, or buck the system they control. Taboo topics, like revolutionary ideas and democracy, may or may not return in time. The first of those topics will be any meaningful address of the differentials of power, and the speakers or talkers will undoubtedly be persecuted. And in this way, Appalachia represents the future, for there is no point in addressing issues about power — all the decisions, all the control, all the power, has already been taken, firmly, completely, and with overwhelming and everlasting force. People may well re-tribalise, not necessarily by choice, but because corporate and private wealth, technological and military power, and elite social status have taken away other options.

ACKNOWLEDGEMENT

Special thanks are due to friends, colleagues, and family members in Elmira, New York, a coal mining region of Pennsylvania, Huntington and surrounding counties in West Virginia, Southeast Ohio, Southwest Virginia and especially those from Sparta and Marion in North Carolina. The thoughts expressed are entirely my own.

REFERENCES

Beaver, Patricia D. and Burton L. Purrington (eds.). 1984. *Cultural Adaptation to Mountain Environments*. Southern Anthropological Society Proceedings, No. 17, Athens, Georgia: The University of Georgia Press.

Berry, Wendell. 1991. *Standing on Earth: Selected Essays*. Ipswich, UK: Golgonooza Press.

De Loria, Vine Jr. 1969. *Custer Died for Your Sins: An Indian Manifesto*. New York: Macmillan.

Gaventa, John. 1980. *Power and Powerlessness: Quiescence and Rebellion in an Appalachian Valley*. Urbana, IL: University of Illinois Press.

————. 1984. "Land Ownership, Power, and Powerlessness in the Appalachian Highlands," (pp. 142-155) in Beaver and Purrington (eds.), op.cit.

Gregory, Robert J. 1997. "Definitions as Power," *Disability and Rehabilitation*, 19 (11): 487-489.

Humphrey, Richard. 1984. "Religion and Place in Southern Appalachia," (pp. 122-141) in Beaver and Purrington (eds.), op.cit.

Korten, David C. 1995. *When Corporations Rule the World*. West Hartford, CT: Kumarian Press.

Langman, R. C. 1971. *Appalachian Kentucky: An Exploited Region*. Toronto: McGraw-Hill Ryerson Ltd.

Mander, Jerry. 1997. *Eleven Inherent Rules of The Great Smoky Mountains*. New York: Promontory Press.

Mc Cauley, D.V. and J.O. Former (Reviewer). 1996. "Appalachian Mountain Religin: A History (review)," *American Historical Review*, 101(5) : 1613.

Morris, William (ed.). 1980. *American Heritage Dictionary of the English Language*. Houghton Mifflin.

Peter, Eliot (n.d.). *Appalachian Wilderness : The Great Somoky Mountains*. New York: Promontory Press.

Quentin-Baxter, Alison. 1998. *Recognising the Rights of Indigenous Peoples*. Wellington: Institute of Policy Studies.

Rothblatt, Donald N. 1971. *Regional Planning: The Appalachian Experience*. Lexington, MA: D.C.Heath and Company.

Staley, Kathryn L. (23/12/1999) Identity in a Mountain Family http://www.acs.appstate.edu/dept/anthro/ebooks/ethno97/staley.html

ILO Convention 169 of the United Nations, http://panda.org/resources/publications/sustainability/indigenous2/annex1.html

NOTES ON CONTRIBUTORS

Bal, Ellen recently completed her PhD thesis at the Erasmus University Rotterdam, The Netherlands. It was published as *'They Ask If We Eat Frogs': Social Boundaries, Ethnic Categorisation, and the Garo People of Bangladesh* (Delft, 2000). Other recent publications are *Manderangni Jagring: Images of the Garos in Bangladesh* (Dhaka, co-authored with Yasuhiro Takami and Johannes Sandgren, 1999) and *Banglar Bohujati: Bangali Chhara Banglar Onnanyo Jatir Proshongo* (Calcutta, co-edited with Willem van Schendel, 1998).

Mailing Address :
C/o. Willem van Schendel
Asian Studies in Amsterdam (ASiA)
University of Amsterdam
O.Z. Achterburgwal 237
012 DL Amsterdam
THE NETHERLANDS
Fax : +31 20 6756437
E-mail : <vanschendel@pscw.uva.nl>

Behera, Deepak Kumar obtainded his Master's and PhD degrees from Sambalpur University, where he has been teaching social anthropology since 1985. Prof. Behera has authored/edited 14 books. Of these, five are jointly with Prof. Georg Pfeffer of Free University of Berlin, Germany and one with Prof. Margaret Trawick of Massey University, New Zealand. He was a guest faculty member in the Department of Anthropology, University of the Orange Free State, South Africa in 1998. Prof. Behera is the editor of the international journal —*Journal of Social Sciences* (website : <www.krepublishers.com>. He has chaired half-a-dozen scientific sessions in different international conferences. Prof. Behera is a member of the Executive Board of International

Union of Anthropological and Ethnological Sciences (IUAES) for the period 1998-2003. He is the chairperson of IUAES *Commission on Anthropology of Children and Childhood.* He is also an Officer-at-Large of the International Sociological Association, Research Committee-53 — *Sociology of Childhood.* Prof. Behera is a member of the Advisory Board of the Journals —*Practicing Anthropology* (Oklahoma, USA) and *Sociological Analysis* (North Carolina, USA). He has participated in a number of international conferences held in North America, Latin America, Africa, Europe, Asia. He attended an International Interdisciplinary course in Children's Rights at Ghent University, Belgium in 1997. His current interests in research are childhood matters, tribal studies, gender issues, and development studies.

Mailing Address :
Department of Anthropology
Sambalpur University
Sambalpur-768019
Orissa
INDIA
Fax : ++91-(0) 663-404000/430158
E-mail : <dkb@vsnl.com>

Berger, Peter (born 1969) is an Assistant Professor of Social Anthropology at the Institute of Ethnology of the Free University of Berlin, Germany. His Master's thesis is on the death rituals of the Toraja, a community living in highland Sulawesi, Indonesia. Mr. Berger recently completed 22 months of fieldwork among the Scheduled Tribe named Gadaba and other Desia communities in a village of the Koraput district of Orissa (India) on which he has published several articles and will complete his doctoral thesis in 2002.

Mailing Address :
Institute of Ethnology
Freie Universitaet Berlin
Drosselweg 1-3
14195 Berlin
GERMANY
E-mail : <peberg@gmx.de>

Braukämper, Ulrich (born 1944) is a Professor at the Institute of Ethnology, University of Goettingen, Germany. He received his PhD on "The impact of Islam on history and cultural development of Adamauas" in the year 1969

(Cologne) and completed his postdoctoral thesis of Habilitation on "Migration and ethnic change —investigations on the Eastern Sudan zone" in the year 1990 (Munich). He has done intensive fieldwork in Nigeria and North-East Africa. One of his recent publications is *Raise and Teasing. Narrative Songs of the Hadiyya in Southern Ethiopia* (Frankfurt/M: Freobenius-Institut, 1999).

Institute of Ethnology
Georg-August Universitaet Goettingen
Theaterplatz 15
37073 Goettingen
GERMANY
E-mail : <ethno@gwdg.de>

Carrin, Marine is a Senior Researcher of the French National Council of Research (CNRS) and based at the Centre d'anthropologie, Toulouse. She has been working among the Santals of Bengal and Orissa since the early seventies. Madame Carrin has also done some substantive work on the Santal texts found in the Oslo University Library. She has furthermore worked on the tribe/caste frontier in Bengal. Her approach combines structural and semantic studies with observation of interaction in the field. She has recently completed fieldwork among Tulu speakers in Karnataka, and published on ritual, possession and the imagery of the forest. Presently she is working on an analysis of the cultural encounter between Scandinavian missionaries and the Santals. Some of her important publications are *La fleur et l'os: symbolisme et rituel chez les Santal* (Paris: EHESS, 1986); *Inner frontiers: Santal responses to acculturation* (Bergen: Chr. Michelsen Institutt, 1991); *Managing Distress: Therapeutic Cults in South Asia.* (New Delhi: Manohar, 1999); *Le Parler des Dieux: Sémantique du discours rituel santal (forthcoming).*

Mailing Address :
182 rue Lemerchier
80000 Amiens
FRANCE
Fax : +33-565302021
E-mail : <MARINE-CARRIN@wanadoo.fr>

Demmer, Ulrich (born 1956) has obtained his PhD in Anthropology at the South Asia Institute, University of Heidelberg in 1993 and his postdoctoral

Habilitation in 2001 in the University of Munich, his thesis bearing the title *Ritual and the Rhetorical Tradition of the Jenu Kurumba (South India).* At present he is conducting a research project on "Visual Culture" at the Department of Anthropology, Univeristy of Munich. His current interests in research are South Asia, ritual theories, oral traditions and social memory, anthropology of praxis, rhetorical theory of culture. Dr. Demmer is also associated with the Orissa Research Programme of the German research Foundation and will conduct fieldwork in the tribal belt of southern Orissa.

Mailing Address :
Institue fuer Voelkerkunde und Afrikanistik
Universitaet Munchen
Oettingenstr.67
80538 Munich
GERMANY
E-mail : <Ulrich.Demmer@-online.de>

Gaenszle, Martin (born 1956) obtained his PhD from Heidelberg University in the year 1982. The topic of his postdoctoral thesis of Habilitation from the same University was *"Ancestral Voices: Oral Ritual Texts and their Social Context among the Mewahang Rai of East Nepal"* in the year 1998. At present he is engaged in field research in Benaris as part of a project of the South Asia Institute, Heidelberg His research interests are ethnolinuistics, studies of identity, literality, studies of ritual, social anthropology, Asia, South Asia.

Mailing Address :
Seminar fuer Ethnologie
Suedasien-Institut
Universitaet Heidelberg
Im Neuenheimer Feld 330
69120 Heidelberg
GERMANY
E-mail : <martin.gaenszle@urz.uni-heidelberg.de>

Glatzer, Bernt (born 1942) is a research fellow at the Centre of Modern Oriental Studies, Berlin; and Programme Officer for Asia section at the German Foundation for International Development, Bad Honnef, Germany. He obtained his PhD from Heidelberg University on *"Nomads of Gharjistan: Aspects of Economic, Social and Political Organization among Durrani*

Pashtuns in Northwest Afghanistan" in the year 1975. Dr. Glatzer's research interests are tribalism, ethnicity and nomadic life. He has done extensive fieldwork in Afghanistan and Pakistan and has engaged himself in the relief work among Afghan refugees for many years.

Mailing Address :
Deutsche Stiftung fuer internationale Entwicklung (DSE)
German Foundation for International Development
Zentralstelle fuer Auslandskunde (ZA)
Lohfelder Str. 128
D-53604 Bad Honnef
GERMANY
E-mail : <bglatzer@web.de>

Gregory, Robert J. is Senior Lecturer in the School of Psychology at Massey University, Palmerston North, New Zealand. As an undergraduate, he studied anthropology at Cornell University and then gained a Master of Arts and a PhD in rehabilitation at Syracuse University. Among other activities, he has worked as a vocational counselor, researcher in a mental health center, director of a multi-disciplinary social science think tank and director of a substance abuse program in North Carolina. Dr. Gregory engaged in a two year post-doctoral study at the Duke University Medical Center, Department of Psychiatry, and subsequently obtained a research grant through the Department of Anthropology and the National Institute on Drug Abuse to examine the classic John Frum Cargo Cult and its relationship to use of the drug, kava, on Tanna, in Vanuatu. More recently, he designed and established the rehabilitation studies programme at Massey University. He now teaches and carries out research on community psychology. He is particularly intrigued with research on alternative futures in our changing world and writes prolifically to share these interests.

Mailing Address :
School of Psychology
Massey University
Palmerston North
New Zealand
E-mail : <rgregory@pop3.massey.ac.nz>

Haddders, Hans was awarded his MA on the Jadopatias of Bengal and Bihar by the University of Trondheim 1999. Since then, he has been teaching anthropology at this University holding a post of temporary teacher. During the eighties Hadders spent six years at the Visva-Bharati University at Santiniketan (West Bengal) studying North Indian Classical Music. At present Hadders is also involved in a project focusing on leave taking and mortuary rituals at a palliative ward of the Regional Hospital of Trondheim.

Mailing Address :
Holbergsgate 42
7015 Trondheim
NORWAY
Fax : 0047 73596555
E-mail : <hanhad@stud.ntnu.no>

Köhler, Ulrich (born 1937) is Professor of Ethnology and Director of the Institute of Ethnology at the University of Freiburg. He obtained his doctoral and Habilitation degrees both from the University of Muenster in the year 1968 and 1976 respectively. His research on Middle America ranging from the pre-Columbian civilizations to fieldwork among present-day indigenous populations focuses on their syncretic religions, problems of cultural change and actual conflict management. Some of his recent publications are *Altamerikanistik* (1990); *Zur Ethnographie der Tzotzil von Chenalhó* (1990); *Santa Catarina Pantelhó* (1997); *Der Chamula-Aufstand in Chiapas, Mexiko, aus der Sicht heutiger Indianer und Ladinos* (1999). Professor Koehler is also on the editorial board of the leading German journal *Zeitschrift fuer Ethnology.*

Mailing Address :
Institut fuer Voelkerkunde
Universitaet Freiburg
Werderring 10
79085 Freiburg
GERMANY
E-mail : <ukoehler@ruf.uni-freiburg.de>

Pfeffer, Georg is Professor of Social Anthropology and Director of the Institute of Ethnology at the Free University of Berlin since 1985. He studied ethnology, sociology and history of religions at Freiburg University, Germany, where he obtained his doctoral degree in 1970 with a thesis on *Pariagroups of the Panjab.* His postdoctoral thesis of Habilitation at the University of

Heidelberg bore the title : *Puri's Sasana Villages : Basis of a Regional Elite.* In 1971 he was appointed Assistant Professor at the South Asia Institute of University of Heidelberg where he was promoted to the position of an Associate Professor in 1979. He has conducted fieldwork for several years in various parts of India and Pakistan. Since 1980 Prof. Pfeffer has undertaken numerous extended excursions to the tribes of middle India. In addition to his teaching and research obligations in Berlin, he is an active member of several national and international academic societies and on the editorial board of the German *Zeitschrift Fur Ethnologie*. Prof. Pfeffer has published a number of articles in reputed international journals. He has brought out five edited volumes on tribal studies, jointly with Prof. D.K. Behera of Sambalpur University, India. Religious cults and kinship structures of the scheduled tribes in the Koraput and Phulbani districts of Orissa (India) are Prof. Pfeffer's key areas of interest.

Mailing Address :
Institute of Ethnology
Free University of Berlin
Drosselweg 1-3
14195 Berlin
GERMANY
E-mail : <gpfeffer@gmx.net>

Soheila, Shahshahani got her B.A. (Philosophy) from University of California and PhD in Anthropology from the Graduate Faculty of the New School for Social Research in New York. She is now Assistant Professor of Social Anthropology at Shahid Behesthi University, Tehran. Her research in urban anthropology has concerned the cities of Kashan, Varameen and Esfahan. She has also studied the Mamassani, a pastoral nomadic population in Iran, and as rural area is concerned, she has done research in the grotto villages of Meymand in central Iran. The *Four Seasons of the Sun, A Bibliography of Iranian Women in Social Sciences, Humanities and Arts,* and *A Pictorial History of Iranian Headdresses* and many articles in Persian and English are her published works. She is the editor of the Iranian journal *Anthropology.*

Mailing Address :
B.P. 19585 - 193
Tehran
IRAN
E-mail : <soheila@kanoon.net>

Suzuki, Peter T. born in Seattle, Washington, U.S.A., studied Anthropology at Columbia University (B.S., M.A.), Yale University (doctoral studies), and Leiden University, Holland (M.Phil and PhD degrees). His post-doctoral work includes studies at Heidelberg University, Germany, and Louvain La Neuve, Belgium. Prof. Suzuki has conducted fieldwork in Turkey, and has done research among Turks in Germany, American Indians in Nebraska, American Blacks in Omaha, and Asian Americans, human relations in eastern Berlin, the Omaha, Winnebagó, and Santee Sioux Reservations in Nebraska. He is the Frederick W. Kayser Professor at the University of Nebraska at Omaha, Nebraska.

Mailing Address :
Department of Public Administration
University of Nebraska at Omaha
Omaha
Nebraska - 68182-0276
USA
E-mail : <psuzuki@FA-CPACS.UNOMAHA.EDU>

Tambs-Lyche, Harald is Professor of Ethnology at the Universite de Picardie— Jules Verne, Amiens, France. Having completed his work on ethnicity among Gujaratis in Britain and his native Norway, he went to Saurashtra for conducting a regional study combining historical and anthropological perspectives. He has several publications on various aspects of religion in Gujarat notably the myths and cults of the Goddess. Recently he has completed a fieldwork in Karnataka. Presently he is working with his wife Marine Carrin on the cultural encounter that has been brought about by Scandinavian missionaries among the Santals. Some of his important publications are *London Patidars. Case Study in Urban Ethnicity* (London: Routledge & Kegan Paul, 1980); *Power, Profit and Poetry. Traditional Society in Kathiawar, Western India* (Delhi: Manohar, 1997); *The Feminine Sacred in South Asia* (Delhi: Manohar, 1999); *The Good Country. Individual, Situation and Society in Saurashtra* (Delhi: Manohar, in print).

Mailing Address :
182 rue Lemerchier
80000 Amiens
FRANCE
Fax : +33-565302021
E-mail : <MARINE-CARRIN@wanadoo.fr>

Tanner, R.E.S. obtained his B.Sc. in Social Anthropology from Oxford University and PhD in Criminology from Stockholm University. He joined the Tanzanian Administrative Service in 1948 and continued to serve there till 1960. Then he joined the University of East Africa as Lecturer in Adult Education. He was the Chairman of East African Institute of Social Research from 1964 to 1967. He served the University of London as Lecturer in Comparative Religion from 1968 to 1980. He has been actively engaged in research works for the last 17 years. He has authored a number of books like *Homicide in Uganda, Transition in African Belief. An East African Problem, the Social Ecology of Religion* and *The Biology of Religion,* etc. He has contributed a large number of articles on translation problems in religion, religious hysteria, ancestor worship, witchcraft, Tanzanian agriculture, cattle theft, gossip, ecumenism, etc.

Mailing Address :
The Footprint
Pudworth Common
Reading
RG 74 QG
UNITED KINGDOM
E-mail : <restanner@kutkai.fsnet.co.uk>

Trawick, Margaret is Professor of Social Anthropology at Massey University in New Zealand. She has held this position since 1992. From 1979 to 1992 she taught at Hobart and William Smith Colleges in Geneva, New York. She received her PhD in anthropology from the University of Chicago in 1978, and her BA from Harvard University and Radcliffe College in 1970. Her area focus is South Asia, with a specialization in the Tamil language and Tamil-speaking peoples. She is author of *Notes on Love in a Tamil Family* (University of California Press, 1990, Oxford University Press, 1996) and numerous articles in journals and edited volumes on the topics of medical anthropology an linguistic anthropology. She has carried out several extensive fieldwork projects in South Asia, and she has presented papers at numerous professional conferences and meetings in the US, South Asia, Australasia, Europe, the UK, and Canada. Her current research concerns the situation of children and youth who live in the conflict zones of Sri Lanka.

Mailing Address :
Social Anthropology Programme
School of Global Studies

Massey University
Palmerston North
NEW ZEALAND
E-mail : <trawick@clear.net.nz>

Van Horn, Lawrence F. obtained his PhD in anthropology from the Graduate School of the City University of New York in 1977. He has taught anthropology at the University of Pennsylvania, Hunter College of the City University of New York, and at Drew University (Madison, New Jersey. Dr. Van Horn is a member of the National Park Service, United States Department of the Interior, at the Denver, Colorado, Service Center where he works in Planning and Design Services as a cultural anthropologist and cultural resources specialist. He serves on interdisciplinary park planning teams and conducts Native American consultations with American Indians and other Native Americans such as Alaska Natives and Native Hawaiians who are neighbours of particular national parks. In the U.S. National Park Service, Dr. Van Horn has prepared reports, using ethnographic interviewing and ethnohistorical research, about peoples or groups associated with national park units, such as the Tohono O'odham (formerly Papago) Indians associated with Organ Pipe Cactus National Monument, Arizona.
Honours include the Phi Beta Kappa National Academic Honor Society (founded December 5, 1776, at the College of William and Mary, Williamsburg, Virginia; Equal Opportunity Award, Denver Service Center; Fellow, Society for Applied Anthropology; Exemplary Service Award, High Plains Society for Applied Anthropology; Certificate of Excellence, Denver Service Center; and American Indian Seminar Fellow, Newberry Library, Chicago. Dr. Van Horn is a past editor of the *High Plains Applied Anthropologist,* the journal of the High Plains Society for Applied Anthropology.

Mailing Address :
Planning and Design Services
Denver Service Center
National Park Service
12795 West Alameda Parkway
Denver, CO 80225-0287

INDEX

Index